Fifty Filmmakers

FIFTY FILMMAKERS

Conversations with Directors from Roger Avary to Steven Zaillian

by Andrew J. Rausch

Michael Dequina, *Contributing Editor*

Foreword by Max Allan Collins

McFarland & Company, Inc., Publishers
Jefferson, North Carolina, and London

LIBRARY OF CONGRESS CATALOGUING-IN-PUBLICATION DATA

Rausch, Andrew J.
Fifty filmmakers : conversations with directors from Roger Avary to Steven Zaillian / Andrew J. Rausch ; Michael Dequina, contributing editor ; foreword by Max Allan Collins.
p.   cm.
Includes bibliographical references and index.

ISBN 978-0-7864-3149-6
softcover : 50# alkaline paper ∞

1. Motion picture producers and directors—Interviews.
I. Dequina, Michael.
II. Title.
PN1998.2.R38   2008   791.43023'30922—dc22   2007046481

British Library cataloguing data are available

©2008 Andrew J. Rausch and Michael Dequina. All rights reserved

No part of this book may be reproduced or transmitted in any form or by any means, electronic or mechanical, including photocopying or recording, or by any information storage and retrieval system, without permission in writing from the publisher.

Cover image ©2008 Stockbyte

Manufactured in the United States of America

*McFarland & Company, Inc., Publishers
Box 611, Jefferson, North Carolina 28640
www.mcfarlandpub.com*

To the memory of
Budd Boetticher, Albert Band, and Robert Wise,
who all passed away before it was completed.

Acknowledgments

The author would like to thank all of the filmmakers who participated in this project, including those whose interviews wound up on the cutting room floor: Allison Anders, Wes Anderson, J.R. Bookwalter, Jeff Burr, Bruce Campbell, Don Coscarelli, Alex Cox, Rusty Cundieff, Stuart Gordon, Craig Hamann, C. Courtney Joyner, Sarah Kelly, Robert Kurtzman, Sheldon Lettich, Steve Miner, John Ottman, Vincent Pereira, P.J. Pesce, John Putch, James F. Robinson, Tom Savini, Darrin Scott, Chris Smith, Scott Spiegel, A.C. Stephen, C.M. Talkington, Guillermo del Toro, David Veloz, and Boaz Yakin.

The author would like to give a very special thanks to Michael Dequina and Don Murphy, without whom this book could not have been completed. Special thanks are also in order for my wife Kerri Rausch, who assisted me in the editing of this project.

The author would also like to thank the following individuals for their assistance, encouragement, and patience: Dan and Sherry Rausch, Marilyn Allen, John White, Steve Spignesi, Mike White, Fred Rosenberg, Sean Westhoff, Josh Barnett, John Perkins, Chris Watson, Ronald Riley, Ryan Hixon, Keith Gordon, Henry Nash, Peter Modesitt, Cyndee and Sam Timmerman, Aron Taylor, Norman and Marion Leistikow, Ryan Robertson, Ryan Kasson, Brad Paulson, Richard Ember, and Mary Reynolds. I would also like to thank my four beautiful children, Jordan, Jaiden, Jalyn, and Julian, for bringing so much sunshine into my life; without you, I'm nothing.

Portions of the interview with Wes Craven appeared as "A Conversation with Wes Craven" in *Ain't It Cool News* on December 16, 1999. Portions of the interview with Daniel Myrick appeared in a much different form as "Hype Survivor: Daniel Myrick and *The Blair Witch Project*" in *Film Threat* on August 30, 2000. Portions of the interview with Roger Corman appeared in a much different form as "Roger Corman on *The Blair Witch Project* and Why *Mean Streets* Would Have Made a Great Blaxploitation Film" in *Images*, issue 9, 2000. Portions of the interview with Robert Wise appeared as "Sure, I'll Do It: An Interview with Robert Wise" in *Bright Lights Film Journal* in January 2002.

Contents

Acknowledgments vii
Filmography Abbreviations xi
Foreword by Max Allan Collins 1
Preface 5

Roger Avary	7	Monte Hellman	96	D.A. Pennebaker	181
Ralph Bakshi	12	Buck Henry	102	Michael Radford	187
Albert Band	18	George Hickenlooper	107	Mark Romanek	192
Harold Becker	24	Mike Judge	112	David O. Russell	197
Josh Becker	29	Lloyd Kaufman	118	John A. Russo	203
Budd Boetticher	34	Barbara Kopple	125	Tony Scott	209
John Carpenter	40	Mark L. Lester	129	Alan Shapiro	216
Jeremiah Chechik	45	Herschell Gordon Lewis	134	Bryan Singer	221
Larry Cohen	50	Richard Linklater	139	John Singleton	227
Roger Corman	56	William Malone	144	Kevin Smith	233
Wes Craven	61	Albert Maysles	149	Betty Thomas	239
Frank Darabont	66	John Milius	155	Robert Towne	244
Ernest Dickerson	71	Floyd Mutrux	161	Robert Weide	250
Jon Favreau	76	Daniel Myrick	166	Wim Wenders	254
Mick Garris	82	Peter O'Fallon	171	Kevin Williamson	259
Keith Gordon	87	Alexander Payne	176	Robert Wise	264
Ethan Hawke	92			Steven Zaillian	270

Index 277

Filmography Abbreviations

A	Actor
AD	Assistant Director
2AD	Second Assistant Director
An	Animator
AP	Associate Producer
C	Composer
CA	Creative Advisor
CC	Character Creator
Cin	Cinematographer
Co-D	Co-Director
Co-Ed	Co-Editor
Co-P	Co-Producer
Co-Sc	Co-Screenwriter
D	Director
Ed	Editor
Ex-P	Executive Producer
L	Lighting
MU	Make-Up Artist/Make-Up Effects
P	Producer
PA	Production Assistant
PD	Production Design
PM	Production Manager
S	Story
Sc	Screenplay
SE	Special Effects/Special Effects Supervisor
SE ED	Sound Effects Editor
SED	Sound Editor
St	Stunts
SUD	Second Unit Director
TA	Technical Advisor
TV	Telefilm/made-for-television
Un	Uncredited

The director is both the least necessary and most important component of filmmaking. He is the most modern and most decadent of all artists in his relative passivity toward everything that passes before him. He would not be worth bothering with if he were not capable now and then of sublimity of expression almost extracted from his money-oriented environment.

—Andrew Sarris

Foreword: "A Reel Cocktail Party"
by Max Allan Collins

I'm pleased to have the opportunity to introduce Andrew J. Rausch's collection of conversations with filmmakers—note that Andrew does not call these exchanges "interviews," and their slightly informal, freewheeling nature justifies that distinction... and your rapt interest.

I've been a reader, and, frankly, a collector, of books about film since my college days. Among my most vivid memories of the University of Iowa in the early 1970s—alongside buying underground comics at head shops and snarfing down subway sandwiches at the Bushnell's Turtle—is checking out various bookstores for the latest volume on film. These included a sudden spate of studies on directors—Howard Hawks, Alfred Hitchcock, John Ford, or any other filmmaker who'd been deemed a worthy *auteur* by Andrew Sarris.

Come to think of it, Sarris' classic *American Cinema* (1968) may well have been the first such book I ever purchased.

The notion of the director as the author of a film was controversial then, and is controversial now. At the Writers Workshop at Iowa City in those years, I thought of myself as a fiction writer, specifically a novelist. Along the way, I took film classes, thinking I might one day write screenplays... and anyway, movies were at least as important to me as books (and comics). As it happened, in the career that followed, I've been able to work in just about every branch of the storytelling art, though I admit the first time Leonard Maltin referred to me as a "filmmaker" I did a double take (and not just because Leonard can appreciate a good double take).

Encountering Sarris and his theories at a tender age, I had to grapple with the notion that the writer of the screenplay might not be the author of the film from that screenplay. I'm sure, at first, Sarris' (intentionally rabble-rousing) view annoyed, perhaps even outraged, me; but I also remember thumbing through his roster of directors, with filmographies and write-ups, thinking how much sense Sarris made in his appreciation of such obscure directors as Joseph H. Lewis, Robert Aldrich, and Don Siegel, who were responsible for some of my favorite films.

And I use the word "responsible" with no reservations. As it happens, I became a director when I had to step in and take over on the first indie film I wrote (*Mommy*, 1995). I'd only got involved with the project—which I also co-produced—because, after an unfortunate Hollywood experience, I wanted to see a screenplay of mine faithfully brought to life.

Partnered with my talented friend Phil Dingeldein—director of photography and editor on most of my projects—I learned how filmmaking works (or, I should say, started learning, because every filmmaker is learning up and through the final picture). I, of course, came from the solitary world of the fiction writer, who—in an office somewhere, behind a word processor (or, when I started, a typewriter)—provides in a novel not just dialogue but casting and art direction and every other creative aspect of bringing a story to life.

Unlike novels, films are not brought to life in an office by somebody sitting at a word processor. They begin life there, but the document that emerges from that solitary exercise—no matter how many drafts the title page might indicate have been written—is a draft.

The second draft will occur on set, in the collaborative atmosphere of actors and art direction and wardrobe and lighting and photography and so much more. The director has already guided a small army of collaborators in the pre-production phase to present the actors and the director of photography with a proper venue from which to craft that second draft.

On set, the director and actors almost certainly will change lines, perhaps throw them away, or substitute variations (or wholly new ones). And even when the writer's words are spoken right down to the commas, undoubtedly interpretations the writer never dreamed of will find their way into this second draft.

In *Mommy*, I had written a scene in which the title character, after committing a murder in front of her young daughter, carries the child away from the bedroom crime scene to a living-room couch. As written, the scene showed Mommy manipulating her daughter as the two get a story together, designed to shield Mommy. As acted, Patty McCormack and Rachel Lemieux found layers of emotion that transformed the scene from something cynical into the moment where mother and daughter finally, truly express their love.

Now I suppose I could have yelled "cut" and informed my actors that they'd gone way off the mark; but thank God I had sense enough to know my collaborators had improved my script without changing a word—that, in fact, they had just helped craft the best, and possibly the central, scene of the piece.

Patty McCormack, one of the greatest and most criminally underused actors of our day, taught me the importance of a second draft being crafted on set—the writer half of the writer/director might be short-sighted and protective of his words, but the director half needs to nurture the motion picture into life... to take advantage of the collaborative process.

During the post-production phase, I soon learned that the final draft, and really the film itself, would be "written" in the editing suite. Perhaps because *Mommy* was a project begun by another director, I took a proprietary stance and supervised every phase of post-production, not just editing but sound editing and mixing.

I came away understanding the dirty little secret of filmmaking: *Andrew Sarris was right.* The auteur theory is about as much a theory as evolution or gravity. The screenwriter is under the director on the filmmaking chain for good reason: what the screenwriter produces is two drafts away from the final result. The author of the film really *is* the director... or, anyway, should be; and I am prepared to deal with the wrath of my fellow screenwriters on this point.

What directing and writing have in common, however, is their solitary nature. True, through much of the process a director is surrounded by collaborators, while the writer of a novel only has to deal with a few minions of the publishing business after the book is finished. A director, after making tens of thousands of decisions, is finally alone with the result that he or she (with the help of an army) has crafted. Those who begrudge directors for having credit heaped upon them should reflect on the singular blame that comes a director's way as well.

I make no claim to be a director of any note—if I were, I'd be in this book instead of writing its foreword. But from this front-row seat I take special delight in hearing the thoughts and the reminiscences of other directors; it's always instructive from a craft perspective, often fascinating from a storytelling stance, and frequently resonant with joys and frustrations unique to directors.

This is not to imply that you have to be a director to enjoy Andrew Rausch's book. Loving movies is really the only requirement here; and you wouldn't be reading this if you didn't have a yen to pay attention to the men (and women) behind the curtain.

My college-era interest in film books has continued on until I have a library that a film school might envy almost as much as a wife deplores the space it takes up. Two of the best film books I've read, in recent years, have been conversational tomes with filmmakers of Hollywood's glory days: Peter Bogdanovich's *Who the Devil Made It: Conversations with Legendary Film Directors* (1998) and *Conversations with Moviemakers of Hollywood's Golden Age at the American Film Institute* (2006), by George Stevens, Jr. These massive works look intimidating, but disappear like a big tub of popcorn at a James Bond movie.

Andrew's book is a worthy third volume for the shelf shared by Bogdanovich and Stevens, whose works practically demand this fine supplement.

Unlike the subjects of those Golden Age volumes, *Fifty Filmmakers*' subjects are a wide-ranging bunch, reflecting the post-studio system emergence of everything from drive-in movies to Sundance independents. That makes this book a particular delight for film buffs — it's a big cocktail party where you may encounter a Hollywood great like Robert Wise or Budd Boetticher at the punch bowl, but on your way to the john could well run into "B" movie maestro Roger Corman or supreme goremeister Herschell Gordon Lewis.

And that's what impresses me about this massive volume: the variety of filmmakers, whether mainstream or cult, with perhaps an emphasis on writers who also direct (Robert Towne, Larry Cohen, Buck Henry), but with room for documentary filmmakers like D.A. Pennebaker and the Albert Maysles, as well as indie superstars Alexander Payne and Richard Linklater. *Fifty Filmmakers* displays a respect and interest in everything and everyone in film, from blockbuster director to Tony Scott to rebel Lloyd Kaufman.

The implicit message here is a wonderfully democratic one, free of snobbery — these are filmmakers. They have worthy things to say in their films.

And in these pages.

Muscatine, Iowa

Preface

Why is a book like this necessary? You may question just how important a director really is and just how much he had to do with the finished film we see up there on the screen. After all, we *see* the actors bringing life to the characters. And surely the screenwriter is the most significant creative force behind the film, right? After all, they wrote and/or conceived the characters, dialogue, and story. I have heard this argument time and time again — that the director is actually little more than a glorified traffic cop, directing crew members to move here and there, instructing actors to hit their marks. But I would contend that the director is one of the most important driving forces behind a motion picture, if not *the* most important. Whether or not one subscribes to the so-called "auteur theory," which states that the director is the singular creative force (or author, if you will) behind a motion picture, he or she must agree that the films of any given filmmaker tend to share many of the same distinctive traits. When we view the entire body of a filmmaker's work, we frequently find a similarity in morality, philosophy, acting styles, and aesthetics. Therefore, we must conclude that a director plays an extremely large role in the outcome of a motion picture, even if we disagree on the exact amount of influence he or she has.

You will notice that the interactions contained within this volume are better defined as conversations than interviews. Rather than focusing solely on aesthetics and technique, I consciously chose to expand the topical horizons a bit. While some of this would appear on the surface to be insignificant, I would contend that these things are of equal importance to film scholarship. Having worked on numerous films myself, I would contend that there are innumerable factors which affect the resulting film. Because of this I would further contend that even the most banal details of a film's production — the working conditions, the relationship between the director and his actors, the occasional random anecdote, and even the director's own cinematic influences — provide us with pieces to the overall puzzle; these details provide clues and help us to learn (a) how the film was made, and (b) why it turned out the way that it did.

You will also notice that the filmmakers I've selected for this project are a bit different from those you would normally find in such a volume. Rather than focusing solely on prestige filmmakers and Oscar winners, which is the norm, I've made a conscious decision to include a wide range of directors. Whereas horror movie directors, low-budget indie filmmakers, animators, and documentarians are most generally overlooked in such projects, I chose to include them, as I found their stories equally as enlightening. Most film academians snobbishly choose to examine only the well-known highbrow works deemed to have the utmost "artistic merit"—films by guys like Orson Welles, D.W. Griffith, Sergei Eisenstein, et al. Within this volume, however, we will examine works both high and lowbrow made by filmmakers with varying degrees of talent (ranging from the merely competent to the most brilliant of artists). It is my belief that a "bad" film can teach us as much about filmmaking as a "good" one — and sometimes more. And certainly every filmmaker who ever shot so much as a single reel of film — from Ed Wood to Akira Kurosawa — can teach us something about the art of cinema, whether these lessons come as a result of their failures or their triumphs. I would assert that no film is unworthy of academic appraisal; surely there is something we can learn from each and every one, even if it's only what we should not do.

Because some of the subjects here are also accomplished screenwriters, producers, editors, cinematographers, and/or actors, the conversations cover not only the films they've directed, but also their most significant works in these other arenas. (After all, it would be a crime to question Buck Henry and not discuss his screenplay for *The Graduate*. Could you imagine an interview with Robert Wise that didn't touch upon his work as editor on *Citizen Kane*?)

Although excerpts have appeared elsewhere, each of the fifty interviews contained in this volume were conducted expressly for this book. This project took seven years to complete, and seventy-nine filmmakers were interviewed in all. These interviews were conducted in offices, homes, restaurants, via telephone, and through correspondence. With the exception of John Singleton, who was interviewed by Michael Dequina, each of the interviews here was conducted by myself. (I did, however, conceive the questions and write the introduction for the Singleton interview.)

Three of the filmmakers here — Robert Wise, Albert Band, and my good friend Budd Boetticher — passed away before this volume was completed. I hold the utmost respect for each of them and am genuinely glad that I had the opportunity to talk with each of them before they left us.

The fifty conversations that are included here were selected for the quality of the conversation rather than the reputation of the filmmaker. It is for this reason that a fairly unknown director such as Josh Becker is included when my interview with Wes Anderson is not. In order to allow readers to get a sense of who these filmmakers are, I have asked each of them to list his or her favorite films as a viewer.

This book was a labor of love and, in the end, belongs as much to the filmmakers whose conversations fill these pages as it does to myself. It is my sincere hope that *Fifty Filmmakers* is both enlightening and entertaining, while at the same time a work which will stimulate intellectual discourse on the subject of film.

—*Andrew J. Rausch*

Roger Avary

In the late eighties, Roger Avary collaborated with his Video Archives co-worker Quentin Tarantino on a number of screenplays, including *Natural Born Killers* (1994) and *True Romance* (1993), which was inspired by Avary's script *The Open Road*. In 1994, Avary made his directorial debut with *Killing Zoe*, the story of a bank heist gone bad. *Killing Zoe* took top honors at the Yubari and Mystfest film festivals, and also won the prestigious Cannes Prix Tres Special. Soon after came *Pulp Fiction* (1994), which Avary co-wrote with Tarantino. After winning the *Palme d'Or* at the Cannes Film Festival, *Pulp Fiction* exploded onto the scene, irrevocably changing the face of independent film. For his work on *Pulp Fiction*, Avary would win a number of awards, among them a Best Screenplay Oscar. In 1998, *Pulp Fiction* was named to the American Film Institute's list of the one hundred greatest American films in the history of cinema.

In 1995, Avary wrote and directed the interesting but troubled television pilot *Mr. Stitch*. To many fans, it seemed as though Avary had disappeared in a cloud of smoke. However low-key he may have appeared, Avary was working on a number of projects. Among them was an uncredited script polish for the French film *Crying Freeman* (1995) and the screenplay for a fifth installment in the *Phantasm* series.

The road to Avary's second directorial feature was a bumpy one. Avary was at one time slated to direct the Alfred Hitchcock remake *Dial M for Murder*, later retitled *A Perfect Murder* (1998). Citing creative conflicts, Avary walked away from the project. Avary then spent a year developing *The Sandman* for Warner Bros., but again wound up leaving the project after creative conflicts with producer Jon Peters. Avary then worked on developing *Gala Dali*, which was to have starred Al Pacino. Unfortunately, this project remains unproduced.

Avary wrote and directed his second feature, *Rules of Attraction*, in 2002. The critically-acclaimed film, adapted from the novel by Bret Easton Ellis, starred James Van Der Beek, Jessica Biel, Faye Dunaway, and Eric Stoltz.

Favorite Films: *A Clockwork Orange* (1971), *Sorcerer* (1977), *M* (1931), *Cabaret* (1953), *Barry Lyndon* (1975), *Apocalypse Now* (1979), *Gregory's Girl* (1981), *Excalibur* (1981), *The Beast* (1988), and his own *Killing Zoe* (1994) ("Why not?").

ANDREW RAUSCH: *I know you're a huge fan of George Romero's "Dead" trilogy. Tom Savini, whom you worked with on* Killing Zoe *and* Mr. Stitch, *did the makeup for* Dawn of the Dead *(1978). As a fan of those films, what was it like working with him?*

ROGER AVARY: When I was working on *Killing Zoe*, I knew I was gonna have lots of bullet hits in the movie. So I told the production staff, "Okay, the guy I need is Tom Savini." And

John Travolta as hitman Vincent Vega in the 1994 film *Pulp Fiction*, written by Quentin Tarantino and Roger Avary (Miramax Films, 1994).

they're like, "Tom Savini? Who's he?" I said, "Tom Savini. He's from *Dawn of the Dead*. He's in Pittsburgh. Look him up." And nobody could find him. Finally I just called information in Pittsburgh, got his number, and called him up. I said, "Hi. My name's Roger Avary. I'm a young filmmaker living in Los Angeles, and I have the opportunity to make my first movie, and I may not ever get to make another movie after this. If I don't, I can't live the rest of my life knowing I haven't worked with you. I would like you to work on my film."

Then he did the most extraordinary thing. We didn't have any money to make the movie. We had so little to make the movie, he flew himself out, and put himself up in Los Angeles, and worked on the movie for the bare minimum. And I swear he saved me, time and time again. He did all this wonderful burn make-up on the guard with Vaseline, paint, and tissue paper. And that's all he used! I watched him do it, and it was like, Jesus Christ, the guy is an artist!

I just love Tom. I think Tom is so brilliant. To me, he's one of the pharaohs. Whether I have make-up or not in a film, I will have him in every single movie I do. I won't do a movie without him! I absolutely refuse to do a movie without him.

You were once approached to direct Spice World *(1997). I understand you now regret not doing it. Why?*

RA: I'll tell you exactly what happened. One day I got a call from my agent at William Morris who said, "There's this girl group called the Spice Girls, and they want you to do their movie, and they'd like to meet you this weekend at their hotel." And I was like, "Who?" At that time, nobody knew who they were. So I go to the hotel and she's saying, "Listen, they're gonna be big. This is gonna be huge, and they're big fans of yours." So I go up to the Four Seasons in Hollywood. I go up to their room, and it's the Spice Girls, you know? They're in full costume and everything. This is actually what they wore.

Jessica Biel and James Van Der Beek appear as promiscuous Camden College students Lara Holleran and Sean Bateman in Roger Avary's adaptation of Bret Easton Ellis' *The Rules of Attraction* (Lions Gate Films, 2002).

The other night I had a dream about Sporty Spice where I was married to her, and this is kind of key. [Laughs]

So I'm sitting there and I'm talking to them, and they start doing their little music and it's like [sings], "I'll tell you what I want, what I really, really want...." They're just doing the whole performance and I'm just sitting there looking at them. I'm a red-blooded male, just like any other heterosexual guy. What they wanted was like *A Hard Day's Night* [1964] or something like that, and I was gonna shoot mine more documentary-style, but kind of fake as a documentary. But as I'm sitting there watching them, I was thinking, If I do this movie, my marriage is gonna fall apart. It's as simple as that. I just know what'll happen — my marriage will fall apart. So they gave me the song on tape, and I left the hotel, and I was walking downstairs, and Geri Hallowell — Ginger Spice — chased me. I actually really, really dug her. She definitely would have been the one to break up my marriage. They were so seductive. They really knew how to play a man and how to manipulate him. If they really wanted it, they could have it. I realized that it was one of those moments where I just had to utilize whatever strength I had to get out of there. They were sirens like Lorelai, who would sing on the rocks and call sailors to their death. You know, you became blinded by the song and you crashed into the rocks and drowned.

But not doing the Spice Girls movie is one of my regrets. That would have been really fun. I know now not to pass up those things. And at the time, I was writing my Dalí film. You know, those are two *completely* different kinds of movies.

Right now Al Pacino is attached to play Dalí. As a fan of his work, what is it like to know you're going to work with him?

RA: I don't know that I'm going to work with him. You never know until you're running film through a camera. He claims to be committed to the project, and right now he wants to make the movie and I want to work with him.

More than anything, I'm friends with Al Pacino now. I've spent months with him and I truly love him. He is a great, great man. He defends the arts. He lives for the work. He's very Strasberg in his origin, and there is nothing else but the work. He holds the artist and the writer of the work above all. You can't really ask for a better guy to work with than Pacino. I'm blessed—even if I don't make the movie—for what I've been through and for what I've learned from him. Should the movie never get made, or should it not work out, or should I die tomorrow, I die a happy man because, just in the readings I've done, I've seen life breathed into my work.

What is your favorite Pacino film?

RA: *Scarface* (1983) is by far my favorite Pacino movie.

In Killing Zoe, *there's a scene where John-Hugues Anglade is riddled with bullets and his body dances almost rhythmically for a moment, just as Tony Montana's does in* Scarface. *Was that influenced by* Scarface?

RA: I would be lying if I didn't say it was influenced by it.

What happened when I wrote that movie, [producer] Lawrence Bender called me up on the phone and told me, "Roger, we have a bank on location, and if you have a script that takes place in a bank, we can get together one, maybe two hundred thousand dollars to make a movie. I immediately said, "Lawrence, this is your lucky day. I just happen to have a script!" I then went out and quickly wrote one, and what I said was that I was going to make a movie in Los Angeles, but I want it to take place in Paris. How am I going to do that? And I literally kind of fell into the movie. I had no idea where the movie was going to go.

I was in a cab driving away from the airport like, Okay, how am I gonna do that? I'm gonna stay tight on Eric Stoltz's face. I'll have a narrow depth-of-field so you won't see the background. I'll just shoot it tight like that, and then when I get to the hotel, that's no problem. I kept the locations at a minimum. It just kind of evolved that way. In the writing, I had no idea how the movie was gonna turn out. I was watching and doing that tunnel thing because I wrote the movie so fast that the ideas and the metaphors just fell out of my head. And so did the references. And, of course, *Scarface* is one of the most glorious references.

When he got shot up like that, it seemed like the only potential ending. And it really wasn't until I started making the movie that I started thinking about how to shoot that. And, of course, *Scarface* came up, and I realized the metaphor and where it had been hidden. If you plan your metaphors and your references, they're never as good as if you simply discover them on your own. And I realized that it was gonna be similar to *Scarface*, so what I made sure to do was to have the maximum potential squibs, which is the explosive device on the body, and I made sure we had two more than *Scarface*.

Pacino's performance in *Scarface* is a brilliant, brilliant performance. You know, "Take a look at the bad guy!" [Laughs] It's that scene in the restaurant where he's like, "Who are you lookin' at? What are you lookin' at? You need people like me, so you can have somebody to point at and say, 'Look, there, that's the bad guy.'" And that was a scene Pacino fought for.

When I first met Pacino, I brought a little bag with my laserdisc of *Scarface* in it because I didn't know if he was gonna do the movie, and it was my first meeting with him. We were having the meeting and we were talking, and I was almost ashamed to bring it up because I didn't want to blow it with him and just seem like a fanboy. Then, at one point, he said there were three roles he knew he had to do. One of them was *Scarface*. Then there was this other one — I can't remember what it was—"and the third one is your film *Dalí*. I *have* to play that character." And I said, "*Scarface*? Really?" And I just pulled out the laserdisc and I was like, "Would you like to sign this?" [Laughs] I just can't say enough good things about Al Pacino.

There are a few similarities between Dog Day Afternoon *(1975) and* Killing Zoe, *as well.*

RA: Yeah, I was kind of getting to that. Now I had seen *Dog Day Afternoon* and, frankly, didn't really care for it that much as a kid. I loved the performances in it, but I was too young when I first saw the movie to really appreciate it. I hadn't really sat down to watch the movie in years. You also have to understand that, at that time, *Dog Day Afternoon* existed not quite in its glorious form on video. Now it's been re-transferred and letterboxed. You can really study it properly now. Before, you'd see bits of it on TV, or on Showtime, or actually back then it was Selectavision. It was really difficult to see the film, so I never consciously tried to do that.

But I can't deny that I went back and watched it because everybody's always been talking about [the similarities between] *Killing Zoe* and *Dog Day Afternoon*. So I went back and rewatched the film and I was stunned. Not the plot similarities, because you've got two bank robbery films, so naturally you're gonna have similarities. I was shocked at how much John Cazale looked like John-Hugues Anglade in the movie. When I was writing *Killing Zoe* I was thinking of John-Hugues Anglade, but I wasn't really thinking about him with long hair, and I didn't know he was gonna have such a pasty face. It just happened that way. It was like a happy accident. I just lucked out and there was that similarity there. That was one of those things I don't think you could plan.

When I look back on it, I love that fact. I really do feel like they're sister films. Cousin films, maybe.

FILMOGRAPHY FOR ROGER AVARY

1. *Maximum Potential* (1987) PA
2. *My Best Friend's Birthday* (1987) Cin
3. *True Romance* (1993) Un Co-Sc
4. *Killing Zoe* (1994) D & Sc
5. *Natural Born Killers* (1994) Un Co-Sc
6. *Pulp Fiction* (1994) S
7. *Mr. Stitch* (1995) [TV pilot] D & Ex-P
8. *Crying Freeman* (1995) Un Co-Sc
9. *Boogie Boy* (1997) Ex-P
10. *Odd Jobs* (1997) Sc
11. *Phantasm IV: Oblivion* (1998) A
12. *The Last Man* (2000) Ex-P
13. *RPM* (2002) Un Sc [removed name]
14. *The Rules of Attraction* (2002) D & Sc
15. *Glitterati* (2005) D, Sc, Cin
16. *Silent Hill* (2006) Sc
17. *Beowulf* (2007) Co-Sc & Ex-P

Ralph Bakshi

Ralph Bakshi's career as an animator began at the Terrytoons studios, where he worked on cartoons such as *Deputy Dawg* and fashioned many short films. Bakshi then went to work at Paramount Studios, where he was head of their animation department until its demise in 1967. He then inked a deal to write, direct, and produce the original animated *Spider-Man* television series. During this time Bakshi also worked on animated series based on other Marvel Comics characters, such as *The Incredible Hulk*, *Captain America*, and *Iron Man*.

After working on these series Bakshi began directing full-length feature animated films. For his work on these films he has been dubbed the "first auteur animator," which is a fitting title. In 1970, Bakshi directed his first feature-length animated film, *Fritz the Cat* (based on R. Crumb's underground comic character). The $700,000 film, which became the first animated feature to receive an "X" rating, raked in more than $90 million and proved that there was a market for adult-themed animation. Bakshi then made a much more personal animated film for the adult audience, *Heavy Traffic* (1973). He then followed this up with the extremely controversial *Coonskin* (1975). The picture, which focused on racism, was itself perceived as being racist by some. This controversy led to distributor Paramount dropping the film. Bakshi then followed *Coonskin* with the fantastical *Wizards* (1977), which remains a cult favorite today.

In an effort to cut costs, Bakshi soon began toying with a process known as "rotoscoping." This process involved the tracing of "live" actors to achieve realistic movement. The first of Bakshi's films to rely heavily upon this process was his 1978 adaptation of J.R.R. Tolkein's *Lord of the Rings*. Unfortunately, the animated epic failed to find a substantial audience at the box office. Nevertheless, Bakshi immediately went to work on his next film, *American Pop* (1981), which found him utilizing rotoscope to an even greater extent. Bakshi kept busy the next few years cranking out *Hey Good Lookin'* (1982) and *Fire and Ice* (1983).

In 1986, Bakshi returned to his Terrytoons roots with the series *The New Adventures of Mighty Mouse*. Despite receiving critical acclaim, the series soon came under fire when it was accused of promoting cocaine usage. In 1987, Bakshi directed the music video for the Rolling Stones' "Harlem Shuffle." That same year he directed the live-action short *This Ain't Bebop* (1987), which starred Harvey Keitel. He next directed the film *Cool World* (1992), which combined live action with animation. Bakshi then wrote and directed the live action film *Cool and the Crazy* (1994), which starred Alicia Silverstone and Jared Leto.

Favorite Films: *Lawrence of Arabia* (1962), *Mean Streets* (1973), *La Strada* (1954), *The Asphalt Jungle* (1950), *The Godfather* (1972), *Apocalypse Now* (1979), *Nights of Cabiria* (1957), and *Five Easy Pieces* (1970).

Animation from Ralph Bakshi's classic 1977 fantasy film *Wizards* (20th Century–Fox Film Corporation, 1977).

ANDREW RAUSCH: *When you were working in the seventies, you were an auteur in the purest sense of the word. How did you manage to maintain creative control over controversial films such as* Coonskin *and* Heavy Traffic?

RALPH BAKSHI: There are many aspects to this. Okay, the first aspect is that I did the films for very cheap. Even in the day I made them, the budgets were amazingly low. Disney was spending $14 to $20 million on an animated feature, and I was the only other feature film company in the business. My budgets were under a million or $1.2 million. So I was making them at very reasonable rates for distributors. Second, I opened up my own company, Bakshi Productions. I wasn't working for anyone. That eventually became my undoing because I was producing, directing, and writing these films. That eventually got me out of the business because it became too tiring. But the director, the writer, and the producer owned the company, so there was no one to tell me I couldn't do something. Thirdly, the motion picture companies had no idea how animation was made. Now they all know how it's made, but then they didn't know they could look at the storyboards to check out what I was doing. They would look at the scripts, right? But over the next year or two I could rewrite the scripts whenever I wanted. So whenever I had a new idea, I just boarded it and handed it out to the artists. There was nothing handed in to the motion picture company. So any changes made to the script they had bought were all right because they had no way of checking up on me. They were very bored with animation. They would rather take a movie star out to lunch. So the minute I sold the film, they forgot about it. The only thing the studios did have tight control over was budget. I couldn't spend more on my films if I wanted to. If I went over budget, it came out of *my* pocket. I was responsible for all over-budgets. Most directors don't take that responsibility, but I knew that by doing that, they would leave me alone even more.

There were those reasons and then, most important, my will to do what I did. In other words, I had automatically made the decision to make the films I wanted to make, as opposed to making films which might be more commercial. I wasn't stupid; I knew I was making my audience smaller and smaller by making these very personal films. But that was the decision I made. The director, writer, and producer all decided to make those sort of films. So that's how it was done.

Do you feel that the atmosphere is more or less restrictive than it was at the time when those films were made?

RB: Oh, yeah, it's absolutely more restrictive today. "The times they are a changing...." Marty Scorsese was making *Mean Streets* and *Taxi Driver* [1976] at that time; Coppola was making *Apocalypse Now*. It was more art for art's sake in those days. I came out of the fifties and into the sixties, which really formed my perceptions of art. You know, Jackson Pollock, Miles Davis, John Coltraine, Diane Arbus, Fellini, rock music, Bob Dylan. There was a tremendous appreciation for what it meant to be an artist. You didn't feel stupid being an artist in those days. You feel stupid being an artist today because artists are generally very poor. I suspect the decision to go for the dollars or do what you felt was right personally began in the abstract expressionist movement in America. There was more experimentation then. Today everything is very commercialized, very sanitized. The large companies were much smaller then, as well. There weren't these conglomerations, like Warner Bros. and Disney, which owned television networks and cable. There wasn't that kind of control then. If someone gave you a hard time in motion pictures, you went to cable. If someone gave you a hard time in cable, you went to independent production. There were more marketplaces for an artist to take his stuff. Times were very different then. Of course, money was always an issue, but it wasn't the *only* issue.

Everyone has become either very smart or very stupid, but I don't know which. Today animators get agents, writers get agents. Everyone says yes to whatever companies want, whereas I fought companies like crazy. I told you the *easy* part of what happened with those films, but when the executives saw these films they went ballistic! When they saw the films, there was trouble — don't get me wrong. I made what I wanted and waited for the explosion at the end. Everyone plays the game of making a fortune today. And now the country is getting much more conservative. So was it different in my time? Oh, yes.

You used rotoscoping rather extensively on a few of your films, yet you've said that you hate rotoscoping. Why is that?

RB: I've got a love/hate relationship with rotoscoping, ending more with hate. The kind of projects I wanted to do at that time couldn't be animated in the truest sense of the word. It wasn't possible to do *Lord of the Rings* or *American Pop* in the truest sense of the word "animation." We just didn't have the ability to do the kinds of the things the story called for. This was before computer animation. I kept searching for a technique that would allow me to do these things on budget.

The downside is that tracing photographs is ugly. Anything that becomes that mechanical gets ugly. With rotoscoping, the great art of animation — drawing and lines, an artist expressing his own feelings— is gone. The live action more or less produces the motion for you. When you're an animator, it gets very boring tracing someone else's motion. I found that

Brad Pitt as Detective Frank Harris in Ralph Bakshi's *Cool World*, a daring film which combined animation with live action (Paramount Pictures, 1992).

it was too much of a technique. I mean, I was able to produce the things I wanted — I got the ring wraith riding and chasing Frodo in a way I never could have done with pure animation — but it wasn't as much fun as *Heavy Traffic* and *Coonskin*. Also, it was much more restrictive creatively.

Adapting Lord of the Rings *seems like it must have been a Herculean task. What were some of the primary difficulties you found in adapting that?*

RB: The biggest difficulty was the budget! We only had $8 million for it. And the amount of work on *Lord of the Rings* was overwhelming because Tolkien was such a great writer. His attention to detail was amazing. In every scene you had nine different characters walking around. In animation, if you have three characters walking around, you try to cut to a close-up to avoid the animation. Even Disney did that. Nine characters to put in every scene — maintaining what they're saying, what they're doing, where they're at respectively — that's an enormous and tremendously difficult task. No one had ever done anything like that in animation at that time. The designing of that was also a challenge. You know, what does a ring wraith look like? What does an orc look like? I had to illustrate Tolkien. I mean, I gave the people who made the live-action version a picture to look at! [Laughs] They could say, "We like that, but we don't like this..."

Peter Jackson borrowed rather liberally from your original version of Lord of the Rings. *Would it have lessened the blow had he acknowledged your contributions?*

RB: Absolutely! When Scorsese remade *Cape Fear* [1962], he acknowledged the original film. I'll be quite frank. What it was, they didn't know whether they had the rights or not. So they started playing very tough with me, and they tried to make believe I was dead. Peter Jackson bought into that because he wanted desperately to make the film. My problem with Peter Jackson is that he never gave me a call. He knew how passionate I was about the film. And did they have the right to make the film? I don't think so. Do you know why? Because their fucking picture is animated! The orcs and everything are made by computer — CGI — which is animation. And I have the animation rights. They *may* have been entitled to make a live action version, but computer animation is not considered live action. And I think they know that, but I'm not interested in spending the remaining years of my life chasing these bastards in the lower courts.

Obviously Peter Jackson doesn't need me to worry about. He's a very rich man, but as a director, he made a huge mistake and a lot of people are aware of that mistake. He fucked me over to get his chance to do the movie, and I'll always maintain that.

You've directed a couple of live action films now. Do you feel that your background as an animator helped you with that, and if so, in what ways?

RB: Live action is easier than animation. Animation is the hardest thing in the world to do because you're the actor, the writer, the producer, the set director... you're everything. With live animation, you have a lot of people helping you. There's a camera man. He points the camera at the actors. The actors do something for you. If you like it, you say, "I like it," if you don't, you say, "Do it again." They do whatever you want them to do without your personally having to do anything to make that happen. Then, the next day you walk in and you see the rushes. In animation, you wait an entire year or two before you see any finished product.

Compared to animation, live action is easy. It doesn't take nearly as long to make live action films, either. My good friend Marty Scorsese used to make two-and-a-half films to my one! Plus, they pay live action directors more. Not only is it easier, they pay the bastards more! [Laughs]

FILMOGRAPHY FOR RALPH BAKSHI

1. *Deputy Dawg* (1959) D & Sc
2. *Mattie's Funday Funnies* (1959) D & Sc
3. *House of Hashimoto* (1960) An
4. *The Hector Heathcote Show* (1963) An
5. *Gadmouse the Apprentice* (1965) D
6. *Don't Spill the Beans* (1965) D
7. *Dress Reversal* (1965) D
8. *The Third Musketeer* (1965) D
9. *Dr. Ha Ha* (1966) D
10. *Scuba Duba Do* (1966) D
11. *The Monster Master* (1966) D
12. *The Mighty Heroes* (1966) D
13. *Dreamnapping* (1966) D
14. *The Sub-Mariner* (1966) D & P
15. *The Mighty Thor* (1966) D & P
16. *The Marvel Superheroes* (1966) D & P
17. *Iron Man* (1966) D, Sc, P
18. *The Incredible Hulk* (1966) D, Sc, P
19. *The Famous Skyscraper* (1966) D
20. *Captain America* (1966) D, Sc, P
21. *Rocket Robin Hood* (1967) D, Sc, P
22. *The Heat's Off* (1967) D
23. *It's for the Birds* (1967) D
24. *A Voodoo Spell* (1967) D
25. *Give Me Liberty* (1967) D
26. *Spider-Man* (1967) D, Sc, Ex-P
27. *Which Is Witch?* (1967) D
28. *Dr. Rhinestone's Theory* (1967) D
29. *All Teed Off* (1967) D
30. *Traffic Trouble* (1967) D
31. *Mr. Winlucky* (1967) D
32. *Fancy Plants* (1967) D

33. *Marvin Digs* (1967) D & Ex-P
34. *Bugged by a Bug* (1967) D
35. *Frozen Sparklers* (1967) D
36. *The Abominable Mountaineers* (1967) D
37. *Loops and Swoops* (1967) D
38. *Judos Kudos* (1967) D
39. *Baron Von Go-Go* (1967) D
40. *The Mini-Squirts* (1967) D
41. *Mouse Trek* (1967) D & Ex-P
42. *The Fuz* (1968) D
43. *The Stretcher* (1968) D
44. *The Frog* (1969) D
45. *The Toy Man* (1969) D
46. *The Ghost Monster* (1970) D & An
47. *The Drifter* (1970) D & An
48. *The Proton Pulsator* (1970) D
49. *The Shocker* (1970) D & An
50. *The Enlarger* (1971) D & An
51. *The Duster* (1971) D
52. *Martin Luther King, Jr.* (1971) D
53. *The Big Freeze* (1971) D
54. *Fritz the Cat* (1972) D & Sc
55. *Heavy Traffic* (1973) D & Sc
56. *Coonskin* (1975) D & Sc
57. *Wizards* (1977) D, Sc, P
58. *The Lord of the Rings* (1978) D
59. *American Pop* (1981) D & P
60. *Hey Good Lookin'* (1982) D, Sc, P
61. *Fire and Ice* (1983) D, Sc, P
62. *Cannonball Run II* (1984) An
63. *Mighty Mouse: The New Adventures* (1987) D, Sc, P
64. *Tattertown* (1987) Sc & P
65. *This Ain't Bebop* (1987) D & Sc
66. *Imagining America* (1989) Co-D
67. *Cool World* (1992) D & Un Sc [removed name]
68. *Cool and the Crazy* (1994) D & Sc
69. *Spicy City* (1997) D & Ex-P
70. *Malcolm and Melvin* (1997) D & Sc
71. *Babe, He Calls Me* (1997) D & Sc
72. *Last Days of Coney Island* (2007) D, Sc, P

Albert Band

Parisian born filmmaker Alfredo Antonini (he later adopted the name Albert Band) moved to Hollywood at a young age and developed an interest in motion pictures. In 1950, his film career began with a stint as assistant director on the classic John Huston film *The Asphalt Jungle*. Under the tutelage of the legendary filmmaker, Band learned the craft of filmmaking. He then reteamed with his mentor Huston the following year — this time working as a screenwriter — on the Audie Murphy starrer *The Red Badge of Courage* (1951). Five years later Band made his own directorial debut with *The Young Guns* (1956). This western was not only the first of Band's fourteen films as a director, but also marked the first of five collaborations with Oscar-nominated screenwriter Louis Garfinkle. Displaying an uncanny versatility, Band next directed the horror film *I Bury the Living* (1958), which starred Richard Boone.

Band then relocated to Sweden, where he helmed the James Whitmore starrer *Face of Fire* (1959). In 1962, Band directed muscleman Steve Reeves in *The Avenger*. Three years later Band would return to the sword-and-sandals genre with *Hercules and the Princess of Troy* (1965). Band also contributed significantly to the spaghetti western movement of the late sixties. He penned two seminal films of this period: Sergio Corbucci's *A Minute to Pray, a Second to Die* (1968) and *The Hellbenders* (1967), which heavily influenced Sam Peckinpah's bloody actioner *The Wild Bunch* (1969). Band also helmed two spaghetti westerns himself, *Massacre at the Grand Canyon* (1965) and *Showdown* (1966). Band then took an eleven year hiatus from filmmaking before returning to helm *She Came to the Valley* (1977), which starred Dean Stockwell, Scott Glenn, and singer Freddy Fender. The following year Band helmed the exploitation film *Zoltan, Hound of Dracula* (1978) for his son Charles' Empire Pictures. Band's later directorial efforts included *Ghoulies 2* (1987), *Dr. Mordrid* (1992), and *Prehysteria!* (1993).

In addition to writing and directing, Band also worked as a producer on a number of films, including *Cinderella* (1977), *Mansion of the Doomed* (1977), *Metalstorm: The Destruction of Jared-Syn* (1983), *Troll* (1986), *The Pit and the Pendulum* (1990), and Walt Disney's *Honey, I Blew Up the Kid* (1992). In the 1990s, Band worked actively with his son, Charles, in operating Full Moon Entertainment, which they co-founded.

On June 14, 2002, at the age of 78, Band died of complications from a stomach blockage coupled with severe lung infection. *Cinescape* journalist John Thomen summed up Band's legacy at the time of his death: "There's not likely to be any retrospectives of Albert Band's work, nor salutes to him by the AFI or the Academy Awards, but he was one of the last breed of writers, filmmakers, and producers who believed that even a low-budget film deserved to be made as professionally as possible and should aim to entertain its audience in addition to turning a profit for its producers. It seems likely that we won't see his kind again."

Favorite Films: *Citizen Kane* (1941), *The Maltese Falcon* (1941), *The Killing* (1956), and *The 400 Blows* (1959).

ANDREW RAUSCH: *One of your favorite movies is* Citizen Kane, *which leads me to an interesting question. You worked with actor Joseph Cotten a couple of times. What was he like to work with?*

ALBERT BAND: He was just adorable! He was a perfect gentleman from Virginia. Very polite and very cooperative.

What directors have most influenced you?

AB: Well, John Huston, of course. I would say Max Ophuls, because I worked with him on one picture. I can't think of too many directors who have influenced me. Stanley Kubrick, of course; Jean Renoir, the French director.

You worked with Huston twice. What was he like to work with?

Audie Murphy as Union soldier Henry Fleming in the 1951 adaptation of Joseph Crane's *The Red Badge of Courage*, written by Albert Band and directed by John Huston (Metro-Goldwyn-Mayer, 1951).

AB: Well, John was John. [Laughs] He was terrific, you know, in many ways. He was a maverick. He was not a man who follows the rules. He simply made his own. He had a wonderful eye for composition. That was his main touch. This was because he wanted to be a painter in his early days. That's why his work is so outstanding when you see it. Whenever you see a Huston picture, you can always tell it is a Huston picture. It's shot in a certain way and composed in a certain way.

I worked with him on a picture called *The Asphalt Jungle*. It was just on TV two days ago. I was sort of shocked to see it there. I could see the beauty of his framing and his composition between people and objects. It's just wonderful. He was also a wonderful writer, as well.

The other project you worked on with John Huston was The Red Badge of Courage, *which you wrote the screenplay for. Did you find adapting a screenplay from a novel to be easier or more difficult than crafting an original script?*

The title character from *Dracula's Dog* scratches at the tomb of its master in this offbeat 1978 offering from Albert Band (Crown International Pictures, 1978).

AB: It's much more difficult because you have a guideline. You've got an absolute devotion to material not written by you. Then, you have this duty to somehow make this material seem unique.

There are an awful lot of similarities between The Hellbenders, *which you wrote, and Sam Peckinpah's* The Wild Bunch, *which was released two years later. Do you think Peckinpah was influenced by* The Hellbenders?

AB: I doubt it. I mean, I wouldn't know. [Laughs] Peckinpah was his own man. That much is for sure.

You worked with director Sergio Corbucci on that film just before he went on to shoot Django *(1967), which would change the entire genre. What was Corbucci like?*

AB: He was a lot of fun. He had one eye. He had somehow lost it while shooting, just like Raoul Walsh. He was very, very funny and full of piss and vinegar. He very rarely lost his temper. We had a very good time. He was very, very professional. An excellent, excellent director.

The spaghetti western films have virtually disappeared, with the notable exception of Sergio Leone's trilogy. Why do you think this is?

AB: They were not shown here in the U.S. in any important place. The Leone picture was a huge success when he made his first one [*A Fistful of Dollars*, 1964]. It was a big hit worldwide. None of the other spaghetti westerns were of that magnitude. Leone's films worked great here, too.

What films do you consider underrated?
AB: All of my films! [Laughs] No, I don't know. That really is not me. Underrated? You got me.

I absolutely adore Little Cigars *(1973), which you produced.*
AB: [Laughs] *Really?*

Since a story about a band of midget criminals is so completely off-the-wall, I was wondering what your initial reaction was upon hearing the storyline for the first time.
AB: I laughed my heart out! It was very funny, a very good comedy. I mean, imagine those midgets running around doing those things! It was so silly that it was genius!

It certainly is an interesting film. [Laughs]
AB: Oh, yes. [Chuckles]

You've worked in the film industry for a long time. What are some of the most significant changes you've seen during that span?
AB: Oh, everything! Are you kidding? For *this* we need a few hours! [Laughs] I started out as an apprentice at Warner Bros. and I was splicing film with acetate. That shows you how far back I go. There are changes every ten years, every fifteen years, every twenty years. Now it's a new ball game entirely in almost all departments except the one that counts the most; this is, of course, the screenplay. Films today are of a different breed both physically and technologically. The pictures may flop, but they don't flop in the screenplay. The only thing that hasn't changed is that you have to have a good screenplay. This has been proven many times. No matter who you put in it, if it's got a lousy screenplay, it'll be a lousy movie! The audiences won't go.

In the editing alone, you can see huge differences. Today we are able to make a picture and edit it on the set; whereas, before this was impossible. So, in many ways it's different. It's faster and more convenient because you're able to see your film back and forth very quickly. Take this out, change that — now you see immediately how it is, as opposed to before when we had to cut it, then splice it, and then look at it, and change it. That's a pretty good example of what's happening in this industry. This is often for the better because you can tell a great story that way.

Have you been happy with the way other filmmakers have shot your screenplays?
AB: Well, yeah, mostly. I haven't had many problems.

You have written, directed, and produced. Which of these aspects of filmmaking do you enjoy the most?
AB: Well, I've most enjoyed editing. Producing is a technically difficult job. Directing is something I love, but I have to love the material. If I don't love the material, then it's pretty much routine. I always enjoyed it because it's still a challenge. No matter how ridiculous you may think it is, it's still a challenge. I mean, I made a picture called *The Robot Wars* [1993]. That picture was very successful. It was well thought out and well-shot. That's a pretty good example of what I enjoy doing. But it's not my favorite thing. My favorite thing is sitting with the film in the cutting room and playing with it.

You directed Steve Reeves in The Avenger, *which was one of the last "sword and sandals" epics. What was Reeves like from a director's standpoint?*
AB: Where do you get all of this information? [Laughs]

An ad sheet from *Little Cigars* (a.k.a., *The Little Cigars Mob*), produced by Albert Band (American International Pictures, 1973).

I do my homework.

AB: Jesus Christ! I even forgot about that! [Laughs] He was extremely conscientious, shall we say. He knew that his voice would not be used. We would use an actor to voice him. He was used just because of his physical beauty. He was very nice. A really nice fellow. He was just a beautiful figure. Directing him was easy because we became pals. Once you become pals, you begin to tell jokes and stuff like that. He then mellowed a lot and he did the best he could. It was, you know, ridiculous!

FILMOGRAPHY FOR ALBERT BAND

1. *The Asphalt Jungle* (1950) AD
2. *The Red Badge of Courage* (1951) Sc
3. *The Young Guns* (1956) D
4. *Footsteps in the Night* (1957) Sc & S
5. *I Bury the Living* (1958) D & P
6. *Face of Fire* (1959) D, Sc, P
7. *The Avenger* (1962) D & P
8. *Gunfight at Red Sands* (1963) Sc
9. *Massacre at the Grand Canyon* (1965) Co-D
10. *Hercules and the Princess of Troy* (1965) D & P
11. *Showdown* (1966) D, Sc, P
12. *The Hellbenders* (1967) S & P
13. *A Minute to Pray, a Second to Die* (1968) Sc & P
14. *Little Cigars* (1973) Ex-P
15. *Texas in Flames* (1977) D
16. *Mansion of the Doomed* (1977) Ex-P
17. *Cinderella* (1977) P
18. *She Came to the Valley* (1977) Sc
19. *Zoltan, Hound of Dracula* (1978) D & P
20. *Auditions* (1978) Sc
21. *Metalstorm: The Destruction of Jared-Syn* (1983) Ex-P
22. *From Beyond* (1986) PM
23. *TerrorVision* (1986) P
24. *Ghost Warrior* (1986) Ex-P
25. *Troll* (1986) P & A
26. *Ghoulies II* (1987) D
27. *The Pit and the Pendulum* (1990) P
28. *Robojox* (1991) P
29. *Trancers II* (1991) A
30. *Trancers III* (1992) P
31. *Honey, I Blew Up the Kid* (1992) Ex-P
32. *Doctor Mordrid* (1992) Co-D
33. *Remote* (1993) P
34. *Robot Wars* (1993) D
35. *Prehysteria* (1993) Co-D
36. *Pet Shop* (1994) P
37. *Oblivion* (1994) Co-P
38. *Prehysteria 2* (1994) D
39. *Castle Freak* (1995) Ex-P
40. *Oblivion 2: Backlash* (1996) Co-P
41. *Zarkorr! The Invader* (1996) Ex-P

Harold Becker

Harold Becker's fascination with cinema developed at an early age. He began making short films at the age of sixteen. He then studied art at the Pratt Institute and began dabbling with still photography. After graduating he went to work in New York City as a commercial photographer, finding great success there. In his mid-thirties, Becker resumed his place behind the movie camera, directing television commercials and short films. One of his shorts, *Ivanhoe Donaldson*, garnered critical acclaim and numerous awards. This breakthrough led to his producing and co-directing (with Souter Harris) the 1972 feature film *The Ragman's Daughter* (1972). After a seven-year hiatus, Becker directed back-to-back Joseph Wambaugh adaptations with the gritty crime drama *The Onion Field* (1979) and *The Black Marble* (1980). The following year, *The Black Marble* received the Edgar Allan Poe Award for Best Motion Picture.

Becker then became recognized as an "A"-list director with his fourth feature, *Taps* (1981). While the film boasted two Oscar-winners as its stars (George C. Scott and Timothy Hutton), it is best remembered today for launching the superstar careers of Sean Penn and Tom Cruise. The film was met with critical praise and quickly became a box-office success. It also garnered a Golden Globe nomination for leading man Hutton. Next, Becker directed *Vision Quest* (1985), as well as the video for Madonna's soundtrack single "Crazy for You." Becker then directed *The Boost* (1988), which examined the perils of drug addiction. However, the film was largely overlooked, as it was overshadowed by the controversy surrounding the tumultuous affair of costars James Woods and Sean Young. Becker next used his talents to revive the careers of Al Pacino and Ellen Barkin with the thriller *Sea of Love* (1989).

In 1993, Becker helmed the Hitchcockian thriller *Malice*, which won both the Audience Award and the Best Director prize at the Cognac Festival du Film Policier. Becker then re-teamed with Pacino for *City Hall* (1996), directed Bruce Willis and Alec Baldwin in *Mercury Rising* (1998), and later John Travolta and Vince Vaughn in *Domestic Disturbance* (2001).

At the time of this writing Becker was preparing to direct his thirteenth feature, a remake of the Jules Dassin classic *Rififi*.

Favorite Films: The works of David Lean, John Ford, Federico Fellini, Michelangelo Antonioni, Ingmar Bergman, and Billy Wilder.

ANDREW RAUSCH: *What was the first film to have a significant impact on you?*

HAROLD BECKER: I think the film that had the most significant impact on me was Antonioni's *L'Avventura* (1960). That was a seminal film for me. It was the first film that showed me that there was such a thing as film grammar. With that film Antonioni opened up doors for me in terms of the way I looked at cinema.

Director Harold Becker contemplates his next scene on the set of the suspense-thriller *Malice* (Castle Rock Entertainment, 1993).

You came to filmmaking from a background in still photography. Certainly these are two completely different mediums, but are there any aspects of that experience which lent itself to directing?

HB: Well, of course. Just the sense of telling a story through visual images.

There is a rumor that you had the cast of Taps *attend some sort of boot camp to prepare themselves to be soldiers. As this story goes, Tom Cruise refused to attend. How much of this rumor is fact and how much is fiction?*

HB: That's absolutely not true. Completely wrong. That's ridiculous! We sent all of the actors to Officer Training School, and we basically turned this group of actors into cadets at a military academy. They were there for about four weeks, and the training was intensive. But quite to the contrary, Tom came into the picture having originally been cast as a background player. At that period of time he really showed his stuff during what you call "boot camp." I always make the joke that I gave him a battlefield commission; I promoted him there to the third lead in the picture.

Taps *was the first of two films you worked on with the late George C. Scott. What was he like to work with?*

HB: He was marvelous. Just a great actor.

Were you a fan of his work coming into the project?

HB: Oh, of course. I love pictures of his like *The Hustler* [1961]. He was one of the all-time great actors on the stage as well as film.

Let's talk about another great theater actor that you've collaborated with twice. From a director's standpoint, what is Al Pacino like to work with?

HB: He's a dream. Any director who gets to work with Al has just been given a great good fortune.

Pacino's been getting some criticism over the past few years. They say his performances are always very similar and that he always does that yelling thing. What's your take on this?

HB: He's a great actor. That's my take on it.

Alec Baldwin's "I am God" monologue from Malice *is certainly one of the most memorable of the past decade. When you read the script initially, was there a sense of how powerful and effective that scene was going to be?*

HB: Yeah, I think there was. Certainly by the time I did rehearsals I knew. Of course, you never really know until you do the scene, but I had a great writer on that — Aaron Sorkin, who is now dominating television with *The West Wing*.

How many takes did you have to shoot to capture that performance?

HB: It wasn't a lot. He really hit it on the nose pretty quickly. Maybe half-a-dozen takes; eight. Something like that.

Are there any films that you consider underrated?

HB: A lot of films are underrated. Many just don't find their audience, and sometimes they find their audience later. Even a great film like *Citizen Kane* [1941] didn't find its audience until years later. It never found its full audience. It's shocking to think that it didn't open up to applause, but it didn't. Another film I never really thought did it was another Orson Welles picture, *The Magnificent Ambersons* [1942]. *Magnificent Ambersons*, I think, really just broke Welles' spirit.

I absolutely adore both films. Obviously The Magnificent Ambersons *didn't reinvent the language of cinema the way* Citizen Kane *did, but in terms of entertainment, I actually enjoy it more than* Kane.

HB: I know others who share that sentiment, but I don't. They're close, but *The Magnificent Ambersons* was never finished the way Welles wanted it done.

Yes, it was actually finished by Robert Wise while Welles was working on It's All True.

HB: That's right.

Are there any films that you consider overrated?

HB: [Laughs] No, I won't go into that! They come out every day! But they have a way of leveling off. A lot of films that are overrated when they open will level off in time. I always feel that films—to some degree, hopefully—find their own level with time. Some films just open at the wrong time; don't get the promotion they should; the spirit or the temper of the times isn't fitting at that moment.

I remember Robert Altman talking about his terrific film *McCabe & Mrs. Miller* [1971]. That film got poor critical reviews and poor audience. Twenty years later it's been named one of the best pictures of the last thirty or forty years. So, how do you know?

If you could remake any film, what would interest you?

HB: I wish I could do *Double Indemnity* [1944] again, but I'd never do it better. I wouldn't

Al Pacino's Detective Frank Keller is on the case in Harold Becker's thriller *Sea of Love* (Universal Pictures, 1989).

even approach it! [Chuckles] It was so perfect. To me, it was one of those films that you look at and say, "You could never do this specific thing better." It just couldn't be done.

Here's a broad question for you: what do you see as being the single biggest problem with the film industry right now?

HB: Well, I think it's that films have become so much a commodity. They've always been a commodity, but now they have to open big on a weekend. It requires tremendous promotion, television, etc. Television is really what's changed the business because it's such a great medium for advertising. But then the tail begins to wag the dog because in order to use television you have to spend enormous amounts of money, so the films you make have to justify those expenditures. So now you're talking about having to have brand-name stars, if you will. It basically produces a kind of negative cycle. So is the tail wagging the dog or what?

There is, of course, a burgeoning independent film market. But it's very tough for independent films to get released because of the pressure, as well as the expense, that goes with releasing any film.

What advice would you give to aspiring filmmakers?

HB: If you want to become a filmmaker, don't let anybody tell you "no." Don't let anything stop you. Be persistent and do it. Set your goals and attain them.

Filmography for Harold Becker

1. *The Ragman's Daughter* (1972) D & P
2. *The Onion Field* (1979) D
3. *The Black Marble* (1980) D
4. *Taps* (1981) D
5. *Vision Quest* (1985) D
6. *The Big Town* (1987) Un D
7. *The Boost* (1988) D
8. *Sea of Love* (1989) D
9. *Malice* (1993) D & P
10. *City Hall* (1996) D & P
11. *Mercury Rising* (1998) D
12. *Domestic Disturbance* (2001) D & P

Josh Becker

By 1979, Josh Becker had already written four scripts, all of which, in his own words, "were in some way inept." In search of a new idea, Becker hit upon an interesting storyline: *the U.S. Marines vs. Charles Manson*! He knew it was a bizarre concept, but Becker also saw potential. He quickly hammered out an early draft with screenwriter Sheldon Lettich, but the script was nearly as problematic as his previous screenwriting attempts. "It was too serious," Becker recalls. "It just wasn't any fun." In an effort to tighten up the story and inject some fun into the project, Becker opted to reconstruct it in the form of "an all–American John Wayne movie." While driving from Tennessee to Michigan in a Ryder truck (on their way home after working on Sam Raimi's *The Evil Dead*, 1982), Becker and actor Bruce Campbell worked out the details of this new revision. After developing every minute detail of the storyline, Becker pulled the truck over at an all-night truck stop. He ordered a cup of java and scrawled everything on the back of a place mat. The film, which he titled *Thou Shalt Not Kill... Except* (1984), would not be made for several years. The film didn't shatter any box-office records, but it did establish Becker as an independent filmmaker with a unique voice. In 1991, Becker helmed his second feature, *Lunatics: A Love Story*. In 1994, Becker served as assistant director on the telefilm *Hercules and the Amazon Women*. He then directed its follow-up, *Hercules and the Maze of the Minotaur* (also 1994). He next wrote and directed the highly innovative thriller *Running Time* (1997), shot in real time with no visible cuts, á la Alfred Hitchcock's *Rope* (1948).

Becker was in postproduction on his fourth feature, *If I Had a Hammer* (2002), at the time this interview was conducted. In addition to his feature work, Becker has directed episodes of the Sam Raimi–produced television shows "Xena: Warrior Princess" and "Jack of All Trades." Becker's motto is "directing with an edge." His films—all produced outside the often meddlesome Hollywood studio system—are unorthodox, sometimes visionary, and quite refreshing in an era of assembly-line filmmaking.

Becker's most recent directorial effort was the Bruce Campbell starrer *Alien Apocalypse* (2005), which he described as being "*Spartacus* with aliens."

Favorite Films: *The Bridge on the River Kwai* (1957), *Lawrence of Arabia* (1962), *Marty* (1955), *The Big Country* (1958), *The Best Years of Our Lives* (1946), and *Unforgiven* (1992).

ANDREW RAUSCH: *In 1994, you directed Anthony Quinn in* Hercules in the Maze of the Minotaur. *During that shoot you recited his* Lawrence of Arabia *monologue for him. As a film buff, what was that experience like?*

JOSH BECKER: The look on his face was pretty priceless. He looked like, "Oh, my God. Kids these days! [Laughs] Boy have they wasted their lives!" He was honestly shocked and impressed, I think, that someone would have gone to the trouble. What can I say? I've seen the movie probably a hundred times. I love that speech of his.

Was it intimidating directing him?
    JB: He made sure it was intimidating! [Laughs] He had to take me on first shot, first day. Once I got past that, it was okay. Once he realized that I was doing everything within my means to get him out of there as fast as possible, then he was okay.

I'd like to talk a little bit about your view of Steven Spielberg. You once said, "The king of the shitmakers is Steven Spielberg. Because he is so good at making shit that looks like steaks, we have bestowed upon him a billion dollars, two Oscars, and his own film studio. Now Spielberg has his own shit factory."

Kevin Sorbo portrays the legendary Hercules in Josh Becker's ***Hercules and the Maze of the Minotaur*** (Universal TV, 1994).

JB: He can't tell a story. It's funny because I saw him on *Inside the Actors Studio* fairly recently. He's forever this humble guy, right? In this interview he says, "Look, there's one thing I can do and that's tell a story." And I just burst out laughing because I think that's the one thing he *can't* do. I think he can set up a camera angle really well or integrate a special effect really well—as well as anyone in Hollywood—but he doesn't understand basic story structure. I'm sorry, but almost no one in town does.

I've written three essays on story structure, and that's sort of my mantra and my philosophy of life. It is the basis of storytelling, and without it you're screwed. I see all of this shit coming down the pike all the time where nobody bothered to pay any attention at all to the basic story structure. Without it, the rest of it doesn't mean anything. It's like telling a joke and telling the punchline first. If you don't tell it right, it just ain't funny.

You want to hear my joke about Spielberg? Okay, have you ever seen *The Train* [1964]? In it you have Paul Scofield, who's a Nazi art expert who's stripping all the artwork out of France during World War II and loves these artworks. Burt Lancaster is the resistance fighter who has to stop the train from getting out of France, and he doesn't know anything about art. As far as he's concerned, he'd rather just blow the train up with all the artwork in it than let it leave France. Well, if this script was presented to Steven Spielberg, he'd *knowingly* say, "See, you fucked up. The resistance guy has to love the paintings and the Nazi has to hate them. You can't have the Nazi love them and the resistance guy not care about them! Don't you see? The good guy has to be entirely good and the bad guy has to be entirely bad!" And he thinks he's really on to something! [Laughs] The idea of there being *any* gray area in a character is something he's completely against. You're good or you're bad. Schindler—he's a bad man *until* he's a good man. No in-betweens in Spielberg movies. Human beings just don't work that way.

You see, I don't have any fear of saying these things anymore because, as I've gotten to this late stage in my career, I know I can't make movies for Steven Spielberg. I don't have to look out for not insulting him because I don't give a shit about him. There is no hope in me that he's gonna hire me to make a film, because I couldn't do it. Within a day or two I'd have insulted him and be gone from the picture! [Laughs] I can't make movies for these assholes. It's not possible for me anymore. I can't go through development. I don't think there's an executive in this town with a decent idea, and I can't pretend that they do. I think the whole system is an insult. You bring in a professional writer and then you say, "Look, we're not interested in anything you have to say. Just take notes." I'm telling you, there's *never* been an executive with a good idea.

Running Time definitely stands as a testament of what can be done outside the studio system. I think it's a brilliant film. What was the inspiration for that?

JB: Alfred Hitchcock's *Rope*. I had always admired the technique, but I never thought Hitchcock pulled it off. The material just wasn't right. So I sat down and tried to analyze why I liked this technique so much and what was wrong with *Rope*. My conclusion was that if it's all done on a soundstage, it doesn't matter. The only thing that's making not cutting cool is that you're on location—that the office building legitimately is next to where the car is parked. I also concluded that if you were gonna use the real-time concept, it had to be part of the story, which it's not in *Rope*. There's no time element in *Rope*. There's a body in the trunk and they have a party. Well, it's not like there's a timer and at that time the trunk's gonna pop open, so where's the fun in that?

You need that time element if you're gonna work in real time. Otherwise, why bother? Since a heist film is always based on a time element, it seemed like a natural fit. Then I just tried to compound it as many ways as I could. He gets a hooker at the beginning. Okay, now you've got an hour and ten minutes left. Time is the issue, and it continues to reestablish itself as the issue.

What are some of the difficulties of writing a screenplay which moves in real time as opposed to something more conventional?

JB: I found writing the script much more difficult than shooting the film. In our cut-happy world we are used to seeing a character say, "Okay, let's go to the store." Then they step out of frame and they're at the store. You don't see their trip to the store, unless there's a scene in the car. So if I need to get people from place to place, that means the stuff in between has to actually mean something. It was very difficult! [Laughs] You're constantly fighting the temptation to illogically place these places too close together.

I think the dialogue you use in the film is much more natural than what we see in most crime films today. You don't use pop culture references or a lot of long-winded moviespeak monologues.

Robbers Patrick (Jeremy Roberts), Buzz (Stan Davis), Carl (Bruce Campbell), and Donny (Gordon Jennison) experience an unexpected delay when a tire blows out on the way to the heist in *Running Time* (Panoramic Pictures, 1997).

JB: I think it's nonsense! Call it what you like, I call it "Quentin Tarantino dialogue." [Laughs] There was a scene in *Running Time* where I could have used it. It would have been funny and I'd have gotten a laugh with it, but it never furthers the story. That's the problem with that. When you go into that self-reflective non-sequitur dialogue your story stops. I'm off on a little point here, but let's say you've got two hitmen who are going to kill someone—which is Tarantino's entire career—but instead of talking about what they're about to do, they're talking about Madonna's latest record. Non-sequitur; it has nothing to do with what's happening!

Anyway, I'll tell you exactly when I could have used that in *Running Time*. The guys pull up in the van in front of the laundry and they're a little bit early. I'd written a whole scene out with all of them, and Buzz was saying, "I'm thinking about buying a new car." And they go, "What kind of car?" And he says, "Well, I've been looking at Fords." And Bruce goes, "No, no, no, you don't want a Ford. You want a GM." And another guy's like, "GM? Forget that! You need a Chrysler." Then the other guy's saying, "No, you wanna go foreign on this," and they just get into this whole thing about this until finally the car pulls up and they all start to pay attention again. To me, that's a Quentin Tarantino scene. It'll definitely get a laugh, but it does nothing to advance your story. So instead I had them discuss the safe, which continues the story. Instead of just making up bullshit sitting there, I actually had to go to the library and look at some books about safes and safecracking.

Filmography for Josh Becker

1. *The Evil Dead* (1982) L
2. *Thou Shalt Not Kill ... Except* (1985) D, Sc, Cin, Ed
3. *Evil Dead II* (1987) A
4. *Lunatics: A Love Story* (1991) D & Sc
5. *Army of Darkness* (1993) A
6. *Real Stories of the Highway Patrol* [episodes: various] (1993) D
7. *Hercules and the Amazon Women* (1994) [TV] AD
8. *Hercules in the Maze of the Minotaur* (1994) [TV] D
9. *Mosquito* (1995) A
10. *Xena: Warrior Princess* [episodes: various] (1995) D
11. *Running Time* (1997) D, Sc, P
12. *Jack of All Trades* [episodes: "Return of the Dragoon" and "The People's Dragoon"] (2000) D
13. *If I Had a Hammer* (2001) D, Sc, P
14. *Alien Apocalypse* (2005) [TV] D & Sc
15. *Stan Lee's Harpies* (2007) (TV) D

Budd Boetticher

Few filmmakers (or anyone else, for that matter) have accomplished as much as the late Budd Boetticher did in his lifetime. After attending Culver Military Academy and Ohio State University, where he excelled as a football player and boxer, Boetticher traveled to Mexico and studied bullfighting, becoming only the third white matador in history. He then, through his friendship with Hal Roach, Jr., managed to land a couple of lower level positions in the film industry — as a horse wrangler on *Of Mice and Men* (1939) and as a technical assistant on the bullfighting film *Blood and Sand* (1941). After learning the craft from director Rouben Mamoulian and editor Barbara McLean, Boetticher served as assistant director on films by noted filmmakers King Vidor and George Stevens. Soon Boetticher moved into the role of director, elevating the "B" film to levels of artistic vision unlike anything seen previously. With producer John Wayne, Boetticher made his first "A" picture, *Bullfighter and the Lady* (1951), a semi-autobiographical film which he also co-wrote. Despite the fact that Wayne and legendary filmmaker John Ford re-edited the film and trimmed nearly forty-five minutes without his approval, Boetticher received an Oscar nod for Best Original Screenplay. Boetticher would have a similar run-in with Wayne on *Seven Men from Now* (1956) when the producer once again recut the film without the director's approval. (Both films have since been restored to the director's original vision.)

Having directed more than forty films, Boetticher is best remembered for a series of westerns he made with stoic actor Randolph Scott. Those films, collectively known as "the Ranown Cycle," are widely considered to be among the finest films the genre has produced. In 1960, Boetticher paid homage to the Warner Bros. crime pictures of the 1930s with *The Rise and Fall of Legs Diamond*, which remains one of the strongest gangster films captured on celluloid. In addition to his feature film work, Boetticher also worked on several television series. He directed the pilot for *Maverick*, as well as episodes of the Sam Peckinpah–produced series *Zane Grey Theater* and *The Rifleman*.

In the early sixties, Boetticher began filming a documentary about his close friend, famed matador Carlos Arruza. In what would be one of the most legendary and problematic shoots in motion picture history, *Arruza* (1972) would take nearly a decade to complete, over which time Boetticher and his crew faced many hardships, not the least of which was their subject's death. After Boetticher's return to the States he formed partnerships with Sergio Leone and Audie Murphy, both of which were cut short due to his partners' deaths. (However, Boetticher and Murphy did complete one film together: *A Time for Dying*, 1971.)

In 1969, Don Siegel was hired to direct Boetticher's screenplay *Two Mules for Sister Sara*. However, the Clint Eastwood vehicle would bear little resemblance to Boetticher's original script. Boetticher, envisioning the project as another potential Oscar nominee, was outraged to learn that Siegel had dramatically rewritten the script and filmed it as a spaghetti western–styled melodrama.

Author Andrew J. Rausch with the late Budd Boetticher at Boetticher's home in 1999 (author's collection).

Budd Boetticher passed away on November 29, 2001— almost two years to the date after this interview was conducted. Although his death leaves a gaping void in the lives of everyone who'd ever met him, Boetticher left behind an incredible body of work.

Favorite Films: *The Treasure of the Sierra Madre* (1948), *Casablanca* (1942), and *The Way We Were* (1973).

ANDREW RAUSCH: *John Wayne produced two of your films,* Bullfighter and the Lady *and* Seven Men from Now. *What was he like to work with?*
BUDD BOETTICHER: A bastard. [Laughs] You know, I never worked with him as an actor. I was supposed to direct *The Comancheros* [1961], but I didn't want to work with him. I would have quit, or he'd have fired me the first day. I'm probably the only guy in the world who ever fought with John Wayne. I was a boxer, an athlete. He could have hit me in the ring with boxing gloves for ten years, but if he'd have hit me in the street in a street fight, he'd have killed me. You know, we argued about a lot of things. I didn't like a lot of the things he did, and we didn't really get along very well, but we loved each other. Anytime I write something about John Wayne, it's always the same sentence: anyone who knows me well knows how much I loved John Wayne. But if they really know me well, they also know that I many times hated his guts. So that's what I thought of John Wayne.

An ad for the infamous Budd Boetticher biopic/documentary *Arruza* (AVCO Embassy Pictures, 1972).

I think Duke played Duke better than anybody in the world could play anybody. I thought he was the all-American guy and a big hero. I did love him, but he was also not that great in some respects.

You served as technical advisor to Tyrone Powers on Blood and Sand *(1941). What was that experience like?*

BB: I hated it. [Director] Rouben Mamoulian was just awful. He was cruel. He had a bell, and if he rang twice, I'd have to come and stand behind him. He would ask me questions about bullfighting, and bullfighting is like Catholicism; it's a religion — there's a right way to do it and a wrong way. And he never did anything right — like the sash that Tyrone Powers had that was sixteen feet long and [made him look] like he was pregnant. By the time he got this thing around, he would have made a nice scene. He told us he wanted Tyrone to die with El Greco colors — the grays and the light greens and stuff. If you die, you don't die in a church, with a beautiful crucifix there; you die in a freezing hospital. But that's not how he wanted it. He wanted to win the Academy Award for color, which he did.

I told Mary after we were married that the only person in the world that I ever really hated — I don't know the word jealousy, I don't know the word hate, I don't know a hell of a lot about the word love — but I *hated* Rouben Mamoulian. He was just a horrible, horrible man.

Mary and I had been married about a week, and we went out for dinner. This was thirty years after *Blood and Sand*. I walked into this restaurant with my beautiful new wife, and here came Rouben Mamoulian. And he looked at me and he said, "Buddy, darling! Oh, my dear, dear people, this is my Budd Boetticher! I started him! He is a great, great director!" And he gave me a hug, and I said to my wife, "Mary, I'd like you to meet my dear friend, Rouben Mamoulian!" [Laughs] How phony can you get? But the years went by, and I thought he was great. He loved what I did, so I thought he *must* be a nice guy! [Chuckles]

You worked with Woody Strode a number of times. Because Strode generally played characters of a stereotypical nature, his contributions regarding the advancement of African-Americans in the film industry are often overlooked. How important do you feel his work was in this context?

BB: Well, I think he was great; because he was such a talented athlete and a great guy, you didn't notice what color he was. I lived in Indiana where the word "nigger" was fashionable, and I never understood it. The only person who ever beat me in the one-hundred-yard dash was Jesse Owens. I never knew what his color was, nor did I care. My mother referred to blacks in a completely different way. The Mason-Dixon line was not just Kentucky; it was terrible in those days. And two of the men that I loved the most in my life were Woody and Sydney Poitier. You know, I did one of Sydney's first pictures [*Red Ball Express*, 1952]. I picked him off the street. And Woody was a dear friend. We never discussed black and white. I put him in every film I could, but I never realized he was contributing because I never thought of him that way.

Some film critics in the late sixties accused Italian filmmaker Sergio Leone of ripping off your work. What's your take on that?

BB: I take it as a great compliment. You know, we were going across France and then over to Milan. I was being honored there and I hadn't paid any attention to what they were doing, other than what they were doing for me. I said, "Oh, my God!" Mary said, "What's the matter?" I said, "Guess who the top judge is? Sergio Leone!" She said, "So?" I said, "They used to say the same thing about Sam Peckinpah — that he'd stolen everything from me. He's gonna hate my guts like Sam did!" She said, "I don't think so." I said, "I know these guys. If you see a short, fat little guy who looks like Sergio Leone, you tell me and we'll get the hell out of there!"

So we were walking up the steps to the hotel in Milan with the bellboys in front of us, and down came Leone. I was halfway up the steps and there was nothing to do but face him. And he looked at me and he said, "Buddy, darling, I stole *everything* from you!" [Laughs] Of course, he didn't really, not that I know of. If you looked at his picture and then looked at mine, I don't know where they got that. Maybe it's because they were good, I hope. From that point on, we became best friends.

How much different was Don Siegel's film Two Mules for Sister Sara *from your original screenplay?*

BB: I was at the premiere with Ron Ely, who played Tarzan, and was just very unhappy. Clint Eastwood is a dear, dear friend of mine now, but at the time I said, "The stupidest S.O.B. in the theater was the leading man because he was the only person who didn't realize this nun was not a nun." Couldn't he smell her breath? When he threw the dynamite to get rid of the three rapists and then *walked* down... It's dynamite, it's gonna blow up! I said, "Jesus Christ!" Don Siegel and Clint were sitting directly behind us, and Ron said, "We ought to get up and hit those two guys sitting behind us." I said, "Well, you hit Clint and I'll hit Don." But Don was a good friend of mine and he called me the day after the premiere and he said, "Budd, thanks for not walking out of the theater last night." I said, "Don, how could you make a

Audie Murphy as Bill Doolin, a.k.a. "the Cimarron Kid," in the Budd Boetticher oater *The Cimarron Kid* (Universal Pictures Company, 1952).

piece of crap like that?" And he said, "It's a wonderful thing to wake up in the morning and know there's a check in the mail." Dead silence. Finally, he says, "I'm talking to the wrong guy, aren't I?" And I said, "Yeah, you sure as hell are. Don, it's better to wake up in the morning and not be ashamed of what you see in the mirror." And he was getting older, and now I'm twenty years older than he was then, and I would *never* do that. And that's why I haven't been working — now I can do as I please.

What's the one piece of advice you wish someone had told you before you became a filmmaker?
BB: [Laughs] Don't sleep with the leading lady until you're almost finished shooting, or you'll end up with two directors on the film!

FILMOGRAPHY FOR BUDD BOETTICHER

1. *Blood and Sand* (1941) TA
2. *Military Training* (1941) 2AD
3. *Submarine Raider* (1942) Un Co-D
4. *The Desperadoes* (1943) AD
5. *Destroyer* (1943) AD
6. *Good Luck, Mr. Yates* (1943) Un A
7. *The More the Merrier* (1943) AD
8. *Cover Girl* (1944) AD
9. *U-Boat Prisoner* (1944) Un Co-D
10. *One Mysterious Night* (1944) D
11. *The Missing Juror* (1944) D
12. *The Girl in the Case* (1944) Un Co-D
13. *Youth on Trial* (1945) D
14. *A Guy, a Gal, and a Pal* (1945) D
15. *Escape in the Fog* (1945) D
16. *The Fleet That Came to Stay* (1946) D
17. *Behind Locked Doors* (1948) D
18. *Assigned to Danger* (1948) D
19. *The Wolf Hunters* (1949) D
20. *Black Midnight* (1949) D
21. *Killer Shark* (1950) D
22. *The Sword of D'Artagnan* (1951) D
23. *The Cimarron Kid* (1951) D
24. *Bullfighter and the Lady* (1951) D, Sc, AP
25. *Horizons West* (1952) D
26. *Bronco Buster* (1952) D
27. *Red Ball Express* (1952) D
28. *Wings of the Hawk* (1953) D
29. *The Man from the Alamo* (1953) D
30. *City Beneath the Sea* (1953) D
31. *Seminole* (1953) D
32. *East of Sumatra* (1953) D
33. *The Public Defender* (1954) D
34. *The Magnificent Matador* (1955) D & Sc
35. *The Count of Monte Cristo* (1955) D
36. *The Killer Is Loose* (1956) D
37. *Seven Men from Now* (1956) D
38. *Zane Grey Theater* (1956) D
39. *Alias Mike Hercules* (1956) D
40. *Decision at Sundown* (1957) D
41. *The Tall T* (1957) D
42. *Maverick* (1957) [TV pilot] D
43. *Maverick* (1957–1962) [various episodes] D
44. *Westbound* (1958) D
45. *Buchanan Rides Alone* (1958) D
46. *77 Sunset Strip* (1958) D
47. *The Rifleman* (1958) D
48. *Ride Lonesome* (1959) D & P
49. *Hong Kong* (1960) D
50. *The Rise and Fall of Legs Diamond* (1960) D
51. *Comanche Station* (1960) D & P
52. *Two Mules for Sister Sara* (1969) S
53. *A Time for Dying* (1971) D & Sc
54. *Arruza* (1972) D, Sc, P
55. *My Kingdom For...* (1985) D, Sc, P
56. *Tequila Sunrise* (1988) A

John Carpenter

Kentucky native John Carpenter began crafting short films in 1962. As a student at USC Film School, Carpenter would make two impressive career-altering short films. For the first, *The Resurrection of Broncho Billy* (1970), Carpenter won an Academy Award in the category of Best Live-Action Short Film. The second short, *Dark Star*, was expanded into a feature film that would be released theatrically in 1974. (When USC refused to give him back the footage from the original short, Carpenter reportedly broke into the college and stole it.) In 1976, Carpenter reworked his idol Howard Hawks's *Rio Bravo* (1959) into a contemporary thriller entitled *Assault on Precinct 13* (1976). Two years later, he wrote, directed, and scored the hit film *Halloween* (1978), which has since spawned eight sequels (to date) and is considered one of the finest horror movies ever produced. The film, made for a mere $300,000, quickly became the most profitable indie picture ever produced. That same year, Carpenter's script *The Eyes of Laura Mars* (1978) was directed by Irvin Kershner, and starred Faye Dunaway and Tommy Lee Jones. Carpenter then directed the seminal Elvis Presley biopic *Elvis* (1979). The telefilm, which starred Kurt Russell, received three Emmy nominations.

The "master of terror" then returned to horror with the genre classic *The Fog* (1980), which starred his then-wife Adrienne Barbeau. He then re-teamed with Kurt Russell for the hit film *Escape from New York* (1981). That same year, he and cowriter Debra Hill collaborated on the sequel *Halloween II* (1981). Carpenter then embarked upon another Hawks remake with *The Thing* (1982). While the film proved to be a box-office disappointment, it has since gained a tremendous following and is—like a good many of Carpenter's films—looked upon today as one of the genre's finest offerings. Carpenter has since worked without pause, writing, directing, composing, and producing. Other notable Carpenter films include *Christine* (1983), *Starman* (1984), *Big Trouble in Little China* (1986), *They Live* (1988), *In the Mouth of Madness* (1995), *Escape from L.A.* (1996), *Vampires* (1998), and *Ghosts of Mars* (2001). In 1993, Carpenter collaborated with *Texas Chainsaw Massacre* (1974) helmer Tobe Hooper on the well-received anthology film *Body Bags*.

Favorite Films: *Only Angels Have Wings* (1939), *Rio Bravo* (1959), *His Girl Friday* (1940), *Touch of Evil* (1958), *Forbidden Planet* (1956), and *The Quatermass Experiment* (1955).

ANDREW RAUSCH: *You once said, "The second you call yourself an artist, you're dead." What did you mean by that?*

JOHN CARPENTER: I meant that you shouldn't allow yourself to become pretentious. For me, at least, that's the death of spontaneity and creativity. You can't take yourself too seriously. I think it's something you see all the time. As a result, a lot of really talented directors are gone now. I pray everyday that I never get to that point.

John Carpenter on the set of his 1986 adventure-comedy-kung-fu-monster-ghost-story *Big Trouble in Little China* (20th Century–Fox Film Corp., 1986).

Your film Dark Star *began as a short film you made at USC. What inspired you to expand that short into a feature-length film, and how many years did you work on that project?*

JC: That was a four-year project. What happened was, my co-creator Dan O'Bannon and I decided that this would be a good chance to try and get a feature out. We started out with something like forty-five minutes of footage, and we had a lot of faith in that footage. We sort of saw an opportunity there, and we took it. Somehow, it all worked out.

You've won an Academy Award and worked in a number of different genres, yet you tend to be typecast as a "horror director." Why do you think that is?

JC: You really get labeled with your first major success. For me, that success came with *Halloween*. I have no problem with that label. I love the horror genre, and I love working in it. It doesn't bother me at all.

Eight sequels have been produced since you made Halloween. *What are your thoughts on those films?*

JC: [Sighs] Well, it's essentially a money-making operation, and all of the major '70s and '80s horror films have spawned sequels: *Friday the 13th* [1980] did; *A Nightmare on Elm Street* [1984] did; *Halloween* did. Part of me says, "That's too bad," because I don't think there was really much more story there that needed to be told. Then another part of me thinks it's okay because I get a check each time they make one. [Laughs] So, that's not bad. I guess I'm a happy capitalist.

Storywise, do you feel that any of the sequels have been true to the original film?

JC: Oh, I don't think I want to comment on that.

Should your not wanting to comment be seen as a statement in itself?
  JC: [Laughs] I don't want to comment on that, either.

Your theme music for Halloween *has really stood the test of time. Today it remains as effective and as chilling as it was when the film was first released. When you were writing the film's score, did you have any idea that you were making something special?*
  JC: [Laughs] No! Of course, you never really know that. It was just a really simple little piano theme which was based on my father's teaching me five-four time when I was young. I had no idea whatsoever that it would be remembered or thought of as being important.
  The other score that people keep bringing up is my score from *Assault on Precinct 13*. Apparently that influenced a lot of people. I wasn't really aware of that until just here in the last few years. It's odd, isn't it? You just never know.

Right now they're making a big-budget remake of Assault on Precinct 13, *which stars Laurence Fishburne, Ethan Hawke, and Gabriel Byrne. What are your thoughts on that?*
  JC: You know, they've got a pretty good script.

Has it changed much from the original?
  JC: Yes and no. It's essentially the same siege movie that I made, only with a few really neat things added. I guess we'll see how it goes. This was a French producer who's been wanting to do this for years, and he's worked really hard to get it right.

Serial killer Michael Myers (Nick Castle) strangles one of his victims (unidentified) in John Carpenter's horror classic *Halloween* (Compass International Pictures, 1978).

In the past, you've also been quoted as saying that in Europe you're regarded as an auteur, but in America you're seen as being a "bum." Why do you think Europeans tend to look at the genre with more respect?

JC: I don't know. America tends to not celebrate its genre directors, be they western directors or horror directors—even comedy to some extent. For some reason, Europeans have always seemed to look at that a little bit differently. They don't look at them as being "B" movies. Instead, they look at them as being their own separate art form. I think it's just a difference in perspective.

American audiences—especially American critics—tend to think that horror films are beneath them. You know, they're junk; they're "pulp." They see them as being like comic books—they could never be serious. There are some exceptions, but those are few and far between.

Like all filmmakers with a body of work as large as yours, you've seen your films praised and you've also seen them drubbed. Do you allow yourself to be affected by criticism?

JC: You can't help but be affected when you read the reviews. I try not to take it too seriously one way or the other. It's usually somewhere in between. I think you have to keep your perspective at all times; perspective meaning that you're in it for the long haul. In the short run, some people aren't going to like this or that, and others are going to love it. You just can't let yourself worry too much about it.

Do you have any dream projects?

JC: No, not really. I had one for many years. It was an adaptation of a novel called *The Star Is My Destination*, by Alfred Bester. But, you know, it didn't work out. The screenwriter who worked on it didn't do a very good job. I just sort of decided that it wasn't really fair to the [original] material. I just said, "I don't want to do that. I'll just fuck it up."

As you know, Hollywood can be a mercilessly demanding, controlling place. How have you managed to remain true to your artistic visions thus far in your career?

JC: Well, I don't know that I always have. In some circumstances I've had less control than I've had on others. Usually, I've just been very lucky. That, and I've tried to stick to my guns as much as possible. In a few cases, I wasn't so lucky, but that's the toughest battle a director has.

What's the funniest thing you've ever seen on a film set?

JC: There was a period of time during the making of both *Christine* and *Starman* where we had a lot of practical jokes going on amongst the crew. That was part of the fun of making films in those days. Probably the funniest thing I can remember is the time I snuck on the ground up to the sound cart and unplugged all of the wires. Then I snuck back. When we rolled sound, there was nothing coming out. The soundman was a very close friend of mine. The look on his face was something I'll never forget. It was probably cruel, but it was extremely funny.

FILMOGRAPHY FOR JOHN CARPENTER

1. *The Resurrection of Broncho Billy* (1970) D, Sc, Ed, C
2. *Dark Star* (1974) D, Sc, P, C
3. *Assault on Precinct 13* (1976) D, Sc, Ed, C
4. *Halloween* (1978) D, Sc, P, Un A, C
5. *Eyes of Laura Mars* (1978) Sc & S
6. *Someone's Watching Me!* (1978) [TV] D & Sc

7. *Zuma Beach* (1978) [TV] Sc
8. *Elvis* (1979) D
9. *The Fog* (1980) D, Sc, Un A, C
10. *Escape from New York* (1981) D, Sc, Un A, C
11. *Halloween II* (1981) Un Co-D, Sc, P, C
12. *The Thing* (1982) D & Un A
13. *Halloween III: Season of the Witch* (1982) P & C
14. *Christine* (1983) D & C
15. *Starman* (1984) D & Un A
16. *The Philadelphia Experiment* (1984) Ex-P
17. *Black Moon Rising* (1986) Sc, S, Ex-P
18. *Big Trouble in Little China* (1986) D, Un A, C
19. *Prince of Darkness* (1987) D, Sc, C
20. *They Live* (1988) D, Sc, C
21. *El Diablo* (1990) [TV] Sc
22. *Blood River* (1991) [TV] Sc
23. *Memoirs of an Invisible Man* (1992) D & Un A
24. *Body Bags* (1993) [TV] Co-D, Ex-P, A, C
25. *In the Mouth of Madness* (1995) D & C
26. *Village of the Damned* (1995) D & A
27. *Escape from LA* (1996) D, Sc, C
28. *Vampires* (1998) D & C
29. *Silent Predators* (1999) [TV] Sc
30. *Ghosts of Mars* (2001) D, Sc, C
31. *Vampires: Los Muertos* (2002) Ex-P
32. *Assault on Precinct 13* (2004) S
33. *Masters of Horror* (2007) [episodes: "Cigarette Burns" and "Pro Life"] D

Jeremiah Chechik

Before MTV became a dominant force in the entertainment industry and music videos were seen as a legitimate art form, Canadian-bred Jeremiah Chechik, a former *Vogue* fashion photographer, made a name for himself shooting music videos for early-eighties bands like Hall and Oates. The Directors Guild Award–winner also found tremendous success directing commercials, but all along he dreamed of making motion pictures. In the late eighties Hollywood began looking upon the world of music videos as a proving ground for fresh young filmmakers. Soon Chechik found himself being wooed by several studios and being bombarded with screenplays. One of these was an early draft of *National Lampoon's Christmas Vacation* (1989), which ultimately became his directorial debut. The film, which features early appearances by actors Juliette Lewis, Julia Louis-Dreyfuss, and Johnny Galecki, was met with critical acclaim and was a box-office hit, earning $71 million for Warner Bros.

The success of Chechik's debut gave him the leverage to explore different types of projects. In 1993, he was again met with critical praise for his sophomore effort *Benny & Joon* (1993). Despite having a less-than-commercial premise — the story of two mentally ill lovebirds, played by Johnny Depp and Mary Stuart Masterson — the film still grossed a respectable $23 million. For his role in the film, Depp received a Golden Globe nod, and the picture was nominated for three MTV Movie Awards. The following year Chechik conceived and executive produced Arturo Ripstein's *The Queen of the Night* (1994), which was nominated for an impressive eleven Mexican Academy Awards, winning six.

Chechik's third film as director was Disney's *Tall Tale* (1995), written by *Saving Private Ryan* (1998) scribe Robert Rodat. Chechik then remade the Henri-Georges Clouzot classic *Les Diaboliques* (1955) — a film Alfred Hitchcock had expressed interest in remaking but never did. (Instead, Hitchcock tapped Pierre Boileau — the author whose work *Les Diaboliques* was based upon — for *Vertigo*, 1958.) Chechik's update, rewritten by Don Roos, boasted a stellar cast which included Sharon Stone, Isabelle Adjani, and Kathy Bates.

In 1998, Chechik helmed his fifth film, Warner Bros.' $60-million adaptation of the cult television series *The Avengers*. As with each of the four projects Chechik directed prior to *The Avengers* (1998), the film featured a stellar cast, starring Academy Award winners Ralph Fiennes and Sean Connery, and Oscar-nominated actress Uma Thurman. In 2004, Chechik directed the telefilm *Meltdown*.

Favorite Films: *Napoleon* (1927), *His Girl Friday* (1940), *Happy Together* (1997), *Harold and Maude* (1971), and *The 400 Blows* (1959).

ANDREW RAUSCH: *When did you first realize that you wanted to make movies?*

JEREMIAH CHECHIK: The realization was not an instant one, but really came out of a convergence of interests I had in life, which was in people, storytelling, music, photography, theater. I realized that those interests, which I had pursued in their simplest forms, could be brought together by making movies. So it seemed that, as a director, I could utilize many of the skills I had learned in those different arenas.

On your first film, National Lampoon's Christmas Vacation, *you worked with John Hughes, who wrote the screenplay and also served as producer. What was Hughes like to work with?*

JC: He was fantastic to work with in terms of his understanding of comedy. I learned a lot about comedy from him. He's a very funny and extremely focused individual. Also, as a producer, he protected me creatively so that I could pretty well work from my instincts without looking over my shoulder.

Given the mediocrity of the film's predecessor, National Lampoon's European Vacation *(1985), expectations were not very high for* Christmas Vacation. *However, I think you made a much better film. What do you see as being some of the problems with* European Vacation, *and how do you think your film managed to avoid those pitfalls?*

JC: I don't know. I never saw *European Vacation.*

Really?

JC: No. I had originally planned to do a different movie as my first movie for Warner Bros., which was a very, very small movie about music and the Apollo Theater. When that didn't happen they started sending me scripts for different projects, and this was the one I thought seemed kind of fun. I had never done any comedy before. Working primarily as a

Director Jeremiah Chechik (center) discusses a scene with actors Johnny Depp (left) and Aidan Quinn (right) on the set of *Benny & Joon* (Metro-Goldwyn-Mayer Inc., 1993).

Chevy Chase's Clark W. Griswald (center) and family unite for the holidays in *National Lampoon's Christmas Vacation* (Warner Bros. Pictures, 1989).

commercial director, my work was much more visual and much more focused on mood, so I thought if I could master this it would be an interesting experience. It was at a point in my life when I really had a desire to make a movie, so I just jumped in and tried to do the best job I knew how to do. I wasn't really thinking of the movies that had come before, so I consciously chose not to look at the other films.

In fact, when John wrote the script, it wasn't initially a National Lampoon film for Chevy Chase. It was just a movie about a family, and then Warner Bros. convinced him to adapt it to that series.

Each of the films you've directed at this point in your career have been completely different. You've worked in comedy, drama, action-adventure. Is this something you intentionally try to do from project to project?

JC: I like working with actors very, very much, and I don't like to repeat myself, for better or worse. I've always enjoyed exploring new frontiers for myself and in my work.

After making a comedy, I made *Benny & Joon*. I didn't consider that a comedy because it has a number of tragic elements, as well, but I wanted to direct it with a light touch so that one could approach the subject matter in a way that wasn't too heavy. It turned out to be funnier than I intended it to be, but it turned out pretty well.

In each of the five films you've directed, you have always aligned yourself with extremely gifted actors or actresses. Even in the smaller supporting roles your films have featured actors such as

Julianne Moore, Kathy Bates, Juliette Lewis, William H. Macy, et al. Is this something you consciously look for going into a project?

JC: Yeah, absolutely. One of the most critical marks for me when I approach any material is, can I pull together a group of actors that will create some very distinctive energy?

Do you think that casting such talents can sometimes be a catch-22? I'm thinking of The Avengers, *where you had two Oscar-winning actors and an Oscar-nominated actress as your three leads. In my mind, that starpower created expectations which were impossible to live up to.*

JC: In a way, I think that was the case. I think part of the problem regarding the process of *The Avengers* was that it didn't start out to be a big summer movie. It just started out to be a quirky, unusual movie with Ralph Fiennes. Because of my luck in landing Sean Connery for the part of the villain, I think the studio started to perceive the film in a different way — maybe started to cast a more greedy eye on the potential of the film — and started to build it in a way that would build false expectations for the audience.

Then there was a very unhappy convergence of these forces in the cutting room, and what resulted was pretty much stillborn.

How much of the film was lost in the studio recut?

JC: Quite a bit. I would have to say that many of my favorite moments in the entire movie were cut out.

After all of these events, how happy were you with the final cut?

JC: I was extraordinarily unhappy. But having said that, I thought Ralph's performance was fabulous and the performances of the supporting cast were really great. The problem was when you rob it of its own internal illogical logic, you really turn it on its head.

I understand the chess moves in The Avengers *are the same as those in* Blade Runner *(1982). Is that true?*

JC: If that's true, it's a coincidence, but it could be not an unusual coincidence. We were looking for a very classic setup, so I had brought in a chess expert to find several point/counterpoint moves that worked out really well. We went through them and chose that one because it just had the best pace, sense of play, and sense of dialogue. When they were making *Blade Runner*, they may have gone through that very same procedure.

Interesting or not, the line "time to die" has also been pointed at as a reference to Blade Runner, *as that line appears in both films.*

JC: As far as I know, that was not intentional. I didn't write that line, Don MacPherson did. If that's true, that's certainly a great tip of the hat.

How did you become involved with The Queen of the Night?

JC: *The Queen of the Night* was an original idea I had when I was traveling in Mexico. I am a great fan of ranchero music, and one night I found myself in a bar. After many bottles of tequila and my Mexican friends surrounding me, I looked up in a daze and saw velvet paintings of the great ranchero singers and mariachi singers over the last fifty years. And only one of them was a woman. So I said, "Well, who's that?" And they told me that she was Lucha Reyes and that she had really originated this form of ranchero music. I said, "Well, what's the story with her?" And they told me, and I said, "Why hasn't anyone made a movie of this?" They shrugged. I said, "Well, let's do it." So we did. I hired Paz Alicia Garciadiego, who is a brilliant writer, and Arturo Ripstein, who is one of the finest Latin American filmmakers, and we made the movie.

Let's talk about Diabolique *for a moment. Alfred Hitchcock once expressed great interest in remaking the original 1955 film, but never got the opportunity to do so. However, you did. How much pressure did you feel in remaking what is essentially considered a classic film?*

JC: Well, I have to be honest. I kind of liked that pressure. This may in hindsight be kind of an odd conceit, but I wanted to take a movie that is perceived as a classic, but is really a very flawed film, and remake it. I thought, If I could take this story and redo it, shifting it from a mysogynistic story into a feminist story without really changing the essence of the plot twist, then I will have achieved something artistically that is satisfying to myself. That was really one of my principal focuses. In a way, the movie was meant to be viewed along with the first one; it's really a nice experience to screen both of them together.

Screenwriter Don Roos and yourself caught a lot of flack for changing the ending of the original film. What were some of the considerations that went into that decision?

JC: I think it was too easy [in the original version] to see her as a victim, and we didn't want to victimize the woman. It was something that we felt very strongly about in our own personal expression of this story. The original movie ended rather abruptly. It just ended. We wanted a little more of a dynamic between the two women that was a little more complex.

Filmography for Jeremiah Chechik

1. *Head Office* (1986) A
2. *National Lampoon's Christmas Vacation* (1989) D
3. *Benny & Joon* (1993) D
4. *The Queen of the Night* (1993) Ex-P & Un S
5. *Tall Tale* (1995) D
6. *Diabolique* (1996) D
7. *Van Halen: Video Hits Volume One* [video: "When It's Love"] (1996) Co-D
8. *Robert Altman's Gun* (1997) D
9. *The Avengers* (1998) D
10. *Meltdown* (2004) [TV] D
11. *Tilt* [episode: "The Whale"] (2005) D

Larry Cohen

In his five decades as a screenwriter, producer, and director, Larry Cohen has established himself as one of the most versatile and prolific filmmakers of the modern film era. He has written and directed films in nearly every genre, and his filmography is almost as lengthy as John Dillinger's rap sheet.

Cohen's screenwriting credits include *The Return of the Magnificent Seven* (1966), *El Condor* (1970), *Body Snatchers* (1993), *Guilty as Sin* (1993), and *Phone Booth* (2002). Cohen's directorial credits include *It's Alive!* (1974), *A Return to Salem's Lot* (1987), and Bette Davis' final film, *Wicked Stepmother* (1989). His 1977 film *God Told Me To*, which features an early cameo by comedian Andy Kaufman, has served as an inspiration to many filmmakers, and its influence can be seen in Chris Carter's popular television series *The X-Files*. Cohen wrote and directed *Black Caesar* (1973) and its sequel *Hell Up in Harlem* (1973), which many film academians consider the best of the so-called "blaxploitation" films of the seventies. Cohen's television writing credits include *Ed McBain's 87th Precinct* and numerous *Columbo* telefilms. In addition, Cohen executive produced and wrote the series *Branded*, as well as the cult sci-fi series *The Invaders*, which continues to influence the genre. In 1988, the Cohen-penned film *Best Seller* (1987) was nominated for Best Picture at the Mystery Writers of America's Edgar Allan Poe Awards.

In 2002, Cohen once again found success as a screenwriter with the Joel Schumacher–helmed thriller *Phone Booth* (2002). In 2004, Cohen returned to the director's chair for the documentary *Air Force One: The Final Mission*. In addition, his script *Cellular* (2004) was produced as a movie starring Kim Basinger and William H. Macy.

Favorite Films: The Warner Bros. films of the thirties and forties, such as *Casablanca* (1942), *Yankee Doodle Dandy* (1942), and *The Adventures of Robin Hood* (1938); "Most of the stuff directed by Michael Curtiz."

Andrew Rausch: *What was it like directing Bette Davis in* Wicked Stepmother? *I've heard there were creative conflicts during filming.*

Larry Cohen: The main conflict was just Bette and her health. She came on the picture a very sick woman. Apparently, the bridge in her mouth broke on the first day of production. She was having trouble keeping the bridge in place, so she was doing very strange line readings with pauses in odd places. I didn't know why, but she did. She was trying to keep her bridge from falling out, and it's a terribly embarrassing thing for a big star like that. After a week of shooting the picture, she saw the dailies, and she could see what she was doing. She said, "I can't live with this. I've got to get this bridge fixed." She said she couldn't come back.

A publicity photograph from the classic television series "The Invaders," depicting Roy Thinnes' David Vincent running from aliens (American Broadcasting Company, 1967).

First her lawyer came in and said she wasn't well-treated and that she wasn't happy with this and she wasn't happy about that. At first, I couldn't figure it out because she'd always been so friendly to me. She always came over and gave me a big kiss at the end of the day, and hung on me most of the time. She always sat down next to me, leaning on me. If it had been a younger woman, it would have been like a romance. She was just very, very nice to me. I enjoyed her quite a lot. But then she had to go off and have these teeth done, and she wouldn't go to a dentist in Los Angeles. She had to go to New York. Then, when she got to New York, they told her they had to pull a bunch of other teeth to make a whole new bridge. That was going to take a month. Then, without the dentures, she lost weight and she went down to about seventy-two pounds, and obviously couldn't return to the picture.

In the meantime, there was a question of whether or not we were going to shelve the film. The insurance company was just going to pay off the cost of the film. I would have gotten paid my directing fee. I said, "Let's try to salvage what we have of Bette Davis. This might be her last film, and having her in the picture would certainly enhance the video sales." I didn't think she had any theatrical draw because she hadn't been in any feature movies to speak of in many years. So, at best, she wasn't going to bring in any big money at the box office. Her big strength was on video because every video store has a Bette Davis section. I convinced them that they shouldn't replace her with someone like Lucille Ball. Let's just keep the Bette Davis footage

New mother Lenore Davies (Sharon Farrell) must come to grips with the fact that her newborn baby is some sort of murderous monster in Larry Cohen's 1974 horror classic *It's Alive* (Warner Bros. Pictures, 1974).

and rewrite the script to fit the situation. So we took her out and changed the plot around a little bit and kept the picture alive. The picture actually did go into profit for MGM and for the investors. They all made a considerable amount of money. It was one of the few successful films MGM made that year. It's not considered a success because it's overshadowed by the stories that Bette Davis walked off the picture.

Have you been asked to do much script doctoring on other writers' work?
   LC: I usually turn those jobs down. I don't really want to go in and rewrite other people. I don't like people to do it to me, and I don't like having to do it to other people. I know it's the whole way of life out in Hollywood, but it's not my way of life.
   I once did a rewrite on a script for a film called *El Condor*. They had built all of the sets and they wanted to make the picture, but they didn't want to use the script they had. They had already built the scenery over in Spain. I had to go over and write a fresh screenplay based on the scenery they had. It was kind of a challenge because I knew all of the cast and crew was waiting to see if I'd be able to come through and deliver. So, that was a rewrite.

What was Lee Van Cleef like to work with on El Condor?
   LC: It was amusing because he didn't want to do the picture. When I came back from having finished the script, everyone was all excited about it. Lee Van Cleef had been approached to do the film and had said he would do it. Then Alberto Grimaldi, who had produced a number of Lee's spaghetti westerns, advised him not to do the picture. Grimaldi apparently told him that he would look foolish because the character was kind of a raggedy, run-down character. It was very different from the kind of cold-blooded killer that Lee Van Cleef was associated with playing. So he told them that he would not do this picture.
   I asked if I could possibly meet him, and they arranged for us to meet in a coffee shop in Los Angeles. He came over and was very hostile at first, saying that he wouldn't do the picture because it would make him look stupid. I said, "Well, you know, Lee, it's supposed to be a comedy. You have a comedic part. It's not supposed to be taken straight." He looked at me and asked, "Well, why hadn't anybody told me that?" I said, "Well, they should have. This is the kind of character Humphrey Bogart played in *The African Queen* [1951], which was completely opposite of what Bogart usually played, yet he won an Oscar for it. Here you have the same kind of broken-down character. It'll give you a chance to act." And he loved it. "That's great! I'll take off my toupee, and I'll play it without my hairpiece. I'm so excited about doing it." By the time we got through with the meeting, he couldn't wait to get on that airplane. Once again I had salvaged the picture. He went on and did the part, and I thought he was very good in it.

Van Cleef was notorious for his drinking, which sometimes got in the way of his film career. Were there any problems with his drinking on El Condor?
   LC: The big problem on that movie was between the director, John Guillerman, and the producer, Andre DeToth, who was also a famous director of westerns. Andre really wanted to get Guillerman fired so he could take over and direct the picture. Guillerman knew what Andre was up to, and they were constantly arguing, and finally came to blows. They actually had a fistfight in the office one day, although I wasn't present at the time. Everything that Gillerman was trying to do, Andre would try to undermine. While Guillerman was shooting, Andre was sneaking out with the second unit crew and shooting scenes himself. I think with all the problems between the producer and the director, nobody really noticed too much about Lee Van Cleef. If he was drunk on the set, it wouldn't have mattered because that was the character he was playing. So if he'd been a little plastered, it wouldn't have hurt his performance.

You did some writing for Columbo. *The structure of that series was very rigid and formulaic. How difficult was it to create something new and fresh while working within that already-established structure?*

LC: It was just something I could do. I had a knack for that show. The producers of that show, [Barry] Levinson and [William] Link, were friends of mine, and they were constantly pestering me to write for that show. They couldn't find writers who could utilize that format. I really didn't want to write television at the time, but it was so easy for me to do it. I was moving to London and I said to them, "I'll write the scripts and send them to you, but I'm not going to come in for any meetings or production sessions. I'll just mail the material to you from London and you can either make them or not make them. I don't care." That was it. It was a nice arrangement for me to be able to do something while I was in London and have some fun with it.

Those puzzle mysteries were just kind of entertaining for me to do. I enjoyed writing those kinds of things. It was like a game to me, devising the perfect murder and then finding the mistake. I thought the show eventually became very repetitious. I can hardly watch *Columbo* anymore. Now when I see Peter Falk go into those gyrations after having seen it so many times before, it becomes somewhat of a bore. They haven't been able to come up with any variations on the form to make it fairly interesting. Now he just seems old and tired doing the part. But what can you do? Everything wears itself out eventually.

FILMOGRAPHY FOR LARRY COHEN

1. *Checkmate* (1960) [episode: "Nice Guys Finish Last"] Sc
2. *Way Out* (1961) Sc
3. *The Nurses* (1962) Sc
4. *Espionage* (1963) [episode: "Medal for a Turncoat"] Sc
5. *The Fugitive* (1963) Sc
6. *Branded* (1965–66) S & P
7. *Return of the Magnificent Seven* (1966) Sc
8. *I Deal in Danger* (1966) Sc
9. *The Invaders* (1967–68) S & P
10. *Scream, Baby, Scream* (1969) Sc & S
11. *Daddy's Gone A-Hunting* (1969) Sc
12. *El Condor* (1970)
13. *In Broad Daylight* (1971) Sc
14. *Bone* (1972) D, Sc, P
15. *Cool Million* (1972) [TV] Sc
16. *Hell Up in Harlem* (1973) D, Sc, P
17. *Columbo: Candidate for Crime* (1973) [TV] Sc
18. *Black Caesar* (1973) D, Sc, P
19. *Griff* (1973) Sc, S, P
20. *Shootout in a One-Dog Town* (1974) [TV] Sc
21. *It's Alive!* (1974) D, Sc, P
22. *Man on the Outside* (1975) [TV] Sc
23. *Columbo: An Exercise in Fatality* (1975) [TV] S
24. *The Private Files of J. Edgar Hoover* (1977) D, Sc, P
25. *God Told Me To* (1977) D, Sc, P
26. *It Lives Again* (1978) D, Sc, P
27. *The American Success Company* (1979) Sc & S
28. *Full Moon High* (1981) D, Sc, P
29. *I, the Jury* (1982) Sc
30. *Q: The Winged Serpent* (1982) D & Sc
31. *Women of San Quentin* (1973) [TV] S
32. *Special Effects* (1984) D & Sc
33. *Perfect Strangers* (1984) D & Sc
34. *Scandalous* (1984) S
35. *The Stuff* (1985) D, Sc, Ex-P
36. *Spies Like Us* (1985) A
37. *A Return to Salem's Lot* (1987) D, Sc, S, Ex-P
38. *It's Alive III: Island of the Alive* (1987) D, Sc, Ex-P
39. *Deadly Illusion* (1987) D & Sc
40. *Best Seller* (1987) Sc
41. *Desperado: Avalanche at Devil's Ridge* (1988) [TV] Sc
42. *Maniac Cop* (1988) Sc & P
43. *Wicked Stepmother* (1989) D & Sc

44. *Maniac Cop 2* (1990) Sc
45. *The Ambulance* (1990) D & Sc
46. *Maniac Cop 3* (1992) Sc
47. *Guilty as Sin* (1993) Sc
48. *Body Snatchers* (1993) S
49. *The Expert* (1994) Sc
50. *As Good as Dead* (1994) [TV] D & Sc
51. *Uncle Sam* (1996) Sc
52. *Ed McBain's 87th Precinct: Ice* (1996) [TV] Sc
53. *Invasion of Privacy* (1996) Sc
54. *Original Gangstas* (1996) D & Co-Sc
55. *Misbegotten* (1997) Sc
56. *The Ex* (1997) Sc
57. *Ed McBain's 87th Precinct: Heatwave* (1997) [TV] Sc
58. *The Defenders: Choice of Evils* (1998) [TV] S
59. *Phone Booth* (2002) Sc
60. *Air Force One: The Final Mission* (2004) Co-D & Co-Sc
61. *Cellular* (2004) Sc
62. *Captivity* (2007) S
63. *Masters of Horror* (2006) [episode "Pick Me Up"] D

Roger Corman

Having produced and/or directed nearly three hundred films, Roger Corman is easily one of the most prolific filmmakers in the history of the medium. In 1954, he and producers Samuel Z. Arkoff and James H. Nicholson joined forces, establishing American International Pictures. The following year, Corman directed *Five Guns West* (1955), the first of his fifty-four films as director to date. As a director, Corman's creative output was astounding; he churned out as many as eight films a year, and his shoots were generally ten days or less. Some of Corman's most memorable films as producer or director are *Machine Gun Kelly* (1958), *A Bucket of Blood* (1959), *Dementia 13* (1963), *Death Race 2000* (1975), *Piranha* (1978), *Saint Jack* (1979), and *Humanoids from the Deep* (1980). In 1960, Corman directed *Fall of the House of Usher*, the first in a series of eight lushly colored Edgar Allan Poe adaptations (although his 1963 "Poe" film *The Haunted Palace* was actually based upon a story by H.P. Lovecraft, not Poe). Other Corman-directed films of note include *The St. Valentine's Day Massacre* (1967) and *Bloody Mama* (1970), starring Shelly Winters and Robert De Niro. In 1967 — the same year the three would go their own way and make *Easy Rider* — Corman collaborated with Dennis Hopper (assistant director), Jack Nicholson (screenwriter), and Peter Fonda (actor) on *The Trip* (1967).

Corman left American International and retired from directing after filming *The Red Baron* (1971). He then established New World Pictures and began focusing on production and distribution. At New World, Corman continued producing "B" movies, as well as distributing arthouse films such as Federico Fellini's *Amarcord* (1974). In addition, Corman has appeared as an actor in nearly thirty films, including *The Godfather Part II* (1974), *The Silence of the Lambs* (1991), *Philadelphia* (1993), and *Apollo 13* (1995). (It should be noted that both *The Silence of the Lambs* and *The Godfather Part II* appear on the American Film Institute's list of the one hundred greatest films in the history of American cinema.)

Besides being the undisputed king of the exploitation market, Corman will be remembered for having an eye for talent, discovering *many* talented young filmmakers, including Martin Scorsese, Francis Ford Coppola, James Cameron, Joe Dante, John Sayles, Robert Towne, Dennis Hopper, Peter Bogdanovich, Jonathan Demme, Jonathan Kaplan, Monte Hellman, and Ron Howard, among others. In this light, one must conclude that Corman has single-handedly altered the course of film history.

Favorite Films: *Battleship Potemkin* (1925), *Grand Illusion* (1938), *The Seventh Seal* (1957), *My Darling Clementine* (1946), and *The Big Sleep* (1946).

ANDREW RAUSCH: *I'm going to read you a quote by Quentin Tarantino and I'd like you to comment on it: "Roger Corman would find a young Jonathan Demme or Jonathan Kaplan or Joe Dante or Francis Coppola or Martin Scorsese, and because they were hungry to make a movie, they'd make the best women-in-prison film ever."*

An angry mob takes to the streets in Roger Corman's *The Haunted Palace* (American International Pictures, 1963).

ROGER CORMAN: [Laughs] In regards to that particular quote, Jonathan Demme is the only one who actually made a women-in-prison picture. But the statement is correct. We did a number of women-in-prison features in the 1970s. We did four or five of them, I think. Jonathan took that assignment [*Caged Heat*, 1971] and said exactly that: "This is gonna be the best one ever made." I think it indicated his enthusiasm and determination to make a good picture. The others did well, but they just took it as an assignment and said, "We'll just make this a prison feature," and just did it. Jonathan took the genre, worked with it, and made something exceptionally good. That indicated from the beginning that he had an extraordinary talent. I think the distinguishing characteristic of all of them, no matter what films they did — Francis Coppola did a horror film [*Dementia 13*], Joe Dante did a satire of a horror film called *Hollywood Boulevard* (1976) and then went on to do a science fiction horror film called *Piranha* (1978) — is that they were all determined to do the best possible work they could do.

I'm going to name some of the filmmakers you've discovered, and I'd like you to comment on each of them as I do.
    RC: All right.

Francis Ford Coppola.
    RC: Francis Coppola came to me as a film editor out of UCLA film school and then advanced rapidly to eventually writing and directing his first film for me. He is one of the

most brilliant all-around filmmakers I have ever met. When I say all-around, I mean that not only can he write and direct, but he can also edit, function as cameraman, and do almost every job connected with filmmaking.

Martin Scorsese.

RC: Martin Scorsese is one of the few directors I gave an opportunity to direct without having worked for me as an assistant. I saw an underground film he'd made in New York, which I liked very much, and gave him the opportunity to do *Boxcar Bertha* (1972). Once more, he tackled a subject he had no personal knowledge of, but he had the great intelligence and creativity to make it a great film.

Peter Bogdanovich.

RC: Peter Bogdanovich has demonstrated brilliance both as a writer and as a director. His first film for me was *Targets* (1968), which was one of the best debut films of any of the directors I've worked with.

Jonathan Demme.

RC: Jonathan Demme has grown continually as a director. His first work was good, and with each additional film he's gotten better, so he's gone from being merely a good director to a great director.

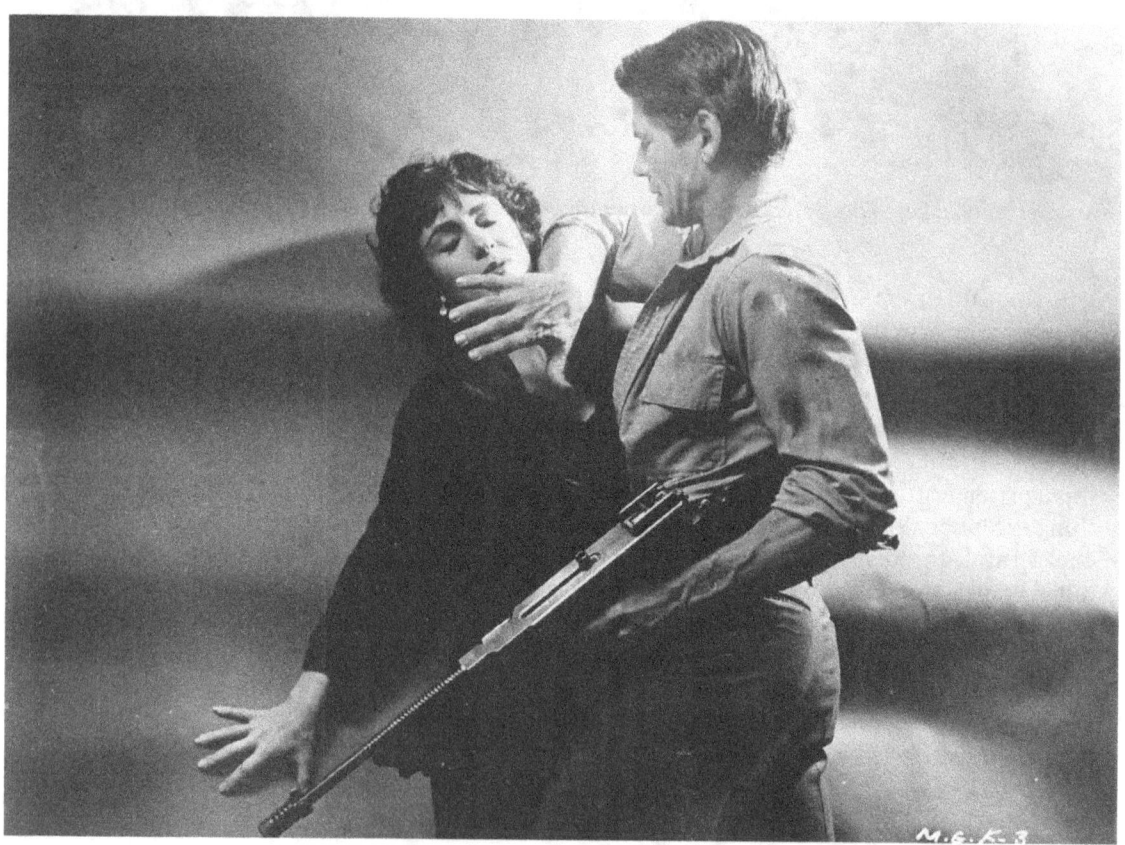

George "Machine Gun" Kelly (Charles Bronson, right) tries to silence Flo (Susan Cabot, left) in a scene from Roger Corman's 1958 crime film *Machine Gun Kelly* (American International Pictures, 1958).

James Cameron.

RC: Jim Cameron is proof that if you are good, you'll get promoted. He started with me as a model maker on *Battle Beyond the Stars* (1980). We were having trouble with the special effects, and I sent my ace assistant, Gale Ann Hurd, down to the set to find out what was going wrong. She came back after a couple of days and said the staff is not as competent as they should be, but there's a young model maker at the bottom of the list who knows more than anyone else. I went down to the set that day and promoted Jim Cameron, and he was head of special effects and second director on the next picture, showing that if you have the ability, it will be recognized quickly.

Joe Dante.

RC: Joe Dante started as a trailer editor and then moved up the traditional way from trailer editor to feature film editor to second unit director and then to director. I think he's one of the best directors in the country. While I have great admiration for Joe and everything he's done, I regret a little bit that I've never, ever been able to find a trailer editor as good since he left! [Laughs]

I've got another quotation for you. Martin Scorsese remembers of Boxcar Bertha, *"Roger just told me to read the script, rewrite as much as you want, but remember Marty, you must have some nudity every fifteen pages." [Laughs] Would you like to comment on that?*

RC: [Laughs] That's close, I think. The statement is *almost* correct. Needless to say, we talked a little bit more than that, and I didn't say every fifteen pages. I think I said two or three times in the picture. [Laughs again] He, possibly on his own, decided to do it every fifteen pages, but I don't particularly remember saying that. He may be remembering the film being a little racier than it was. I think there was only nudity in there two or three times.

Something else interesting I remember reading was that you had expressed interest in financing Mean Streets *(1973) as a black exploitation film. Is that right?*

RC: Yes. Marty came to me with the idea and I liked it, but at that time the black films were really very successful. I'd been thinking that I wanted to make a black film, and I thought this film would really work well as a black film. What most people don't know about *Mean Streets*—even the New York critics commented on how much of a New York picture it was—is that he shot most of that picture in Los Angeles, utilizing my crew.

You put this in. [Laughs] It was a great Italian film, but it would have been just as great a black film!

Today those films tend to get a bad rap from a lot of people who don't understand the term "blaxploitation" or "black exploitation." A lot of people, completely ignorant of film history, tend to think that black actors were being exploited because they don't understand that label. How would you define black exploitation?

RC: Blaxploitation is exactly the same as the word exploitation, which you could call "whitesploitation." It's the same type of picture, except that you have blacks instead of whites. There's no particular difference. If you look at them, you see that they followed the same basic genres as any other exploitation film. Crime stories, action stories, mystery, adventure, so forth. These are the same genres, but they appealed specifically to the black audience.

We used black actors because of their talent—not because they were black. For instance, Carl Franklin, as a director, started with us and did several films with us, and I don't think he ever made what you would call a "black film" for us. I chose him as a director, not because he was black, but because he was good. After he left us, he began making black films for the majors. They saw him as a black director. I just saw him as a director.

Filmography for Roger Corman

This listing includes only Roger Corman's directing credits, as his complete filmography would contain more than three hundred films.

1. *Swamp Women* (1955) D
2. *Five Guns West* (1955) D & P
3. *The Beast with a Million Eyes* (1955) Co-D & Ex-P
4. *Apache Woman* (1955) D & P
5. *The Oklahoma Woman* (1956) D & P
6. *The Gunslinger* (1956) D & P
7. *The Day the World Ended* (1956) D & P
8. *It Conquered the World* (1956) D & P
9. *The Undead* (1957) D
10. *Teenage Doll* (1957) D & P
11. *Sorority Girl* (1957) D & P
12. *Rock All Night* (1957) D & P
13. *Naked Paradise* (1957) D & P
14. *Carnival Rock* (1957) D & P
15. *Not of This Earth* (1957) D & P
16. *Attack of the Crab Monsters* (1957) D & P
17. *War of the Satellites* (1958) D & P
18. *Teenage Cave Man* (1958) D & P
19. *She Gods of Shark Reef* (1958) D & P
20. *The Saga of the Viking Women and Their Voyage to the Waters of the Great Sea Serpent* (1958) D & P
21. *Machine Gun Kelly* (1958) D & P
22. *I, Mobster* (1958) D & Co-P
23. *A Bucket of Blood* (1959) D & P
24. *The Wasp Woman* (1960) D & P
25. *Ski Troop Attack* (1960) Co-D & P
26. *The Little Shop of Horrors* (1960) D & P
27. *Last Woman on Earth* (1960) D & P
28. *The Fall of the House of Usher* (1960) D & P
29. *Atlas* (1960) D & P
30. *The Pit and the Pendulum* (1961) D & P
31. *The Intruder* (1961) D & P
32. *Creature from the Haunted Sea* (1961) D & P
33. *Tower of London* (1962) D
34. *Tales of Terror* (1962) D & P
35. *The Premature Burial* (1962) D & P
36. *The Young Racers* (1963) D & P
37. *X: The Man with the X-Ray Eyes* (1963) D & P
38. *The Terror* (1963) Co-D, Un Sc, P
39. *The Raven* (1963) D & P
40. *The Haunted Palace* (1963) D & P
41. *The Secret Invasion* (1964) D
42. *The Masque of the Red Death* (1964) D & P
43. *The Tomb of Ligeia* (1965) D
44. *The Wild Angels* (1966) D & P
45. *The St. Valentine's Day Massacre* (1967) D & P
46. *The Trip* (1967) D & P
47. *A Time for Killing* (1967) Un Co-D
48. *Target: Harry* (1969)
49. *De Sade* (1969) Un Co-D
50. *Gas-s-s-s* (1970) D & P
51. *Bloody Mama* (1970) D & P
52. *The Red Baron* (1971) D
53. *Deathsport* (1978) Un Co-D & Ex-P
54. *Frankenstein Unbound* (1990) D, Sc, P

Wes Craven

Whether or not you're a fan of the horror genre, chances are good that you've heard of Wes Craven. The man is a household name — a brand name for horror, if you will — the cinematic equivalent of Stephen King. Craven has directed a number of genre-altering films, including *Last House on the Left* (1972), *The Hills Have Eyes* (1978), *A Nightmare on Elm Street* (1984), and *Scream* (1996), all of which are considered horror classics. When all is said and done, despite having directed more than twenty films, *A Nightmare on Elm Street* and its sweater-clad, steel-clawed antagonist, Freddy Krueger, is likely to be the project he is most remembered for.

Unlike most filmmakers who begin working in the field at an early age, Craven, a former college humanities professor, was nearly forty when he made his directorial debut with the controversial indie film *Last House on the Left*. One reason for Craven's long-term success in the horror genre is his uncanny knack for combining humor with terror. "It's an instinct," Craven explains. "The sense that it's time to get scary, or have a clock go off in the background, or take a breather and laugh where it would be appropriate."

In 1995, Craven tried his hand at straight comedy, directing comedian Eddie Murphy in *Vampire in Brooklyn*. Craven further proved his versatility with the Academy Award–nominated film *Music of the Heart* (1999), which starred Meryl Streep, Aidan Quinn, and Angela Bassett. In 1999, he also published his first novel, *The Fountain Society*. His most recent directorial effort is *Cursed* (2005), on which he re-teamed with *Scream* scribe Kevin Williamson.

In addition to his successes as a screenwriter, director, and novelist, Craven is also an accomplished producer. His credits as a producer or executive producer include *The Outpost* (1995), *Wishmaster* (1997), *Carnival of Souls* (1998), *Don't Look Down* (1998), and the revisionist tale *Dracula 2000* (2000).

Favorite Films: *Citizen Kane* (1941), *Juliet of the Spirits* (1965), *The Third Man* (1949), *Shoot the Piano Player* (1960), *The Treasure of the Sierra Madre* (1948), *Casablanca* (1942), *The 400 Blows* (1959), and *Red River* (1948).

ANDREW RAUSCH: *I find it interesting that everyone is so amazed by your decision to step away from the horror genre. It seems to me that your last pure horror film was* Wes Craven's New Nightmare *(1994), which was six years ago.* Vampire in Brooklyn *had some elements of horror, but it was really a comedy at heart, and* Scream, *by your own admission, is really a thriller disguised as a horror film.* [Editor's note: When this interview was conducted in 2000, Craven had announced that he would no longer be directing horror films. In the years since, Craven would ultimately reconsider.]

WES CRAVEN: Well, it's very difficult for me to even define what a horror film is. I think a lot of the films I've done are quite far from the "classical horror film." You know, the car stalling in the middle of the woods in a dark night beside a haunted mansion, and things of that sort. Even the Hammer films. I've never really felt that close to that particular part of the genre. A lot of the films I've made are just kind of using the genre to talk about violence and hallucinative reality and kind of the irrational curve of the twentieth century. *Last House on the Left* didn't feel like a horror film, so much as a bizarre political commentary in a "B"

A publicity photograph of director Wes Craven for the release of the horror film *The Serpent and the Rainbow* (Universal City Studios Inc., 1988).

movie format. *The People Under the Stairs* (1992) was certainly very political. I'm kind of talking about the ones that I wrote myself, because I kind of did some real dogs in there, too. [Laughs] And even the end of *A Nightmare on Elm Street*— the seventh one I did — was already kind of deconstructing the whole format, and looking behind the scenes at the people who made it, and confronting issues of censorship and everything else. I don't know if anyone in the genre has, but I've never felt — especially since I didn't have a big background in the genre — that I was ever consciously making "horror films."

You mentioned Wes Craven's New Nightmare, *which brings me to an observation. As that film and* Scream 3 *both deal with a movie-within-a-movie, you seem somewhat interested in that concept.*

WC: It did fascinate me. I think in my own work I kind of pushed the use of the genre beyond where it didn't want to stretch without kind of going to that next step of talking about what we were doing in a sense, in a way that the viewer was aware of you as a filmmaker. That was part of it, and part of it was just a frustration that in the years during which I hadn't been associated with the *Nightmare* series, it felt like it had drifted so much that I couldn't find a recognizable theme anymore. I would always confront myself when asked to do something like that, when given the chance, with whether or not there was a way to take this up to the next level. When I was called and given the chance to work on *Nightmare on Elm Street 3: Dream Warriors* [1987], I felt I could do that by using a character that was melded with other characters of the same sort of psychic gift, or someone who had this vision of the way things could work. But once it was past that level, I didn't know a way to take it up any further without going outside of it. So that idea of talking with a film-within-a-film sort of started early. In that case, it was watching characters watching a film they had made and seeing the effect it had on children, or, as a whole, reflection on an earlier work in a time it was being watched in currently. So that was kind of my interest in that.

For whatever reasons, Kevin Williamson sort of hit on that same theme with *Scream 2* [1997], so I just felt very much at home with it, and I liked it a lot. It gives you a way to talk about your own film or similar films without being completely tied to your own body of work. [Laughs] You can kind of say, "Here's how it can be done badly," which is kind of fun.

You've sort of become the cinematic equivalent to Stephen King in that your name has become a brand name for horror. Now these films that you've produced become labeled as "Wes Craven's" Wishmaster *(1997) or "Wes Craven Presents"* Carnival of Souls *(1998). What is that like?*

WC: It's kind of a mixture of fun with a very cautionary feeling about the danger of selling out. You know, "How can I exploit this?" I've worked so damned hard, how can I cash in on this legitimately? There's kind of a feeling of wanting to give back a little to the community of young filmmakers by shepherding something through that might give a young filmmaker a chance. It's kind of a mixture of all of those things. It's strange in a way because you don't have your hand on it the way you're used to doing with your own films, where you want every frame to kind of have your own initials on it someplace, and you feel responsible for it and want to use every ounce of your strength to make it something that is completely your own. With this other kind of film we're talking about, you're kind of taking everything you've earned from that process, and kind of lending it, in a way, to someone else. It's either a very good feeling or a queasy feeling, depending on how you feel about the end product.

In the past you've discussed the horror genre's penchant for churning out instant rip-offs of every successful film that comes along. Certainly there are examples of these rip-offs in every genre, but horror seems to take that to the next level. In horror, whenever there's something new and refreshing, you can almost count on at least half-a-dozen or so rip-offs coming out within the following year. Why do you think this practice is so much more prevalent in the horror genre?

WC: I think it's the financial inducement that exists in the horror genre because they tend to make a lot of money when they're good, and they generally cost very little to make. *The Blair Witch Project* [1999] would be a great example of that currently. This kind of makes the dollar signs light up in the eyes of a lot of people that usually wouldn't be drawn to the genre for the sake of loving it or for the sake of expressing any feeling about violence or whatever in the world at large. It's just, "How can we make one of those and make some money?" That's the difference between a guy or an organization that sits down to make a Rolex and a guy who just sits down to make something that *looks* like that so he can make some money. The result is that the genre is almost immediately engulfed by bad copies after something innovative has come along, and I don't think that's usually true with films that sort of fall in the midpoint, which could be real artistic expressions, but nobody would ever think of trying to copy them. But with genre films that do well, you can just bet that there are twenty-six or one hundred versions of *Blair Witch* in the works, and they're going to be done by everybody with no real impulse to do it except that it made so much money and they want to be on that gravy train. I think that's the curse of the genre, really. Those who love the genre—or have come to love it as I have—kind of wince at it, and kind of forgive the genre because that's not really its fault. It draws those kinds of films because of that financial payoff when it works.

Director Wes Craven discusses a scene with actress Rachel McAdams and actor Cillian Murphy on the set of the film *Red Eye* (Dream Works, 2005).

Filmography for Wes Craven

1. *You've Got to Walk It Like You Talk It...* (1971) Ed
2. *Together* (1971) AP, Cin, Ed
3. *Last House on the Left* (1972) D, Sc, Ed
4. *It Happened in Hollywood* (1973) Ed
5. *The Carhops* (1975) Ed
6. *Tales That Will Tear Your Heart Out* (1976) Co-D & Co-Sc
7. *Stranger in Our House* (1978) [TV] D
8. *The Hills Have Eyes* (1978) D, Sc, Ed
9. *Deadly Blessing* (1981) D & Sc
10. *Kent State* (1981) [TV] P
11. *Swamp Thing* (1982) D & Sc
12. *A Nightmare on Elm Street* (1984) D & Sc
13. *Invitation to Hell* (1984) [TV] D
14. *The Hills Have Eyes Part II* (1985) D & Sc
15. *The Twilight Zone* [episode: various] (1985–88) D & A
16. *Chiller* (1985) [TV] D
17. *Deadly Friend* (1986) D
18. *Casebusters* (1986) [TV] D
19. *A Nightmare on Elm Street 3: Dream Warriors* (1987) Sc, S, CC, Ex-P
20. *A Nightmare on Elm Street 4: The Dream Master* (1988) CC
21. *The Serpent and the Rainbow* (1988) D
22. *A Nightmare on Elm Street 5: The Dream Child* (1989) CC
23. *The People Next Door* (1989) Sc & Ex-P
24. *Shocker* (1989) D, Sc, Ex-P, A
25. *Night Visions* (1990) [TV] D, Sc, Ex-P
26. *Freddy's Dead: The Final Nightmare* (1991) CC
27. *The People Under the Stairs* (1992) D, Sc, Ex-P
28. *Body Bags* (1993) [TV] A
29. *Laurel Canyon* (1993) [TV] Ex-P
30. *Wes Craven's New Nightmare* (1994) D, Sc, CC, Ex-P, A
31. *The Outpost* (1995) Ex-P
32. *The Fear* (1995) A
33. *Vampire in Brooklyn* (1995) D
34. *Scream* (1996) D & A
35. *Wishmaster* (1997) Ex-P
36. *Scream 2* (1997) D & A
37. *Hollyweird* (1998) [TV pilot] D
38. *Hollyweird* (1998) Ex-P
39. *Carnival of Souls* (1998) Ex-P
40. *Don't Look Down* (1998) Ex-P
41. *Music of the Heart* (1999) D
42. *Scream 3* (2000) D
43. *Dracula 2000* (2000) Ex-P
44. *Jay and Silent Bob Strike Back* (2001) A
45. *Kamelot* (2003) Ex-P
46. *Freddy vs. Jason* (2003) CC
47. *Cursed* (2005) D & P
48. *Red Eye* (2005) D & P
49. *Paris, je t'aime* (2006) Co-D
50. *The Hills Have Eyes II* (2007) P

Frank Darabont

Frank Darabont began his career in the film industry in 1980, serving in the humble role of production assistant on *Hell Night* (1981). He worked in a similar capacity on *The Seduction* (1982), *Crimes of Passion* (1984), and *Trancers* (1985). The young filmmaker made his directorial debut in 1983 with the short Stephen King adaptation *The Woman in the Room* (1983), for which he also wrote the screenplay. Darabont soon began working as a screenwriter, writing or co-writing *A Nightmare on Elm Street 3: Dream Warriors* (1987), *The Blob* (1988), *The Fly II* (1989), and an episode of *Tales from the Crypt*. In 1990, Darabont directed Tim Matheson and Jennifer Jason Leigh in the telefilm *Buried Alive*. Darabont then found work writing episodes of the Steven Spielberg–executive produced series *The Young Indiana Jones Chronicles*.

In 1994, Darabont directed his first theatrical feature, *The Shawshank Redemption*. The film, which stars Tim Robbins and Morgan Freeman, garnered seven Oscar nominations, including nods for Darabont's screenplay and Best Picture. Darabont then began focusing on his writing again, contributing heavily to the critical favorite *Saving Private Ryan* (1998).

In 1999, Darabont helmed yet another Stephen King prison story with *The Green Mile*, which starred Tom Hanks. The film received four Oscar nominations, including two nominations for Darabont in the categories of Best Adapted Screenplay and Best Picture. Darabont then followed this up with the Jim Carrey starrer *The Majestic* (2001), which served as a nod to legendary director Frank Capra. In 2004, Darabont served as executive producer on the hit film *Collateral*, starring Tom Cruise and Jamie Foxx.

Favorite Films: *The Third Man* (1949), *Amistad* (1997), *It's a Wonderful Life* (1946), *2001: A Space Odyssey* (1968), *The General* (1927), and *Close Encounters of the Third Kind* (1977).

ANDREW RAUSCH: *You're one of the only filmmakers who seems to understand the art of adapting Stephen King to screen. Why do you think so many of the King adaptations fail?*

FRANK DARABONT: I think, in many cases, the people making these movies simply can't see past the fur and the fangs—the things that make the marketing people excited. There are many layers and substories interwoven in Steve's writing, and I think a lot of people forget about that, and a lot of that gets discarded. That's why so little of the feeling from King's original writing comes through in those films.

Little things like character development and story get lost in favor of the more horrific elements that have become associated with King. It becomes, "We've got a story by Stephen King," and then they begin focusing on all of those things instead of the story itself.

In some ways, weren't you guilty of focusing on the horrific elements associated with King in The Woman in the Room, *where you added a horror scene which wasn't present in the short story?*

Directors (from left to right) Robert Rodriguez, Quentin Tarantino, Frank Darabont, and Scott Spiegel pose together for this photograph at Tarantino's home (courtesy Scott Spiegel).

FD: Yeah, I suppose so. How old was I when I made that? Twenty-one? Man, here we are twenty years later ... I think I wrote that scene because I wanted to keep the film from being a talking-head movie. I mean, that's mainly what it is: thirty minutes of these characters sitting and talking. I just felt like I needed something else there.

After The Woman in the Room, *you were going to adapt Stephen King's short story "The Monkey" for Granite Entertainment. What happened with that project?*

FD: You know, it's funny that you mention that because I was just talking with Steve about that not too long ago. I might still be making that one of these days. In fact, I'm still interested in developing a number of Steve's stories, such as *The Mist*. Sometimes one project takes off and another gets put on the backburner. Time just flies so fast, and five years have come and gone before you know it. So I don't know what will happen with that, but I might still film "The Monkey."

In your King adaptation The Shawshank Redemption, *your voice is very much in sync with King's. I don't think I've ever seen a better example of this. How do you think you pulled that off?*

FD: Well, I think when you're adapting something from a very good source, you have to sort of pretend to be that writer and to not let your own voice take over. With *Shawshank*, that's an example of me doing my Steve King impression, kind of like Rich Little doing Johnny Carson.

With that film, even the scenes you wrote which weren't present in the original source material could have been in there. What comes to mind for me is the scene where Andy plays the record player over the loudspeakers and Red reflects on the Italian operetta. Although that wasn't part of King's original story, it sounds like it could have been. It's a very beautiful scene.

FD: Thank you. I take that as a great compliment. I love it whenever someone tells me that *Shawshank Redemption* is the most faithful adaptation of a Stephen King story, because it's really not that faithful. It just *feels* faithful. As a writer, I actually took a lot of liberties with the original story, but I tried to maintain the essence of King's original story.

Such as making the character Red a black man.

FD: Exactly. You have to find a way to tell the story you want to tell while still serving the original material. So it's really a matter of imitating the writing style of the author, which is what I tried to do with both *Shawshank* and *The Green Mile*.

In The Shawshank Redemption, *Red says that speaking of freedom is "just a shitty pipe dream." Considering that Andy escapes through a sewage pipe, I was wondering if this was a conscious act of foreshadowing on your part?*

FD: [Laughs] Yeah, that was my little joke.

Did very many people pick up on it?

FD: Oh, yeah. I think there was something in King's novella — something said about a pipe dream. In fact, he may have even said "shitty pipe dream." I can't remember. It might have been Stephen King's joke first, but I'll take credit for it. [Laughs] I really can't remember.

I'm sure that by now you've seen Natalie Van Doren's spoof, The Shark Tank Redemption *(2000). What are your thoughts on that?*

FD: I thought it was a terrific little film. Very professionally made.

Ellis Boyd "Red" Redding (Morgan Freeman) and Andy Dufresne (Tim Robbins) discuss prison life in Frank Darabont's ***The Shawshank Redemption*** (Columbia Pictures, 1994).

The casting of Alfonso Freeman was perfect.

FD: Yes, it was. You know we had Alfonso on *The Shawshank Redemption*, right?

Yeah.

FD: I just thought it was a terrific, very funny little film. I also found it very flattering to be parodied. That was like when *Mad* magazine parodied *The Green Mile*. They called it "The Yellow Mile," which was actually a joke we used to make on the set.

I used to say, "This movie is about pain because Tom Hanks' character can't pee, Wild Bill can't stop peeing, and the audience has to hold their pee and sit with their legs crossed through this movie for three hours." [Laughs] I guess *Mad* magazine kind of picked up on that. But you know you've become a part of cultural reference when you find yourself being parodied in *Mad* magazine.

What is your collaboration process with King like?

FD: There really isn't one. It's really become more of a friendship now. I express interest in a property, he gives me permission to use it, and I go off and write the screenplay. Although I always send him the script and ask him for his input, I think the most I've ever gotten from him was, "Read the script. Loved it. Go make the movie and good luck. Can't wait to see the film!"

In what ways does being a screenwriter yourself affect the way you handle another writer's work as a director?

FD: Well, I try to bring out the story I want to tell. So far I have only directed two screenplays by other writers, but I'm not the kind of guy who's afraid to rewrite. Hopefully the story

Frank Darabont in deep thought on the set of *The Majestic* (Warner Bros. Pictures, 2001).

I want to tell and the story the writer wants to tell are the same. With *The Majestic*, I liked Michael Sloane's script from the beginning, and I just helped him develop it a little bit. I felt that was a very good script, and I thought he did a good job telling that story. I think a director has to take charge and has to have a strong vision, and if a director has a strong enough vision, he's going to end up with good results.

Stephen King has always been annoyed when writers ask him, "So, where do you get your ideas?" What oft-asked interview question makes you cringe?

FD: I like this question because there are a few. Maybe one day I should make a list of them. One of the top ones is, "Why do you keep coming back to Stephen King stories?" Another is, "What attracts you to prison films?" Another stupid one that I hear a lot at junkets is, "What does this film mean?" Then I'm expected to pontificate and spoon-feed this reporter my idea of what the film means. Can't the film just be art? Shouldn't it be up to the audience to leave the theater with their own ideas of what the film is or isn't? When you go to the art museum and you look at a painting, you don't have the artist standing right there saying, "You know, this is what this painting means. This is why I used blue paint here...." Audiences have grown lazy because they're used to having someone else tell them what the film is supposed to represent rather than to formulate their own opinions.

Another very, very stupid question that I get a lot is, "So, why did you make this movie?" I have absolutely no respect for that question. I always want to say, "Well, gee, obviously I liked it, huh?" [Laughs] I hear quite a few dumb questions at junkets. I realize that the reporters are just trying to do their jobs and get some kind of sound bite, so I don't humiliate them by telling them how stupid that question really is. I mean, after all, if I spent nearly two years of my life working on a film, logic would dictate that it's because I liked the project, right? Obviously it said something to me as a person and as a filmmaker.

FILMOGRAPHY FOR FRANK DARABONT

1. *Hell Night* (1981) PA
2. *The Seduction* (1982) PA
3. *The Woman in the Room* (1983) D & Sc
4. *Crimes of Passion* (1984) PA
5. *Trancers* (1985) PA
6. *A Nightmare on Elm Street 3: Dream Warriors* (1987) Sc
7. *The Blob* (1988) Sc
8. *The Fly II* (1989) Sc
9. *K-9* (1989) Un Sc
10. *Tales from the Crypt* (1989) [episode: "Showdown"] Sc
11. *Buried Alive* (1990) [TV] D
12. *Till Death Do Us Part* (1990) [TV] D
13. *Two-Fisted Tales* (1991) [TV] Sc
14. *The Rocketeer* (1991) Un Sc
15. *The Young Indiana Jones Chronicles* (1992) [episodes: various] Sc
16. *The Shawshank Redemption* (1994) D & Sc
17. *Frankenstein* (1994) Sc
18. *Young Indiana Jones Travels with Father* (1996) [TV] Sc
19. *The Fan* (1996) Un Sc
20. *Eraser* (1996) Un Sc
21. *Stephen King's The Shining* (1997) [TV] A
22. *John Carpenter's Vampires* (1998) A
23. *Saving Private Ryan* (1998) Un Sc
24. *Black Cat Run* (1998) [TV] Sc, S, Ex-P
25. *The Green Mile* (1999) D, Sc, P
26. *The Majestic* (2001) D & P
27. *The Salton Sea* (2002) P
28. *Collateral* (2004) Ex-P
29. *King Kong* (2005) A
30. *The Mist* (2007), D, Sc, P

Ernest Dickerson

After graduating from Howard University, Ernest Dickerson enrolled in the New York University graduate film program. There he became a skilled cinematographer and discovered a kindred spirit in another student named Spike Lee. Dickerson and Lee then collaborated on the first "Spike Lee Joint," *Joe's Bed-Stuy Barbershop: We Cut Heads* (1983). Dickerson and Lee then formed a solid partnership which would last another decade. Together they crafted a solid body of work, which includes the films *She's Gotta Have It* (1986), *School Daze* (1988), *Do the Right Thing* (1989), *Jungle Fever* (1991), *Mo' Better Blues* (1991), and the epic biopic *Malcolm X* (1992). During this period Dickerson became one of the youngest members of the American Society of Cinematographers. Not only was Dickerson recognized as one of the finest cameramen in the film industry, but he also held the distinction of being Hollywood's only prominent African-American cinematographer. His cinematography credits also include John Sayles' *The Brother from Another Planet* (1984), *Krush Groove* (1985), and *Eddie Murphy Raw* (1987).

In 1992, Dickerson made his directorial debut with the gritty urban crime drama *Juice*, which featured the debuts of actors Omar Epps and Tupac Shakur. In the fourteen years following, the prolific filmmaker has directed an astounding seventeen features. These include *Surviving the Game* (1994), *Demon Knight* (1995), *Bulletproof* (1995), *Futuresport* (1998), *Bones* (2001), *Monday Night Mayhem* (2002), and the neo-noir Donald Goines adaptation *Never Die Alone* (2004).

Following studio interference in the making of films such as *Bulletproof* and *Bones* (both were badly damaged by studio recuts), Dickerson has vowed to work more within the realm of independent cinema. "One of the things I'm always doing is trying to find some way to put my stamp on the material," he has said. "For me, it's a way of dealing with the material to make it more interesting to work with. I love working in film and stretching the medium. I see myself as an independent filmmaker. I don't think I have the patience to work with a lot of studios now. It's gotten really bad doing studio films because it's almost like the filmmaker isn't trusted anymore. The corporate mentality has really come down. All the jokes we make about executives are true, but the jokes haven't helped make them shape up. I just don't like the idea of filmmaking by committee."

Favorite Films: *2001: A Space Odyssey* (1978), *The Godfather* (1972), *The Godfather Part II* (1974), *Raging Bull* (1980), *Kiss Me Deadly* (1955), *Blade Runner* (1982), *Brazil* (1985), *The Seven Samurai* (1954), *The Searchers* (1956), and *Pulp Fiction* (1994).

ANDREW RAUSCH: *You came to directing after working as a cinematographer. Do you feel that that experience gave you an advantage?*

ERNEST DICKERSON: Maybe in my case it did because a lot of the filmmakers that I shot for also acted in front of the camera. My very first film was a film called *The Brother from Another Planet*, and John Sayles had a small role in it. Usually, whenever that happens, the cinematographer becomes the director's eyes and alter-ego in a way. He's kind of like the co–director at that point because he brings objectivity. Then, working with Spike — even though we worked together in film school — he really didn't start acting in his films until *She's Gotta Have It*. Whenever Spike was in front of the camera he would always rely upon me to give him my opinion about what was going on in the scene, and help him out in directing it, and being his objective eye.

In some of those films you worked on with Spike, most notably Malcolm X, *you did something very interesting that I had never seen before. A character was shown moving forward as if he was on a conveyor belt and shot from below. Who came up with that shot?*

ED: Well, Spike and I kind of worked it out together. The first time we actually did it was in *Mo' Better Blues*. Spike wanted an interesting point-of-view when his character, Giant, was moving. There's a scene where he's on his way home and he realizes that the gangsters are staked out in front of his house, ready to catch him and beat him up because he owes them a lot of money. The idea was to come up with a very interesting point-of-view, so we tried sitting Spike up on the dolly with the camera and have him mimic the moves of walking. We wanted something that was kind of twisted, and that felt right. His character is twisted, addicted to gambling. That just seemed like an interesting way to go. We tried that, shooting from the front and from behind, and it gave a very, very interesting effect.

Director Ernest Dickerson (center) discusses a scene with actors Omar Epps (left) and Khalil Kain (right) on the set of *Juice* (Paramount Pictures, 1992).

Mookie (Spike Lee, left) and Sal (Danny Aiello, right) on the hottest day of the summer in Spike Lee's *Do the Right Thing*, shot by cinematographer Ernest Dickerson (MCA/Universal Pictures, 1989).

Then the next time we did it was in *Jungle Fever*. Spike wanted to do the same thing, but really just give more of a floating effect. I think at the time the idea was to get the effect you would have if you were really walking with somebody. When you're walking with somebody, you don't really get the sense of up and down like you might get with a handheld camera. I don't know. When we saw it in the dailies, it just seemed like a very interesting way to film a conversation between two people and give it a different feeling. Even though we were trying to give it that walking feeling, we realized we were getting something else. So we tried it again. I think it has varying degrees of success.

I think it really worked the best in *Malcolm X* right before he meets the lady in the street. There we just wanted to give the feeling that he felt something was happening. He felt that his life was coming to an end, which is the way the real Malcolm X really felt.

In 1992, you directed Juice, *starring charismatic rapper-turned-actor Tupac Shakur. What was Tupac like to work with?*

ED: Tupac was high-energy. With his co-workers and everybody else he was a very generous actor. He worked great with everybody. The only trouble I found that he had was that he sometimes made himself too accessible to other people. In some of the neighborhoods we were shooting in I think he made himself accessible to some of the wrong people, and they wound up taking advantage of him. That's when trouble occurred.

There was a guy that he'd befriended in the Harlem neighborhood we were shooting in, and Tupac reported that some jewelry he'd been wearing was missing. He said he knew who did it, and decided he would deal with it himself. One day Tupac started having this huge bodyguard hanging out with him, and the producers kept offering to pay him back for the jewelry he'd lost. He just said, "Nah, I got it. Don't worry about it."

Then one day I was setting up a shot and I noticed the producers were kind of huddled in the corner talking. I just sensed something was up. I went over and said, "What's up, guys?" They said, "Ernest, you don't wanna know." [Laughs] I said, "Yo, come on and tell me because it might affect everything I'm doing for the rest of the day. Tell me." They said, "You know Tupac said he knew who took his jewelry, right?" I said, "Yeah." They said, "You know that big bodyguard he's got hanging out with him?" I said, "Yeah?" They said, "Well, Tupac and the bodyguard were just stomping the kid out in the street ten minutes ago. Right out in the middle of the day, in the middle of the street." There was a car speeding up the street, and the guy jumped onto the back of a moving car to get away!

What do you think is the biggest misconception about Tupac?
ED: I guess that he was just this relentlessly hardcore guy. Tupac was actually a very sensitive and caring person. I'm glad that his genius is acknowledged. When we were shooting, between takes, he would sit on the side and write in his notebook. He always had this little notebook with him and he would always go off in the corner and write. I later on found out that what he was writing was what would eventually become his first album.

I think casting Tupac as this hardcore roughneck gave people that impression. Yeah, there was a little of that roughneck about him, but I think there was a lot of sensitivity and true artistry there.

Much of Bishop's transformation in the film comes from his viewing James Cagney in White Heat *(1934). What made you choose that particular film?*
ED: We wanted to show that gangster films are something kids look at. And *White Heat* is the kind of film that you might see at home in the afternoon. Plus, it was a personal favorite of mine. [Laughs] I like the movie. I guess if we were really going to be realistic the movie we should have shown at that time was *Scarface* (1983). But first of all, we couldn't afford the rights. Second of all … well, that was the primary reason we didn't use *Scarface*! [Laughs again] But *White Heat* was always in the script. I guess because it's such a classic film. Even though it's more likely a film that kids would watch, I don't think *Scarface* has the same resonance.

You worked with F. Murray Abraham on Surviving the Game. *What was he like to work with?*
ED: He really was a big inspiration because he almost lost his life making the film. We were four days into shooting and we had been shooting the dinner scene at the cabin. All of our locations were about an hour away from the hotel. Normally, Murray would be driven to and from the set. And it's really strange because one night Murray decided he wanted to drive himself. Maybe he wanted to be by himself or whatever, but when he was driving, all of a sudden a drunk driver ran a stop sign and slammed into his car. It was a green car that hit him, and Murray said that all he caught was a flash of green in the corner of his eye. Bam! The next thing he knew he was turned around one-hundred-and-eighty degrees and on the other side of the road. The driver in the other car was killed, and the two passengers had to be airlifted out to a hospital because we were four hours away from Seattle.

Murray had three broken ribs, a broken hand, and his face had hit the steering wheel, so he was really banged up badly. He was in quite a bit of pain and he couldn't shoot because he was in the hospital. Murray insisted on coming back to work after three days. He insisted. I know his agent tried to tell him to stay in the hospital, but Murray's attitude was like, "If I stay in the hospital, I'm gonna think about what almost happened, and it's gonna drive me crazy. I've got to get back to work."

God bless him. He was a real trooper and a good friend. He came back and completed the role with quite a bit of discomfort to himself because we were in pretty rough terrain. Just walking was difficult for anybody, let alone someone with three broken ribs. A real trooper. Really, really a great guy.

FILMOGRAPHY FOR ERNEST DICKERSON

1. *Joe's Bed-Stuy Barbershop: We Cut Heads* (1983) Cin
2. *The Brother from Another Planet* (1984) Cin
3. *Day of the Dead* (1985) Un Cin
4. *Krush Groove* (1985) Cin
5. *She's Gotta Have It* (1986) Cin
6. *Almacita di desolato* (1986) Cin
7. *Enemy Territory* (1987) Cin
8. *Eddie Murphy Raw* (1987) Cin
9. *School Daze* (1988) Cin
10. *Do the Right Thing* (1989) Cin
11. *The Laserman* (1990) Cin
12. *Def by Temptation* (1990) Cin
13. *Ava & Gabriel* (1990) Cin
14. *Law and Order* (1990) Cin
15. *Mo' Better Blues* (1990) Cin
16. *Jungle Fever* (1991) Cin
17. *Sex, Drugs, Rock & Roll* (1991) Cin
18. *Cousin Bobby* (1992) Cin
19. *Visions of Light* (1992) A
20. *Malcolm X* (1992) Cin
21. *Juice* (1992) D, Sc, S
22. *Surviving the Game* (1994) D
23. *Demon Knight* (1995) D
24. *Bulletproof* (1995) D
25. *Blind Faith* (1998) D
26. *Ambushed* (1998) D
27. *Futuresport* (1998) [TV] D
28. *Strange Justice* (1999) [TV] D
29. *Night Visions* [episodes: "Still Life" and "My So Called Life and Death"] (2000) D
30. *Bones* (2000) D
31. *Big Shot: Confessions of a Campus Bookie* (2002) [TV] D
32. *Monday Night Mayhem* (2002) [TV] D
33. *Our America* (2002) D & Cin
34. *The Wire* [episodes: various] (2002–2006) D
35. *Good Fences* (2003) D
36. *Never Die Alone* (2004) D
37. *Miracle's Boys* (2005) [TV] D
38. *Invasion* (2005) D
39. *For One Night* (2006) [TV] D
40. *Masters of Horror* (2006) [episode: "The V Word"] D
41. *Weeds* (2007) [episodes: various] D

Jon Favreau

Jon Favreau made his acting debut in the 1993 pigskin drama *Rudy*. It was there on the set that he met friend and future collaborator Vince Vaughn. Three years later, Favreau stepped into the spotlight with the release of Doug Liman's breakout indie hit *Swingers* (1996). Favreau, who appears in the lead alongside Vaughn, also wrote and co-produced *Swingers*. The largely-autobiographical film garnered critical acclaim and was quickly embraced by the so-called "Generation X," as evidenced by Liman's winning Best New Director honors at the MTV Movie Awards. Favreau was also recognized for his performance and was dubbed "Most Promising Actor" by the Chicago Film Critics Association. He soon found himself appearing in a recurring role on NBC's wildly-popular sitcom *Friends*, and starring with Morgan Freeman, Robert Duvall, and Vanessa Redgrave in the disaster thriller *Deep Impact* (1998). That same year Favreau played actress Cameron Diaz's beau in Peter Berg's delightful ultra-black comedy *Very Bad Things* (1998). (When Favreau was approached about the project, Christian Slater and Diaz were already attached. Favreau has since commented that his first reaction — understandably — was, "You want *me* to be Cameron Diaz's groom?" Needless to say, he took the role.)

Favreau's ascent to stardom continued with his career-defining turn as legendary boxer Rocky Marciano in the MGM biopic *Rocky Marciano* (1999), which co-starred legendary actor George C. Scott. Favreau followed up *Rocky Marciano* with appearances in Valerie Breiman's indie film *Love & Sex* (2000), the big-budget Warner Bros. comedy *The Replacements* (2000), and on HBO's hit series *The Sopranos*, on which he appeared as himself.

Today Favreau has become a true renaissance man, working as an actor, scribe, producer, and director. Favreau made his directorial debut with *Made* (2001), which he also wrote, produced, and starred in. His second film, the Will Ferrell vehicle *Elf* (2003), proved to be a tremendous hit and was amongst the top moneymakers of 2003. He next directed the big-budget children's adventure film *Zathura* (2005). In addition to his continuing work as an actor, screenwriter, and director, Favreau also hosts the popular Independent Film Channel series *Dinner for Five*.

Favorite Films: *Mean Streets* (1973), *The Godfather* (1972), *Miller's Crossing* (1990), and *The Cameraman* (1928).

ANDREW RAUSCH: *You recently observed that more fans seem to recognize Vince Vaughn and yourself from* Swingers *than from the big-budget blockbusters in which you've both appeared. Why do you think that is?*

JON FAVREAU: Because independent films live on the small screen, and everybody gets to watch it on cable over and over again, and on DVD and video. I mean, the movie itself made less than ten million dollars, but in the years since, people have really gotten to not only watch it, but watch it time and time again.

How often do fans approach you quoting the "You're money, baby" line from Swingers? *I would imagine this is something you get quite a lot.*

JF: It's dwindling, thankfully. [Laughs] But people recognize me from *Swingers* just about every time I go out. It depends. If I go out at night, it happens constantly. If I'm out during the day, less so.

Swingers *feels like a very personal film. To what extent was that screenplay autobiographical for you?*

JF: Well, it was based on what my life was about at the time. I had moved out to Los Angeles from Chicago (after growing up in New York). We shot it in my apartment. You know, that was my car and those are my friends; those are the places I hung out. So in that sense, it was *very* autobiographical. But the actual events that occurred in the film were all fictional.

While writing Made, *did you approach the screenplay from that same perspective? What I mean to say is that obviously you and Vince haven't done the things in that film — you're not connected with the mob — but were the characters themselves fashioned from some sort of an autobiographical perspective?*

JF: No, not really. I tried to base it somewhat on my relationship with Vince. There was a lot of the same chemistry. I tried to preserve that chemistry without making a sequel, so I tried to find two different characters in a different situation, where I could still maintain the relationship that I have with Vince.

From a director's standpoint, what's Vince like to work with?

JF: Well, it's always tricky when it's with someone who's a peer of yours, a close friend that you came up with. Because then the relationship isn't the traditional director/actor relationship. And on *Made*, Vince was a producer on the film, too, so all the creative decisions we kind of went over and discussed beforehand. But on the set — not just with Vince, but in general — I don't really try to do too much with the performers. I don't try to change things that much. I just try to create a nice environment for them to try things and trust that I'm going to put the best stuff in the finished film. So with Vince there's a lot of improv, and we tried to do things we hadn't planned on doing.

When you're directing yourself, is it ever difficult to objectively assess your own performance?

JF: No, not really. Because with my style of acting, I usually give myself — or another director, for that matter — a range of performance, knowing that they won't know until they're in the editing room what they need. I'm confident enough as an actor to know that my performance is going to be pretty honest, so I just try to give a range of performance. A lot of times when you're the lead in a film, your job is to do very little; you try to underplay a lot of stuff because you're on the screen so much. And the audience is seeing through your eyes. When you're a supporting character, your performance becomes much more crucial.

Obviously coming from a background in acting helps you as a director. What are some of the areas of filmmaking where that experience seemed to make the biggest difference?

JF: I think to be a director you should probably come from another aspect of the business, because the director runs the show. If you're a writer or an actor or any part of the crew,

Trent (Vince Vaughn), Mike (Jon Favreau), and Sue (Patrick Van Horn) strut their stuff in the cult favorite *Swingers* (Miramax Films, 1996).

you'll have had on-set experience, so you'll get to learn the game before you have to run the show. So as an actor, all the time I spent on the set and observing other directors was like an apprenticeship. That was very useful. Plus, as an actor, it's helped me as a writer because I have that knowledge of what makes a role good and what makes a role believable. It taught me to interact with other actors, as well. What I need when I'm an actor is what I try to give other actors when I'm directing.

What were some of the advantages in casting Sean "Puffy" Combs, a musician who had no real prior acting experience?

JF: Well, the advantage was that you have the opportunity to present someone fresh to your audience. It's an opportunity to introduce somebody new to the industry, and that's always a big thrill. You know, with Vince in *Swingers*, and now in this film [*Made*], I'm introducing new people.

What's nice about Puffy is that people are very aware of his persona and very aware of him in the music industry, so it was interesting to play off of that and introduce him in a different way. He's actually a very dedicated performer who takes everything he does very seriously. It's always a pleasure to work with people who are that committed.

How did you hook up with him?

JF: We met through a manager I had just started working with, and who had a relationship with Sean. He had known that Sean was looking to become involved with independent film, and they were very smart in that he wanted to play a part that was a supporting role and not try to carry a movie his first time out. So he was on the lookout for a role like this, and he had also had meetings over at Artisan and had expressed an interest in collaborating with that company. So between all that, a meeting had been set up. Vince had met him on the set of *The Cell* (2000), so I knew he was a stand-up guy; Vince had had a good experience meeting him through Jennifer [Lopez].

So we sat down and talked about it, and he was very earnest and sincere, and I really liked where he was coming from, his take on the character. I knew it was worth a shot. He also had a great reputation from the people who had cast him originally on *Any Given Sunday* (1999). And I had worked on *The Replacements*, and I had spoken with people who had worked with him before the schedules were such that he couldn't continue to do the role that Jamie Foxx went on to play. His reputation was good with everyone I had talked to who had worked with him. In this business, like any business, it's really word-of-mouth and your reputation that determines how successful you're going to be. His reputation was *very* good.

In Swingers *there were a number of homages to other films. Were those your idea, or was that something Doug Liman came up with?*

JF: All of that was in the script. As a matter of fact, Doug hadn't really wanted to include the *Reservoir Dogs* (1992) shot. And his whole thing was, "If you want to do it, then you shoot it." So that sequence I sort of set up and storyboarded. And as those little film references got good responses in the preview screenings we had, everybody began to embrace them, and those became the set pieces of the film. But I felt it was very much in character with this ensemble piece because the characters themselves are film fanatics. So when you have the characters sort of fantasizing about their own lives, I thought it was really appropriate for them to project themselves into that world of a [Quentin] Tarantino or [Martin] Scorsese film.

How much did your being a fan of Martin Scorsese's work, such as Raging Bull *(1980), play a role in your decision to appear in* Rocky Marciano?

JF: Well, Irwin Winkler produced *Raging Bull*, and his company produced *Marciano*, with his son Charles Winkler directing it. It was very exciting because Charles was a P.A. on *Raging Bull*, and he showed me the original script for *Raging Bull*. So it was very exciting. And also Jimmy Nickerson, who was a boxing coordinator and taught [Robert] De Niro how to box and coordinated *Raging Bull*, was the guy who coordinated the boxing in our movie. He also did *Rocky* (1976). So it was very exciting in that way.

You know, it ended up being a Showtime movie and never really getting the kind of exposure or theatrical release I had hoped for. So that kind of bummed me out, but *Raging Bull* is one of my favorite films. I think it's probably one of the top five films ever made. It was exciting. It's also incredibly big shoes to fill. Once it's been done like that, then what are you going to do?

What advice would you give to someone aspiring to become a filmmaker?

JF: Just do it, and don't plan on doing it. Nowadays with digital filmmaking and video and all of these people who have an understanding of film, there's no reason not to go out and just make something. But do *something*, whether it's getting a job on the set as a crew member or getting a camera and a bunch of friends together and actually making something. There are enough festivals out there that if you do something that's of any value, it's going to be discovered. My only film school was watching movies; I never went to film school. This is not to say that that's not a way to learn. People spend a lot of time and money on film school, and sometimes it sort of gets them off track of what they should be pursuing, which is actually making movies.

Actor Will Ferrell and director Jon Favreau discuss the scene they're about to film on the set of the comedy *Elf* (New Line Cinema, 2003).

FILMOGRAPHY FOR JON FAVREAU

1. *Folks!* (1992) A
2. *Rudy* (1993) A
3. *PCU* (1994) A
4. *Seinfeld* [episode: "The Fire"] (1994) A
5. *Chicago Hope* [episode: "Genevieve and Fat Boy"] (1994) A
6. *Notes from Underground* (1995) A
7. *The Larry Sanders Show* [episode: "Hank's Sex Tape"] (1995) A
8. *Swingers* (1996) Sc, Co-P, A
9. *Just Your Luck* (1996) A
10. *Persons Unknown* (1996) A
11. *Dogtown* (1997) A
12. *Friends* (1997) A
13. *Deep Impact* (1998) A
14. *Very Bad Things* (1998) A
15. *Rocky Marciano* (1999) [TV] A
16. *Buzz Lightyear of Star Command* (2000) A
16. *Love & Sex* (2000) A
17. *The Replacements* (2000) A
18. *The Sopranos* [episode: "D-Girl"] (2000) A
19. *Dinner for Five* (2001-) A
20. *Made* (2001) D, Sc, P, A
21. *The First $20 Million* (2002) Sc
22. *The Big Empty* (2003) Ex-P & A
23. *Daredevil* (2003) A
24. *Elf* (2003) D & A
25. *Something's Gotta Give* (2003) A
26. *Wimbledon* (2004) A
27. *Zathura* (2005) D
28. *My Name Is Earl* (2006) A
29. *The Break-Up* (2006) A
30. *In Case of Emergency* (2006) [Pilot] D & Ex-P
31. *The Break-Up* (2006) A
32. *Open Season* (2006) A
33. *Iron Man* (2007) D

Mick Garris

After fronting for a San Diego rock band known as Horsefeathers, and contributing film essays and celebrity interviews to publications such as *Fangoria* and *Starlog*, Mick Garris landed a job as host of the weekly television series *Fantasy Film Festival*. This led to a brief stint as an assistant to filmmaker George Lucas. Garris then went to work at Avco Embassy Pictures, first as a publicist and later as a project coordinator. Garris soon left Avco Embassy to work at Universal, where he met Steven Spielberg. The noted filmmaker then hired Garris to direct behind-the-scenes shorts for Amblin films. Through these $8,000 shorts Garris learned the craft of filmmaking. After Garris wrote *Coming Soon* (1982) with John Landis, Spielberg tapped him to pen an episode of his weekly television series, *Amazing Stories*. Impressed, Spielberg then hired Garris to work as story editor on the series. Garris eventually wrote eight episodes for the series, winning the Mystery Writers of America's Edgar Allan Poe Award for one of them ("The Amazing Farnsworth"). Garris also made his directorial debut when he helmed an episode of the series ("Life on Death Row"). On the heels of this success, Garris wrote and directed the telefilm *Fuzzbucket* (1986).

During this period Garris found work as a writer working on projects as varied as **batteries not included* (1987), *Hocus Pocus* (1993), and *The Fly II* (1989), which he cowrote with Frank Darabont. In 1988, Garris made his big-league directorial debut with the cheesy horror sequel *Critters 2*. While the film may not have been Academy Award material, it established Garris as a competent filmmaker and paved the way for his career as a director. After directing episodes for a number of television series, Garris followed up *Critters 2* with the impressive *Psycho IV: The Beginning* (1991). He then directed *Sleepwalkers* (1992), from an original script by best-selling novelist Stephen King. While working on this project, Garris and King became friends. This led to five more collaborations: *The Stand* (1994), *Stephen King's The Shining* (1997), *Quicksilver Highway* (1997), *Riding the Bullet* (2004), and *Desperation* (2006). In 2001, Garris directed his first non-horror film with the Steve Martini adaptation *The Judge*.

Garris has also directed episodes of television series such as *Freddy's Nightmares* and *Tales from the Crypt*. He was the co-creator of the syndicated series *She-Wolf of London*, which was later retitled *Love & Curses*. Garris also reunited with Steven Spielberg on the short-lived television series *The Others*, on which he served as a director and producer.

Favorite Films: The works of Billy Wilder, Alfred Hitchcock, and Frank Capra.

ANDREW RAUSCH: *Was it ever intimidating following in the footsteps of legendary director Alfred Hitchcock on* Psycho IV: The Beginning, *and then Stanley Kubrick on* The Shining?

MICK GARRIS: That's a question to ponder that I only really think about afterwards because, had I thought I was trying to fill the shoes of Alfred Hitchcock, I never would have taken the job. He was one of the greatest filmmakers of all time, and I'm somebody who's still learning what he's doing and trying to grow. He'd already done all of his growing long before *Psycho* (1960). *Psycho IV* was an opportunity to work with a lot of people who'd worked with Hitchcock, including Joe Stefano, who'd written the original *Psycho* and our movie as well. Hilton Green was Hitchcock's first assistant director on *Psycho*, and he was my executive producer. And, of course, there was Tony Perkins. It was more exciting and challenging to a naive filmmaker like me than something to regret or be intimidated by. I think my naiveté got me through that. It also prepared me a little bit with a suit of armor for when we went into *The Shining*, but that was a *very* different circumstance there.

Anthony Perkins (left), Henry Thomas (center), and Olivia Hussey (right) pose in front of the infamous house in this publicity photograph for Mick Garris' ***Psycho IV: The Beginning*** (Universal City Studios, Inc., 1990).

A lot of the Kubrick fans hate King because he didn't like *The Shining* (1980), so they really resent anybody treading on his "sacred ground." I'm a huge Kubrick fan myself, but I saw *The Shining* a few days before it came out and it was a huge disappointment to me. I like the movie a lot now, seeing it as Kubrick's movie rather than King's book. But at the time I felt like a wife who'd been cheated on by her husband because I so admired that book, and that wasn't what I got. Rather than looking at it as a competition between what I did and what Stanley Kubrick did — I would never win a competition like that — I just looked at it as a chance to tell the book as it was written. With King writing the screenplay, as he had with *The Stand*, we had an opportunity to do that. And I know there was no way a lot of these Kubrick fans could have liked our movie, no matter what we did. They felt that we took the sacrosanct and lifted our leg on it, whereas the King book existed first. The book will always exist, so I'm always going to feel a little bit defensive about it, but I think the miniseries we did was very faithful to it, and I feel it was the best work I've ever done as a director. It's also the best script I've ever read that I've had the opportunity to work with.

There are mother and son incestual relationships in both Psycho IV: The Beginning *and* Sleepwalkers. *You're creating a rather interesting niche for yourself as "the incest guy!" [Laughs]*

MG: Yeah, don't tell my mom! [Laughs] Actually, there was a third project that actually had that theme! But you see, those two films are projects that came to me. They didn't originate with me, so I plead innocence on that. But I do think one of the reasons Steve wanted me to do *Sleepwalkers* ultimately was because that theme was touched upon in *Psycho IV*. It did have some relevance to *Sleepwalkers*.

What was Anthony Perkins like to work with?

MG: Educational would probably be the best word. I really liked him a lot. He was by far the most difficult and challenging actor I've ever worked with. That, in itself, was worth it for the education. I say educational glibly, but I mean it that you have to learn to deal with every type of person. I have a lot of respect for Tony. He really wanted to direct *Psycho IV*, and *Psycho III* (1986) had been so unsuccessful that the studio wouldn't let him. I know there had to be resentment there, but he ended up really liking the movie and going on and on to embarrassing lengths about how much he liked it. But during the production of the film, he was *very* challenging. I mean that in the strictest sense of the word. Whenever I would discuss things with him — give him direction or just discuss an approach — he would take a contrary position and challenge it just to see that I was asking him to do something for more reason than it looks good on camera. He wanted to know that there was a basis for the direction more than just the visual. That's a long way of saying it was very difficult but very rewarding, and he has passed away. I don't have to say it was rewarding, except that it truly was. I do cherish having had that experience. As tough as it was at the time, I'm glad it happened. I think he gave a really good performance that I think was not nearly as campy as he had done in the previous film.

You've collaborated with Steven Spielberg a couple of times. What was that like?

MG: He is one of the most creatively generous people you could ever hope to be around. Ideas drip off him like sweat. I just finished doing a pilot for his series *The Others*. I've never done a pilot, and I don't particularly like network television; I really don't like or watch series television. He was very happy with it, and when the network bought the pilot to be a series, he asked me to be a directing producer on the series.

That's interesting that you don't really care much for network television, considering that's pretty much what you've become known for. [Laughs]

Brian Krause as the creepy Charles Brady in *Stephen King's Sleepwalkers*, directed by Mick Garris (Columbia Pictures Industries, Inc., 1992).

MG: That's true. I'll tell you, before I did *The Stand*, I'd maybe watched one miniseries in my life. After *The Stand*, I've watched that and *The Shining*, and maybe one other miniseries. I know it's biting the hand that feeds me, but I'm hoping that not being a TV watcher can possibly elevate, or at least remove it, from the standards of television. I don't want to be pretentious about it in any way because I know it is network television, and it's a huge place in the social and cultural cognizance of the world, but truthfully, I've seen *E.R.* once. I've never seen *Homicide* or *NYPD Blue*. I've never seen any of these shows. Even if I know they're good, I just don't have the time or the interest to get to know that family in my living room.

Obviously, television provides some advantages, such as the time needed to properly do a project as large and complex as The Stand, *but how limiting is the medium? It seems like it would be hard to sustain a sense of dread within a film when you're forced to go to a commercial every twenty minutes.*

MG: Very well put. I mean, first of all, your financial limitations are enormous, although *The Stand* cost $28 million. I know that sounds like a lot of money, and in the TV universe it's a huge amount of money, but we had to shoot it in sixteen millimeter to save $300,000. The second biggest problem is censorship; but the first biggest problem is, as you say, trying to create a sense of dread or a dramatic arc that has to start and stop seven times each night. You have seven acts where you basically have to start over every break. It's nice to know you're telling something in chapters, but you can't maintain. The longest you can maintain is a twenty minute stretch. Then your audience is deflated by five minutes of maxi-pad commercials screaming at them. Then you have to start over and begin trying to knit that sweater back.

It is limiting, but it's the only way to tell a story like *The Stand*. King became a convert with *The Stand*. We were able to do something that was so faithful to his book, and that was the self-imposed mandate — to create something that the people who had read the book would love, because no one ever loves a film or a TV show based on a book, especially something as beloved as *The Stand* was to all the fans, not the least of which being me. It was incumbent on me to take one of my favorite books of all time and do it justice. There were a lot of things that tried to get in the way of that, but with the group of people we had working on it, I think we were able to do something that shocked a lot of people because it was faithful to the book as much as it could be.

FILMOGRAPHY FOR MICK GARRIS

1. *Coming Soon* (1982) Sc & P
2. *Amazing Stories* (1985–1987) D, Sc, SE
3. *Fuzzbucket* (1986) D, Sc, P
4. **batteries not included* (1987) S
5. *Critters 2: The Main Course* (1988) D & Sc
6. *Freddy's Nightmares* [episode: "Killer Instinct"] (1988) D
7. *Tales from the Crypt* [episode: "The Mirror"] (1989) D
8. *The Fly II* (1989) Sc & S
9. *She Wolf of London* (1990–93) Sc, S, TA
10. *Psycho IV: The Beginning* (1991) [TV] D
11. *Sleepwalkers* (1992) D
12. *Hocus Pocus* (1993) Sc, S, Ex-P
13. *The Stand* (1994) [TV] D & A
14. *The Quick and the Dead* (1995) A
15. *The Stupids* (1996) A
16. *The Shining* (1997) [TV] D & A
17. *Michael Jackson's Ghosts* (1997) S
18. *Quicksilver Highway* (1997) [TV] D, Sc, P
19. *Virtual Obsession* (1998) [TV] D, Sc, P
20. *The Others* (2000) D, Sc, P
21. *The Judge* (2001) [TV] D
22. *Riding the Bullet* (2004) D, Sc, P
23. *Desperation* (2005) [TV] D
24. *Masters of Horror* (2005–) [episodes: various] D & P

Keith Gordon

Keith Gordon's career began as an actor when he appeared as Roy Scheider's son in *Jaws 2* (1978). The following year, Gordon worked with Scheider again, portraying the younger version of Scheider's character in Bob Fosse's hit film *All That Jazz* (1979), which was nominated for nine Academy Awards. Next, Gordon worked with director Brian De Palma on back-to-back films, *Home Movies* (1979) and *Dressed to Kill* (1980). Gordon then appeared in a number of TV movies before playing the human lead in *Christine* (1983). Having had the opportunity to watch noted directors such as Fosse, De Palma, and Carpenter at work, Gordon then embarked upon a second career as a filmmaker.

His first film behind the camera was the critically-acclaimed but largely-unseen *The Chocolate War* (1987). His sophomore feature was an adaptation of William Wharton's *A Midnight Clear* (1991). The film is very haunting and stark, and Gordon's direction is superb. In 1993, Gordon co-directed the ambitious Oliver Stone–produced miniseries *Wild Palms* with Peter Hewitt, Phil Joanou, and Kathryn Bigelow. In 1996, Gordon finally gained widespread recognition with the release of his brooding third feature, *Mother Night*. With this Kurt Vonnegut adaptation, Gordon's direction began to mature, and a distinctive style began to emerge. From its opening scene, few will (or can) argue *Mother Night*'s brilliance. It also stands as one of the only Vonnegut adaptations to receive the author's full approval, a testament to both Gordon and screenwriter Robert Weide's talents and hard work. In some ways, the work of Gordon and Vonnegut are quite similar: both men are uncompromising in their search for truth; their work is often filled with a dark humor; and while their respective bodies of work are amazingly solid, their work doesn't generally translate into commercial success.

The year 2000 saw the release of Gordon's fifth film, an adaptation of Scott Spencer's novel *Waking the Dead*, executive-produced by Oscar-winning actress Jodie Foster. Gordon's most recent project was *The Singing Detective* (2003), which starred Robert Downey, Jr., Mel Gibson, and Katie Holmes.

Favorite Films: Anything directed by Stanley Kubrick.

ANDREW RAUSCH: *You began your film career as an actor. Was directing always a goal for you?*

KEITH GORDON: Yeah, but I didn't know how I would get there. Frankly, I didn't know that I would get there. I didn't come from a rich family. The only people I knew that ever got to make movies were people whose families had paid for their first shorts. But I had always loved films and filmmaking — probably more than I loved the idea of being an actor. But I was lucky enough that I was in a school play and somebody saw me. So I auditioned for a professional play and I got the job. That led to my getting an audition for a movie, and I got that job. And I started working as an actor. I certainly loved it, enjoyed it, and took it very seriously, but I always tried to use the experience to learn about directing and filmmaking, with the hopes that I would get back to being involved more with that side of the process. I just didn't know if I'd take forty years to get there, and I'd make my first film at the age of fifty-five and it would be something like *Teenage Beach Blanket Bimbo Killers*. [Laughs] But I always had that dream of getting back to it. I was just fortunate that I was able to do it a lot more quickly and painlessly than I had expected. I was also very lucky to have had directors like Brian De Palma and John Carpenter and Michael Bennett, as well as people I worked with on stage and in theater who were very patient with my endless questions about what they did. They really let me be a bit of an apprentice while I was acting for them.

What was Carpenter like to work with?

KG: At the time we did *Christine*, he just really seemed to enjoy making movies. He seemed to love that process and it was very infectious. His sets had a very light atmosphere about them. People didn't get angry, and there was no yelling or screaming. He would play elaborate practical jokes in the middle of trying to make this movie, which I thought was really great. He wasn't an actor's director in the sense that he didn't want to sit around and talk about motivation for ten hours, but I was also self-motivated enough, no pun intended, that I didn't necessarily need that. But he was very encouraging of me experimenting with the character and trying different things, pulling me back if I went too far and pushing me here and there. He wasn't an actor's director in that he didn't speak the actor's language, but on the other hand, he seemed to have an appreciation for what actors did. He seemed to enjoy that

Keith Gordon as actor, with movie dad Rodney Dangerfield in the comedy *Back to School* (Orion Pictures Corporation, 1986).

and he seemed to want to help guide you, but he wasn't going to sit around and help you break down the character's history. People think a director has to speak in that actor's language, and it's probably best for an actor; but there are so many directors that are downright destructive and negative, that having someone like John, who is excited about what you're doing and has good taste, that's eighty percent of the battle right there. And if somebody really knows acting inside and out, yeah, that's another additional premium. But the kinds of movies John makes are not primarily about acting, anyway. Now if John was going to try to make a film like Ingmar Bergman, it might be a problem. But when you're directing a horror movie, those broad strokes are fine. That's what you need.

On the subject of your acting, I had read that you took the small role in I Love Trouble *(1994) so that you could get the script for* Mother Night *to Nick Nolte. Is that true?*

KG: That is true. It was one of those rare instances of good luck that happened to come up. Trying to raise the money for *Mother Night* was a very, very long process. We had all sorts of ups and downs. At one point we had Robert Duvall and couldn't get it financed with Robert Duvall. We had Anthony Hopkins, and by the time we got the money together we'd lost Anthony Hopkins. But Nick was the first actor we'd ever tried to go to. At that time his agents were like, "He's not interested in small movies." So we came full-circle, and Nick was one of the very few actors that we'd make the movie with. He was always the guy we wanted to play that role.

As it happened, Bonnie Zimmerman was casting *I Love Trouble*, and she called me up and said, "We're trying to get some interesting people in the movie in little cameo parts. Would you want to do it?" I said, "Can you get me in a scene with Nick?" And she said, "Sure." That was how it happened. So basically I have one line in the movie as "Andy the Photographer." I went up to Nick and just said, "Just so you know, I'm not really here to do this one line. I'm here to give you a script." He looked at me very oddly, but he'd never heard of the project. It had never gotten past his agency; they'd never really told him about it. Luckily, he liked Kurt Vonnegut's work, and, luckily, his assistant Eric knew my films and said, "Look, this guy's for real. He's not some lunatic." So Nick took the script, and three months later I finally heard back from him and he loved it. Had that little part never come up, *Mother Night* probably never would have been made.

Nick Nolte is a very versatile, very complex actor. What was Nolte like to direct?

KG: God. [Laughs] Nick is the most amazing actor I've ever worked with. If someone wanted a design in a textbook for what an actor should be for a director, you would see a picture of Nick Nolte. He does so much homework and puts so much of his heart into what he's doing. And here we were doing this little movie with a budget that was less than his salary on *I Love Trouble*. He could have just come in and done schtick; he could have just done what he'd done in his other movies and simply relied on his tricks. I mean, he was fifty-six when we made this film. But he approached this like a twenty-year-old just getting his first break.

First of all, he invited us to his house to do rehearsals and casting. He made himself the center of production, which was incredibly generous of him. Second of all, in the room where we were rehearsing, he already had up all of these cork boards with index cards breaking down the script into chronological order and script order. He had notebooks full of historical facts about Germany at the time he would have been there. He had biographies of other playwrights who would have lived in the era that Howard Campbell would have lived in. He studied what German playwrights of that era would have looked like and who they would have had to be friends with in the government. He did his own biography of the character beyond what was in the novel. It was like a ten-page type-written document. He then put all of this together

Brother Leon (John Glover) makes an example out of one of his students, Jerry Renault (Ilan Mitchell-Smith), in *The Chocolate War* (MCEG Virgin Home Entertainment, 1988).

in a book and gave me a copy, and he gave [screenwriter/producer] Bob Weide a copy. You looked at this thing and you said, "My God, he's done my research for me!" [Laughs] Nick basically did a lot of my homework! And this was before we had even started rehearsal. Then, throughout the process, Nick had this amazing combination of complete openness and flexibility in being the classic method actor who never does the scene the same way twice and always being open to trying something new, but at the same time being incredibly technically competent and enjoying the technicality of the medium. A lot of actors, even great actors, especially who come out of theater, kind of resent the medium. They resent the camera. They resent the lights. They resent having to hit a very specific mark for focus. Nick enjoys it, and Nick knows his stuff. If Nick wanted to, he would be a terrific director. He knows the technology of filmmaking really well, but I don't think he wants to do it.

FILMOGRAPHY FOR KEITH GORDON

1. *Jaws 2* (1978) A
2. *Home Movies* (1979) A
3. *All That Jazz* (1979) A
4. *Studs Lonigan* (1979) [TV] A
5. *Dressed to Kill* (1980) A
6. *Kent State* (1981) [TV] A
7. *Silent Rebellion* (1982) A
8. *Christine* (1983) A
9. *Single Bars, Single Women* (1984) [TV] A
10. *Static* (1985) Sc, Co-P, A
11. *The Legend of Billie Jean* (1985) A
12. *Back to School* (1986) A
13. *Combat High* (1986) [TV] A
14. *The Chocolate War* (1987) D & Sc
15. *Miami Vice* [episode: "Leap of Faith"] (1989) A

16. *A Midnight Clear* (1991) D & Sc
17. *Homicide: Life on the Street* [episode: "Extreme Unction"] (1994) D
18. *Wild Palms* (1993) [TV] Co-D
19. *I Love Trouble* (1994) A
20. *Hoggs' Heaven* (1994) [TV] A
21. *Mother Night* (1996) D
22. *Waking the Dead* (2000) D & Sc
23. *Delivering Milo* (2000) A
24. *Gideon's Crossing* (2000) D
25. *Night Visions* [episodes: "Bokor" and "Patterns"] (2001) D
26. *Jaws 2: A Portrait by Keith Gordon* (2001) A
27. *The Singing Detective* (2003) D
28. *House, M.D.* [episode: "Sports Medicine"] (2004) D
29. *Dexter* (2006) [episodes: various] D

Ethan Hawke

Austin, Texas, native Ethan Hawke made his screen debut at the age of fourteen in the forgettable sci-fi romp *Explorers* (1985). Four years later Hawke graced the screen, alongside Robin Williams, in Peter Weir's *Dead Poets Society* (1989). Hawke also appeared in *Dad* (1989) the same year, garnering accolades for his performances in both films. These successes led to a string of films which allowed him to fully display his acting chops: *A Midnight Clear* (1991), *Waterland* (1992), *Alive* (1993), *Reality Bites* (1994), and *Before Sunrise* (1995). Other notable credits in Hawke's filmography include *Gattaca* (1997), *Great Expectations* (1998), *The Newton Boys* (1998), *Snow Falling on Cedars* (1998), *Hamlet* (2000), *Waking Life* (2001), *Tape* (2001), and *Training Day* (2001), for which he received a Best Supporting Actor Oscar nomination. In addition to his screen work, the dedicated actor also continues to work in theater.

The versatile Hawke is also an accomplished novelist and director. Thus far in his writing career Hawke has published two novels, *The Hottest State* and *Ash Wednesday*. In 1994, Hawke emerged as a filmmaker, directing the short film *Straight to One* and also a music video for Lisa Loeb's single "Stay." In 2001, Hawke made his feature directorial debut with *Chelsea Walls*. The avant-garde project featured a remarkable ensemble that included Kris Kristofferson, Robert Sean Leonard, Christopher Walken, Vincent D'Onofrio, Tuesday Weld, and Hawke's then-wife Uma Thurman.

At the time of this writing Hawke was back in the director's seat crafting an adaptation (for which he also wrote the screenplay) of his own novel *The Hottest State*. (His decision to adapt the novel into a feature film makes the discussion about this possibility found within this interview all the more enlightening.) Despite his many accomplishments, renaissance man Hawke downplays his talents, saying, "I think most people are good at more things than the world gives them opportunity to do."

Favorite Films: *Reds* (1980), *The Right Stuff* (1983), *The Dreamlife of Angels* (1998), *Paris, Texas* (1984), and *One Flew Over the Cuckoo's Nest* (1975).

Andrew Rausch: *Do you find from your own experiences that an actor can become so consumed by a role that it affects his or her personal life?*

Ethan Hawke: Yes, I have seen an actor's role affect his or her personal life, but I must say that everyone's work affects the rest of their day. It is, however, particularly difficult to be portraying a human going through some kind of mental collapse in the afternoon, and then have yourself all put together for dinner at eight. When I was younger, each role would have a deep impact on my sense of self — a situation that was often confusing, and it usually worked in subtle ways. The role needs to be a complex and interesting one for this to even be an issue. Most people, however, try on different attitudes, highlighting different elements of their

Celine (Julie Delpy) and Jesse (Ethan Hawke) share their love for the unrehearsed, and their appreciation for the unexpected, in the romantic drama *Before Sunrise* (Castle Rock Entertainment, 1995).

personality at certain stages of their life. Growing older, some roots start to take shape underneath you, and it becomes easier and easier to stay close to your own sense of self through alternating situations. More than anything else, this is the great gift of getting to be an actor — having windows into other peoples' worlds and getting a taste of their experiences. Each job is an opportunity for a larger education.

Tape and Before Sunrise *feature two of your finest performances. Those films also showcase some of Richard Linklater's best work. What is it about your collaborative process with Linklater that brings out the best in each of you?*

EH: I appreciate that you think some of my best work is in *Tape* and *Before Sunrise*. Rick Linklater is one of the few people working in film today that has any real sense of how to utilize rehearsal. We also have a shred sensibility; working with Rick is the closest I've come to feeling like I was in a band. I'd like to think we inspire one another; certainly I know that he inspires me. The great benefit of working with people again and again — if it doesn't put too much pressure on your friendship — is that there is a trust, respect, knowledge, and love at the base of the work, where people can really feel safe enough to be at their most creatively liberated.

Sadly, I have to admit that he does do fantastic — perhaps better — work without me. *Slacker, Dazed and Confused,* and *Waking life* are phenomenal.

You've published two novels thus far in your career as a writer. Has the thought of directing an adaptation of your own writing crossed your mind?

EH: I work so hard putting the novels together that I could never find the energy to take them apart again the way I would need to make a movie. But yes, I do think about it constantly.

Obviously your experiences as an actor gave you a special insight when it came time to direct your first film. After making Chelsea Walls, *do you feel that having directed has given you new insight in regards to your acting?*

EH: I would say that the major insight, if I may be so bold, in directing *Chelsea Walls* was a renewed interest for acting. I had been acting for so long that I completely bought into the "it's a director's medium" thing, and I saw myself as being used effectively in one film and used less effectively in another. The whole acting process had begun to bore me. I also felt I had come to the wall of my gifts and was disappointed. But directing illuminated for me how much actors contribute to the set, the script, the mood, the tone; they each changed the shape of the day and the film. And the more they put into it, the more they got out of the experience.

So that was the major insight. Well, that and the unbelievable joys of editing.

You mentioned many directors not knowing how to effectively utilize rehearsal. What was your rehearsal process on Chelsea Walls *like?*

EH: I really didn't rehearse at all for *Chelsea Walls*. It is my belief that you either need a lot of rehearsal time or none at all; film is about spontaneity and catching it. I knew most of the actors extremely well before we began shooting, so there was an understanding between us which had already been cultivated. Then I took the time to get to know the actors I hadn't known as well prior to the shoot. If you empower actors, they will almost always reward you. Let them drive the character. They are, in effect, telling the story.

Chelsea Walls *is a pretty ambitious project for a first-time filmmaker. What attracted you to the project?*

EH: I guess *Chelsea Walls* was a pretty ambitious first film in that it is so non-linear, but it was also quite humble, as it was shot entirely in and around one building for around $100,000. I wanted to start out in a way that would give me an opportunity to learn as much as possible and to be free of any commercial pressures. If you accept $30 million dollars from somebody to finance your film, you have a built-in obligation to be responsible so they at least have a solid chance to make back their investment. I wanted the experience of getting to make a movie without giving up the creative freedom that you get when writing or working in the theater. I do the bulk of my acting in a commercial atmosphere and had no desire to be a "professional" filmmaker.

One of the aspects I liked most about the film was your giving each story its own visual style. What considerations went into that decision?

EH: The visual style of the film is one I harbor a lot of pride in. We gave each of the main storylines, as you commented, it's own visual dynamic. First off, I wanted the audience to be unclear as to what year it was exactly — like the movie was taking place in one day or over forty years. There have been people just like the characters portrayed floating in and out of these rooms for the last hundred years. And when you are in the hotel you lose track of time; parts of the hotel haven't been renovated in fifty years. A timelessness, I hoped, would evoke a kind of ghost-like atmosphere for the characters. So we gave each story its own decade. Not literally, but I hoped to evoke that feeling: for Bud, the sixties, void of primary colors and shot in a very conventional fashion; Grace, the seventies — we gave her whole story a gold/yellow pallet, and her room, if you remember, was all hippied out; Audrey and Val were the eighties, shot primarily with a steady cam and with a watery blue saturation; Terry and Ross were the nineties, all handheld and saturated in red. All of this was done in the hopes of achieving the timeless aspect I mentioned, as well as the hopes of creating a dynamic feeling when cross-cutting from room to room. Also, I hoped it would help articulate a theme of the film, which was separateness. Together they made up the whole pallet, but each room individually was separate and consumed with itself.

Sorry you asked? [Laughs] It's a long-winded answer, but when you're working with a piece that structurally has no rules you have to start making definitions in hopes of leading the audience. The film is too non-linear for most people, anyway. But if you watch it a lot—which I think everyone should—it actually makes a lot of sense. One of my favorite scenes is with Uma standing alone in an empty hallway talking on a yellow phone to a boyfriend who refuses to listen to her as a blue Mark Webber floats past one direction, red Wall strides the other way, and the black Kris storms back the other direction. The film, to me, was always a collective consciousness piece—all these people trapped in a transient residence bouncing around like electricity. They're all desperate to be heard, but none are listening to the other.

The advantages to shooting on digital — and there are many — are often discussed. Are there any disadvantages to shooting on DV?

EH: You're right; the advantages, such as economy and intimacy of performance, are much discussed. However, there are many disadvantages. Linklater has a saying that what DV giveth, it also taketh away. First off, if you are going to blow the film up to 35mm and try to release it, the post-production is still a nightmare. The technology is changing so rapidly that in a couple of years it may be vastly improved, but blowing up *Chelsea Walls* for release was expensive (equal to the cost of shooting the film) and extremely time consuming. Also, I believe that when audiences hear that something is DV, they assume it'll look like shit and not be very interesting: "If the script was really good they would've shot it on film." Exteriors, I think, are still really ugly. The biggest disadvantage, in my opinion, is how hard you have to work to make it look dynamic. You can take snapshots at Christmas with a 35mm camera and a couple of the photos will turn out magic, but on DV there is little natural poetry; too much information. As the emperor in *Amadeus* (1984) says, "Too many notes."

FILMOGRAPHY FOR ETHAN HAWKE

1. *Explorers* (1985) A
2. *Dead Poets Society* (1989) A
3. *Dad* (1989) A
4. *White Fang* (1991) A
5. *Mystery Date* (1991) A
6. *A Midnight Clear* (1991) A
7. *Waterland* (1992) A
8. *Rich in Love* (1992) A
9. *Alive* (1993) A
10. *Reality Bites* (1994) A
11. *Quiz Show* (1994) Un A
12. *Floundering* (1994) A
13. *Straight to One* (1994) D
14. *Before Sunrise* (1995) A
15. *Search and Destroy* (1995) A
16. *Gattaca* (1997) A
17. *Great Expectations* (1998) A
18. *The Newton Boys* (1998) A
19. *The Velocity of Gary* (1998) A
20. *Joe the King* (1998) A
21. *Snow Falling on Cedars* (1999) A
22. *Hamlet* (2000) A
23. *Tell Me* (2000) A
24. *Waking Life* (2001) A
25. *Tape* (2001) A
26. *Training Day* (2001) A
27. *Chelsea Walls* (2001) D & Un A
28. *The Jimmy Show* (2001) A
29. *Taking Lives* (2004) A
30. *Before Sunset* (2004) Co-Sc & A
31. *Assault on Precinct 13* (2005) A
32. *Lord of War* (2005) A
33. *The Hottest State* (2007) D, Sc, S, A
34. *Before the Devil Knows You're Dead* (2007) A

Monte Hellman

Monte Hellman's career began in the theater, where he directed the Los Angeles production of *Waiting for Godot*. After his theater was torn down, he directed *Beast from Haunted Cave* (1959), a film he half-jokingly refers to as his version of *Key Largo* (1948) "with a monster added."

Although Hellman's directorial resume is rather expansive, he is best known for westerns, such as the existential classics *Ride in the Whirlwind* (1965) and *The Shooting* (1967), which he shot back-to-back in 1964. These classic films showcased a lean and mean Warren Oates, and a hungry young actor named Jack Nicholson. Hellman's 1971 rock-and-roll-on-wheels picture *Two-Lane Blacktop*, which starred James Taylor, Beach Boys drummer Dennis Wilson, Laurie Bird, and Warren Oates, has also gained cult status. Ironically, if you look under the hood, *Two-Lane Blacktop* is a western at heart. Although *Two-Lane Blacktop* was largely overlooked in its time, today it's considered a bona fide classic. *American Cinematheque* critic Dennis Bartock believes it to be the definitive American road movie. "I think *Two-Lane Blacktop* will look better and better [with the passing of time]," Bartock has said. "That's not to say *Easy Rider* won't, but I don't think people have even begun to realize how great a film *Two-Lane Blacktop* is."

Other Hellman classics include *Back Door to Hell* (1964) and *Flight to Fury* (1966), which he shot back-to-back in the Philippines with Jack Nicholson, and the spaghetti western *China 9, Liberty 37* (1978), which starred Fabio Testi, Jenny Agutter, Warren Oates, and Sam Peckinpah. In 1974, Hellman filmed an adaptation of Charles Willeford's novel *Cockfighter*, which is generally regarded as the finest Willeford adaptation to date. In addition to these efforts, Hellman also directed additional footage for the 1975 ABC television debut of Sergio Leone's *A Fistful of Dollars* (1964), with Harry Dean Stanton.

In 1992, Hellman further solidified his already-respectable credits by executive producing Quentin Tarantino's *Reservoir Dogs*. Like Tarantino, Hellman's talents aren't bound to any one aspect of filmmaking; Hellman has written, directed, produced, and acted in numerous pictures. In addition, the versatile filmmaker has served as editor on a number of movies, including Jonathan Demme's *Fighting Mad* (1976) and Peckinpah's *The Killer Elite* (1975). He is also the subject of the George Hickenlooper documentary *Monte Hellman: American Auteur* (1997).

Favorite Films: *The Sentinel* (1992), *Outcast of the Islands* (1952), *Broken Blossoms* (1936), *Casablanca* (1942), *It's a Wonderful Life* (1946), *Annie Hall* (1977), *The Wild Bunch* (1969), *The Bicycle Thief* (1948), *Shoot the Piano Player* (1960), and *Dodsworth* (1936).

Andrew Rausch: *With the advent of video, a lot of your older work has become much more recognized and you've become somewhat of a cult figure. What's it like when younger filmmakers such as Quentin Tarantino say your work has heavily influenced them? How do you react to that?*

MONTE HELLMAN: It makes me feel very friendly toward them! [Laughs] I'm like anybody in that I like people who like me. If someone comes up to me and tells me they like my films, that immediately makes me like them.

How did you end up shooting Beast from Haunted Cave *for Roger Corman?*

MH: Roger had been one of the backers of a theater company I had where we did the Los Angeles production of *Waiting for Godot*. Then I got notice from my landlord that the theater was being torn down and was being converted into a movie theater. Roger said, "You should take that as a sign!" [Laughs] "The handwriting is on the wall...." Then he used a very funny phrase in terms of what my life has been like. He said, "Why don't you make a movie and get healthy." [Laughs again] It hardly made me healthy!

Cockfighter *was based on the novel by Charles Willeford. I was wondering what Willeford's creative involvement on the film was, and how he came to appear in it?*

MH: He wrote the screenplay before I came onboard. Roger had bought the rights and hired Charles to write the screenplay. I was hired to direct the film. I then brought in another writer to do some rewriting. Then Charles came on the set as kind of an advisor, and I fired one of the actors and asked Charles to take over at the last minute. I did that because I felt the actor I'd hired wasn't authentic. I just felt he didn't fit into the milieu.

Frank Mansfield (Warren Oates, left) and Jack Burke (Harry Dean Stanton, right) prepare their animals for battle in *Cockfighter* (a.k.a. *Born to Kill*) (unidentified actor in center; New World Pictures, 1974).

I'm going to name a couple of actors that you've worked with. As I do, I'd like you to comment on each of them briefly.

MH: Okay.

Harry Dean Stanton.

MH: Well, Harry Dean is totally unique, and he's a great actor. He was always living in the shadow of Warren Oates. He would constantly ask me why he had to play second banana to Warren. He had a great kind of constantly griping personality. He was very amusing to be around. He never stopped complaining on any of the pictures we did together! [Laughs]

Warren Oates.

MH: Warren Oates is my alter ego. He was the actor I felt closest to. I think most directors find an actor that they can relate to who can be their voice in their films. Warren was that for me. He was irreplaceable. I feel a tremendous creative and personal loss not to be able to continue making movies with him.

Warren Oates was great in anything. However, you consistently managed to pull some of the finest performances of his career from him. How did you do this? Was there a certain way you worked with him, or was it simply that he felt comfortable with you?

MH: I think we were both comfortable. The first film we did together was *The Shooting*, and we probably had more conversations about the work on that one movie than we ever did again. We actually had some arguments, and then finally he would say, "Okay, let's shoot it both ways." And I would agree. After that, he knew that once it got into the editing room, it was gonna be my way! [Laughs] So we didn't argue any more after that. In fact, we barely talked. After you've worked together a few times, it's kind of a silent language that takes place between an actor and a director. We just had a communication that didn't require a lot of words.

James Taylor.

MH: James Taylor was one of the most professional actors I've ever worked with. There's a tremendous advantage to using someone before they develop a lot of bad habits. James just took to it naturally, and he had a way of working in his music that perfectly fit what he was doing in the film, other than the fact he felt strange about it. He felt strange because he was used to being in control. He felt uncomfortable giving that responsibility to someone else.

Jack Nicholson.

MH: Jack is like most actors in the sense that he really wants someone to watch his performance and guide him in a way. But he's different in the sense that he really does respect the director. When I worked with him, his ego never got in the way, as with some actors today. I can't vouch that Jack never changed over the years. I haven't worked with him since the two westerns [*Ride in the Whirlwind* and *The Shooting*].

You were involved with a couple of back-to-back shoots, which was a much more common practice at that time. What were those like?

MH: Well, it's very energizing. [Laughs] In the Philippines, it was very difficult because the first shoot was in the jungle and I had contracted some sort of rare tropical disease. In the three weeks I should have been preparing for the second film, I was mostly in the hospital. They didn't even know if I'd be able to get out to do the movie. Finally, Jack Nicholson came to my hospital bed and he put his hand on my forehead and said, "I'm laying hands on you. You will be well." The next day I jumped out of bed and went scouting locations, and that was it. He made me well.

Jack Nicholson's Billy Spear (left) lays down the law to a character played by Wally Moon in Monte Hellman's classic western *The Shooting* (Jack H. Harris Enterprises, Inc./Continental Distributing Incorporated, 1967).

I understand that you and Jack Nicholson wrote a screenplay called Epitaph, *which was never produced. What can you tell me about that?*

MH: When Jack and I first started talking about working together, we decided to work on this script. It's essentially autobiographical to the extent that we were using Jack's experience as a young actor for the foundation of his character. In fact, we actually intended to use clips from the many small movies and TV shows he had done at that time. Then the story becomes fictional in the sense that it's about this character, Jack, whose girlfriend has become pregnant. It's about him trying to raise $300 for an abortion. It's a search movie. It's picaresque travels through his friends, trying to borrow $300.

Eventually the film itself was aborted. What happened?

MH: What happened was, Jack and I had gone off to the Philippines to do two movies, *Back Door to Hell* and *Flight to Fury*. Before that, we had an agreement with Roger to back *Epitaph*. When we came back, he told us he'd changed his mind. He didn't think it was commercial, but he didn't want to totally renege. He told us if we wanted to make a western, we could. Then one western grew into two westerns.

You worked with Sam Peckinpah on both The Killer Elite *and* China 9, Liberty 37. *I'd like you to describe Peckinpah as you knew him.*

MH: I think he was a man who was afraid to face himself. He had all these ruses to keep you from getting close to him, yet somehow you got close to him. He was really an amazing, tormented genius. When I worked with him as an editor, he seemed like he was barely able to walk, function, or do anything. You would expect that there was no one inside. Then he would come into the editing room and just come up with these things that were so brilliant. He would solve all the problems. You didn't know where [the ideas] were coming from because he seemed so out of it. But he wasn't out of it. He was always there. He had just built up defenses against the world.

You served as executive producer on Reservoir Dogs. *Is it true that you initially considered directing that yourself?*

MH: Yes. I had been approached indirectly by Lawrence Bender through a friend of mine. They felt that having a director attached would make it easier to get the picture made. They set up a meeting between me and

Harvey Keitel as the tough-as-nails Mr. White in *Reservoir Dogs*, produced by Monte Hellman (Live Entertainment/Miramax Films, 1992).

Quentin. I met with him, and, just by coincidence, on the day we met, he had sold *True Romance* (1993). He apologized for making me come to the meeting. He said that as much as he admired my work, he was now going to direct the movie. He could afford to do it now that he'd sold his screenplay. I told him I thought that was great, and that he would be the right director for it. He asked me if I would help him get it made, and that's what I did.

Just for fun, how might you have directed the film differently?

MH: I think I probably would have done the whole thing differently, but that doesn't mean that I would have made a better film. I think he made the film exactly as it should have been made.

Filmography for Monte Hellman

1. *Beast from Haunted Cave* (1959) D
2. *Ski Troop Attack* (1960) Un Co-D
3. *The Wild Ride* (1960) Ed
4. *The Terror* (1963) Un Co-D
5. *Back Door to Hell* (1964) D & Un Ed
6. *Bus Riley's Back in Town* (1965) Ed
7. *Ride in the Whirlwind* (1965) D, P, Ed
8. *Flight to Fury* (1966) D, S, Un Ed
9. *The Wild Angels* (1966) Ed
10. *The Shooting* (1967) D, P, Ed
11. *Target: Harry* (1969) Ed
12. *Two-Lane Blacktop* (1971) D & Ed
13. *The Christian Licorice Store* (1971) A
14. *Shatter* (1974) Un Co-D
15. *Cockfighter* (1974) D & Un Ed
16. *The Killer Elite* (1975) Ed

17. *A Fistful of Dollars* (1975) [additional footage for TV broadcast] Un Co-D
18. *Baretta* (1975) [TV pilot] Co-D
19. *Harry and Walter Go to New York* (1976) Un Ed
20. *Fighting Mad* (1976) Ed
21. *The Greatest* (1977) Un Co-D
22. *China 9, Liberty 37* (1978) D, P, Un Ed
23. *Avalanche Express* (1979) Co-D
24. *The Awakening* (1980) Un Ed
25. *Chambre 666* (1982) [TV] A
26. *RoboCop* (1987) Un SUD
27. *Someone to Love* (1987) A
28. *Iguana* (1988) D, Sc, Ed
29. *Silent Night, Deadly Night 3* (1989) D, Sc, Ed
30. *Reservoir Dogs* (1992) Ex-P
31. *Love, Cheat & Steal* (1993) Un Ed
32. *The Killing Box* (1993) Ed
33. *L.A. Without a Map* (1998) A
34. *Trapped Ashes* (2006) Co-D

Buck Henry

The son of actress Ruth Taylor, Buck Henry began acting at the age of sixteen in a traveling production of *Life with Father*. In the late fifties, Henry began writing for *The Garry Moore Show* and *The Steve Allen Show*, occasionally appearing on the latter. In 1964, he became a regular on *That Was the Week That Was*. The following year, Henry and Mel Brooks co-created the popular TV series *Get Smart*. In 1966, Henry was awarded an Emmy for his work on the show.

Henry came to national prominence with his screenplay *The Graduate* (1967), which was directed by Mike Nichols. The film was immediately showered with praise and received seven Oscar nominations. Henry received a Best Screenplay Oscar nomination, a Golden Globe nomination, a British Academy Award, and a Writers Guild Award (his first of four WGA nominations). In the years following the film's release, *The Graduate* has become recognized as a bona fide classic. In 1996, the film was listed to the National Film Registry. Two years later, *The Graduate* was listed at number seven on the American Film Institute's list of the one hundred greatest films in the history of American cinema.

Following the success of *The Graduate*, Henry stayed busy. He wrote two more scripts for Nichols, *Catch-22* (1970) and *Day of the Dolphin* (1973), appearing as an actor in both films. In 1972, Henry co-wrote Peter Bogdanovich's *What's Up, Doc?* which paid homage to Howard Hawks' classic screwball comedy *Bringing Up Baby* (1938). Henry and co-writers David Newman and Robert Benton received a Writers Guild Award for their work on *What's Up, Doc?* The film was a box-office success and became the second highest grossing film of 1972 behind *The Godfather*. Other notable screenplays Henry has written or co-written include *The Owl and the Pussycat* (1970), *Protocol* (1984), *To Die For* (1995), and *Town and Country* (2001). In addition, Henry penned an Edgar-nominated episode of *Alfred Hitchcock Presents*, and created the two short-lived television series *Captain Nice* and *Quark*.

Renaissance man Henry is also an accomplished actor and director. In 1970, he co-directed the short film *I Miss Sonia Henie* with Milos Forman and Paul Morrissey. In 1979, Henry was nominated for a Best Director Oscar for his feature-length directorial debut, *Heaven Can Wait* (1978), which he co-directed with Warren Beatty. In 1980, Henry directed the comedy *First Family*, which he also wrote. Having appeared in more than forty features, Henry's acting credits include films as diverse as Paul Bartel's *Eating Raoul* (1982), *Grumpy Old Men* (1993), and *Serendipity* (2001), and he's worked with such noted filmmakers as Nicolas Roeg, John Cassavetes, Milos Forman, Albert Brooks, Robert Altman, and Gus Van Sant. In the late 1970s, Henry became an unofficial member of the *Saturday Night Live* Not Ready for Prime Time Players, appearing in many of the show's most memorable skits with the likes of John Belushi, Chevy Chase, Dan Ackroyd, Gilda Radner, and Jane Curtin.

Buck Henry directing on the set of his second directorial effort, *First Family* (Warner Bros. Pictures, 1980).

Favorite Films: "There are just too many to list."

ANDREW RAUSCH: *How did you become involved with* The Graduate?
  BUCK HENRY: Mike Nichols asked me if I'd like to read the book, and what I thought of it. I thought it was terrific, and I felt it would make a great movie.

I understand that Mike Nichols and yourself originally envisioned the character Benjamin Braddock as being a blonde-haired, blue-eyed man, á la Robert Redford. I was wondering if you could tell me a little bit about this earlier characterization, and how Dustin Hoffman, who is obviously none of these things, wound up in the role?
  BH: Well, that's what those people tended to look like in the imagination: the golden folks of California. I think everyone's idea—certainly our idea—when reading the book was that everyone was blonde and beautiful. But when it comes to actually casting blonde and beautiful people, you get into a bit of trouble because there are only a few of them that can act. [Chuckles] So you either go for all of it, or you just forget about it and go for the best actors.

I remember reading that Mike Nichols and yourself initially brought in a few other actors—actors you already knew—to read for the part. Who were some of those actors?
  BH: We knew *everybody* better than we knew Dustin! But there were at least six tests made: Redford, Tony Bill, Charles Grodin, Dustin, and one or two others that I can no longer

remember. We were familiar with all of them except Dustin; he was the one we were the least familiar with, and certainly the furthest from the average conception of what the character looked and sounded like.

But the truth is that Dustin was more interesting than anyone else.

While a lot of people remember the film's ending as being a happy one, director Mike Nichols has said that he believes the couple will grow apart just as their parents have. In the film's final scene, Nichols implies that this is already happening, as Benjamin's smile quickly fades and we're shown separate shots of them both as "The Sounds of Silence" plays. This doesn't really come through in the script, so I was wondering if you agree with Nichols' interpretation?

BH: Oh, yeah. I mean, in the original screenplay I think I included one or two words of dialogue between them. I can't remember any longer, but I know there was something. They were really perfunctory. It was like two people who don't have much more to talk about. [Laughs]

But, you know, it's no big revelation. Well, perhaps it was a revelation in terms of contemporary filmmaking because people tended to want neat, tidy endings. And this was neither neat nor tidy, and much more, it seems to me, like life. But you have to remember also that, in the book, Benjamin breaks up the wedding before it takes place and runs off with Elaine. In the film, he gets there *after* they've been married and runs off with her. It was a change that author Charles Webb did not like *at all*.

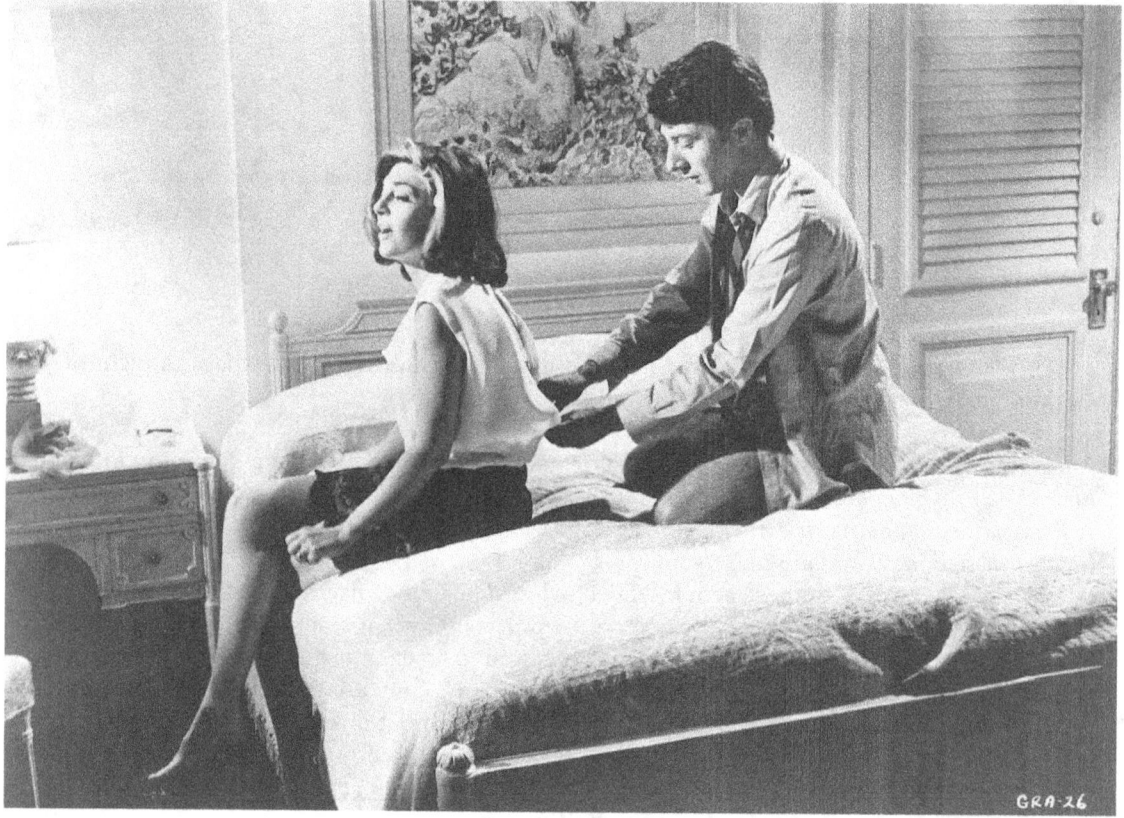

Benjamin Braddock (Dustin Hoffman) finds himself being seduced by Mrs. Robinson (Anne Bancroft) in *The Graduate*, written by Buck Henry (AVCO Embassy Pictures Corporation, 1967).

What were some of the considerations that went into that change?

BH: Well, one of the considerations—Nichols' consideration—was that it was too much like, "Ah, the cavalry to the rescue!" It's just an enormous cliché. But wouldn't it be more interesting if he got there too late?

I think the scene in The Player *(1992), in which you pitch* The Graduate 2, *is hilarious. How did that come about?*

BH: Robert Altman asked a few writer friends of his if we'd come and improvise a pitch. The only rule was that we should mention Julia Roberts as a possible part of the project. That was the only rule: we had to find a way to fit her in. But it was up to us what we wanted to pitch.

On your first film, Heaven Can Wait, *you were directing what was largely someone else's material. On your second project,* First Family, *you directed your own script. Do you find it more constraining when you're bringing someone else's writing to the screen?*

BH: Not at all. The two experiences felt completely the same.

I remember reading that Cary Grant was considered for the role of Mr. Jordan. Is that true?

BH: Of course. And also, so was Senator Eugene McCarthy and Muhammad Ali. [Laughs] So there you are. Take your pick.

From a director's point-of-view, what was James Mason like?

BH: Oh, he's fabulous! I mean, just a really great man with a real actor's intelligence. You didn't have to tell him anything. Very professional.

One of the films you've worked on that I really enjoy is Peter Bogdanovich's What's Up, Doc? *Bogdanovich has always called this his homage to* Bringing Up Baby. *When you were writing that, how conscious were you of the Hawks film?*

BH: I actually wasn't conscious of it at all. It doesn't interest me to do homage. But you know, that was Peter's thing. Actually, the unfinished screenplay by Benton, Newman, and Peter, from which I took off, had a *lot* of movie stuff in it. I imagine those were mostly Peter's contributions. Well, I guess it could have been Newman and Benton, too, because they were very *Esquire*-oriented in those days—using quotes and popular culture and those kinds of things. And the references were very clever, but I took them all out except for the obvious *Casablanca* (1942) piece, where Barbara Streisand sings to Ryan O'Neal. Peter had a real fondness for that scene. But the only piece that I know of that is directly borrowed [from *Bringing Up Baby*] is the tearing of the jacket, which I would not have left in if I'd had total control.

Charles Grodin as Tony Abbott in a scene from *Heaven Can Wait*, co-directed by Warren Beatty and Buck Henry (Paramount Pictures Corporation, 1978).

I have to add that I absolutely love what Peter did. I think he made the film brilliantly. I'm very, very fond of *What's Up, Doc?* But now that I'm older and maybe a little wiser — perhaps just more cynical — I'd take out everything that referred to other movies in every film I've ever worked on. And there have been a lot of references. *The Troublemaker* (1964), which you are probably — and should be *happily* — unfamiliar with, is *filled* with film references. It plays quite frequently on Bravo, much to my horror! [Laughs] It's a real collegiate kind of film. It's jammed purposely with film references that I now find very irritating.

FILMOGRAPHY FOR BUCK HENRY

1. *The Steve Allen Show* (1956–61) Sc & A
2. *The Garry Moore Show* (1958–67) Sc
3. *The Troublemaker* (1964) Sc & A
4. *That Was the Week That Was* (1964) A
5. *Get Smart* (1965–1967) Co-Sc & P
6. *The Graduate* (1967) Co-Sc & A
7. *Candy* (1968) Sc & Un A
8. *Captain Nice* (1968) Sc & P
9. *The Secret War of Harry Frigg* (1968) A
10. *Jailbird* (1969) Co-Sc
11. *Catch-22* (1970) Sc & A
12. *The Owl and the Pussycat* (1970) Sc & Un A
13. *Is There Sex After Death?* (1970) Co-Sc & A
14. *Taking Off* (1971) A
15. *I Miss Sonia Henie* (1971) Co-D
16. *What's Up, Doc?* (1972) Co-Sc
17. *The Day of the Dolphin* (1973) Sc
18. *The Man Who Fell to Earth* (1976) A
19. *The Absent-Minded Waiter* (1970) A
20. *Saturday Night Live* (1975–1980) A
21. *Heaven Can Wait* (1978) Co-D, Un Sc, A
22. *Quark* (1978) Sc & P
23. *Strong Medicine* (1979) A
24. *Old Boyfriends* (1979) A
25. *Gloria* (1980) A
26. *First Family* (1980) D, Sc, A
27. *Eating Raoul* (1982) A
28. *The New Show* (1984) A
29. *Protocol* (1984) Co-Sc
30. *Alfred Hitchcock Presents* (1985) [episode: "Wake Me When I'm Dead"] Sc
31. *Aria* (1987) A
32. *Rude Awakening* (1989) A
33. *Dark Before Dawn* (1989) A
34. *Murphy Brown* (1989) [episode: "My Dinner with Einstein"] A
35. *Tune in Tomorrow...* (1990) A
36. *Defending Your Life* (1991) A
37. *The Linguini Incident* (1991) A
38. *Shakespeare's Plan 10 from Outer Space* (1991) A
39. *The Player* (1992) A
40. *Keep the Change* (1992) [TV] A
41. *Mastergate* (1992) [TV] A
42. *The Lounge People* (1992) A
43. *Even Cowgirls Get the Blues* (1993) A
44. *Short Cuts* (1993) A
45. *Grumpy Old Men* (1993) A
46. *To Die For* (1995) Sc & A
47. *Shotgun Freeway* (1995) A
48. *Kurt Vonnegut's Harrison Bergeron* (1995) [TV] A
49. *The Real Blonde* (1997) A
50. *1999* (1998) A
51. *I'm Losing You* (1998) A
52. *The Story of X* (1998) A
53. *Breakfast of Champions* (1999) A
54. *Curtain Call* (1999) A
55. *Dilbert* (1999–2000) A
56. *Famous* (2000) A
57. *It's a Girl Thing* (2001) [TV] A
58. *Town and Country* (2001) Co-Sc & A
59. *Serendipity* (2001) Un A
60. *The Last Shot* (2004) A

George Hickenlooper

In 1991, George Hickenlooper garnered critical acclaim with *Hearts of Darkness: A Filmmaker's Apocalypse*, which he co-directed with Fax Bahr. The film — a documentary about the making of Francis Ford Coppola's epic war film *Apocalypse Now* (1979) — is widely regarded as the quintessential documentary on filmmaking. *Hearts of Darkness* won the National Board of Review's award for Best Documentary, as well as the American Cinema Editors' Award (known as the "Eddie") for Best Edited Documentary. In 1993, Hickenlooper helmed the Roger Corman executive-produced romp *The Killing Box*. Much to the director's dismay, the film would be trimmed substantially in the producer's final cut. However, New Horizon later released the director's cut under the title *Grey Night*. Hickenlooper's next project would be the short film *Some Folks Call It a Sling Blade* (1993), starring Billy Bob Thornton, who later made a full-length version of the tale as *Sling Blade* (1996).

Other Hickenlooper-directed features include *The Low Life* (1994), *Persons Unknown* (1996), and *Dogtown* (1997). The latter, which features Jon Favreau in an unusually dark role as a racist, took home top honors for Best Director and Best Screenplay at the 1998 Hermosa Beach Film Festival, as well as Best Director honors at the Newport International Film Festival. For his next project, Hickenlooper and film critic-turned-screenwriter F.X. Feeney reworked an unfilmed script by Orson Welles and Oja Kodar for *The Big Brass Ring* (1999). *The Big Brass Ring*, which debuted on Showtime, was nominated for Best Television Feature at the Edgar Allan Poe Awards, and Best Film at the Newport International Film Festival. Hickenlooper then crafted his most polished feature to date, *The Man from Elysian Fields* (2001), which starred Andy Garcia, James Coburn, and Mick Jagger.

Like his book *Reel Conversations*, many of Hickenlooper's documentaries reveal his fascination with filmmakers and their craft; such films include the aforementioned *Hearts of Darkness*, *Picture This: The Life and Times of Peter Bogdanovich in Archer, Texas* (1991), *Art, Acting, and the Suicide Chair: Dennis Hopper* (1988), and *Monte Hellman: American Auteur* (1997). Hickenlooper's most recent documentary is *The Mayor of Sunset Strip* (2004).

Favorite Films: *On the Waterfront* (1954), *Wild Strawberries* (1957), *Sunset Boulevard* (1950), *The Magnificent Ambersons* (1942), *Glen or Glenda* (1953), *The Best Years of Our Lives* (1946), *Rules of the Game* (1939), *The American Friend* (1977), *Walkabout* (1971), *Touch of Evil* (1958), *The Third Man* (1949), and *Rashomon* (1950).

ANDREW RAUSCH: *You co-directed* Hearts of Darkness, *which documented the filming of* Apocalypse Now. *In your opinion, how do you think a masterpiece resulted from such a disastrous shoot?*

GEORGE HICKENLOOPER: Well, I would argue whether or not *Apocalypse Now* is a masterpiece; it's a perceived masterpiece. I think it's a great war film, but, in my own personal opinion, I think it's seriously flawed.

I think the flaw is simple: I think the dynamic that Coppola failed to bring into it — particularly the closure of the third act — is simply the coda at the end of the film, in [Joseph] Conrad's *Heart of Darkness*, when Marlowe goes to see Willard's widow. Her question to him is, "What were his last words?" He says, "They were of you." Really, that moment embodies the irony of Western civilization. Really, that one small scene at the end of the novella is completely what *Heart of Darkness* is. Coppola was immersing himself in Conrad's material; he was trying to bring the original [John] Milius script back closer to the Conrad novella, whereas Milius just borrowed the river metaphor. The original Milius script intonally was just more in line with *Dr. Strangelove* (1964) — it was more of a satire, where Coppola kept many of the satiric elements but was trying to make a more serious film. But he failed to shoot that coda. He had scripted it, and he was going to shoot it with Martin Sheen, and Willard's widow was going to be Michael Learned. But he didn't shoot it. Instead, he chose to end the film with the slaughter of Kurtz, which was, in a way, a much more narcissistic ending; the ending was really more about Coppola defeating the beast — the beast being the making of this picture — and I think he lost perspective. That's why it fails to be a masterpiece, in my mind.

The Big Brass Ring is based upon Orson Welles' screenplay of the same name. Welles' biographer, Joseph McBride, who also appears in the director's unreleased film *The Other Side of the Wind*, recently called your film a bold adaptation "that Welles himself would have been proud of." He went on to say that "Hickenlooper did a damned good job adapting Welles." What is your reaction to this praise?

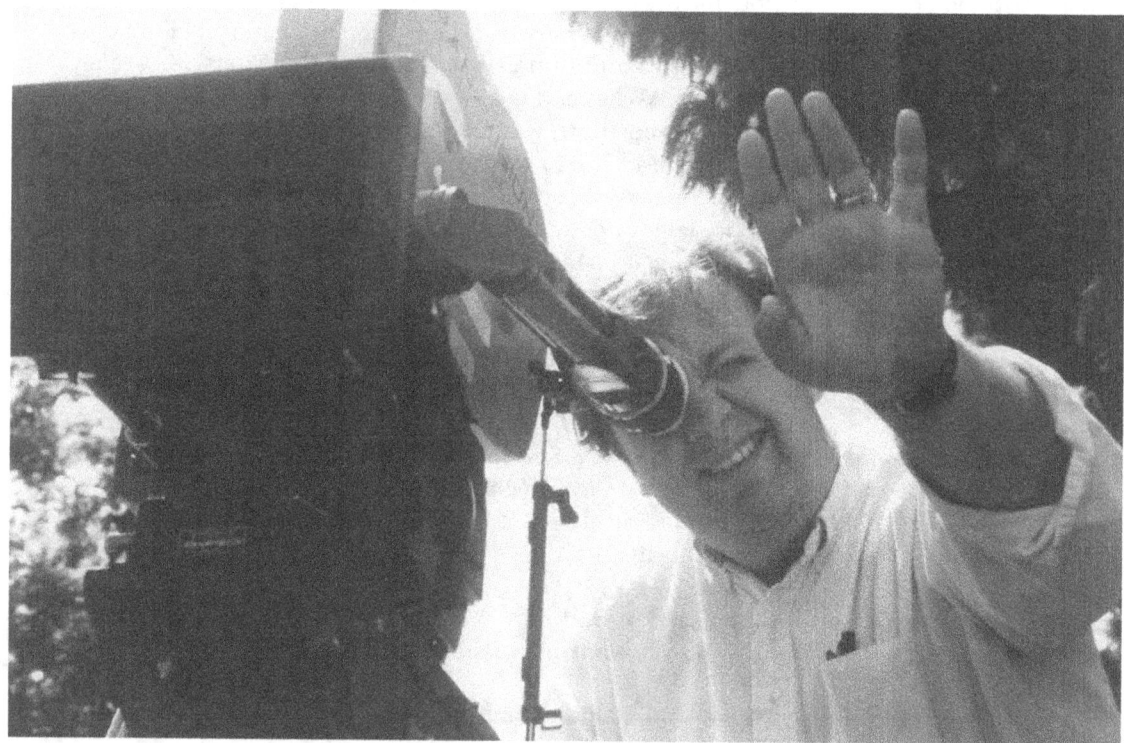

Director George Hickenlooper takes a look at a shot on the set of his film *The Low Life* (Cabin Fever Entertainment, 1995).

Marlon Brando and Martin Sheen in *Apocalypse Now*, which served as the basis of the 1995 documentary *Hearts of Darkness: A Filmmaker's Apocalypse* (United Artists, 1979).

GH: Well, first of all, I'm very flattered.

Let me say that going into *The Big Brass Ring*, knowing that Welles had written his script with the intention of it being a bookend to *Citizen Kane* (1941), I knew that the perception would be that I was meddling with the forces of nature, that what I was doing would be sacrosanct. My intention was never to try and step into Orson Welles' shoes or to fulfill his vision. I think [co-writer] F.X. Feeney and I, our intention was to pay homage to Orson Welles the writer, and bring attention to his work, and to adapt Welles just as we would adapt William Shakespeare. And it has always been my view—ever since I was a young boy—that Orson Welles is the Shakespeare of cinema. He, in my mind, is the greatest filmmaker who ever lived. So by making *The Big Brass Ring*, I knew that people would perceive me as meddling with Orson Welles the icon, that I was somehow meddling with his talent. Because he is such an icon, his talents as a writer are not really well-known. And Pauline Kael certainly did her best to destroy his reputation as a writer with her damning, unscholarly essay "Raising Kane." So I simply wanted to bring attention to his work as a writer, and I approached this the same way one would when adapting the work of any great writer, from William Shakespeare to Tennessee Williams. So I knew coming out of the gate we'd be compared to *Citizen Kane*—certainly by the popular press—and that it was a losing battle. So I never really went into this worrying about the reviews, because I knew that more than likely all of them would be negative. But I felt I needed to make this film because it spoke to me on a personal level; my own great uncle had been the governor of Iowa, and I understood the public versus private persona. But going into this, I knew there would be big guns aimed at me. Considering the fact, I thought we did pretty well. We got great reviews in *The Washington Post, The L.A. Times, New York Magazine.*

So when I hear someone like Joseph McBride, who wrote the first biography of Welles and knew the man well enough that he knew Welles' tastes, it was certainly one of the most flattering comments I received regarding *Big Brass Ring*. Gary Graver and Oja Kodar also said very great things, which meant a great deal to me, and made me feel as though I had, hopefully, in my humble way, served Orson Welles' legacy well.

Some Folks Call It a Slingblade launched Billy Bob Thornton's film Slingblade. *How did you become involved with that?*
GH: Billy Bob and I struck up a friendship while working together on *Grey Night*. He was from Arkansas and I was from Missouri. The basis for our friendship was that we had a mutual love for the St. Louis Cardinals baseball team. We used to hang out together, and we were going to collaborate on a number of projects. He had a script called *The Gulf* he wanted me to direct. He had another script called *The Sounds of Country*, which he wanted me to direct. He was going to take a pass at *The Big Brass Ring* script. In the meantime, he told me he had this character he had performed in a showcase. It wasn't part of a play, just something he played in a showcase of characters. He performed this for me one time in his apartment, and it sent chills down my spine. I said, "This is a great character. We should really, really make a movie out of this, Billy Bob." And he said, "Well, I was thinking of shooting something for my acting reel," because he was trying to get work as an actor. And I said, "No, let's make this a short film. Let's write something that will give this character some shape." So he wrote a short twenty-five-page script, using a lot of ideas we came up with together, such as its setting. So I raised the money, and we shot this over three days in 1993, and we finished the film, and Billy Bob and I had a huge, huge falling out over the edit of the short. He wanted his whole monologue in close-up, and I wanted to start off wide and move in with a slow tracking shot. We had a huge argument, and he disassociated himself with the short until it got into the Sundance Film Festival. Then he tried to be my best friend.

So we got back together, and based on the response we got from Sundance, we'd always intended to shoot this film as a feature together. I was going to direct it, and he was going to write and star in it. We were going to use the twenty-five-minute short as the first act of the feature. When he was released from the prison mental hospital, the film would gradually, over a series of a couple of scenes, fade to color. He had a lot of ideas I didn't think worked, so I gave him a lot of ideas that did, some of which, quite frankly, ended up in the feature. After we reconciled at Sundance, we went to a number of producers, talking about the financing of the picture. One producer was interested, in particular. In the meantime, shortly after the New York Film Festival, I got financing together for a script I'd been working on for a couple of years called *The Low Life*. So I went to Billy Bob and said, "I'd love for you to do a cameo in this while we're getting the financing together for *Slingblade*." And he said, "I don't want to be in a cameo. I want to star in it." And he told me he wanted to play a part which was not right for him at all. He wanted to play the role which Sean Astin ended up playing, which is like a twenty-two-year-old. He was far too old for it, and I told him, "No. You're not right." We had a huge blow-up, and he was very insulting to both me and my wife. He was physically threatening. He was psychotic. He scared the shit out of me, and I basically told him I never wanted to see him again. And I never did.

He went on and made *Sling Blade*, and had great success with it — much to my dismay, frankly. But the story and the feature is something we'd discussed together for a long time. What ended up on the screen was based entirely on the short film, in my view.

FILMOGRAPHY FOR GEORGE HICKENLOOPER

1. *Art, Acting, and the Suicide Chair: Dennis Hopper* (1988) D
2. *Picture This: The Times of Peter Bogdanovich in Archer City, Texas* (1991) D
3. *Hearts of Darkness: A Filmmaker's Apocalypse* (1991) Co-D & Co-Sc
4. *Some Folks Call It a Sling Blade* (1993) D, Ed, P
5. *The Killing Box* (1993) D & A
6. *The Big Brass Ring* (short version) (1994) D
7. *The Low Life* (1994) D, Sc, A
8. *Persons Unknown* (1996) D & A
9. *Sling Blade* (1996) Un S
10. *Monte Hellman: American Auteur* (1997) D
11. *The Last Express* (1997) A
12. *Dogtown* (1997) D & Sc
13. *The Big Brass Ring* (1999) D & Co-Sc
14. *Karen Black: Actress at Work* (1999) A
15. *The Man from Elysian Fields* (2001) D
16. *The Mayor of Sunset Strip* (2004) D
17. *Bizarre Love Triangle* (2005) D & Sc
18. *Factory Girl* (2007) D

Mike Judge

Mike Judge was born in Ecuador and then grew up in Albuquerque, New Mexico. He attended U.C. San Diego, where he received a degree in physics. After graduation, Judge found work as an engineer for a government contractor. In 1990, Judge created a series of short animated films featuring a nebbish desk jockey named Milton. These shorts garnered Judge a great deal of attention and were then purchased by Lorne Michaels, who aired them as part of *Saturday Night Live*. The following year Judge sold another animated short to Comedy Central.

In 1992, Judge crafted a short entitled *Frog Baseball*. This short introduced the world to the characters Beavis and Butthead, who soon landed their own MTV series (written, produced, and animated by Judge). The series, which drew criticism after an act of adolescent pyromania was blamed on the show, became incredibly popular and spawned the feature film *Beavis and Butthead Do America* (1996). In 1997, *Beavis and Butthead* was cancelled, and Judge created the popular television series *King of the Hill*. The series has—to date—been nominated for five Emmys, winning two.

In 1999, Judge wrote and directed his second film, *Office Space*. The live-action comedy, which featured Ron Livingston and Jennifer Aniston, failed to create sparks at the box office but has since become a bona fide cult classic. Judge then collaborated with Don Herzfeldt on the compilation film *The Animation Show* (2003), for which the duo was awarded the prestigious Annie Award.

The versatile Judge is also an accomplished actor whose credits include *Airheads* (1994), *South Park: Bigger, Longer, and Uncut* (1999), and all three of Robert Rodriguez's *Spy Kids* films.

At the time of this writing Judge was collaborating with Hertzfeldt and *King of the Hill* co-writer Etan Cohen on his third directorial effort, *Idiocracy* (2006).

Favorite Films: *A Clockwork Orange* (1971), *Badlands* (1973), *Pulp Fiction* (1994), and *Ace Ventura: Pet Detective* (1994).

ANDREW RAUSCH: *A lot of really great filmmakers, such as Robert Rodriguez, David Lynch, and Tim Burton, began in animation. Do you think animators possess a certain sensibility that somehow lends itself to filmmaking?*

MIKE JUDGE: Yeah, I think that's probably true. It's all the same in that you're making the same decisions—the way you stage something. When you're actually animating a character you're doing the physical acting yourself. It's the same thought process, really. I don't know if it's necessarily a better step toward live-action filmmaking than just making a film, but it's not as different as people think.

Director Mike Judge maps out a scene during the filming of *Office Space* (20th Century–Fox, 1999).

Your animated work has always been a little bit edgy, with some mature themes. Were you a fan of Ralph Bakshi's work?

MJ: I haven't seen all of it. I remember seeing *Wizards* (1977) in my senior year of high school. I remember thinking it looked really cool. I don't remember much about the story or anything like that, but just the way animation looked on the big screen made an impression on me. I haven't really seen much of Bakshi's work. What really influenced me was the first time I went to an animation festival. I'd just loved cartoons as a kid — the old Warner Bros. stuff. I'd assumed that that was just a bygone era. I thought it was something that just happened back in the Fifties, and now animation just looked horrible, you know? Then I went to an animation festival and saw that there were people doing really cool things independently. Just seeing it on the big screen blew me away. Animation shot on film and projected just looked amazing to me. It still does. But that's what really made it click for me.

Also, there were a lot of still cartoonists that I was into — stuff like *National Lampoon*, Bill Griffith's Zippy, and Robert Crumb. Mary Kay Brown was another one I was really into. I would look at that stuff and just think, Man, I wish this was animated. I could just hear how it would sound.

I had wanted to do claymation since high school, but I didn't have a camera and I couldn't afford one. [Laughs] It just seemed like something I wanted to do if I became rich one day. Then I realized that individuals could do it when I was living in Dallas and I saw this story about this guy there who had something in the animation festival. Then I started thinking, "Hey, you can rent time on a camera and work for two months to get two minutes."

In a review for Beavis and Butthead Do America *one critic praised the film for being a calculated study of the twentieth century in American society. [Laughs] Do you ever feel like critics over-analyze these things?*

MJ: [Laughs] Yeah, sometimes. But I'm glad they're saying things like that. I'm glad that somebody's analyzing it. I have to be careful not to read too many reviews. Especially on something like that where it's my drawings, my voices, and my writing. There's nobody to hide behind. Yeah, sometimes they get a little bit too heavy. But every now and then I read something and I'm like, "Wow!" It's like I've just been to a psychologist or something!

Was it at all surreal having Robert Stack ordering "cavity searches, hard and deep"?

MJ: [Laughs] Yeah. I had written all of those scenes, and I heard this voice in my head of what the character was supposed to sound like. I couldn't think of who it was. At first I thought it was Alec Baldwin. Suddenly I just realized it was Robert Stack I was hearing. Then he agreed to do it and I tell you, he came to the studio a really nice guy, but I was so nervous that by about the fifth cavity search line he was gonna storm out of there. And he was getting a little irritated. At one point he said [perfect Robert Stack impression], "Ah, so this movie's all just about cavity searches?" [Laughs again] So I kind of raced through it, thinking if I can get every line a couple of times, I can go back and work with him on some of those things. Then a camera crew showed up about midway through it and he really kicked it into high gear. He was great.

It's really funny. He's been a big movie star for decades and he's been in all these old movies, and at the test screening all of the kids were like, "That's cool that they got the voice of that *Unsolved Mysteries* guy."

An animated publicity still from Mike Judge's *Beavis and Butthead Do America* (Paramount Pictures, 1996).

Animated characters Luanne, Peggy, Bobby, and Hank Hill "pose" for this publicity shot from Mike Judge's Emmy Award–winning series *King of the Hill* (Fox Broadcasting Company, 1997).

I wanted to comment that I love the way the characters in Office Space *devise their method of embezzlement from watching* Superman III *(1983). As a writer that always kind of seems like cheating, but I must say that you pulled it off better than most.*

MJ: That scam had actually been done back in the seventies, so I wrote it into the script. I used to program a little bit; I did software stuff. A friend of mine who still does that was telling me that it was a big concern when they were updating everything for Y2K. So originally I had that in the script, but they mentioned the seventies thing. Then someone mentioned *Superman III* and I checked it out. I was about to change it, but then I thought, truthfully, today that's a reference point. That's how people learn about things.

The popular culture reference was really funny as a joke unto itself.

MJ: Yeah. I actually think if you get too heavy handed with it.... Sometimes it bothers me when you get the feeling that the director is using the movie as a platform to rag on another movie or something. I think it was actually just thrown away as something that could be realistic. Then it's okay.

The music you selected for Office Space, *which included Ice Cube, Scarface, and the Geto Boys, was very interesting, as one does not generally associate such a suburban white-collar scenario with so-called "gangsta rap."*

MJ: I had always been into hip-hop off and on. I kind of got out of it for a while around the time MC Hammer and all that stuff was happening. When NWA hit, there was something about it that really struck a chord with me. I went and bought their stuff, and then I started buying the other albums. I was kind of thinking, "Why do I like this stuff so much?" [Laughs] Pretty gnarly, violent lyrics, but it's really just the anger and the passion behind the music that appealed to me. I think that's what music is—a release of emotions and passions, be it angry or whatever. Also, that music always just seemed so cinematic to me. Whenever I hear it I see images and everything. I thought it would actually be really great for an office because there's all this really deep-rooted anger and hatred inside these cubicles. I just thought it would be really cool to hear that playing over these kind of white-collar scenes.

Also, those albums sell millions and there are only a small handful of real gang members. [Laughs again] It's really people like me buying those albums.

I think that opening scene is funny as hell where the guy is acting like a badass, pumping the Geto Boys, and then when a black guy walks past the car, he locks the door nervously!

MJ: That's one scene when I was editing that I never got tired of.

I was driving in my car once. After I got the *Beavis and Butthead* money, I decided I was going to buy a Saab. You know, I thought, I can't drive a Toyota anymore. I was driving around in my Saab cranking the Geto Boys and I just thought, "This is ridiculous! [Laughs] I'm driving around Austin singing this stuff in my Saab."

A few years ago, a pornographic film called Beaver and Buttface *(1997) was released. As one writer lamented in* The Austin Chronicle, *you know you've "made it" when the porn industry satirizes your life's work. [Laughs] What are your thoughts on that?*

MJ: [Laughs] I was flattered. It was also a little freakish to see that! Boy, that's a...

Quite an honor!

MJ: Yeah. I know of at least one other filmmaker who has seen his work become pornized. *Regarding Henry* [1991]. It was *Regarding Heiny* [1992]. [Laughs]

These titles are funny. Things like Saving Ryan's Privates *(1998).*

MJ: Yeah. The one I remember seeing in the video store was *Romancing the Bone* [1985].

Those titles always stick with you. They're good for a laugh. I remember Rambone *(1985).*

MJ: *Absence of Phallus*! [Laughs] My composer that I've used on my two movies always tries to anticipate what the porn title of his film will be. So on *Office Space*, I figure it's probably going to be *Orifice Space*. He had another one, if, God willing, it ever gets that far.

As someone who has faced the criticism with Beavis and Butthead *regarding the "monkey see, monkey do" theory of television, how do you see the relationship between screen violence and real-life violence or misconduct?*

MJ: When people bring that up, I'm always surprised how they never have statistics. The very best they ever have is one incident, and it's always hearsay. There's never any proof of the incident. Being a guy with a physics degree who's taken a lot of probability and statistics classes, I always point out that the years *Beavis and Butthead* were on the air, virtually every kind of crime dropped. The crime rate dropped!

Also, all of this time people have been complaining and correlating violence to real life, violence has gone down this whole time. That's an argument that's been around forever. Except that I don't remember ever hearing that Abraham Lincoln was complaining about Edgar Allan Poe's violent imagery!

FILMOGRAPHY FOR MIKE JUDGE

1. *Saturday Night Live* (1990) [shorts] D
2. *Beavis and Butthead* (1993) D, Sc, P, A
3. *Airheads* (1994) A
4. *Beavis and Butthead Do America* (1996) D & A
5. *The Simpsons* (1997) A (voice)
6. *Space Ghost Coast to Coast* (1997) A
7. *King of the Hill* (1997-) D, Sc, P, A
8. *Office Space* (1999) D & A
9. *South Park: Bigger, Longer and Uncut* (1999) A
10. *Monsignor Martinez* (2000) D, Sc, A
11. *Spy Kids* (2001) A
12. *Spy Kids 2: The Island of Lost Dreams* (2002) A
13. *Serving Sara* (2002) Un A
14. *The Animation Show* (2003) Ex-P
15. *Spy Kids 3-D: Game Over* (2003) A
16. *Idiocracy* (2006) Co-D, Sc, P

Lloyd Kaufman

Lloyd Kaufman's film career began in 1968 with *Rappaccini*, which he produced while attending classes at Yale. The following year Kaufman wrote, directed, and produced his first feature film, *The Girl Who Returned* (1969). He then worked as production assistant on two John G. Avildsen films (*Joe* and *Cry Uncle!*, both 1970). In 1974, Kaufman and former classmate Michael Herz established their own independent studio, Troma Films.

While Kaufman flirted with the majors, working in various capacities on noted films such as *Rocky* (1976), *Saturday Night Fever* (1977), and Louis Malle's *My Dinner with Andre* (1981), his heart remained with the lower-budget Troma releases. In 1985, Kaufman and Herz found success with the cult classic *The Toxic Avenger*, which they co-directed. Kaufman has since directed or co-directed a number of highly-successful indie films, including *Class of Nuke 'Em High* (1986), *Troma's War* (1988), *The Toxic Avenger: Part II* (1989), *The Toxic Avenger III: The Last Temptation of Toxie* (1989), *Sgt. Kabukiman N.Y.P.D.* (1992), the ambitious *Tromeo & Juliet* (1997), *Terror Firmer* (1999), and *Citizen Toxie: The Toxic Avenger Part IV* (2000). The prolific filmmaker has also appeared as an actor in a number of features, including *Rocky V* (1990), *Orgazmo* (1997), and *Zombiegeddon* (2006). In addition, Troma Films serves as the international distributor for hundreds of films, including *Cry Uncle!*, Japanese animator Hayao Miyazaki's *My Neighbor Totoro* (1988), and Trey Parker's *Cannibal! The Musical* (1996).

In 2000, Kaufman established the TromaDance Film Festival as an outlet for low-budget independent filmmakers to display their work. Kaufman has also penned the books *All I Needed to Know About Filmmaking I Learned from the Toxic Avenger*, *Make Your Own Damn Movie*, and *Toxic Avenger: The Novel*.

Today Kaufman is seen as one of the most important figures of the independent film movement, and has been recognized by the British Film Institute, the American Film Institute, and the American Cinemateque. Filmmakers as diverse and respected as Peter Jackson, Quentin Tarantino, Mike Judge, and Kevin Smith credit Kaufman's work as an influence.

Favorite Films: "*Princess Yang Kwei-fei* [1955], which I consider to be the greatest film ever made." Also anything directed by Charles Chaplin, Buster Keaton, or John Ford.

ANDREW RAUSCH: *You once said "The Sundance Film Festival is bogus, they hate filmmakers, and they're not really independent." What did you mean by this?*

LLOYD KAUFMAN: Trey Parker, who is a buddy of mine, took me there because we had helped him with *Cannibal! The Musical*. He had submitted the film to Sundance and paid the entry fee, but hadn't even received a response saying "Get fucked." When we were there, from what we could see, they hate filmmakers. They're interested in Mercedes cars and bald, fifty-year-old guys with pigtails dressed in black and carrying cell phones. Those are also the

Lloyd Kaufman displays his acting chops as a homophobic janitor in *Zombiegeddon*, executive-produced by author Andrew J. Rausch (courtesy Rosie Zwaduck).

people *The New York Times* seems to be interested in; whenever *The New York Times* writes about Sundance, they say, "the independents are in great shape," and then the first thing in the article is a P.R. guy who says he's got eight movies at Sundance! Of course, those eight movies are usually being distributed by Miramax, Fine Line, or HBO. Miramax is owned by Disney; Miramax is *not* an independent, no matter what they would have you believe! Fine Line and HBO are part of AOL/Time Warner. These films are not independent, and, if anything, they're using their cartel power to destroy the true independents.

As a result of Trey Parker's inspiration, we formed our own festival called TromaDance, which takes place at Park City at the same time as Sundance. There is no entry fee. I mean, why should an independent festival, which is supposedly encouraging independent filmmaking, charge money to filmmakers just to submit a movie? You, Mr. Rausch, know how hard it is to make a movie; you're doing it. You have to donate a kidney to get a movie made! It's very expensive. These film festivals are fixed, in my opinion. Let's face it: most of the movies in Sundance already have distribution, or they're made with Sundance in mind and they take absolutely no risks. Half of these movies are going to be in theaters a week or two after Sundance! So, TromaDance was founded so that anybody can send a movie in without having to pay a penny.

The other horrifying thing about Sundance, which hardly makes it aimed at independents, is that the tickets are ridiculously expensive. They're not aimed at the young independent filmmakers or students of film who are the real locomotive of creative energy in the world of art. When you go to the headquarters of the Sundance festival, they truly hate you if you are an independent filmmaker! No question about it.

In fact, we had an incident where the volunteers of TromaDance were trying to get personal handwritten notes to Elvis Mitchell and some of the other panelists, and Sundance wouldn't let them. They also had two of our people arrested for passing out leaflets about the TromaDance festival. Because of the conspiracy between Park City and Sundance, it's illegal to hand out leaflets or even to inform people by mouth in the street about your movie there unless it's a Sundance film. It's also illegal to post any type of notice there. It's a very ugly and clearly non-independent environment.

There are a number of major film critics who have a strict policy against reviewing Troma releases. What is your reaction to that?

LK: Well, the idea is to marginalize and deny the American public of not only Troma movies, but truly independent movies. But, in the process, they are marginalizing themselves because, as you may have noticed, Roger Ebert now has to say in his reviews, "Two thumbs *way* up." It's no longer two thumbs up, because that doesn't mean anything; these guys give everything a good review. So now it's two thumbs *way* up. How many "best films of the year" is Peter Travers of *Rolling Stone* going to pick each year? They are marginalizing themselves. Nobody under the age of eighty-three listens to guys like Joel Siegel or Gene Shalit. These guys have a policy that they will not review anything released or produced by Troma; we could release *Gone with the Wind* [1939], and they wouldn't review it! They've told us that. They won't review *My Neighbor Totoro*, which is a Hayao Miyazaki masterpiece. Now, Disney has released a number of Miyazaki's films, and these critics are more than happy to review *those* films! There is a conspiracy at work here which is going to put people out of business.

Troma is the oldest continuously-running independent movie studio. If you look at what HBO is airing, it's all either HBO-produced or major releases with Mel Gibson. They have no independent movies. If they don't own you, they would like to put you out of business.

Through the years, the Toxic Avenger *franchise has gained a tremendous following. What do you think it is about Toxie that resonates with audiences?*

LK: Well, there are very few people doing satire today. For a while we were the only ones. A lot of people want to see that. They want to laugh at something intelligent. Another thing, as Stan Lee and many of the journalists who've given Toxie good reviews have suggested, is that like the Marvel comic book heroes, we've put a new face on the traditional superhero. Just as Marvel's Spiderman has his own personal problems to contend with, so does Toxie. He doesn't have any major superpowers; he's got a mop, and he can jump. Toxie has to worry about paying his rent; he's true to his girlfriend; he's got a mother that's a pain in the ass; he has skin problems. What makes Toxie such an interesting superhero is that he's able to conquer his worldly problems. His superhuman activities are not what makes people interested in his story. *Citizen Toxie* deals with issues like the Columbine shooting, the abortion issue, the fact that MTV and the media are brainwashing kids into spending billions of dollars on plastic surgery when their bodies are not yet formed, racism — these are issues that are dealt with in *Citizen Toxie*. I think these are issues that the mainstream doesn't want to deal with. They wouldn't even consider it. The Farrelly brothers are doing things that we did in movies twenty years ago! You'll see things in reviews for movies like *There's Something About Mary* (1998) where the critics say something along the lines of, "Troma did this twenty years ago."

I think that's why Toxie is as popular as he is. He deals with those points I just mentioned. Also, he's Chaplinesque. There is — obviously — a major Chaplin influence on Toxie — things like *City Lights* [1931], in particular. I think you can definitely see the influences of guys like Chaplin and Preston Sturges on the *Toxic Avenger* series.

What inspired you to update Shakespeare in your film Tromeo & Juliet *(1997)?*

LK: Well, Michael Herz and I went to Yale. We both have a great appreciation for the

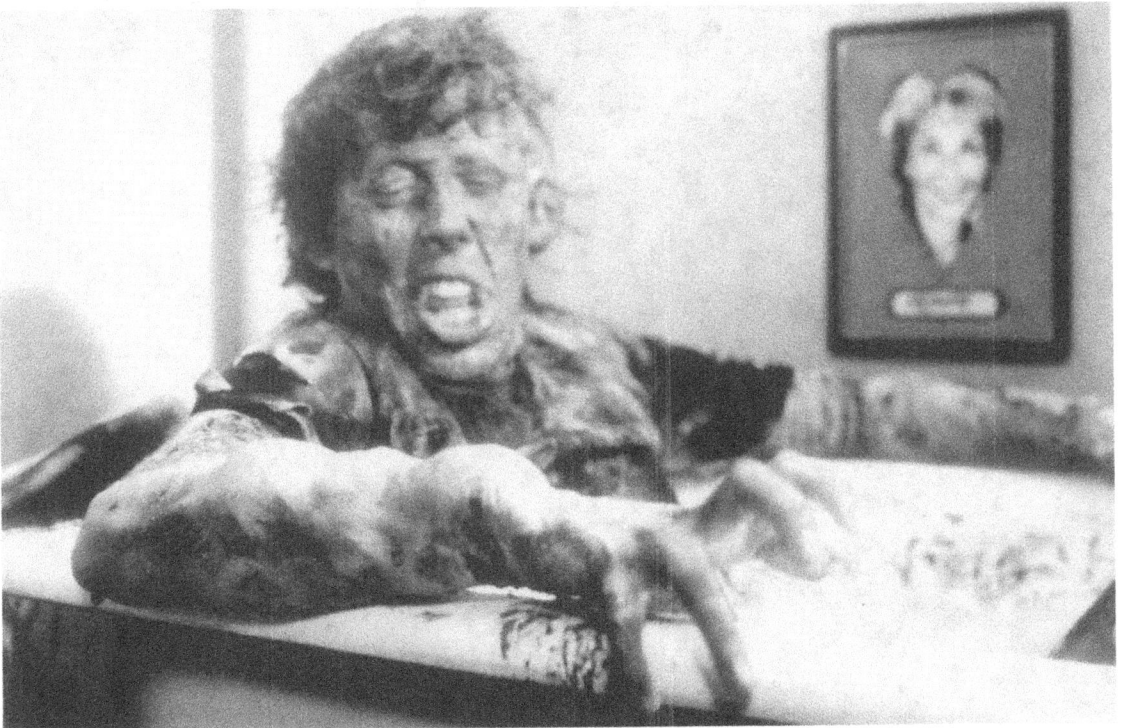

Mild-mannered Melvin Junko (Mark Torgl) finds himself transforming into the title character of the cult film *The Toxic Avenger* (Troma Films, 1985).

The Toxic Avenger (Ron Fazio) and his new bride Claire (Phoebe Legere) in *The Toxic Avenger Part III: The Last Temptation of Toxie* (Troma Films, 1999).

Bard. The British Film Institute did a major retrospective of Troma in London about ten years ago. I visited Stratford-upon-Avon — the birthplace of Shakespeare — while I was there. And, I guess, Shakespeare's spirit entered my body! I cannot reveal from which orifice he exited my body.... [Laughs] The result was *Tromeo & Juliet*. It took us about five years to develop the script that we felt was truly the right path. As you know, the film is entirely in iambic pentameter. We did rewrite about eighty-five percent of Shakespeare's text, but he would have approved.

There's a very important underlying theme to that movie which corresponds a great deal with the original story *Romeo & Juliet* — namely, that true love is a subversive force. Romeo and Juliet were rebelling for love against rules and formalities that, in some cases, they didn't even understand. *Tromeo & Juliet* is based upon the problems the younger generation today face. Young people today are different from my generation — the postwar yuppie Sixties generation. It's my opinion that the postwar generation — the "Clinton generation" — worships the ultra-cool. You know, Clinton sitting on the Presidential airplane with Ted Koppel, wearing his $800 boots and his $300 jeans; he and Koppel with their $80 haircuts and their feet up on the table. They're just so cool, cool, cool. And, as a result, their marriages suck, and they don't know what love is, and they fucked it up. And the postwar baby boom generation — being the most populous, and most aggressive, and most hypocritical of all time — has smothered the next generation. The baby boom generation have brainwashed the young people, and have shown by example that emotion is unwarranted; fifty percent of marriages end in divorce, so emotion is unnecessary. This is the reason that young people are tattooing themselves, piercing themselves, engaging in autoerotic asphyxiation... The kids are turning inward; they're concentrating on themselves. So Tromeo and Juliet come along, and they are using love to fight against the rules and conventions of the previous generation, rules about which they don't fully know or understand.

FILMOGRAPHY FOR LLOYD KAUFMAN

1. *Rappacini* (1968) P
2. *The Girl Who Returned* (1969) D, Sc, P
3. *Joe* (1970) PA
4. *Cry Uncle!* (1970) PM & A
5. *Silent Night, Bloody Night* (1971) P
6. *The Battle of Love's Return* (1971) D, Sc, P, A, Ed
7. *Big Gus, What's the Fuss?* (1972) D & P
8. *The Newcomers* (1972) P
9. *Sweet Savior* (1973) PM & A
10. *Sugar Cookies* (1973) Sc, Ex-P, A
11. *Divine Obsession* (1975) D
12. *Rocky* (1976) PS & A
13. *My Sex-Rated Wife* (1977) Cin
14. *Slow Dancing in the Big City* (1977) PS
15. *Saturday Night Fever* (1977) LM
16. *The Final Countdown* (1979) P & A
17. *Squeeze Play* (1979) D, P, Cin
18. *Waitress* (1980) Co-D, P, Cin
19. *Mother's Day* (1980) P
20. *My Dinner with Andre* (1981) PM
21. *Stuck on You* (1981) Co-D, Co-Sc, P, Cin
22. *The First Turn-On* (1983) Co-D, P, Cin
23. *Screamplay* (1984) Ex-P
24. *When Nature Calls* (1985) P
25. *The Toxic Avenger* (1985) Co-D, Co-Sc, P
26. *Blood Hook* (1986) Ex-P
27. *Girls School Screamers* (1986) Ex-P
28. *Class of Nuke 'Em High* (1986) Co-D & P
29. *Combat Shock* (1986) P
30. *Lust for Freedom* (1987) Co-Sc & Ex-P
31. *Monster in the Closet* (1987) Ex-P
32. *Jakarta* (1988) Ex-P
33. *Troma's War* (1988) Co-D, Co-Sc, P
34. *The Toxic Avenger: Part II* (1989) Co-D, Co-Sc, P
35. *Fortress of Amerikkka* (1989) Co-Sc & P
36. *The Toxic Avenger III: The Last Temptation of Toxie* (1989) Co-D, Co-Sc, P

37. *Class of Nuke 'Em High Part II: Subhumanoid Meltdown* (1990) Co-Sc & P
38. *Rocky V* (1990) A
39. *The Good, the Bad, and the Subhumanoid: Class of Nuke 'Em High Part III* (1991) Co-Sc & P
40. *Toxic Crusaders* (1991) Co-Sc
41. *Sgt. Kabukiman N.Y.P.D.* (1991) Co-D, Co-Sc, P
42. *Tromaville Cafe* (1995) D, Sc, P, A
43. *Cannes Man* (1996) A
44. *Tromeo & Juliet* (1997) D, Co-Sc, P
45. *Orgazmo* (1997) A
46. *Troma's Edge TV* (1997) D, Sc, P
47. *Sucker* (1998) Ex-P
48. *Decampitated* (1998) Ex-P
49. *Rowdy Girls* (1999) P
50. *Terror Firmer* (1999) D, Co-Sc, P, A
51. *Midnight 5* (1999) A
52. *Citizen Toxie: The Toxic Avenger Part IV* (2000) D, Co-Sc, P
53. *Waiting* (2000) A
54. *Class of Nuke 'Em High IV* (2000) P
55. *In Bad Taste* (2000) A
56. *Phantom of the Ferris Wheel* (2001) P
57. *Parts of the Family* (2001) P
58. *All the Love You Cannes!* (2002) D, Sc, P, A
59. *Tales from the Crapper* (2002) D, Sc, P, A
60. *Slaughter Party* (2005) A
61. *Zombiegeddon* (2006) A
62. *Slither* (2006) A
63. *Poultrygeist* (2006) D, Sc, P, A

Barbara Kopple

Two-time Academy Award–winning documentarian Barbara Kopple is easily one of the most respected and accomplished filmmakers working today. Her feature documentaries have explored the social, cultural, and political fabric of American life. Her impressive filmography has brought her numerous awards and fellowships from such organizations as the Guggenheim Foundation and the National Endowment for the Arts.

Kopple learned her craft working as a protégé of Albert and David Maysles after graduating from Northeastern University. She directed her first documentary, *People's Tribunal*, in 1971. The film, which explored the Attica prison riots and their bloody aftermath, was never released. Undaunted by this setback, Kopple then documented a violent miners' strike with her now classic film *Harlan County, U.S.A.* (1976). This brilliant documentary received widespread critical praise and earned Kopple an Oscar for Best Feature Documentary. (In 1991, the film was named to the National Film Registry by Congress as an American film classic.) Displaying a rare talent for directing quality work both fictional and non-fictional, Kopple next directed the telefilm *Keeping On* (1981). The film, scripted by *To Kill a Mockingbird* (1962) scribe Horton Foote, starred Danny Glover, James Broderick, and Rosalind Cash.

With her next documentary, *American Dream* (1991), Kopple once again turned her camera on a labor strike. This film, which analyzed the effects of the economic decline of America's industrial heartland, proved that Kopple's earlier success was no fluke. She was once again showered with critical praise, and was awarded her second Oscar. With this second win, Kopple became the first female filmmaker ever to be awarded multiple Oscars. *American Dream* won a slew of other honors, including a clean sweep at the 1991 Sundance Film Festival, winning the Grand Jury Prize, the Filmmaker's Trophy, and the Audience Award. *American Dream* also landed Kopple her first Directors Guild Award. (This was the first of three DGA Awards Kopple has won to date.)

The following year, Kopple and co-director Danny Schechter examined the controversial assassination of President John F. Kennedy in *Beyond JFK: The Question of Conspiracy* (1992). She then found a real-life subject as interesting and complex as any fictional character in *Fallen Champ: The Untold Story of Mike Tyson* (1993). Kopple then co-directed the ambitious 1994 miniseries *A Century of Women* (along with Judy Korin, Sylvia Morales, and Christen Harty Schaefer), for which she received an Emmy nomination. In 1998, Kopple once again found success with her film *Wild Man Blues*, which followed auteur-turned-musician Woody Allen around Europe as he toured with his jazz band. At a time when Allen's controversial relationship with his former stepdaughter, Soon-Yi Previn, was still considered news, Allen and Previn gave Kopple full access to their personal lives.

Kopple has since directed acclaimed episodes of the television series *Oz* and *Homicide: Life on the Street*. Her most recent documentaries include *Woodstock '94* (1998), *A Conversation* with *Gregory Peck* (1999), *My Generation* (2000), and *The Hamptons* (2002). Kopple made her feature directorial debut with the Stephen Gaghan–penned *Havoc* (2005).

Favorite Films: "*Battle of Algiers* [1965] is my favorite film."

ANDREW RAUSCH: *You're the first female filmmaker ever to win two Academy Awards. That's got to be overwhelming to some degree.*

BARBARA KOPPLE: No, I don't think it's overwhelming at all. In the non-fiction category, the awards are given more to the people who are part of the film. For me, it's more important to have non-fiction films really get out there and to get people to really feel who these characters are. It's important that they discover that non-fiction films can be as entertaining and as incredible as any fiction film. So I see it in a whole different way. I see it as a badly needed gift to the kind of work we do, and a wonderful gift to the people who are involved with these films and have sacrificed so much of themselves for what they believe in. It's terrific and uplifting. It allows you at your worst times when you're struggling to move on because people will get to see these people's stories. I find it very important in that way.

With the commercial successes of your film Wild Man Blues *and Chris Smith's* American Movie *(1999), the past year has been an important one for documentary films. Do you feel that projects such as these are stripping away the stigma which is often associated with documentaries?*

BK: Yeah. We don't call them documentaries anymore. We call them "non-fiction films." And I think the more films that we can get out there, and the more people write about them, the more people can have more of an alternative of the kind of movies we want to see. I think it's very good for this craft, which I think takes you through the whole gamut of emotions. What's exciting is that it's a journey, and you don't know what's going to happen because it's real life. It's the kind of craft that is going to stick with us as to determine who we are as people.

Now you're beginning to do some work in fiction films and television. Coming from a background in non-fiction films, how different is that?

BK: So far I've done some episodes of *Homicide*, and I did the season finale of *Oz*. Hopefully soon I'll be starting on two fictional films, *In the Boom Boom Room*, David Rabe's film, and *Joe Glory*, which is a love story set against a political backdrop. So I'm sort of just getting my feet wet. But for me what's most important is a sense of truthfulness, which I've dealt with in my whole career making non-fiction films. If I can get to that essence and get to that feeling with actors in fiction films, then I'll feel very good about this progression.

Let's talk about Wild Man Blues. *Were you a fan of Woody Allen's work prior to making this film?*

BK: Yeah, I've always liked his work very much. My favorite of his films is definitely *Annie Hall* [1977]. Also, his new film [*The Sweet and Low Down*, 1999] is pretty wonderful — particularly after doing *Wild Man Blues*. I really feel like I see a lot of insights in that I love jazz, and a lot of the tunes he used in his new film, like "Clarinet Marmalade" and "Shine," are music that was used in *Wild Man Blues*. So, it was a totally different Woody Allen film.

You know, a lot of people believe his films are interchangeable. What are your thoughts on that?

BK: I think they're all totally distinct and different. I think that what's so amazing about many of his films for me is that he says the things that all of us think or are our deepest fears, and they do them. That's what makes them so remarkable for me. They just hit those very

Woody Allen playing the clarinet in Barbara Kopple's highly acclaimed documentary *Wild Man Blues* (Fine Line Features, 1997).

subtle places that make it very real. It's as if he's really tuned in to our worst nightmares of human nature.

I'm with you. I disagree that his films are interchangeable, although I do think he pretty much plays the same character in all of those films. Even in Celebrity *(1998), which he's not in, I think it's clear that Kenneth Branagh is playing that Woody Allen character.*

BK: Right, right. But they still go in different directions. So they're still the same schnook, and that same schnook is wonderful and interesting! [Laughs] I can never get enough of him. I love to see where he goes, and what he does, and what situations he presents himself with, and also having that contrast of having seen who he is in real life when he's being himself. That makes it all the more interesting and revealing for me.

Although he's a much more complex person in real life, Wild Man Blues *shows us that a lot of what we see onscreen in his films is, in effect, Woody Allen. When you were shooting the film, did you ever for even a moment lose yourself and feel like you were watching a Woody Allen movie?*

BK: No! [Laughs] When you're working sixteen hours a day, you don't forget where you are. I was holding a wireless mic on him, and I realized very much that I was not in one of his films ... *at all*! It was *very* real. But it made it that much more wonderful because it was real. He was very funny, and very sharp, and very nervous about a lot of things.

There are some very funny moments in Wild Man Blues. *Did you ever have a sense that he might have been playing up to the camera, or is he just like that all the time?*

BK: There could have been those times where he was, but I had him wired all the time, and I was with him literally sixteen hours a day. Sometimes he didn't even know when I was filming because we're very good guerrilla filmmakers.

FILMOGRAPHY FOR BARBARA KOPPLE

1. *Harlan County, U.S.A.* (1976) D & P
2. *No Nukes* (1980) Co-D
3. *Keeping On* (1981) [TV] D
4. *American Dream* (1990) D
5. *Civil Rights: The Struggle Continues* (1990) D
6. *Out of Darkness* (1991) D
7. *Beyond JFK: The Question of Conspiracy* (1992) Co-D
8. *Fallen Champ: The Untold Story of Mike Tyson* (1993) [TV] D & P
9. *Homicide: Life on the Street* [various episodes] (1996) D
10. *A Century of Women* (1994) [TV] Co-D
11. *Woodstock '94* (1998) D & P
12. *Wild Man Blues* (1998) D
13. *Nails* (1998) [TV] D
14. *A Conversation with Gregory Peck* (1999) [TV] D
15. *Oz* (1999) D
16. *Friends for Life: Living with AIDS* (1999) [TV] D
17. *My Generation* (2000) D
18. *The Hamptons* (2002) [TV] D
19. *American Standoff* (2002) P
20. *Havoc* (2004) D
21. *WMD: Weapons of Mass Deception* (2004) Ex-P
22. *The Edge of Madness* (2006) D
23. *Dixie Chicks: Shut Up and Sing* (2006) D
24. *Addiction* (2007) Co-D & P
25. *Kevorkian Chronicles* (2008) D & P

Mark L. Lester

Mark Lester is, in many ways, a throwback to filmmakers of yesteryear like his idol Howard Hawks. Like Hawks, Lester has produced quality work in virtually every genre. Also, in an era where most filmmakers' filmographies will never approach twenty or more films, Lester is continuously working. With twenty-nine films already under his belt, the prolific director shows no signs of slowing down anytime soon.

San Fernando Valley native Lester attended college at California State University, where he earned a degree in political science. In 1971, Lester made his feature directorial debut with the documentary *Twilight of the Mayas*. The film won the award for best documentary at the Venice Film Festival. Lester then wrote, produced, and directed a daring satire of then–President Richard Nixon. The film, *Tricia's Wedding* (1972), featured a cast of male actors appearing in drag. While it didn't win him many fans in Republican quarters, the film established Lester as a bold new talent. (Lester would later return to the subject of politics with *White House Madness*, 1975.)

Lester has since worked on low-budget indies, telefilms, and big-budget actioners. Some of his most popular films are *Commando* (1985), *Armed and Dangerous* (1986), *Showdown in Little China* (1991), *The Base* (1999), and *Firestarter* (1984), which featured a stunning cast that included George C. Scott, Martin Sheen, Art Carney, Louise Fletcher, David Keith, and Drew Barrymore.

Through the years Lester has received his fair share of press for reasons of notoriety, as well. After he adapted Stephen King's *Firestarter*, the novelist began taking potshots at him, which led to a well-publicized battle of words between King and Lester in a 1991 issue of *Cinefantastique* magazine. In 1996, Lester found himself once again at the center of controversy when Presidential hopeful Phil Gramm came under fire in the media for having financed the early Lester film *Truck Stop Women* (1974).

Today Lester continues to churn out films. Recent movies include *Stealing Candy* (2004), *Pterodactyl* (2005), and *White Rush* (2003), which won the New York International Independent Film & Video Festival award for Best Feature Film.

Favorite Films: *Doctor Zhivago* (1965), *Lawrence of Arabia* (1962), *The Conformist* (1970), *The Battle of Algiers* (1965), *Casablanca* (1942), and *Juliet of the Spirits* (1965).

Andrew Rausch: *On* Firestarter *you worked with a remarkable cast. What was it like directing such a brilliant ensemble?*

Mark L. Lester: It was a wonderful experience. We always said that we had more Academy Award winners than any other picture that had been made up to that point. And all of them on that same film. They were all extremely cooperative and were very, very exciting to work with. Especially George C. Scott, whom I had long admired since seeing him in films like *The Hustler* [1961] and *Patton* [1970]. It was an exciting moment to have lunch with him and discuss the movie, and then direct someone of his stature.

Stephen King made some rather damaging remarks about Firestarter.

ML: The movie was still very successful, and I would have taken it personally except that Stanley Kubrick was subject to the same attack [with *The Shining*, 1980]. In fact, so was just about every other person who had adapted anything by Stephen King. What's interesting is that Stephen King read the script and he loved it. He was on the set of the movie. He made comments all along the way. He saw the rough cut of the film and said he really liked it. He said it was the finest script of anything that had been written [based on his work]. But then, some mental disturbance inside Stephen King's mind makes him hate everything that's made into a film. I don't know what that little quirk in him is. *His* film was the worst of all; *Maximum Overdrive* is a terrible movie! So, when he tried to do it himself, he failed miserably. For some reason, he just feels the need to attack all of these movies. He's never liked any of the adaptations as far as I know.

A publicity photograph of director Mark Lester for the release of *Firestarter* (Universal City Studios Inc., 1984).

It was strange that he turned on the movie in the press after having said all these wonderful things after seeing it. In fact, he even did a premiere in his own home town for charity. He invited everyone to come see this film in his home town of Bangor, Maine. That's where the premiere was that he set up. So why later he decides to attack all of these movies, I don't know. I think he has an evil side to him from writing too many horror books. [Laughs]

You've said that King himself came up with the idea of having Charlie's hair blown by the wind each time she uses her powers. That's interesting because that's one of the things King has criticized about the film. He said it makes no sense that her hair blows as if she's caught in the wind each time she starts fires.

ML: He makes up stories for a living. He's gotten so good at making up stories that he can say anything, I suppose. I was at least a little perturbed about his whole change to the press when in person he would say something completely different. I told him that he needed to go to a psychiatrist, you know, to figure out why he was the way he was.

In 1996 Presidential hopeful Phil Gramm was lambasted after it was discovered that he helped line up financing for your film Truck Stop Women. *What are your thoughts on this?*

ML: I think it was quite an amazing story that came out. He was originally a Democrat in Texas. I met him when his brother was raising money for me. He'd told me about this congressman from Texas who was going to invest. He ended up investing in that movie, as well as another movie, which was a spoof of Richard Nixon.

Of course, later he ran for President and this came out, but what disturbed me was that people were saying that he invested in pornography. These were R-rated "B" movies that had nothing to do with pornography at all. All of a sudden, I was on CNN saying that my films weren't pornographic. [Laughs]

Aside from that, I thought it was a very funny story, being lampooned in *Doonesbury*. They ran a comic strip about it all week that showed Phil Gramm telling me how to direct the films.

I think it was something that was blown way out of proportion.

ML: Completely, but it was a Democratic plot to get him out of the race. They tried to depict his investment as an investment in sex pictures. Here I came, all of a sudden, on the side of this conservative Republican. I found myself on television defending Phil Gramm after being a lifelong Democrat! [Laughs] It was a funny position to be in.

You worked with the late John Candy on Armed and Dangerous. *What was he like to direct?*

ML: He was a lot of fun. He had a lot of ideas and he was very cooperative. He was a very funny guy. That was a sad situation. He definitely had a lot of personal problems with drugs and alcohol, which ultimately defeated him.

I know a lot of people don't like Armed and Dangerous, *but I actually liked it. It had a great cast with Candy, Eugene Levy, Robert Loggia, and Meg Ryan. I have a lot of fun with that movie.*

ML: I thought it was a very funny movie, but I haven't attempted a comedy since 1986. All the movies I make now are more thrillers or action pictures. I probably wasn't the right director for a comedy. John Candy just kept saying, "Just make if funny. Don't worry what the story is." As one who was involved with suspense thrillers and action movies, I kept trying to develop the plot. The more story and plot, the less funny things become.

How do you approach editing a comedy as opposed to an action film?

ML: With comedy you have to edit with an audience. You have to preview them over and over and find out where the laughs are. If you hit a certain shot a certain way, you might get a laugh if it's edited a certain way. Comedies require a lot of previewing, whereas with an action movie, I pretty much know what I can do without a preview.

You directed Arnold Schwarzenegger in Commando. *At the time, he was the prototypical action star of the eighties. You recently worked with Mark Dacascos on* The Base. *As there aren't really many contenders, he may well be the prototypical late-nineties action star. As someone who's worked with them both, I'd like you to compare and contrast these two actors and the styles of action films they are associated with.*

ML: Arnold is an incredible presence. He has a great sense of humor, which I was able to utilize in *Commando*. He's more of a regular action actor, with fights and stunts and so forth. Dacascos is more of a martial artist. He's much better with the physical martial arts–type work. Schwarzenegger's not really a martial artist at all. In reality, he's not even a fight person. The athletic world he comes from was more weightlifting and things like that.

They're both very talented, but obviously Schwarzenegger's a lot farther ahead of Mark when it comes to Hollywood star power. They're both talented guys, and very enjoyable to work with.

I understand the scene in Commando *where John Matrix chops off the soldier's arm in the shed was longer in the initial cut?*

ML: Yeah, it was. The ratings board gave *Commando* an X-rating, so we had to go in and cut some of the violence out. [The original scene] was just more bloody and gruesome. We stayed longer on the arm hanging from the soldier's shoulder, and he staggered around for awhile, missing one arm.

In Commando *there are quite a few continuity problems. For instance, one soldier can be seen being killed in the distance more than once. I don't think these instances are obvious and I don't think they hurt the film, but they seem very uncharacteristic of your work. I was curious as to why so many instances pop up in this one film?*

ML: Jesus, I didn't even know about what you're telling me! Did you notice this because you can run it back and forth on the DVD?

It was one of my favorite films when I was about thirteen, so I've seen it a few times.

ML: Did you catch any of that the first time you watched the film?

No, not at all. In fact, a friend of mine showed me some of them. There are a few of them listed on the internet, as well.

ML: That's the problem now. Everyone's got VCRs and DVDs where they can go back and watch these things so closely. You have to be very careful making a movie now because

Arnold Schwarzenegger's Col. John Matrix engages the enemy in the Mark Lester actioner *Commando* (20th Century–Fox Film Corp., 1985).

people can watch them a hundred times. In 1986 you'd make a film and people would watch it once or twice. You'd think, "They're not gonna catch this." [Laughs]

There's a scene where Schwarzenegger pulls the seat out of Rae Dawn Chong's car, right? Then we see the car later and the seat's in there again!
    ML: I didn't think so.... I haven't looked at the movie since then, so I can't tell you.

I only asked because continuity problems are often a sign of a rushed or troubled shooting. Conflicts on set. Things like that.
    ML: No. Nothing like that on *Commando*. We just usually figure no one's gonna catch those things. Obviously we were wrong.

There's another scene where his shorts change colors from shot to shot.
    ML: Wow. I never noticed it. I never noticed any of those things. [Laughs] I'm gonna have to look at my films more closely before I finish editing!

FILMOGRAPHY FOR MARK LESTER

1. *Twilight of the Mayas* (1971) D
2. *Tricia's Wedding* (1972) D
3. *Steel Arena* (1973) D, Sc, P
4. *Truck Stop Women* (1974) D, Sc, P
5. *White House Madness* (1975) D
6. *Bobbie Jo and the Outlaw* (1976) D & P
7. *Stunts* (1977) D
8. *Roller Boogie* (1979) D
9. *Gold of the Amazon Women* (1979) [TV] D
10. *The Funhouse* (1981) Ex-P
11. *Class of 1984* (1982) D & Sc
12. *Firestarter* (1984) D
13. *Commando* (1985) D
14. *Armed and Dangerous* (1986) D
15. *Class of 1999* (1990) D, S, P
16. *Showdown in Little Tokyo* (1991) D & P
17. *Extreme Justice* (1993) D
18. *Night of the Running Man* (1994) D & P
19. *Public Enemies* (1996) D & P
20. *Misbegotten* (1997) D & P
21. *The Ex* (1997) D & P
22. *Double Take* (1997) D & P
23. *Hitman's Run* (1999) D
24. *The Base* (1999) D & P
25. *The Base 2: Guilty as Charged* (2000) D & P
26. *Blowback* (2000) D & P
27. *Sacrifice* (2000) D
28. *Bad Karma* (2001) Ex-P
29. *Stealing Candy* (2002) D & P
30. *The Wisher* (2002) Ex-P
31. *Betrayal* (2003) D
32. *White Rush* (2003) D
33. *Pterodactyl* (2005) D & P

Herschell Gordon Lewis

Dubbed "the Godfather of Gore," filmmaker Herschell Gordon Lewis is best known for horror classics such as *Two Thousand Maniacs* (1964), *Color Me Blood Red* (1965), *A Taste of Blood* (1967), and *Blood Feast* (1963), with which he single-handedly invented the subgenre of the gore horror film. While movies such as *The Texas Chain Saw Massacre* (1974) and *Halloween* (1978) certainly owe a huge debt to Lewis, his influence has hardly been confined to horror. "Lewis is the man who put red meat into the American cinematic diet," film writer Joe Bob Briggs explains. "Ultimately, Herschell made Quentin Tarantino possible." Director John Waters, who has always been vocal regarding Lewis' influence on his own work (even going so far as to incorporate footage from *Blood Feast* into his own *Serial Mom*, 1994), takes this declaration a step further. "Without [Lewis] you wouldn't have *Jurassic Park*," he observed. "You wouldn't have any of these films where gore is accepted."

Despite Lewis' reputation as a master of terror, he also directed films in a number of other genres: family films (*Jimmy the Boy Wonder*, 1966), sexploitation (*Suburban Roulette*, 1967), and even one of the earliest blaxploitation pictures (*Black Love*, 1972). After 1972's *The Gore Gore Girls*, Lewis walked away from the film industry, focusing instead on a career in marketing. Today Lewis is a respected marketing strategist who lectures around the country, consults for major companies like Barnes & Noble, writes for numerous publications, and is the author of nearly thirty books. (His seminal 1984 tome *Direct Mail Copy That Sells!* is currently in its seventeenth printing.)

After a thirty year hiatus, Lewis returned to the director's seat for the long-awaited film *Blood Feast 2: All You Can Eat* (2002). At the time of this writing, Lewis was in preproduction on his thirty-seventh directorial effort, *Win, Lose or Die*.

Favorite Films: *King Solomon's Mines* (1950), *The Bridge on the River Kwai* (1957), *Short Circuit* (1986), *The Wicker Man* (1973), and *The Music Lovers* (1971).

ANDREW RAUSCH: *You were once quoted as saying, "[I] pity anyone who regards filmmaking as an artform and spends money based on that immature philosophy." Could you elaborate?*

HERSCHELL GORDON LEWIS: I object to the auteur attitude. I object to any public-be-damned attitude, whether it pertains to what we sometimes laughingly refer to as "fine art," music, or motion pictures. The purpose of a motion picture, in my opinion — especially a low-budget motion picture — is to compete for playing time. It's the low-budget producers who are constantly caterwauling about audiences' lack of understanding. What they're saying is that audiences don't understand *them*, and my position is that they've got this absolutely inside out. It's their function to understand the audience, and not the other way around. This idea that I am creating a work of fine art, and the public be damned if they don't understand

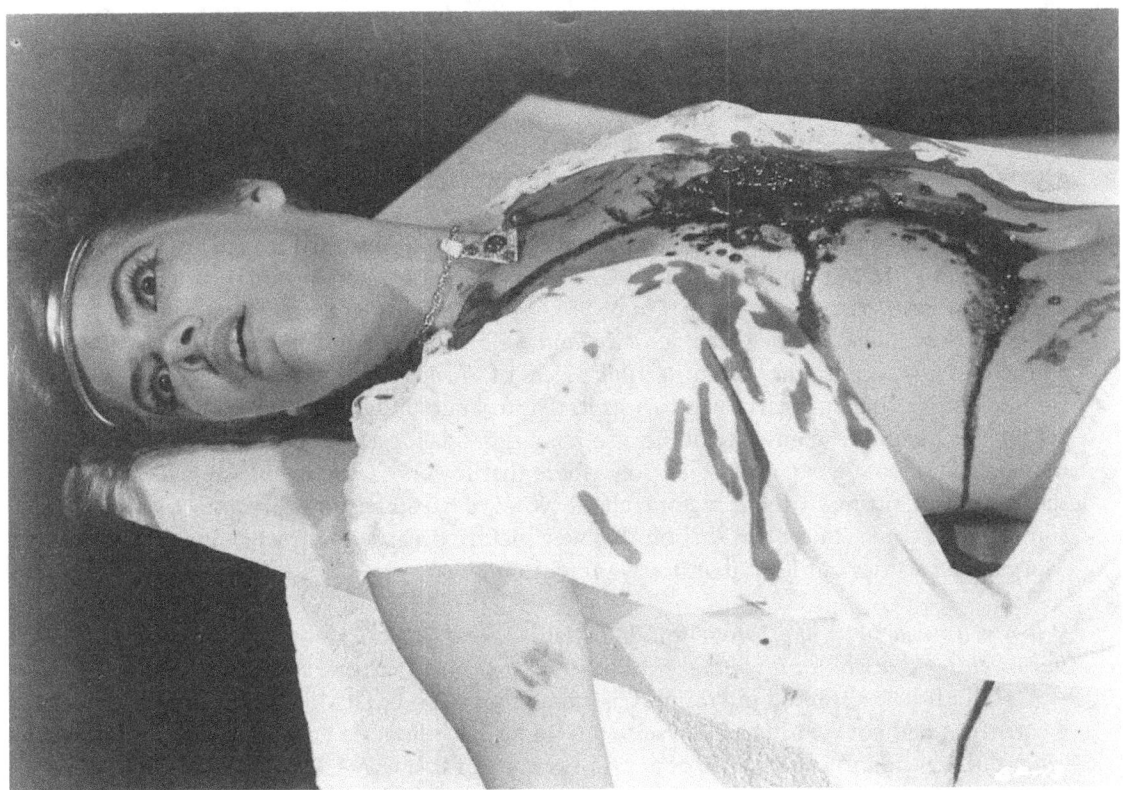

Playboy Playmate Connie Mason meets her bloody demise in the cult classic *Blood Feast* (Box Office Spectaculars, 1963).

it, is backwards. "If they can't come to my level, those poor saps, they deserve to miss out on what I have prepared for them!"

Look, if I prepare a gourmet feast of monkey brains for vegetarians, I deserve to go out of business because I have totally misread the people who are supposed to be my targets. And one area in which I've had good fortune in the motion picture business, perhaps because I've treated it like a business, is producing what an audience is looking for. Sure, if I'm making *Harry Potter* [2001] or *Shrek* [2001] and I have that kind of promotional power behind me, I know my movie's going to get opened. But if I'm making a movie that represents something where I'm trying to compete and I completely misread the audience, then I'm on a level with *Ishtar* [1987] or *Town & Country* [2001].

Another factor I would like to point out is that almost invariably these pictures have confounding titles which have no intention of drawing people into the theater. That puzzles me, too.

On several films you served as screenwriter, director, producer, composer, cinematographer, and special effects technician. Did this result more from necessity or from a conscious desire to personally control the quality of the product?

HGL: Well, you have an interesting point there. Of course I wanted to control the product. I think that becomes important in exact ratio to budget, which was the overriding factor in almost every decision I made. There are many places where I would give almost anything for another take. In the movie we just finished, oh, what I would have given for a zoom lens!

That seems like a nominal expenditure, but apparently it was beyond the budget. What I would have given to have been able to have ripped this thing open in a different way, but we couldn't do it.

I wanted the control, but the reason I would, for example, write the score for these pictures, which was a much more brutal job than directing a movie — any damned fool can direct a movie — was because I didn't want to pay someone else to do it. Here's a movie that cost under $100,000 to make, and a professional composer would want $80,000 to score it! That's nonsense. Proof of my posture that I didn't really want to be regarded that way was the number of times I did this under a pseudonym. Yeah, I am absolutely proud of the background music for *Blood Feast*, for example. I'm proud of the theme songs from *Two Thousand Maniacs, Suburban Roulette, The Girl, the Body, and the Pill* [1967], and *Living Venus* [1960]. I'm proud of them because they're not *terrible* pieces of music.

So I suppose that control was part of it. Control and budget go together. When a director lets his hands loose on control, he also lets his hands loose on budget. I never felt it was denigrating to load a camera. I don't see where that lowers the image of whoever is behind the camera or sitting in the director's chair. Now we have assistant directors who say "roll sound" and "cut." Yeah, I had that on this new picture because that's what [producer] Jacky Morgan had set up, but I felt that it was pretentious.

When you made films like Two Thousand Maniacs *and* Blood Feast, *were you aware of how unconventional it was for a filmmaker to serve in so many capacities?*

HGL: It never entered my mind. I assumed that Cecil B. DeMille never did that, but so what? No, I had not surrounded myself with underlings. It was a non-issue. We were on the set and these things needed to be done. An example of this was *A Taste of Blood*. We needed someone with a "limey" accent and nobody could do it. We hired an actor who didn't show up. Because that was his only line, he was only being paid $25 or $30. He never showed up and I had to shoot the scene, so I put on a stocking cap and borrowed some hair from one of our long-haired crew people and I took that role. I thought nothing of it. I didn't use my name on that. It was simply a matter of getting the job done. I did things like carrying cable. So what?

On my first two films, on which we used union crews, there was very little I could do. "This is my job. You get your hands off of that." I felt that was foolish, too. Here were a whole bunch of guys standing around because the two people whose job it was were working at a slow pace. And you try to get an assistant cameraman to load a magazine at 5:25 in the afternoon! It cannot be done because at 5:30 we go into overtime and you get at least an extra hour, so the eye is on the clock. Well, my eye was on the clock, too. One of the little regulations I imposed on our pictures was that we shoot till we're done, so I was able to surround myself with people who loved making movies, people who loved the idea of looking at the dailies and saying, "Wow! I had a part in that!" They would say, "You want me to hold this or that on camera? Yeah, what the heck." That's increasingly hard to come by, although making movies today is light years easier than it was then. Among other things, we have film speed. Much of what I was shooting was ASA-125, which is now called ISO. On this new film, we used 250. That's ten times as fast. And I'm looking at a TV monitor so I can tell if there's a microphone in the picture! It's easier than it was, which I like, I admit.

I like being a big shot as much as anybody else does, but I sure don't like having a half-finished picture and running out of money.

Regarding the constant evolution of filmmaking, you once cited changes in the industry in the 1970s from when you first began making features in 1960 as being one of the reasons for your 1972

An advertisement for Herschell Gordon Lewis' *Blast Off Girls* (Box Office Spectaculars/Creative Film Enterprises Inc., 1967).

retirement. What were some of the most significant changes which most affected the exploitation market?

HGL: Well, what happened was—and I suppose to some extent I should take responsibility for it—the major companies lost their virginity relative to audience shock. Until we came along, audience shock consisted of someone suddenly having a strange hand poke them on the shoulder or opening a door and then recoiling in horror. The dimension that we added was what you might call hyper-realism. And while we had that area to ourselves as outlaws in the business, theaters regarded the playing of our pictures not just as an adventure, but almost the kind of adventure that you have going over Niagara Falls in a barrel. If you succeed, you sign autographs for the rest of your life. If you don't, your heirs sign autographs.

When the major companies began to ask themselves how long this had been going on; they invaded that turf with the kind of equipment and effects that made it impossible for the independents to compete. The independents also had, for example, bare breasts to themselves for years and years. Once the major companies said, "There's really nothing wrong with a bare breast as long as we rate the picture accordingly," the independents were driven out of that little niche. And what they had to do was to go deeper into that particular gulch. When I saw what was happening with that element, I got out of that because I could see that there was just one direction in which those movies were going. In the case of the gore movies, I just felt I had run my course. The playing time was diminishing. If a theater could play one of my movies, which had Joe Glutz in it, or a Sam Peckinpah movie which had William Holden in it, which film would that theater play? I had no clout to say, "Hey, play this one and I'll give you that one, too." The time had come, and I felt I'd had a good run.

Who could have ever dreamed of this Renaissance which has taken place, where instead of an outlaw I've become a prophet?

FILMOGRAPHY FOR HERSCHELL GORDON LEWIS

1. *The Prime Time* (1960) P & C
2. *Living Venus* (1960) D, Co-Sc, P
3. *The Adventures of Lucky Pierre* (1961) D, Cin, C
4. *Daughter of the Sun* (1962) D & Cin
5. *Nature's Playmates* (1962) D
6. *Goldilocks and the Three Bares* (1963) D
7. *Boin-n-g!* (1963) D & Co-Sc
8. *Scum of the Earth* (1963) D & Sc
9. *Bell, Bare and Beautiful* (1963) D & Cin
10. *Blood Feast* (1963) D, P, Cin, C, SE
11. *Two Thousand Maniacs* (1964) D, Sc, S, Cin, C
12. *Moonshine Mountain* (1964) D, P, Cin, C
13. *Color Me Blood Red* (1965) D, Sc, Cin
14. *Monster a-Go-Go* (1965) Co-D, Co-Sc, P, PD
15. *Sin, Suffer and Repent* (1965) Co-D & P
16. *Alley Tramp* (1965) D & Cin
17. *An Eye for an Eye* (1966) D & P
18. *Jimmy the Boy Wonder* (1966) D
19. *The Magic Land of Mother Goose* (1967) D & Cin
20. *Suburban Roulette* (1967) D & Co-Sc
21. *A Taste of Blood* (1967) D, P, A
22. *Something Weird* (1967) D
23. *The Gruesome Twosome* (1967) D & P
24. *The Girl, the Body and the Pill* (1967) D, P, C
25. *Blast-Off Girls* (1967) D, Sc, S, P
26. *She-Devils on Wheels* (1968) D, P, C
27. *Just for the Hell of It* (1968) D, P, C
28. *How to Make a Doll* (1968) D, Co-Sc, S, P
29. *The Psychic* (1968) Cin
30. *Linda and Abilene* (1969) D & Cin
31. *The Ecstacies of Women* (1969) D & Cin
32. *The Wizard of Gore* (1970) D, P, MU
33. *Miss Nymphet's Zap-In* (1970) D & P
34. *This Stuff'll Kill Ya!* (1971) D, Sc, P, C
35. *Black Love* (1972) D & P
36. *Year of the Yahoo!* (1972) D, P, C
37. *The Gore Gore Girls* (1972) D, P, MU
38. *The Blood Trilogy Outtakes* (1986) D
39. *Blood Feast 2: All You Can Eat* (2002) D
40. *2001 Maniacs* (2005) S & Ex-P
41. *Chainsaw Sally* (2005) A

Richard Linklater

Richard Linklater exploded onto the Indie scene with *Slacker* (1991), a $23,000 film that would become a cult classic. Linklater's first studio film, *Dazed and Confused* (1993), quickly became another cult hit. The film received critical acclaim and earned Linklater a first-look production deal with Castle Rock Entertainment. His next feature, the daringly unconventional romance *Before Sunrise* (1995), further established Linklater as one of the most gifted auteurs of his generation. In 1997, Linklater adapted Eric Bogosian's play *SubUrbia* into a film of the same title. Ironically, according to Bogosian, the play was originally inspired by *Slacker*. Like Linklater's debut film, *SubUrbia* focuses on what Linklater calls "the youth rebellion continuum." The following year Linklater made *The Newton Boys* (1998) with an all-star cast which included Matthew McConaughey, Skeet Ulrich, Ethan Hawke, and Vincent D'Onofrio. Linklater has been nominated for Best Director honors at both the Berlin International Film Festival (for *Before Sunrise*) and the Independent Spirit Awards (*Slacker*).

The year 2001 saw the release of not just one, but two groundbreaking films crafted by Linklater. First came the surreal *Waking Life*, featuring live action combined with animation. Following on the heels of *Waking Life* was the superb drama *Tape*, which was filmed entirely in one room, featuring only three actors, and was shot on digital video.

The prolific Linklater has since managed a rare feat in successfully shifting back and forth between commercial fare and arthouse pictures, directing such diverse films as *School of Rock* (2003), *Before Sunset* (2004), *The Bad News Bears* (2005), *A Scanner Darkly* (2006), and *Fast Food Nation* (2006).

Favorite Films: *Citizen Kane* (1941), *The Hall of Mirrors* (1916), *2001: A Space Odyssey* (1968), *Some Came Running* (1958), and *Carmen Jones* (1954).

ANDREW RAUSCH: *Both Kevin Smith and Sarah Kelly have told me that* Slacker *was the film that inspired them to become filmmakers. How does that make you feel as an artist?*

RICHARD LINKLATER: Well, I've heard that from a lot of people. That's pretty great because I certainly had those films in my own past. They weren't necessarily the best films, but they were the ones that made me think I could go out and do it. When I was first getting into film, it was the films I saw that were kind of 16mm with a low budget. In the early eighties when I was starting to get interested in film, things I saw that had that effect on me were *Return of the Secaucus 7* [1980], *Chan Is Missing* [1982], and a Texas film called *Last Night at the Alamo* [1983]. Those all inspired me in that same kind of way.

When you see something like *Raging Bull* [1980] or *Eraserhead* [1977], and you say, "Oh my God, that's brilliant," you don't feel like tomorrow *you* could go out and make that. When you see these others you start thinking, "I'm a good writer; I could maybe do that."

Do you feel that living in Austin rather than Hollywood has helped you maintain your artistic integrity?

RL: I hope so. It's not a real conscious thing. I'm just following my own instincts. I like living here. Los Angeles just depresses me because you're outnumbered. More people are interested in the business out there. It comes down to the weekly totals, the grosses, per-screen averages, and all that shit. It's a place where bad films become good films if they make a lot of money, and vice versa. That's a real sticky trap to get into. I can be a little blissfully ignorant, you know? Even with my own films. I can just think that this is a film that did make money, so I don't have to walk around town thinking I'm a failure.

You once called Universal a "compromised mediocrity machine," which I find very interesting. Although you were talking directly about Universal, I think you could take that a step further and really apply that label to pretty much all of the big studios these days.

RL: When you're in the heat of production and someone is telling you to compromise something, you kind of blame it on that whole system. Speaking from experience after coming out of that situation, you kind of realize that it's up to you to fuck up, and not to let that get to you. [Laughs] Some people read that article and said, "Oh, you got really screwed over." I thought they weren't reading the same article because in my mind, I didn't. I had to deal with all of that shit on a psychological level, but I won every battle. I really did. You're kind of pressured from the get-go, but that's sort of part of the deal. And that was just my experience with making a film for the first time with a real schedule, and a budget, and all of that. That was a leap for me. If you can go through that and still come out with the film that you set out to make, you're doing pretty good. A lot of people kind of lose that on that level. It's

Director Richard Linklater directs Giovanni Ribisi on the set of his film *SubUrbia* (Castle Rock Entertainment, 1996).

kind of hell! [Laughs again] Where I'm sitting here years later, I would never point that at Universal and single them out. My God, it's all different people over there today. That was from the perspective of someone who was deep in the trenches with his blinders on.

Despite the so-called "creative process" of the big studios, your films always seem so fresh and creative. Especially in this era of assembly line filmmaking...

RL: I would say there are ten to twenty really refreshing and creative films that come out every year. No matter what else. People are always ragging about how many bad films come out, but every year there are a good number of good films that somehow get made.

Of course, I made *Dazed and Confused* at Universal, so it's not really where you're making the film. I've seen a lot of these independent films that were made with very little money that are just compromised from their conception. It really makes no difference. There are some people with a strong enough will who actually envision what the film they want to make is, and there are others who don't. My experience is that if your vision is strong enough — you really have a strong enough film in your head that you're trying to achieve — you'll do that no matter how many studio notes and bullshit that you get. You're the one making the film. What's your excuse? The day I say [mock whining voice], "Oh, the studio made me do this and this," I'll quit. That's just pretty weak. There's no excuse. You can't blame the system. The system is what it is, and what it will always be.

What would you consider the perfect movie for a first date?

RL: Once I took a girl to see *Raging Bull*, and we broke up over it. She said it was boring. I wouldn't choose a romance. It would have to be something that really confronts relationships. Maybe *Bad Timing* (1980). [Laughs]

I think my idea of the perfect first-date movie would be Before Sunrise. *I say this because Julie Delpy and Ethan Hawke kind of go through all of the motions and awkwardness at the beginning of a relationship before your eyes, so you don't have to go through them. That really breaks a lot of those initial barriers.*

RL: Right. You can just say "Let's go straight to bed now" after watching this excruciatingly-extended courting process. [Laughs] My God, it takes them thirty-five minutes of screen time before they even kiss, which is, of course, what I was trying to do anyway.

That's a film that I'm amazed got made in today's studio system. It's so dialogue-driven, with very little action, and you have at least one shot that takes something like six minutes without a cut. I think the film is just brilliant.

RL: Yeah. That's a film that is really special to me. It felt like a gift from the film gods. I'll tell you how it got made — with a $2.7 million budget. Castle Rock really liked the concept. It was so much the antithesis of the modern romance. Every film I do in a genre, I try to do something with it. You can't just be in the genre. *Dazed and Confused* was sort of my reaction to the teenage film. *Before Sunrise* was my reaction to the romance film. If I'm gonna do a film about it, I wanna make it real. This is my own experience. You don't meet someone and go to bed with them five minutes later. Whether that's screen time or not, that's not natural. The real way is through spending time with them and talking. I was interested in that courting, that they could go through an entire relationship in one night and hit all of the bumps along the way. It's really just two people getting to know each other in kind of a magical atmosphere.

You've stated in the past that you're a big fan of the Western genre. The Newton Boys *was kind of a hybrid of that genre. Will we ever see a full-blown Richard Linklater–directed Western?*

RL: It depends on how you define Western. At the end of the day, *The Newton Boys* is really more of an action crime film or a heist film than it is a Western. Of course, it starts out as a Western, and I would like to think that it has that spirit.

I don't know; I have some vague feelings about doing some films in the nineteenth century. Some have to do with Native Americans in the Texas territories and settlers and things like that. So I don't know if that would be considered a Western. You know, I don't think you can really make a straight-up Western today. With *The Newton Boys*, I really tried to make a straight-up old-time movie, and I don't think you can really do that today. I think the only guy who can pull that off is Clint Eastwood, and that's because everyone wants him to be able to do that. That's his persona. I think you have to MTV-ize it or something; make it ridiculously modern.

I think the violence is really up today. It's just a different world now.

It's an interesting contrast to go back and watch some of the pre–[Sam] Peckinpah Westerns. When they shot someone at point blank range, there would be no visible blood.

RL: They really weren't that violent. You have to bring in a modern sensibility with a lot of violence to bring in an audience. I'm just saying this from perhaps a bitter perspective. I mean, I really tried to go all the way with an old-timey movie that really didn't give into modern sensibilities in that way. I wasn't going to modernize the violence and the effects. I made them like old effects up to the montage, which is like an old movie effect.

I think the problem with The Newton Boys *was that the studio marketed it toward the wrong audience.*

Slater (Rory Cochrane), Pink (Jason London), and Don (Sasha Jenson) are three pillars of learning in *Dazed and Confused* (Gramercy Pictures, 1993).

RL: The unfortunate thing with the studios is that they only know one audience, which is a teenage boy. So if you've made a film that appeals to older people — and *Newton Boys* played best with audiences over fifty — it always has to be seen in terms of a mass-market film, and when you don't deliver that, they still try to sucker in that audience. That simultaneously alienates the real audience because the studio has made it look like this MTV piece of shit thing, and then it ultimately doesn't appeal to that audience that they're lying to. I had a very traditional old-fashioned movie poster that we had made which looked like a movie poster from the twenties and thirties. An illustrated poster with all of the action and the characters' faces. It's beautiful. You see that and you say, "Oh, my God! That's the movie." And then Fox didn't want to use that because it was Western and old-fashioned an all that kind of stuff. [Laughs] So we ended up with *Young Guns* [1988] meets *Mobsters* [1991] as their poster. What person with a brain in their head would wanna go see that? I wouldn't!

FILMOGRAPHY FOR RICHARD LINKLATER

1. *It's Impossible to Learn to Plow by Reading Books* (1988) D, Sc, P, Cin, Ed
2. *Slacker* (1991) D, Sc, P
3. *Dazed and Confused* (1993) D, Sc, P
4. *Before Sunrise* (1995) D & Sc
5. *SubUrbia* (1997) D
6. *The Newton Boys* (1998) D & Sc
7. *Spy Kids* (2001) A
8. *Tape* (2001) D & Sc
9. *Waking Life* (2001) D, Sc, Cin
10. *Live from Shiva's Dance Floor* (2003) D
11. *School of Rock* (2003) D
12. *Before Sunset* (2004) D, Co-Sc, P
13. *The Bad News Bears* (2005) D
14. *A Scanner Darkly* (2006) D & Sc
15. *Fast Food Nation* (2006) D & Sc

William Malone

William Malone has been a horror aficionado ever since he donned 3-D glasses for a screening of *Creature from the Black Lagoon* (1954) as a child. That love of the genre led him to filmmaking. At the age of fourteen Malone began shooting his own Super-8 versions of *Dr. Jekyll and Mr. Hyde* and *This Island Earth*. At the age of nineteen Malone went to work for Don Post's FX studio, helping to design monsters and masks (including that of *Halloween*'s Michael Myers). In the late seventies, Malone sold his car and mortgaged his home to raise the $80,000 he needed to make *Scared to Death* (1980), which he wrote and directed. Five years later, Malone wrote and directed his second feature, *Creature* (1985), a frightening sci-fi thriller that predated the similarly-themed *Alien* (1979) by a year. *Scared to Death* would later spawn a sequel — the dreadful *Syngenor* (1990) — which Malone wisely steered clear of.

After *Creature*, Malone worked primarily in television for a number of years, writing and directing for series such as *Freddy's Nightmares*, *New York Undercover*, and *Dream On*. After directing a 1994 episode of *Tales from the Crypt* entitled "The Mask," executive producers Joel Silver and Robert Zemeckis called him back to write and direct a second episode ("Report from the Grave"). The producers then invited him to direct for their series *Perversions of Science*. Increasingly impressed with his work, Silver and Zemeckis asked Malone to helm their 1999 remake of the William Castle frightener *House on Haunted Hill* (1958). Malone co-wrote the script with Dick Beebe, with whom he'd collaborated previously on "The Mask." The film, which stars Geoffrey Rush, Famke Janssen, and Peter Gallagher, opened at number one.

Malone next worked as a screenwriter on the films *Universal Soldier: The Return* (1999) and Walter Hill's *Supernova* (2000). Malone then did directorial work for television on series such as *Law and Order* and *The Others*.

In 2002, Malone directed the *Ringu* (1998)-inspired chiller *FeardotCom* (2002), starring Stephen Dorff, Natascha McElhone, and Stephen Rea.

Favorite Films: *The Black Cat* (1980), *Creature from the Black Lagoon* (1954), *Alien* (1979), *Forbidden Planet* (1956), and *Chinatown* (1974).

ANDREW RAUSCH: *You once worked with Klaus Kinski on* Creature, *which I understand was a very bizarre experience.*

WILLIAM MALONE: He was definitely a weird guy! [Laughs]

You once commented that "Klaus Kinski is dead now and the world is a better place for it."

WM: He was a psycho. He was definitely a psychotic character. He was a funny guy, and I think he would be happy that I said the world was a better place without him! [Laughs] He reveled in that kind of thing.

William Malone and actress Natascha McElhone listen to feedback from others on the set of the film *FeardotCom* (Warner Bros. Pictures, 2002).

I'd read that he kind of bragged to you about having raped his daughter, Nastassia. Is that right?
 WM: He absolutely did tell me that.

Oh, my God! That's terrible. [Laughs]
 WM: That was the first thing that came out of his mouth on the set.

Was that the first time you'd met him?
 WM: Actually I'd met him briefly when he'd come in for costume fitting, but this was the first time I'd had any real conversation with him. He put his arm around me on the set and those were the first words out of his mouth. Things sort of deteriorated from that point on....

And they say the first impression is the lasting one!
 WM: [Laughs] Yeah, he was definitely on some kind of a trip.

I just saw The House on Haunted Hill, *and I enjoyed it quite a bit, although there were no Emergos! [Laughs]* [Editor's note: Emergos were fake skeletons which were dropped from theater ceilings to frighten unsuspecting moviegoers during the release of the original film.]
 WM: No, we didn't have any Emergos in the movie! [Laughs] This is probably a fortunate thing, I suppose.

The movie has certainly changed quite a bit from the William Castle original. I liked the changes. As a fan of the original, I thought they were very interesting — especially changing the house into an asylum. That worked brilliantly. It really opened up a lot of doors for you storywise.

WM: That came from my doing an episode of *Tales from the Crypt* in England, which I wrote, called "Report from the Grave." We actually wound up using a former mental institute as a location. It was just the creepiest place I've ever been in. In fact, the location manager asked us if we would mind if he hired an exorcist to come in and exorcise the place before we shot there. I went, "Sure, I guess if it needs it." [Laughs] But, even so, a lot of the crew members wouldn't go down in the basement. They would go down there for a couple of minutes and come running upstairs. Nobody wanted to go down there. It was definitely a creepy place. I thought, "What a great place to set a movie!"

Did you ever see anything strange while you were shooting there?

WM: I didn't, but there was definitely a weird vibe there. It was just a really odd place. You wouldn't believe the basement. It was just downright medieval. There was just a strange aura about the whole place.

You've been quoted as saying that the Castle original was "the kind of movie that should be remade." What did you mean by that?

WM: Well, I don't mean to denigrate that in any way. The original film is a great deal of fun, but generally it's not regarded as a classic the way a film like *The Day the Earth Stood Still* [1951] would be. I think if you're going to remake a film, these are the kind you should remake.

Geoffrey Rush was terrific in the picture. He really seemed to have channeled Vincent Price for that role.

WM: Yeah, I really thought he did a terrific job. He was a joy to work with. Actually, as far as I know, he didn't attempt to be Vincent Price. He just seems to have that aura about him. He actually wanted to play him sort of as John Waters. I think that was his notion.

How did Rush become involved with this film? It's quite a departure from his previous work in films such as Shine *(1996) and* Elizabeth *(1998).*

WM: Well, you know what? He was on the top of my list. I'd mentioned him to [producer] Joel Silver, and Joel thought he was great, too. After mentioning it, I dropped it. I never figured we'd get him in a million years. I guess Joel went after him with a vengeance and got him to do it. That was definitely a coup. He really adds a cool thing to the picture. He really enjoyed making it, too. At no time did he hold back. I mean, here we've got this Academy Award–winning actor and we're wrapping his head with rubber and steel wire and throwing him in a tank of water! [Laughs]

The chemistry within the film was exceptional. It certainly retained that feeling of the love/hate relationship between the husband and the wife.

WM: That was something we tried to retain because that was one of the better things about the original film. Particularly the one bedroom scene, which I thought was very good. There was talk early on about dumping it. I said, "No, no, no. We've got to keep that." It's a key scene and I think it really adds a lot to the film.

You used the audience's knowledge of the original film to your advantage. Anyone familiar with the original film knew that the wife wasn't really dead and that she and Peter Gallagher were lovers. But then, just when we thought we knew what was happening, you added a twist to the original story.

WM: [Co-writer] Dick Beebe and I were actually spending a lot of time just throwing around ideas about things to do to the film. It was kind of a lot of "what ifs." We both got to

Actor Geoffrey Rush (left) and director William Malone (right) map out a scene on the set of the horror film *House on Haunted Hill* (Warner Bros. Pictures, 1999).

the point where she was in league with the doctor. We both liked that, but what if she kills him? She needs another body. I thought that was kind of a fun notion, which we both liked a lot. We just went with it. I think it is a nice twist in the sense that if you are familiar with that film, it's not something you're going to expect.

I understand that the "powers that be" wanted you to make the film a comedy. Is that right?
　　WM: Yeah. I don't know if they wanted me to make a comedy, but they wanted it to be a lot funnier than we made it. *Scream* [1996] had been out at that time and was a big success. I think they wanted it to be a lot more tongue-in-cheek. I'm a great fan of horror films, and my notion was that we should keep it scary. Let's make it as scary as we can. It's pretty hard to make a movie that's hysterically funny *and* scary. That's a tall order and I didn't think I could pull it off! So, I just thought, "Let's make it as scary as possible, and if there are funny moments in it, it'll be a good thing."

Why do you think studio execs have such a difficult time understanding the genre? Sometimes it just seems like they don't have a clue.
　　WM: I guess it's just not the kind of movie they normally make. I suspect that a lot of them are just not fans of the genre. I've always thought studios are kind of set up in a funny way. It's sort of in a direct line-up. It seems like what they really need to do is set off and have different departments. You know, have a horror/science fiction department; have a drama department, and a mystery department, and a comedy department. I mean, as a director, I wouldn't presume to be able to direct every kind of genre there is. In that same way, I don't

know how an executive could make a decision for every kind of film. How could they possibly know that? I don't know.

I guess they do research and stuff, and then there's a certain amount of flying by the seat of your pants. It just seems to me like it would be smarter if they would just set up different departments and assign people who really knew those particular genres to run them, and then give them a free hand. That would seem smart to me. Of course, I'm just a filmmaker! [Laughs]

[Laughs] Yeah, so what do you know about making movies?
    WM: Yeah, I don't know *anything* about making movies! [Laughs]

Chris Kattan really seemed to play up the comedic aspect of the original Elisha Cook Jr. role. In the original, that comedic aspect was there. Of course, Cook played it seriously, but the paranoia of his character was quite humorous. It seemed like Chris just kind of took it up another notch.
    WM: Elisha Cook was funny in it. [Laughs] I don't know if *he* thought he was funny.... Actually, that was Joel Silver's idea to bring Chris Kattan in, and it ultimately turned out to be a great idea. I think Chris played it straight, but it's funny just because it's Chris.

House on Haunted Hill was an intelligent horror film, which is certainly rare these days. It seems like a lot of horror filmmakers don't give the audience any credit at all.
    WM: I have a great respect for the audience. I think the audience is a lot smarter than a lot of people give them credit for. I think they do know when you're talking down to them. I think some filmmakers do that and I think it's a big mistake. I think the audiences do get it.

FILMOGRAPHY FOR WILLIAM MALONE

1. *Scared to Death* (1980) D, Sc, Ex-P, A
2. *Creature* (1985) D, Sc, P
3. *Freddy's Nightmares* (1988) D
4. *Syngenor* (1990) CC
5. *Dream On* (1990) D
6. *Tales from the Crypt* (1994) D & Sc
7. *New York Undercover* (1994) D
8. *W.E.I.R.D. World* (1995) [TV] D
9. *The Big Easy* (1996) D
10. *Perversions of Science* (1997) D
11. *Honey, I Shrunk the Kids: The TV Show* (1997) D
12. *House on Haunted Hill* (1999) D & Un Sc
13. *Universal Soldier: The Return* (1999) Co-Sc
14. *Supernova* (2000) S
15. *Law and Order* (2000) D
16. *The Others* (2000) D
17. *FeardotCom* (2002) D
18. *Parasomnia* (2008) D & Sc

Albert Maysles

In an era when the term "legend" is bandied about rather loosely, few filmmakers are more deserving of this distinction than documentarian Albert Maysles. As *Movie Maker* journalist Travis Crawford once observed, "If Albert Maysles's name doesn't immediately register as one of the most significant American moviemakers of the last half-century, this comparative lack of recognition can only be explained by the predictable short shrift afforded documentarians in relation to their fiction director counterparts."

With his late brother David, Albert Maysles pioneered the style of filmmaking now known as *cinema verité* (also known as "direct cinema") in the early 1960s. (Practitioners of *cinema verité* discarded the traditional narratives, musical scores, and onscreen interviews, and utilized smaller, less intrusive film equipment to record their subjects.) After crafting the films *Psychiatry in Russia* (1955) and *Youth in Poland* (1957), Maysles made his first significant film, *Primary* (1960). This film, which he co-directed with David Maysles, Robert Drew, and Richard Leacock, followed Presidential hopefuls John F. Kennedy and Hubert H. Humphrey. In 1964, Maysles documented the day-to-day exploits of the Fab Four in *What's Happening! The Beatles in the U.S.A.* (1964). Through his work on these films, Albert Maysles soon became recognized as a top-notch cinematographer. French New Wave auteur Jean-Luc Godard, who later called him America's finest cameraman, enlisted Maysles's talents for his vignette in the anthology film *Six in Paris* (1965). That same year, Albert and David Maysles turned their cameras on actor Marlon Brando for their film *Meet Marlon Brando* (1965). The team then embarked upon short films focusing on writer Truman Capote (*With Love from Truman*, 1965) and filmmaker Orson Welles (*Orson Welles — Spain*, 1965).

After filming Jimi Hendrix at the Monterey Pop Festival in 1968, Albert Maysles co-directed the feature film *Salesman* (1969) with David Maysles and Charlotte Zwerin. The film, often called the quintessential documentary, follows four down-and-out door-to-door Bible salesmen. Of the film, which was selected to the National Film Registry in 1992, author Norman Mailer once observed, "I can't think of many movies which have had as much to say about American life and have said it so well." Another great American writer, Arthur Miller, whose own *Death of a Salesman* is often seen as a companion piece to the film, called *Salesman* "an adventure into the American dream." The Maysles brothers then followed up *Salesman* with *Gimme Shelter* (1970), which documented the Rolling Stones's ill-fated free concert at the Altamont Speedway. (Their cameras captured a spectator's horrific murder at the hands of the Hell's Angels.) This incident, which has often been called "the end of the sixties," caused the Maysles to draw fire from some critics (chiefly, *New Yorker* scribe Pauline Kael) for creating a setting for violence.

Albert Maysles has since crafted numerous standout documentaries, including *Christo's Valley Curtain* (1973), *Grey Gardens* (1975), *Running Fence* (1978), *Muhammad and Larry*

(1980), *Christo in Paris* (1990), *Soldiers of Music* (1991), *Abortion: Desperate Choices* (1992), and *Lalee's Kin* (2001). Between 1986 and 1987, Albert Maysles enjoyed a fruitful period in which he collaborated on three acclaimed films—*Ozawa* (1986), *Horowitz Plays Mozart*, and *Islands* (both 1987). In addition to directing his own films, Maysles has continued to work as a cinematographer. (His credits as a cinematographer include Leon Gast's Oscar-winning film *When We Were Kings*, 1996).

While amassing an impressive list of credits, Maysles has received countless accolades and awards, including an Oscar nomination, a pair of Emmys, a Directors Guild Award, the American Society of Cinematographers' President's Award, three Sundance Grand Jury Prize Award nominations (two in the same year), an Independent Spirit Award nomination, two Sundance awards, and a handful of grants and career achievement awards.

Favorite Films: *Devil in the Flesh* (1946), *The Bicycle Thief* (1948), *Bus 174* (2002), *La Strada* (1954), *Death in Venice* (1971), and *L' Avventura* (1960).

ANDREW RAUSCH: *Prior to becoming a filmmaker, you taught psychology at Boston University. How did you make that leap from college instructor to filmmaker?*

ALBERT MAYSLES: In 1955, I borrowed a movie camera with the notion that if I could get into mental hospitals in Russia, I could make a film. So, with my tourist visa in hand, I borrowed the camera, went to Russia, and got into mental hospitals. That was my first film, and it was called *Psychiatry in Russia*. So far it's only shown on one TV station.... [Laughs]

Do you feel that your background in psychology has helped you in capturing the natural behaviors of people in everyday life?

AM: Well, there are two things. First, I went into psychology because I liked people and wanted to understand them. My ability to understand people made it all the more profound. When you understand people, the possibilities for loving them are all the more. The empathy that you yield to the subjects is very important in establishing and maintaining trust and rapport; they know they don't have to worry about you. They put themselves in your hands. Along with that, the filmmaker has to have a great devotion to his or her responsibility so that discretion plays a large part in revealing the true personality of the individual, rather than trying to do so in an intrusive and exploitative fashion.

Do you feel that love for the subject is something which is lacking in many of today's documentaries?

AM: Well, yeah. If you're really going to respect a person fully, then you have to get behind the scenes with them. You should be devoted to directly engaging yourself in the process of revealing who that person really is. Unless you have a genuine desire to like that person, you're probably going to fail in doing an honest job of it.

Two years ago, I made a film called *Lalee's Kin*, which was about a very poor black family in the South. When Grandma—the main character—saw the film after we had finished it, she said, "Yeah, that's the truth." Then she followed that by saying, "Couldn't you make it longer?" That wouldn't have happened if she hadn't felt we'd done her justice.

Have you maintained relationships with many of your subjects?

AM: Oh, yeah. That goes from the famous to ordinary people. I maintained a relationship with Paul Brennan—the main character of *Salesman*—which lasted throughout his life. He died something like twenty-five years after we had filmed him.

Muhammad Ali trains for his big rumble with George Foreman in the Leon Gast documentary *When We Were Kings*, which features cinematography by Albert Maysles (Gramercy Pictures, 1996).

The Heisenberg Principle states that the behavior of a subject changes under observation. Do you believe this to be true?

AM: The Heisenberg Principle says that the introduction of another element causes everything to change. I don't believe anything has to change if that extra element is myself or another documentary filmmaker who sort of blends in with the people he's filming and has a special relationship where there's mutual trust, and the person being filmed feels confident that the filmmaker is going to portray them in a truthful, honest manner.

You once observed that a documentary filmmaker must "rely on coincidences." An obvious example of this would be the murder which transpired during the concert at Altamont. Are there any other spectacular examples of this which stand out in your mind?

AM: In the Beatles film, there's this wonderful, romantic scene between Ringo and an eight-year-old child who comes up to him and plants a kiss on his cheek. She says, "I've always wanted to meet a famous singer." [Laughs] It's just a lovely, spontaneous moment. How it was that those two should meet was just pure chance.

How did your brother and yourself become involved with the Beatles?

AM: I got a call one day from Grenada Television saying that the Beatles were arriving at Idlewild Airport in two hours. They asked if I'd like to make a film of them. I put my hand over the phone and asked my brother, "Who are the Beatles? Are they any good?" Fortunately, my brother knew, and he said, "Yeah, they're good." [Laughs] We then both got on the phone, made the deal, and rushed out to the airport just in time to catch the airplane as it was coming down. We spent the next six or seven days—day and night—filming them.

You and your brother once planned a collaboration with Orson Welles, which was ultimately aborted. Can you tell me about that project?

AM: In 1963, my brother and I were at the Cannes film festival. Somebody said, "You know, Orson Welles is here. He's in a barroom about twenty miles away." So we rushed out there and introduced ourselves. He said he'd heard of us and our work, and he asked, "Where are you going from here?" He said, "Why don't you stop off in Madrid for a week?" So we spent the whole week with Orson Welles. Shortly after we got together, we went to a bullfight with him. He said, "You know, there's a film we've got to make together." We said, "Wait a minute," and we started filming. We made this little ten minute film of him talking about a film we would make about people who come to bullfights.

The project wasn't aborted. It just never got made.

I'd like to talk about another interesting collaboration you were involved with. You served as cinematographer on Jean-Luc Godard's segment in Six in Paris. *How did that come about, and what was that experience like?*

AM: Barbet Schroder was the film's producer, and we were very good friends. One day he began to tell me about the project. He said, "You and Jean-Luc Godard would get along great. In fact, he's putting together his sequence for the film. Why don't I call him up and see if he'd be interested?" So he called him up and told Jean-Luc enough about me that he said, "Please send him over." So I went to Paris and he explained what he had in mind. He had rehearsed with the actors and made sure the two sets were properly lit, but he wasn't going to tell me what was going on in the scenes. I would just go in with the camera on my shoulder and shoot the way I always shoot a documentary. I was to film it as it happened without knowing what was about to happen next. In the end, it just worked out beautifully.

I think it may have been something like what Orson Welles had in mind, too. Both the

Welles thing and *Six in Paris* happened in 1963. I don't think Welles and Godard were in communication with one another, but they were thinking along the same lines.

I understand that George Lucas worked as a second unit cameraman on your film Gimme Shelter. *Is that right?*

AM: Yes. We didn't know we would be making the film until about twenty-four hours before Altamont was in the works and actually happening for sure. During that twenty-four-hour period we had to get skillful camera people and their equipment together. You can see it on the credits—there were something like ten or fifteen camera people. We took a chance and called Mr. Lucas up, and he said, "Fine." Unfortunately—and we didn't know it at the time—but the equipment we gave him wasn't working correctly, so none of his footage was useful. It wasn't his fault. It was just that, in the rush, we did the best we could to get the best equipment.

In 1964, your brother David was quoted as saying, "We don't want people to say, 'It's a documentary, isn't it?' If we reach that day, something will have been accomplished." Forty years after the fact, do you feel that you've been successful in that endeavor?

AM: The name "documentary" still doesn't convey enough of what people want. It still conveys some sort of archival thing tucked away with a lot of dust on it. It sounds like something academic. It doesn't sound like it's breathing life. The next best thing—or maybe better—is "non-fiction," but that's a negative. So, I've never been able to find a suitable expression for what I do. The films I've made have been labeled *cinema verité*, or "direct cinema," but who knows what that means? [Laughs]

The Rolling Stones perform in *Gimme Shelter*, widely considered one of the finest rock films ever made (20th Century–Fox, 1970).

And now, I don't know what to think of this sudden interest in the so-called "reality" shows. It's interesting that, when those programs first came out, there were quotations around the word reality in the *New York Times*. Then, after awhile, they dropped the quotation marks. That shows, again, how little respect we have for what is really real. The networks haven't caught up with us yet. Television journalism is more than fifty years behind itself, if only because it isn't direct cinema. They still need the anchorman — Peter Jennings or whoever — to explain what's going on. They're not capturing the thing itself, and the news becomes a spoon-fed type of thing. It isn't nearly what it could be.

If you could select only one of your films to carry on the legacy of your work fifty years from now, which one would it be? Which project would you like for people to see and say, "This was Albert Maysles, and this was what he did"?
    AM: *Salesman*, without a doubt.

FILMOGRAPHY FOR ALBERT MAYSLES

1. *Psychiatry in Russia* (1955) D
2. *Youth in Poland* (1957) Co-D
3. *Primary* (1960) Co-D & Cin
4. *Yanki No!* (1960) Cin
5. *Showman* (1963) Co-D & Cin
6. *What's Happening! The Beatles in the U.S.A.* (1964) [TV] Co-D
7. *Sean O'Casey: The Spirit of Ireland* (1965) Cin
8. *Six in Paris* (1965) Cin
9. *Meet Marlon Brando* (1965) Co-D & Cin
10. *Orson Welles — Spain* (1966) Co-D & Cin
11. *With Love from Truman* (1966) Co-D & Cin
12. *Monterey Pop* (1968) Cin
13. *Salesman* (1969) Co-D, P, Cin
14. *Gimme Shelter* (1970) Co-D & Cin
15. *Christo's Valley Curtain* (1973) Co-D & P
16. *Grey Gardens* (1975) Co-D, P, Cin
17. *Running Fence* (1978) Co-D & Cin
18. *Muhammad and Larry* (1980) Co-D
19. *Jimi Plays Monterey* (1986) Cin
20. *Vladimir Horowitz: The Last Romantic* (1986) Cin
21. *Ozawa* (1986) Co-D & Cin
22. *Horowitz Plays Mozart* (1987) Co-D & Cin
23. *Islands* (1987) [TV] Co-D & Cin
24. *Jessye Norman Sings Carmen* (1988) Co-D
25. *Christo in Paris* (1990) Co-D & Cin
26. *Soldiers of Music* (1991) Co-D & Cin
27. *Abortion: Desperate Choices* (1992) [TV] Co-D & Cin
28. *Baroque Diet* (1992) Co-D
29. *Sports Illustrated: Swimsuit '92* (1992) D
30. *Umbrellas* (1994) Co-D & Cin
31. *The Beatles: The First U.S. Visit* (1994) Co-D & Cin
32. *Conversations with the Rolling Stones* (1994) Co-D, Ex-P, Cin
33. *Christo & Jeanne-Claude* (1996) Cin
34. *Letting Go: A Hospice Journey* (1996) Co-D & Cin
35. *When We Were Kings* (1996) Cin
36. *Concert of Wills* (1997) Co-D, Sc, Cin
37. *Lalee's Kin: The Legacy of Cotton* (2001) [TV] Co-D & Cin
38. *On Common Ground* (2001) SUD
39. *Paris Review: The Early Chapters* (2001) Cin
40. *With the Filmmaker: Portraits by Albert Maysles* (2001) D
41. *A Dog's Life: A Dogamentary* (2004) Cin
42. *In Good Conscience* (2004) Cin
43. *The Gates* (2005) [TV] Co-D, Ex-P, Cin
44. *This Is an Adventure* (2005) Co-D & Cin
45. *The Jew on Trial* (2005) D, Sc, P, Cin
46. *Stolen* (2005) Cin
47. *Addiction* (2007) Co-D
48. *Sally Gross: The Pleasure of Stillness* (2007) D, P, Cin

John Milius

John Milius has worked as a scribe and/or director on more than thirty films. He has been dubbed "Mr. Macho" for a body of work film critic/author Leonard Maltin calls "high-octane movies populated by characters whose political leanings would not win them positions in Bill Clinton's cabinet." These tendencies brought his films under constant fire from film critic Pauline Kael, prompting Milius to humorously conclude many times in print that she was "obviously" masking a sexual desire for him.

After being rejected from the military for chronic asthma, the former surfer then attended USC film school, where he became a member of a collective known as the "USC Mafia," which also includes George Lucas, Steven Spielberg, and Francis Ford Coppola. While in film school, Milius garnered accolades for his first short, *Marcello, I'm So Bored*, which parodied the art-house fare of European avant-garde auteurs such as Francois Truffaut, Ingmar Bergman, and Federico Fellini. In 1968, Milius penned his first full-length screenplay, which was a contemporary adaptation of Joseph Conrad's novella *Heart of Darkness*. Originally written for George Lucas to direct, Francis Ford Coppola wound up helming this script, which became *Apocalypse Now* (1979). Filming began on the Marlon Brando–starrer in 1976, but because of numerous difficulties, it would not be completed until 1979. The script, rewritten by Coppola, earned both writers an Academy Award nomination for Best Screenplay in 1980. Other screenplays written or co-written by Milius include *The Life and Times of Judge Roy Bean* (1972), *Jeremiah Johnson* (1972), *Magnum Force* (1973), *1941* (1979), *Clear and Present Danger* (1994), and *Geronimo: An American Legend* (1993). In addition, the screenwriter has performed uncredited rewrites on *Dirty Harry* (1971), *Jaws* (1975), and *Saving Private Ryan* (1998). It should be noted that both *Apocalypse Now* and *Jaws* appear on the American Film Institute's list of the one hundred greatest films in the history of American cinema.

Milius made his feature directorial debut with the revisionist gangster film *Dillinger* in 1973. He has since directed eight more films, writing or co-writing all of them. His directorial credits include the epic film *The Wind and the Lion* (1975), *Big Wednesday* (1978), *Conan the Barbarian* (1982, which he co-wrote with Oliver Stone), *Red Dawn* (1984), and *Farewell to the King* (1989). In addition, Milius is also an accomplished producer. Among his production credits are Paul Schrader's *Hardcore* (1979), Robert Zemeckis' *Used Cars* (1980), and Spielberg's *1941*.

In 2005, Milius returned with the hit HBO series *Rome*, which he wrote, directed, and executive produced.

Favorite Films: The films of David Lean, Akira Kurosawa, and John Ford.

ANDREW RAUSCH: *Why do you think there are so many bad films made today?*
JOHN MILIUS: Because the people who are making them are frauds.

What do you think of the big-studio "creative process" which is used today?

JM: It's all bullshit. They're just frauds. They're no fuckin' good.

[Laughs] I think Apocalypse Now *is brilliant. What inspired you to adapt Joseph Conrad's novella into a Vietnam setting?*

JM: I had read that novel when I was seventeen. My writing teacher at USC had said that a number of people had tried writing it and failed. He said that it could never be licked. Orson Welles had tried it, as well as some others. They said it could never be done, which, of course, is just like waving a red flag in front of a young bull. [Laughs] And I wanted to do a Vietnam movie really bad. I was always fascinated with that story.

Why do you think those others had failed? How did you approach adapting the novel differently than your predecessors?

JM: I don't know. I think *Apocalypse Now* takes it on a different level in the sense that it's about the war, but it isn't about the war. It's a story that, obviously, could work at different times. It works best at that time. When you see the film that Nicolas Roeg made with John Malkovich [*Heart of Darkness*, 1994], it's a pretty good film. It's a pretty good depiction of that story. But it doesn't work, because it's not the same. It doesn't work because finding a dead elephant is different than finding the tail of a B-52.

What inspired you to incorporate the T.S. Elliot poem "The Hollow Men" into the script?

JM: That was Francis' addition. He wanted to prove to the world his literacy. [Laughs] I had a speech in there in that part that I later used in another movie, *Red Dawn*. The speech

John Milius directing the 1982 Arnold Schwarzenegger–starrer ***Conan the Barbarian*** (Universal Pictures, 1982).

at that part of the movie was supposed to be Brando telling of the great hunt of the Mongols, which was where they surrounded an enclosed area and then drove all animals and men before them, and then finally there was an orgy of killing. Then the young son of the great Khan pulled upon his father's sleeve and said, "Let the last creature alive go free."

The line from Conan the Barbarian *in which Conan speaks of "vanquishing one's foes" is a quotation from Genghis Khan.*

JM: It's always been one of my favorite quotes. I remember a million quotes, and I'm always spouting them off. I'm kind of an amateur historian. I don't know, I think it just sounded like such a wonderful thing.

How often have you been pleased with other directors' handling of your screenplays?

JM: I eventually became happy with *Jeremiah Johnson*. At the time it was made, I wasn't at all pleased with it. But I was wrong. Sidney Pollack made a good film. It was just a different film than the one I would have made. I've talked with Clint Eastwood about it. He's seen the original script and said, "Let's do it again." But I think Sidney made a good film and probably a better one than I would have made. Mine would have been a lot more harsh.

Of course, I never liked *The Life and Times of Judge Roy Bean*.

Yeah, I was extremely surprised to see a poster for that hanging outside your office.

JM: I never liked that film, although I liked John Huston a great deal. I don't consider that one of his better works.

I think *Clear and Present Danger* is fine for what it is. [Thinks for a moment] Actually, I don't like it. I think the ending is a little bit.... The original ending was much better than what they did. For the most part, they're okay, but the good ones are made by the good directors. On *Jeremiah Johnson*, Sidney Pollack was a good director. He understood something about that script and was true to it. And Francis was a *great* director. So, if I could work with people like Francis all the time, I'd never be a director.

You mentioned John Huston, who was also in your film The Wind and the Lion. *What was he like to work with?*

JM: He was tough — really, *really* tough. He tortured you. That was his favorite thing. He was a sadist who liked to torture writers, and he hated them. He hated me, and he told me that once. He said, "I despise you because you can write better than I can." He didn't like that. And he said, "I'm gonna make you pay for that talent."

What he did was he would torture you, and if you survived the torture.... But his torture was rough. He would beat you. It was like being somewhere in North Vietnam in a prison; you were gonna talk — it was just a matter of how long you were gonna make him torture you before you talked. But Huston knew he was gonna get you eventually. He had all the power. If you lasted long enough, and fought well enough, you became one of his sons, whom he treated much better than his real sons. Then you became a treasured friend for life.

Your screenwriting credits are quite diverse. How does one go from the drive-in fare of Evel Knievel *(1971) to* Apocalypse Now *and then to* 1941, *all within only a few years? [Laughs]*

JM: *Evel Knievel* was written in just five days, you know? That was an assignment.

Ultimately, everybody does the same thing over and over again. And there are similarities between *Evel Knievel* and *Apocalypse Now* and what I'm doing right now. There are similarities between *Jeremiah Johnson* and those. They're all about a man broken off from himself and broken off from society. The most honest line in *Apocalypse Now* is, "He broke off from all of them. Then he broke off from himself. I'd never seen a man so broken up."

Is that a theme that you consciously write, or does it just kind of find its way into your work?

JM: It just kind of finds its way in. Nobody wants to be that guy. If you look at all of William Faulkner's work, or John Steinbeck, or any of these guys…. In Steinbeck's work, there's always this sad, failed character like Doc in *Cannery Row*. That's the brighter side, the darker being Tom Joad. But you always end up with that same guy with no place to go!

Just how weird was Marlon Brando on the set of Apocalypse Now?

JM: I never had much to do with him. Francis had *that* problem. He was only there a short time. [Laughs] And Francis said he was *very* difficult to work with!

I've heard that Brando's being filmed in the shadows was actually a stipulation of his contract because he was overweight. Is that true?

JM: I don't know. I've heard so many different stories. I've heard that it wasn't that way, that the whole thing was just that they were going to shoot it.

As a matter of fact, I remember doing some drawings here. Francis had me work here with an artist doing some drawings and some scenes with Kurtz, and we sent them to him.

Matt (Jan-Michael Vincent) riding a wave in the John Milius masterpiece *Big Wednesday* (Warner Bros. Pictures, 1978).

And I always drew Kurtz as Lee Marvin. So here, when this guy gets there, and he's terribly overweight for a Green Beret colonel, I think the effort here was to put him in black pajamas and big block shoes to make him taller, so as to thin him out. [Laughs] Because he wasn't going to be there long enough to lose the weight. He was only going to be there for a month, or something. Even with full dysentery, he wasn't going to lose enough!

Actor Ben Johnson on the set of *Dillinger*. Director John Milius can be seen standing behind him to the right (American International Pictures Export Corp., 1973).

Filmography for John Milius

1. *The Reversal of Richard Sun* (1966) D & Sc
2. *Glut* (1967) Sc
3. *Marcello, I'm So Bored* (1967) D & Sc
4. *The Emperor* (1967) Sc
5. *The Devil's 8* (1969) Sc
6. *Dirty Harry* (1971) Un Co-Sc
7. *Evel Knievel* (1971) Sc
8. *Jeremiah Johnson* (1972) Sc
9. *The Life and Times of Judge Roy Bean* (1972) Sc
10. *Deadhead Miles* (1972) A
11. *Dillinger* (1973) D & Sc
12. *Magnum Force* (1973) S
13. *Melvin Purvis: G-Man* (1974) [TV] S
14. *Jaws* (1975) Un Co-Sc
15. *The Wind and the Lion* (1975) D & Sc
16. *Big Wednesday* (1978) D & Sc
17. *Apocalypse Now* (1979) Co-Sc
18. *1941* (1979) Ex-P & S
19. *Hardcore* (1979) Ex-P
20. *Used Cars* (1980) Ex-P
21. *Conan the Barbarian* (1982) D, Co-Sc, Un A
22. *Uncommon Valor* (1983) P
23. *Lone Wolf McQuade* (1983) TA
24. *Red Dawn* (1984) D & Sc
25. *The Twilight Zone* (1985) [episode: "Opening Day"] D
26. *Extreme Prejudice* (1987) S
27. *Farewell to the King* (1989) D & Sc
28. *Flight of the Intruder* (1990) D & Un Co-Sc
29. *Hearts of Darkness: A Filmmaker's Apocalypse* (1991) A
30. *Geronimo: An American Legend* (1993) Co-Sc & S
31. *Clear and Present Danger* (1994) Sc
32. *Motorcycle Gang* (1994) [TV] D & Sc
33. *Rough Riders* (1997) [TV] D & Sc
34. *Saving Private Ryan* (1998) Un Co-Sc
35. *Hell Hath No Fury* (1999) A
36. *Texas Rangers* (2000) Un Co-Sc [removed name]
37. *Rome* (2005) D, Sc, Ex-P
38. *The Last Region* (2006) Ex-P

Floyd Mutrux

Floyd Mutrux spent his childhood growing up in Houston and later Los Angeles. He then worked as an improvisational actor as part of Second City in Chicago and New York City. After leaving Second City, Mutrux enrolled in classes at Columbia University. In the late 1960s, Mutrux resumed his acting career with bit parts in the films *Rosemary's Baby* and *Maryjane* (both 1968), and a handful of television series. In 1971, Mutrux made his directorial debut with the critically-acclaimed docudrama *Dusty and Sweets McGee*. Despite the film's rave reviews, Warner Bros. pulled the picture from release after only one week after *Time* magazine questioned its graphic depiction of drug addiction. That same year, Mutrux wrote and produced *The Christian Licorice Store* (1971), and found screenwriting work on Monte Hellman's classic *Two-Lane Blacktop* (1971). He then co-wrote the Al Pacino/Gene Hackman buddy picture *Scarecrow* (1973), which was awarded Best Picture honors at the Cannes Film Festival. The following year, Mutrux continued his winning ways with the hit comedy *Freebie and the Bean* (1974), which he wrote and produced. During this period, *Variety* predicted that the five greatest directors to emerge from the so-called "New Hollywood" era would be Steven Spielberg, George Lucas, Floyd Mutrux, Martin Scorsese, and Terrence Malick. In 1975, Mutrux wrote and directed *Aloha, Bobby and Rose* for Columbia Pictures. Filmed for a mere $60,000, Mutrux's homage to Jean-Luc Godard's *Breathless* (1960) grossed an astounding $35 million (at a time when tickets still cost three dollars), making it the sixth biggest moneymaker of the year. Mutrux then helmed the seminal rock-and-roll film *American Hot Wax* (1978). The movie, which has since become a cult hit, despite its noticeable absence on the video market, earned Mutrux accolades and rave reviews. (For his work on the film, *Village Voice* dubbed him the year's Best Director.) That same year, Mutrux also co-wrote the Cheech & Chong pot comedy *Up in Smoke* (1978).

As *LA Weekly* film writer Chuck Stephens observed, Mutrux was a "white-light guy in the white-heat moment of New Hollywood" who "seemed for a blink like the rightful heir to Kenneth Anger's *Scorpio Rising*: His films were funny, freaky, dangerous as rock-and-roll, and portended a potential combination of *Mean Streets* edginess and *Badlands* beauty." However, due to a string of films which have been shelved, rewritten by others, or continue to languish in development hell, Mutrux remains a virtual unknown, despite his many successes. After directing the hit comedy *The Hollywood Knights* (1980), Mutrux took a lengthy hiatus from filmmaking. During that time, he continued writing. (It's interesting to note that Mutrux has sold nearly two dozen screenplays — some of them for $1 million or more — which have not yet been produced.) He conceived and co-wrote Brian De Palma's hit film *The Untouchables* (1987), but did not receive screen credit. In 1990, Mutrux served as executive producer on Warren Beatty's film *Dick Tracy*. He then wrote and executive produced the gritty drama *American Me* (1992). In 1994, Mutrux returned to the director's chair for the coming-of-age comedy *There Goes My Baby*. While the film was well-received, it fell victim to a bankruptcy at Orion Pictures and received little publicity and a limited release.

Favorite Films: *Jules et Jim* (1962), *Shoot the Piano Player* (1960), *Breathless*, *One Flew Over the Cuckoo's Nest* (1975), *Chinatown* (1974), *Doctor Zhivago* (1965), *Pulp Fiction* (1994), *From Here to Eternity* (1953), *Giant* (1956), and *Goodfellas* (1990).

ANDREW RAUSCH: Variety *once predicted that the five greatest directors to emerge from the seventies would be Steven Spielberg, George Lucas, Martin Scorsese, Terrence Malick, and yourself. After* The Hollywood Knights, *you took a fourteen-year hiatus from filmmaking. What happened?*

FLOYD MUTRUX: Look, I have a lot of regrets. I made a lot of choices that were not smart. I went off to work on a lot of projects that never got made, and wound up feeling sorry for myself. Well, not feel sorry for myself, but kind of play this rebel.... I never wanted to make anyone else's stuff. In that period in the late seventies, early eighties, I just sort of dropped out. The pictures I cared about weren't getting made. I just disappeared from the scene.

Then I sort of reemerged; I wrote a lot of scripts. I've written fifty-five scripts. Executives from studios got fired or moved, and the pictures I'd written got shelved. In fact, I've just now gotten four scripts back in turnaround. They were all big sales, but all the executives who greenlit them got fired.

Future stars Tony Danza and Michelle Pfeiffer, who play Duke and Suzie Q, in a publicity photograph from Floyd Mutrux's ***Hollywood Knights*** (Columbia Pictures, 1980).

If you had it to do over again, what would you do differently?

FM: I'd behave better. [Laughs] I guess I wouldn't have given away so many projects; I wouldn't have walked away from them. I'd have gone forward and finished them. But, you know, you really can't say, "I would have done this or this differently...." I mean, all of the things that happened got me to where I am right now. Today I'm writing and producing a number of Broadway shows, and it's everything I've ever wanted. I'm having the time of my life. The work I'm doing right now is absolutely the best work I've ever done.

Sometimes I feel like the movie business betrayed me, but that's kind of a whiny attitude. Basically, I don't give a fuck because the movie business betrayed itself. It makes a lot of shit now. It's unwatchable. There are no longer any movies you want to go see. Name your ten best pictures of the last five years, and they don't compare to the best of the fifties, the sixties, or the seventies.

You emerged in the early seventies as part of what has come to be known as "the New Hollywood." At that time the film industry was producing small, personal, character-driven films en masse.

FM: I did those types of films, and I'm very proud of them all.

In the latter part of that decade, those films disappeared. Why do you think that is?

FM: The faces at the studios changed. [Warner Bros. president of production] John Calley, who was smarter than anybody, retired. [Paramount Pictures President] Michael Eisner, who was as smart as anyone, left to run Disney.... Television executives began moving into the studios. Here's an interesting story about a television executive who came to work at Tri-Star. He had an interview with [legendary filmmaker] Fred Zinnemann. The executive sits down, and he looks at Fred Zinnemann, right? The executive says, "So, how do you do, Mr. Zinnemann? Why don't you tell me about yourself?" And do you know what Fred said? "You first." [Laughs]

I think the concept of the personality changed in terms of the studio executives. They were all people who were there for one or two years. MGM was sort of out of business. Fox had something like five different players. Those guys didn't want to make any personal films because those are made from an emotional point of view; they were made from a personal take. The mindlessness of the Hollywood executives changed. Now the goal became trying to capture a franchise. They could have Christmas and summer franchises, and have eleven different writers come in and each write two or three scenes. That's the mindset today. "We can get enough good scenes from good writers that we can just paste it all together," which is why these pictures *look* like they've been pasted together!

Your film American Hot Wax *is regarded as one of the most significant rock-and-roll films ever made. It definitely enjoys a cult status today, yet the film has never had an official VHS or DVD release. Why is that?*

FM: This is the twenty-fifth anniversary! You'd think Paramount would want to do something. You know why they don't do anything with it? Because the other people made it. Eisner made it. They didn't, so why would they want to promote Eisner's project?

William Fraker has served as director of photography on each of the five films you've directed. How would you describe your collaborative relationship?

FM: He's my best friend in the world. We drink the same kind of gin! [Laughs] Billy has a good sense of me. Billy was cinematographer on *Rosemary's Baby*, which was where we first met. He was directing *Monte Walsh* (1970) right next door to where I was directing *The Christian Licorice Store*. That's when we decided to make *Dusty and Sweets McGee* together. Billy is just the kindest, nicest human being in the world. He also has a great eye. I mean, the double-glass scene in *American Hot Wax*— they still talk about that. I remember Steven Spielberg talking about how much he loved that, and then he used that on his film *1941* (1980).

Billy is a great guy, and he's going to work on every film I do.

You've conceived and worked on a number of films on which you weren't credited. There are a lot of people who don't know that you were involved with films such as The Untouchables, Urban Cowboy (1980), Up in Smoke (1978), Ford Fairlane (1990), Dick Tracy....

FM: I was the original writer and original director on a few of those.

So, what happened?

FM: Well, I'll give you an example. I was flying up to Lake Tahoe. [Producer] Irving Azoff and I were doing a picture called *Happy Hour* at Universal. It was about a baseball player, a country singer, a rodeo rider, and a high school beauty queen — one week in their lives. This was a very personal film. By this time, this project had been purchased and set up five or six different times by different producers and studios. Jon Voight was going to star in it, and I was going to direct. Irv Azoff read that script and said it was one of the best he'd ever read. The Eagles read it, and they were going to write the score for it. So, we were flying up to Lake Tahoe to see one of Irv's acts, Boz Skaggs. During that trip, I read an *Esquire* article on *Urban Cowboy*. I came back, called, and said, "I'd like to do the picture." At that time, I had a big

Louise (Lorraine Newman) in a scene from Floyd Mutrux's 1978 Alan Freed biopic ***American Hot Wax*** (Paramount Pictures, 1978).

deal at Paramount where I could kind of do anything I wanted. I made a deal to direct and rewrite the script with [original writer] Aaron Latham. We brought him out, and we started working on it.

I had two different pictures going at once—*Happy Hour* and *Urban Cowboy*. Azoff was being approached by [producer] Bob Evans, who was saying, "Why don't we get somebody else to direct *Urban Cowboy*?" Azoff was thinking he could make two pictures at once rather than waiting for me to complete one and then going to work on the other. We got into a big hassle about it, and I had to make a decision regarding which one I wanted to do. Again, if I had been smarter and not been like, "Fuck you, you can keep it," which is what I did, things might have been different. I went in to Universal and said, "Okay, I'm going to leave *Urban Cowboy* and go with *Happy Hour* because I care more about it. But I'm not going to unless you promise me that you're going to make the picture." They said, "Absolutely. You've got our word." So, I walked away from *Urban Cowboy*. Although I didn't know it at the time—this was something I found out about later—[producer] Ned Tanen gave the [*Happy Hour*] script to Burt Reynolds. Tanen decided he was only going to make the picture if he could get Burt Reynolds to star in it. Burt Reynolds didn't, and ten days later Universal put the picture in turnaround. And, just like that, I had walked away from *Urban Cowboy* to make a picture that would never get made. And I did the same thing with *Up in Smoke* right around that same time.

FILMOGRAPHY FOR FLOYD MUTRUX

1. *Adam-12* (1968) A
2. *Felony Squad* (1968) A
3. *Maryjane* (1968) A
4. *The Outsider* (1968) A
5. *Rosemary's Baby* (1968) Un A
6. *Run for Your Life* (1968) A
7. *Cover Me Babe* (1970) A
8. *Dusty and Sweets McGee* (1971) D, P, Sc
9. *The Christian Licorice Store* (1971) P & Sc
10. *Two-Lane Blacktop* (1971) Un Sc
11. *Scarecrow* (1973) Un Sc
12. *Freebie and the Bean* (1974) Sc & P
13. *Aloha, Bobby and Rose* (1975) D & Sc
14. *American Hot Wax* (1978) D
15. *Up in Smoke* (1978) Un Sc & S
16. *Urban Cowboy* (1980) Un Sc
17. *The Hollywood Knights* (1980) D & Sc
18. *The Untouchables* (1986) Un Sc
19. *Drug Wars* (1989) [TV] Un Sc & S
20. *Dick Tracy* (1990) Ex-P
21. *The Adventures of Ford Fairlane* (1990) Un Sc & S
22. *American Me* (1992) Ex-P, Sc, S
23. *Blood in, Blood Out* (1993) Sc
24. *There Goes My Baby* (1994) D & Sc
25. *Mulholland Falls* (1996) S

Daniel Myrick

Sarasota, Florida, native Daniel Myrick worked extensively in the commercial market before slowly making the transition to feature filmmaker. He and his future *Blair Witch Project* (1999) collaborators Eduardo Sanchez and Gregg Hale crafted *40 Miles Salvation* (1997), a trilogy of shorts combined to make a feature-length film. In 1993, Myrick founded the Filmmaker's Alliance at Universal Studios in Orlando, Florida, established to combine the talents of local indie filmmakers in hopes of establishing a viable indie film community. In 1997, Myrick was hired to write and direct the award-winning promotional trailer for the Florida Film Festival. Noted indie film guru and author John Pierson hired Myrick as a cinematographer for his Independent Film Channel program *Split Screen*.

In 1997, Daniel Myrick and Eduardo Sanchez scripted *The Blair Witch Project*, which they would co-direct as their feature film debut, the story of a would-be documentarian and crew who set out searching for evidence of a mythological witch. The film crew eventually finds all the proof they need when they are systematically killed one by one by the Blair Witch. Myrick and Sanchez opted to film *The Blair Witch Project* from the documentary crew's point of view. Doing something that had never been done before, Myrick and Sanchez actually used the footage shot by the actors as the film itself. In the beginning, the two directors told the actors very little about the project. They simply handed them a camera and sent them out into the woods to spend several nights with little initial direction. Always remaining out of sight, Myrick and company would leave small notes for each of the actors, giving the plot new twists. The directors also served as the ghosts in the woods, making noises outside the tent and leaving piles of stones and bundles of sticks (with human body parts enclosed) outside the tent. As the actors had no idea what was going on, their reactions in the movie are genuine.

In an ingenious move, *The Blair Witch Project* was marketed as the discovered footage from a real-life film crew lost in the woods. Myrick and Sanchez also filmed a documentary called *Curse of the Blair Witch* (1999) to promote the film. The documentary serves as a wonderful companion piece to the movie and is equally as entertaining. After seeing *Curse of the Blair Witch* on the Sci-Fi Channel, many people believed *The Blair Witch Project* was a true story. After an extensive internet campaign which began a year before the film's release, the $50,000 film made history and a lot of money for Artisan.

Myrick and Sanchez were nominated for a number of awards, including the Young Cinema Award at the Cannes Film Festival and Best First Feature (Under $500,000) at the Independent Spirit Awards, winning both.

Myrick has since returned to the director's seat for the indie horror feature *The Strand* (2005).

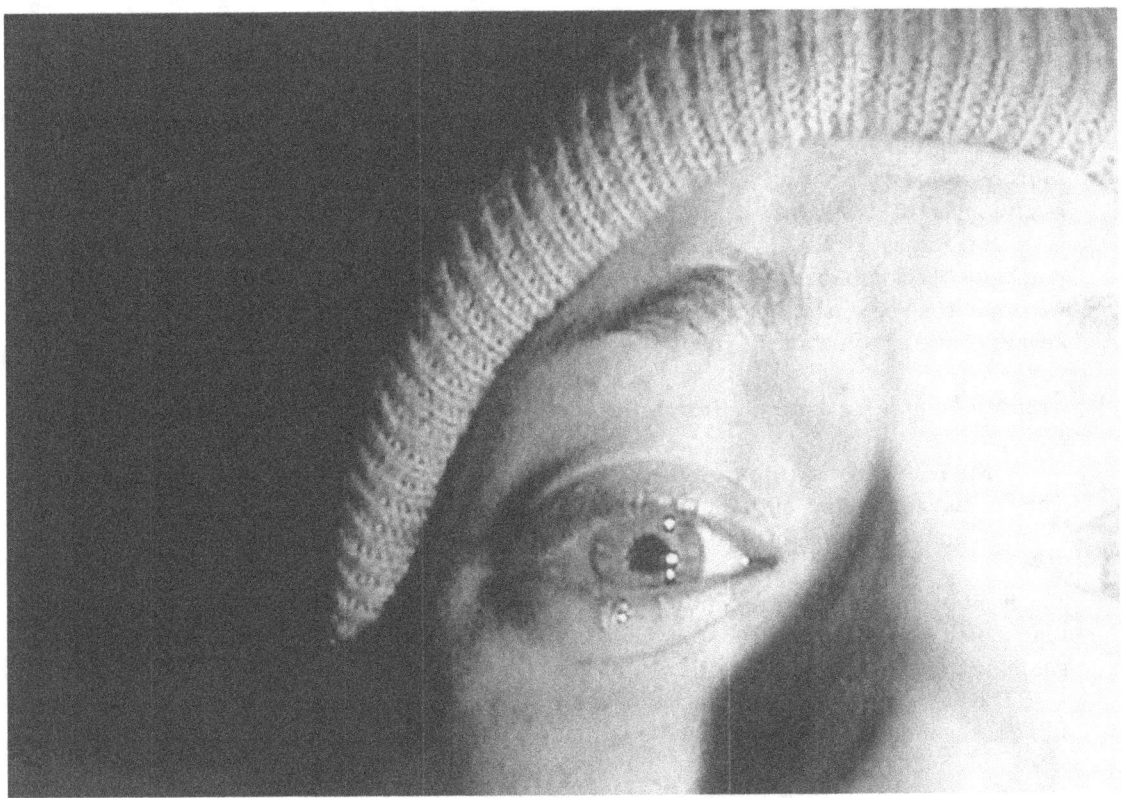

"I am so sorry," Heather Donahue tells the camera in this iconic scene from *The Blair Witch Project* (Artisan Entertainment, 1998).

Favorite Films: *The Omen* (1976), *The Exorcist* (1973), *The Shining* (1980), *The Amityville Horror* (1979), *It's Alive!* (1969), and *Henry: Portrait of a Serial Killer* (1986).

ANDREW RAUSCH: *The name of your production company is Haxan, which I'm guessing came from the classic Benjamin Christensen film of the same name?*

DANIEL MYRICK: *Witchcraft Through the Ages*, which was originally titled *Haxan* (1922). Yeah. It's a great film. It was originally shot in 1922, and was later—around '53 or so—remixed with [William] Burroughs' voice-over, with this great jazz-fusion mix soundtrack.

It seemed to have kind of inspired The Blair Witch Project *in that there's a scene in Haxan where there is a bundle of sticks—*

DM: Not really. The stick man thing, I'm not sure where that came from. It's something that we've seen probably throughout history. But really it was just an idea that I came up with early on. It was one of the earliest scene ideas that we had. I just thought it would be creepy as hell to kind of have the actors walking though the woods and they emerge and see these kind of humanoid icons hanging from the trees. I just thought it would be creepy. It really had no subtext or meaning beyond that.

What I was referring to in Haxan *was a scene in which there is a bundle of sticks with a severed human hand inside, which is pretty similar to the scene in* Blair Witch *where they find the human teeth wrapped in twigs.*

DM: I kind of remember that. Actually, our production designer came up with that, and I don't think he'd seen the film before that. It was just kind of coincidental.

I've got to admit that I didn't see The Blair Witch Project *until after all the hype. I didn't see it until it came out on video. Because of all the hype, I went into the film expecting it to not live up to its reputation. I personally thought it was brilliant. But once the film got so big, it began to receive some backlash. Did that surprise you?*

DM: [Sighs] Not really. It's just a part of doing business. It's a good problem to have, you know? Backlash exists because you're doing something right. It's just something you deal with, but it can be frustrating at times. If you let it really bother you, it'll drive you nuts. There's always gonna be somebody trying to knock it down.

I think a lot of it is the media. It seems like they kind of build up a film just to knock it down later.

DM: Yeah. That's kind of sad in a way. People don't really form their own opinions. They're just contingent on the current fashion or anti-fashions. You just kind of wish that people would learn to think for themselves.

You mentioned films like The Shining *and* The Exorcist *as being amongst your favorites. The* Blair Witch Project *has now been compared to some of those classic films. What is that like? That's got to be flattering.*

DM: Oh, it is! What can you say? To ever be mentioned in the same sentence as those films is beyond anything we ever expected.

Now there are tons of Blair Witch *parodies and rip-offs. Have you seen any of these?*

DM: Yeah, we've seen a few of them. We try to watch as many of them as we can.

What have your thoughts on them been so far?

DM: It's hard to say. We've seen some pretty bad ones. [Laughs] Those will remain nameless. *The Scooby Doo Project* is one of my favorites. The ESPN parody was good. I think one of my favorites was the parody in *Mad Magazine*. For me, I knew I had made it when our movie was in *Mad Magazine*. That was a staple of mine growing up. When you see a movie parodied in there, you know it's become a part of the pop culture consciousness. That was pretty cool.

I read about a new rip-off the other day that I found humorous. It was called The Erotic Witch Project *(1999), which is about a crew of filmmakers who end up having lesbian sex in the woods. [Laughs] And, of course, all that's found is the tape of their sexual escapades. Now you're even influencing softcore porn! What in the world are your thoughts on that?*

DM: [Laughs] Well, it's great! However you want to make the movies, come on and ride the bandwagon! It's just so funny to think about those guys out there in the woods shooting their porno movie and referencing our film! [Laughs again] We never had that much fun when we made ours, you know, but as long as *somebody's* having fun....

Now that you've given a lot of people nightmares with The Blair Witch Project, *I wondered what you consider to be the scariest film you've ever seen?*

DM: It's a tough call, but *The Exorcist* is definitely up there somewhere. *It's Alive!* is probably in the running somewhere, as well. But I was so young when I saw that. When you're young, things like that have such an impact on you. Those are probably a couple of films that had the biggest impact on me as far as the fear factor is concerned. There's also a little-known film called *The Legend of Boggy Creek* (1972), which was kind of inspirational to *Blair Witch*. It was about Bigfoot. That was probably one of the scariest movies of all time for me. It totally creeped me out. When I look back on it now, it looks pretty cheesy. But when you're a ten-year-old or whatever and you saw that film.... It just had a residual effect on me up until just recently when it finally subsided.

What has the phenomenal success of The Blair Witch Project *taught you about the film industry?*

DM: Well, it's definitely reaffirmed a lot of our fears. I don't think I'm as cynical about the film industry as a lot of people want to be because we came into this business with a commercial background. We had kind of a business sense already, so a lot of the things we're seeing now aren't really surprising us. They were half-expected. Nothing's really thrown us a curveball yet. We already expect people to kind of screw us over! [Laughs] We're kind of prepared for that when we see those signs. On the upside, we've met a lot of good people. We've met some fascinating, passion-filled, really driven people in all walks of the industry, whether they be executives or fellow filmmakers or whatever. So there are glimmers of hope wherever you look, and those are the people we try to associate ourselves with. Hopefully we can keep our feet on the ground with *Blair Witch* and continue to maintain good solid relationships with ourselves and whomever we get involved with in the future. You just have to sit through all of the bullshit, and there is a *lot* of bullshit out there. We're the flavor of the month right now, and everybody wants to do business with us, and we just have to kind of take that into consideration when anyone talks to us.

I hate to ask this because so much has already been made of it, but what is your take on the whole controversy surrounding The Blair Witch Project *and* The Last Broadcast *(1998)?* [Editor's note: directors Lance Weiler and Stefon Avalos had made public allegations that *The Blair Witch Project* was a direct rip-off of their film *The Last Broadcast*.]

DM: We're kind of baffled in a way as to why there's even a controversy. The *Last Broadcast* guys maintain that they came up with this idea first, and we're kind of baffled by that because if anyone was going to maintain who came up with this premise first it was *Cannibal Holocaust* [1979], which was an Italian movie out in the seventies and was banned from the United States. We didn't find out about that until Sundance, but this film was out long before our movies were. And with regards to us and *The Last Broadcast*, it's strictly a coincidence that there's even a similarity at all. We conceived our idea back in 1992. We had a broadcast on *Split Screen* in 1996. *The Last Broadcast* wasn't even in the public awareness until late 1997. I can understand them being frustrated, and I can understand their wanting to generate publicity for their movie in order to sell videos. I would probably be doing the same thing, but if you watch both movies, there's really no comparison. That's what we tell people....

Who came out first isn't the issue. I don't know when they came up with their idea, but I know when we came up with ours. Quite frankly, I don't care. There's a reason why we got into Sundance and they didn't. Make your own choice and make your own decision, but watch both movies and decide for yourself. I've met Lance and Stefon, and they were cool to me when I met them. If they have a problem out of frustration or whatever, that's their deal. It doesn't really affect us here. We're gonna continue making movies, and all you have to do is watch both films [to decide if plagiarism occurred].

It would be like Steven Spielberg being upset with Renny Harlin for making a shark movie! I mean, how many shark premises are out there? How many premises of kids getting lost in the woods can there be? Just move on with your lives.

Filmography for Daniel Myrick

1. *40 Miles Salvation* (1997) Co-D, Co-Sc, Ed
2. *Split Screen* (1997–98) D
3. *The Blair Witch Project* (1999) Co-D, Co-Sc, Ed
4. *Curse of the Blair Witch* (1999) [TV] Co-D & Co-Sc
5. *Sticks and Stones: Investigating the Blair Witch* (1999) Co-D, Co-Sc, A
6. *All Shook Up* (1999) Ed
7. *Blair Witch 2: Book of Shadows* (2000) P
8. *The Strand* (2005) D, Co-Sc, Cin, Ed, P
9. *Believers* (2007) D & Sc

Peter O'Fallon

After making a name for himself directing episodes of the popular television series *Thirtysomething* and *Northern Exposure*, Peter O'Fallon made his full-length directorial debut with the 1991 telefilm *Dead Silence*. After showcasing his considerable talent there, O'Fallon returned to series television, directing various episodes of *Party of Five*, *Profiler*, *American Gothic*, and *Northern Exposure*. In 1997, the Emmy-winning director teamed up with *Pulp Fiction* (1994) scribe Roger Avary for a television pilot titled *Odd Jobs*. That same year O'Fallon helmed a second pilot, *Prey* (1997). He then served as executive producer on the resulting series.

In 1998, O'Fallon made his feature directorial debut with the dark comedy *Suicide Kings*. Due largely to inadequate marketing on the part of Artisan Entertainment, the Christopher Walken–starrer came and went virtually unnoticed at the box office. It has been said that video is the savior of overlooked films, and certainly Peter O'Fallon is a believer; almost immediately after *Suicide Kings* hit the shelves of video stores, the film began to develop a rather substantial fan base.

In 2000, O'Fallon directed the television pilot *Mysterious Ways*, which he also wrote. This pilot then spawned a series, which he executive produced. That same year saw the release of O'Fallon's second feature film, *A Rumor of Angels* (2000), which he also wrote. The film starred Vanessa Redgrave, Ray Liotta, and Ron Livingston, and was based upon Grace Duffie Boylan's novel *My Son Liveth: Messages from a Soldier to His Mother*. Finally seeing this film made was a dream come true for O'Fallon, who had shepherded the project for more than a decade.

Favorite Films: *The Godfather* (1972), *Apocalypse Now* (1979), *Little Big Man* (1970), *Jeremiah Johnson* (1972), and *American Beauty* (1999).

ANDREW RAUSCH: *A lot of critics picked on you in their reviews of* Suicide Kings *because of your background in television. What are your thoughts on that?*
PETER O'FALLON: Myself, I think it's bullshit. If you look back at some of the all-time best filmmakers, like John Ford, you'll see it's the same thing. John Ford came from two-reelers first. So did most of the famous filmmakers of the forties, fifties, and sixties. George Cukor and a number of them — almost all of them — started with two-reelers, which were little thirty minute movies that they would make for the studios. Ford did somewhere around one hundred of them. I don't remember the exact number of them, but he did a tremendous number of them. What you do is learn your craft.

Hollywood is one of the few places where directing is an entry-level position. [Laughs] I think that's a bad thing. Peter Weir wrote this great thing I read about the Sundance-type movies, saying he thought there were some really great writers but there weren't very good directors. And if they spent a bit more time on their script and going through the process and then go out and get more experience, like in television or cable movies or whatever, they'd be better off. You have to learn your craft. It's an amazingly difficult craft because you have every discipline. A lot of people get lucky with one film, particularly a film of passion. The trick is to do it consistently. That's again one of my goals, like John Ford or one of those other filmmakers. John Ford's stuff was amazingly consistent over the years. He had a certain genre that he was better at than others, but the man was really an amazing director in his consistency. So having come from that idea, I started in commercials, originally for the money. There's a lot of money in commercials. Then when I came to Hollywood, my commercial reel was very well received and my agent asked me what I wanted to do. At the time I wanted to do the TV show *Thirtysomething* because I thought it was extremely well-done, which it was. I really wanted to go and learn there.

Filmmakers like Tony Scott, who came from a background in commercials, have constantly had to deal with that being thrown up in their faces. Because of your work in television, a lot of critics use that as a means to criticize your film work. Ironically, when these inexperienced "wunderkinds" emerge each year, no one ever questions their validity as a filmmaker. It almost seems as though you lose points for having experience.

PO: Exactly. It's a bizarre thing in Hollywood, and it shouldn't be. The reason is because Hollywood is ultimately obsessed with the newest, youngest, greatest thing.

Every six months there's another wunderkind who's hailed as being the next Kubrick.

PO: It's one of the reasons that [Steven] Spielberg is around. He started it, just as he started a lot of different things. Well, not just him.... These wunderkinds have been around forever. Orson Welles was a wunderkind. And that's good, but if you notice, most of them don't make it. If you really look back and take a look at the wunderkinds— with the exception

Director Peter O'Fallon sets up a scene with actors Trevor Morgan and Vanessa Redgrave on the set of *A Rumor of Angels* (Cinetel Films, 2000).

of Spielberg and maybe Lucas—most of them don't make it. They do one or two good movies, and then they fall away.

You mentioned Orson Welles, which brings me to a question. There are a couple of shots in Suicide Kings *in which the composition reminds me very much of shots from* Citizen Kane *(1941)—particularly where the kidnappers are surrounding Christopher Walken, and you see the design on the ceiling above them.*

PO: One of the reasons we shot it that way was because we shot with very wide lenses and we wanted to show all five or six characters at once. So we caught it "Rembrandts." One of the fascinating things that I found out when I was in film school was when we would watch [Alfred] Hitchcock movies our film professor would get into this whole thing about "What do you think Mr. Hitchcock meant here?" And I would always irritate him by raising my hand and saying, "I think he thought it looked good." [Laughs] And, being a director, that is a lot of it. The ceiling was overwhelming and I wanted to show affluence. I wanted to show that these kids were actually in over their heads, that they were actually little kids in a big background. All those things are subtle, but it also looked good.

The balance of the five figures onscreen looked very impressive. It's a pretty shot.

PO: Well, almost every shot we caught it Rembrandts, which goes back to the Dutch Masters. You know the Dutch Master cigars? It means it's half-lit. Five guys sitting around at different levels.

A French advertisement for Peter O'Fallon's crime thriller *Suicide Kings* (Artisan Entertainment, 1998).

You managed to pull some really great performances from the actors in that film. How do you personally approach working with actors?

PO: Well, it depends on which process. If you have a star, it's a different process. If you get a cast, it's a better process because you can get more accurate about exactly what you want, as opposed to shaping a role for a certain star. Denis Leary's a great example. He was supposed to have a very small part, and we shot him for eight days. Denis Leary is known for, and is notorious for, ad-libbing. I love that, myself. I enjoy it tremendously. As I kept telling him, my job was to keep him in the right area code. "We're talking about New York here, Denis, not L.A." [Laughs]

I tend to let actors have a lot of room. I shoot a lot of film. I do a lot of on-camera direction. Sometimes to bump them, sometimes to bump them back. It takes a lot of actors a while to get used to it. Johnny Galecki didn't like it at all at first. But then he got used to it. Galecki's character had to be just perfect tone-wise or else he was an obnoxious jerk or a wimp. So it was pretty important. I kept telling him he had a two or three-degree window and everybody else had twenty degrees.

You talked about Denis Leary doing a lot of improv. The line "Me and Mr. Mantle are gonna pay you a visit, my friend" sounds a lot like a Leary line. That and the line he has where he asks the guys if rap music drove them to kidnap Walken's character.

PO: Yeah, both of those were his. [Laughs] Leary riffs. When he gets going, he's fucking hilarious. The whole boot thing was his. None of that was scripted. That started out by my wanting the character Lono to wear big black cowboy boots, and Denis came on the set and, being an Irishman like myself, said, "I'm not wearing any fucking cowboy boots!" [Laughs] And he says, "Let me tell you about acting. Acting is comfort and if I'm not comfortable, I can't act." And he was being facetious and a little bit funny, but a little bit serious. So I said, "Let me tell you about directing. Directing is about power and you're gonna wear the boots." [Laughs] So it became this running gag that every time I saw him he would always ask the operator, "Are you seeing the fucking boots?" Otherwise he would take them off. So I would always make sure that even the shots in the car would start on the boots. So one day he was sitting there and he was riffing on the boots, so I came on the walkie-talkie and I said, "That's funny." He goes, "I'll tell you what's fucking funny. Shut up and roll the camera." That's when he hit this whole thing about the boots.

You know, I think it's a shame the film doesn't get more recognition. The thing that's amazing about the film is that it's really come around. It's doing extremely well for me now. A year-and-a-half later, it's actually become very well-respected. I mean, we got great reviews. Of course, we got a couple of people who said "TV background," and there were a couple of people who called me a Quentin Tarantino wannabe, which really pissed me off because I did everything in my power to avoid making a Tarantino film. God bless Quentin, but there's no point to his movies. They're interesting and they're fascinating, but what was *Pulp Fiction* (1994) really about? Nothing! [Laughs] It's like a really good two-hour *Seinfeld*. It's a funny, funny movie with incredible dialogue, and a really hard thing to pull off by the way — having a movie with very little plot and all these characters.

Initially I thought the script was quite Tarantinoesque. Of course, that idea came from those long comical monologues of Leary's. However, now that you've told me that Leary just improvised all that, and it wasn't scripted, it makes sense.

PO: Well, it's funny dialogue in the middle of a very serious scene. The big joke we had was that you can't have two men talking in a car anymore, or you're Quentin Tarantino! [Laughs] So part of it is that, and part of it is the genre. I understand the point, but for me as a filmmaker, it was very frustrating because that was far from what I wanted it to be.

A lot of people seem to forget that this is a genre that was around long before Quentin Tarantino was even born.

PO: Well, Quentin ripped it! [Laughs] On the other hand, Roger Avary, as you know, is a good friend of mine.... The *Pulp Fiction* shadow falls on a lot of people. A lot of people say it was one of the greatest films ever for the independent world. In my opinion, it was actually one of the worst things that's ever happened to independent filmmaking — in the same way that *Star Wars* [1977] and *Jaws* [1975] were bad for Hollywood. They were good on one hand, but on the other it turned into this blockbuster mentality which is exactly what happened to the independent world with *Pulp Fiction*. Once it hit the $100 million mark, all of us in the independent world began being compared to Quentin.

You shot a couple of different endings for Suicide Kings. *Why did you do that, and what factors led to the decision to go with the ending you chose?*

PO: The initial reason was because I wanted it to end happily. [Laughs] The original script wasn't this way, but I wanted to have it where the two people got away with it. They got away with it because Walken had a tender spot for women. We set up this whole thing with Laura San Giacomo, who ended up being cut way down in the film, which was to show that he had a soft spot for women. Especially women who stand up for themselves and are smart. At the end she looks at Walken and he says, "Whoa!" in that Chris Walken way, and says, "This was your idea, wasn't it?" And she says yes very confidently, knowing she's going to be shot for saying yes. Then Walken turns to Sean and says, "You were right about her" and lets them go.

On paper, it sounded great. [Laughs] It's just that ultimately, you want them to get their just desserts. When I finally cut this last version, which is the version that ended up being in the movie, it suddenly all worked for me, and made a lot more sense. It was a story about people who were stupid from the beginning, and basically end up committing suicide.

The movie almost seems to make a statement about a lack of honor among the wealthy, and the code of honor which is upheld by the gangsters.

PO: Yeah, but it's not necessarily the wealthy. The wealthy are a metaphor for us. The idea is that groups of people, even close friends, will sell their souls. The fable in the movie is that the bad guys are good because they have a code. They try to stick by that code, and they can trust one another when no one else can.

FILMOGRAPHY FOR PETER O'FALLON

1. *Thirtysomething* (1987) D
2. *Northern Exposure* (1990) D
3. *Dead Silence* (1991) [TV] D
4. *Party of Five* (1994) D
5. *American Gothic* (1995) D
6. *Profiler* (1996) D
7. *Suicide Kings* (1997) D
8. *Prey* (1998) D & Ex-P
9. *Cupid* (1998) D
10. *Rumor of Angels* (2000) D, Sc, P
11. *Mysterious Ways* (2000) D, Sc, Ex-P
12. *The Twilight Zone* (2002) D
13. *MDs* [episode: "Reversal of Fortune"] (2002) D
14. *That Was Then* (2002) D
15. *Kingpin* (2003) D
16. *Wonderfalls* (2003) D
17. *Las Vegas* [episodes: various] (2004) D
18. *House* [episodes: various] (2004–2005) D
19. *Ghost Whisperer* [episode: "Lost Boys"] (2005) D
20. *Blade* (2006) D
21. *Eureka* (2006) D

Alexander Payne

After graduating from Stanford University, where he double-majored in literature and history, Alexander Payne attended UCLA Film School. His 1990 thesis film, *The Passion of Martin*, secured him a blind deal with Universal as both a writer and director. In 1994, Payne directed his studio debut, *Citizen Ruth*. The controversial film, which he co-wrote with frequent collaborator Jim Taylor, satirized America's ever-raging abortion debate.

In 1999, Payne's second big-league offering, an adaptation of Tom Perrotta's novel *Election*, was showered with critical praise. The scathingly-funny black comedy quickly made a name for both Payne and co-writer Taylor as screenwriters with a wealth of talent and a unique perspective. The film also established Payne as one the most exciting young filmmakers in Hollywood. For their work on *Election*, Payne and Taylor received many accolades, including an Oscar nomination and an impressive three Independent Spirit Awards. After *Election*'s "hat trick" at the Spirit Awards, Payne's stock began to soar. So much so, in fact, that the Omaha, Nebraska, native was embarrassed to find himself named to *People*'s "100 Most Eligible Bachelors" list.

Next, Payne helmed the critically-acclaimed Jack Nicholson–starrer *About Schmidt* (2002). In 2004, Payne continued his winning ways with *Sideways*, for which he received an Oscar nomination for Best Director and took home an Oscar for Best Adapted Screenplay. He then co-directed the anthology film *Paris, je t'aime* (2006).

In addition to his work as a director, Payne has done writing-for-hire work on *Meet the Parents* (2000) and *Jurassic Park III* (2001). He has also served as producer on the films *The Assassination of Richard Nixon* (2004) and *Gray Matters* (2005).

Favorite Films: "Today, certainly in no particular order, these come to mind: *Viridiana* [1961], *The Seven Samurai* [1954], *The Godfather Part II* [1974], *The Wild Bunch* [1969], *The Good, the Bad, and the Ugly* [1966], *The Treasure of the Sierra Madre* [1948], *La Notte* [1960], *City Lights* [1931], *Seconds* [1966], and *McCabe & Mrs. Miller* [1971]."

ANDREW RAUSCH: *Who would you say have been your biggest influences?*

ALEXANDER PAYNE: I feel I've been influenced as a human being by so many films—possibly every film I've ever seen. It's difficult to say what filmmakers have a direct influence on one's work, since in the moment of making a film, you're completely on your own; it's you, the camera, and the actors. No "great master" is going to help you. You're like an infantryman. You've gone through basic training and perhaps even received awards for marksmanship, but there you are on the battlefield, and they're shooting at you. But possibly this question is better than the previous question regarding my favorite films, since I think more often of directors' bodies of work that I admire, rather than of individual films. I can say that I find

Actress Reese Witherspoon and director Alex Payne on the set of the acclaimed film *Election* (Paramount Pictures, 1998).

inspiration both in life and film from certain directors whose bodies of work reflect a deep and ferocious humanist exploration of self and world. But then, it's like asking me who my favorite novelists or painters are, since I feel that my work is influenced not only by films I've seen, but also books I've read, art I admire, and people I've known.

I admire many, many directors. But for your purposes, I'll limit it to six: Akira Kurosawa, Luis Bunuel, Stanley Kubrick, Michelangelo Antonioni, Billy Wilder, and Anthony Mann. But that's just the tip of the iceberg. You'll notice, for example, as I just have, that I list Wilder as one of my favorite directors, yet not a single film of his appeared on my "top twelve" list of the day. I suppose that's because I admire his body of work more than any one particular film. Similarly, I see Anthony Mann's films over and over again — his Westerns above all — and I could have put *The Man from Laramie* (1955) on this list to reflect that, but it's more his work in full that I adore.

Having said that, I guess there are some individual films I admire more than the director's opus. *Room at the Top* is a near-perfect film, but I can't say that I'm a huge Jack Clayton fan. But that film is a powerful and exquisite tragedy in a way that relates to the Greeks and to all of human experience.

I've also just realized that five of the films on my list are films about men on a quest for futile, questionable, or ignoble goals. One of those films on my list is, I feel, the more rarified expression of that director's work, and, unlike what I did with Anthony Mann, I did instinctively look to include one — *La notte*. In my twenties, I had long love affairs with Kurosawa, seeing all of his films at least twice, except for one (*The Idiot* [1951], which I've still never seen, although I'll mention that I've seen *The Seven Samurai* at least forty times), and with Bunuel, again seeing all of his films. Don't get me wrong — there are many directors whose oeuvres I've seen in their entirety, but there are salient ones who dominated my thoughts over periods.

In my thirties, I've had a long love affair with Antonioni, and I've seen all of his films except one—*Il Grido* [1957]. No, make that two. I didn't see his short about returning to Ischia, the island where *L'Avventura* [1960] was shot. What is it about Antonioni? The elusive and oneiric quality of his narratives, the quietly-striking widescreen compositions, the beautiful actors, the deep sense of shattered romanticism? People often apply the word "alienation," with a sense of respect, to his work, but I see so much love in his films—love of experience, of film, of women, of literature, of observing people, and of course the love of love, the basic need of the human heart, even if it is rarely attained.

Anyway, this is all a long-winded way of saying that I mention *La Notte* as the film of his that comes first to mind, since I think it summarizes a lot of what I love in his work. And that letter that Jeanne Moreau reads at the end....

Speaking of endings, I include *City Lights* on this list not because it's Chaplin's best film, but rather specifically because of its ending, which is one of the purest achievements ever of cinematic beauty. Great endings are like a needle perfectly supporting an immense balancing pyramid. Examples of this are *I Am a Fugitive from a Chain Gang* [1932], *The Bicycle Thief* [1948], and *The Godfather Part II*. *The Iron Giant* [1999] almost got there.

I'll add that *The Good, the Bad, and the Ugly*, which I've also seen at least thirty or forty times, has one of the greatest performances ever in a film. Eli Wallach's Tuco, rarely mentioned, has its place in my book with the most accomplished acting ever in the cinema, a perfect screen performance. I'd say it's right up there with Marlon Brando in *Last Tango in Paris* [1972], Walter Huston in *The Treasure of the Sierra Madre*, Robert Ryan in *Clash by Night* [1952], and Anna Magnani in everything.

Many of your favorite films are foreign films. I was wondering if that's any kind of statement on American cinema?

AP: No. There are many American films I love. When I'm asked what my favorite films are, I don't even think in terms of American and foreign. These are just films that I've seen, regardless of their origin. I've just seen a lot of films from a lot of different countries. As a film viewer, there's no reason why I should give primacy to American films. I like all films.

Are there any contemporary films that excite you?

AP: At the Independent Spirit Awards I said something to the effect that American cinema now can allow auteurist cinema within the commercial realm like it was in the seventies. In that respect, I thought *Erin Brockovich* [2000] was a very good commercial film. In the seventies, you had thrillers like that by directors like Alan Pakula, Martin Ritt, and Mike Nichols. You had really great directors making intelligent thrillers which met commercial needs. They hit the commercial marks, but were realistic and gave the audience credit for being intelligent. And we have an opportunity now to have auteurist cinema like that again.

It was a time when commercial cinema was being given over to auteurs. Costs were not as prohibitive, and films were allowed to be more human. It wasn't just escapism. We need a mirror of our society, and cinema after that ceased to be a mirror and became exclusively an escapism. Cinema is so crucially important for a culture. We seek out art to see reflections of ourselves. And I think that now we are in need of that again. We never stopped needing it, but right now I think there are opportunities for a more humanist cinema in America.

What are your thoughts on Election's *recent Academy Award nomination?*

AP: It's fun stuff and it's for entertainment purposes only. It doesn't make your writing any easier. It maybe makes some of the struggles to get your films made a little easier. Maybe

I will now be able to struggle a little bit less, but it doesn't change how difficult the work is. That kind of stuff is exhilarating, but it isn't as exhilarating as actually making a film.

Election is interesting because, despite its misleading marketing campaign, which promoted it as being somewhat of a teen movie, it's actually a very dark adult-themed film.

AP: Well, I certainly didn't set out to make a high school movie. I set out to make an adult-themed movie, which just happens to be set in a high school. I think the marketing department at Paramount had a challenge to let adults know that this movie, set in a high school, is actually an adult movie, and vice-versa, to reel in kids to see something which was actually an adult theme. It was a tough one. It needed word of mouth and awareness that it's actually a good movie to kind of sink in.

What are your thoughts on all of these "teen angst" films?

AP: I don't see them, and I have no interest in them. [Laughs] I'm completely uninterested in high school movies unless it's something like *Carrie* (1976) or *Fast Times at Ridgemont High* (1982). Those are good movies. Otherwise, I'm just not interested. All of these things that came out this year, like *American Pie* (1999). I didn't even see it.

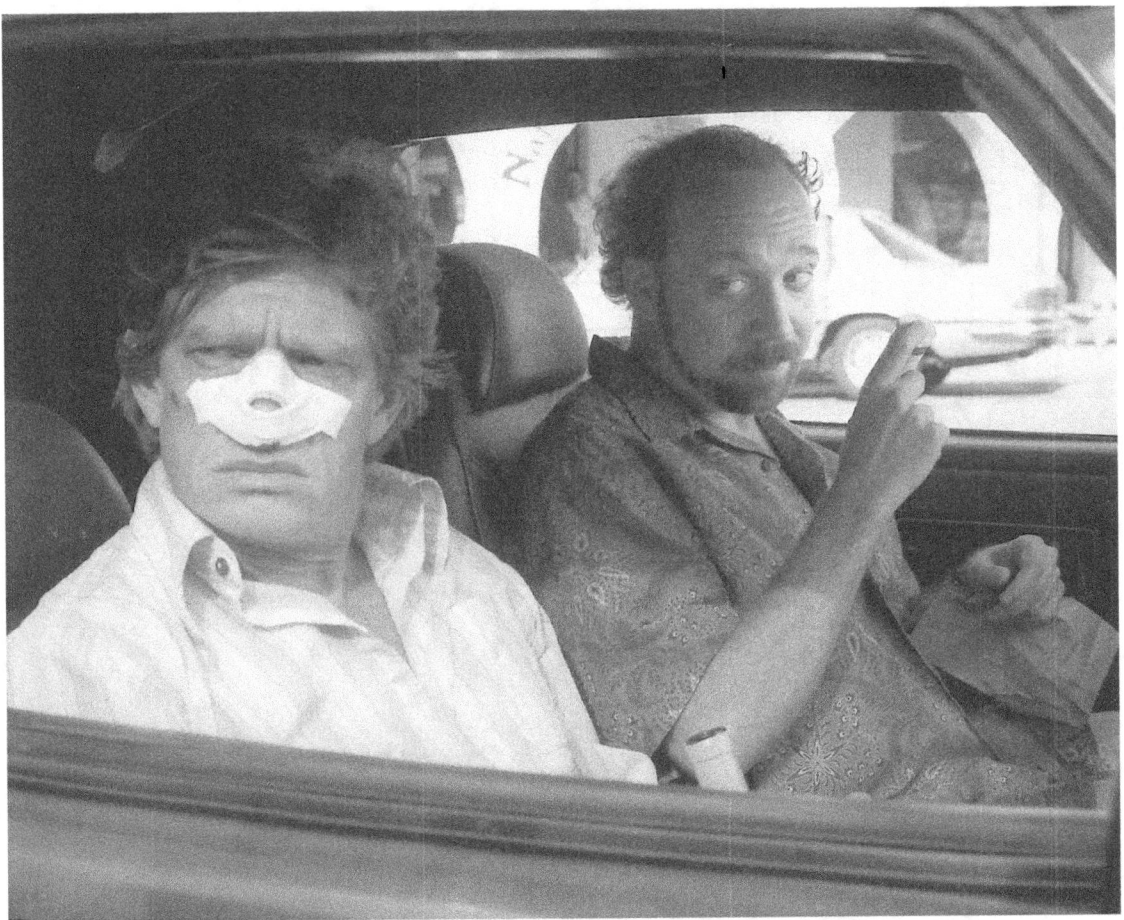

Jack (Thomas Haden Church) and Miles (Paul Giamatti) are old friends reuniting for one last road trip before Jack's wedding in *Sideways* (20th Century–Fox, 2004).

Tracy Flick is, of course, the overachieving character from Election *played by Reese Witherspoon. Did you go to school with anyone like Tracy?*

AP: I'm sure I did, but my high school was an all boys Jesuit! [Laughs] But ambition is everywhere. I get asked this all the time, and I think we all know someone like Tracy Flick.

Where would you like to be ten years from now?

AP: Still making movies. I hope that within that time I might have learned how to make a really good movie. I'd like to make at least one really good movie. And I'm still learning. I'm always a student of film. Right now I've made just two feature films, but I think that they are minor works, and I'm still just trying to figure it all out.

What advice would you give to aspiring filmmakers?

AP: I can only think of what Luis Bunuel said, which was about style: "I can say nothing because everyone figures out his or her own film style. The only thing is that the work has to be sincere, and you can't do anything you don't believe in." Once you do that, you're lost.

Filmography for Alexander Payne

1. *The Passion of Martin* (1991) D & Sc
2. *Inside Out* (1992) D & Sc
3. *Citizen Ruth* (1996) D & Co-Sc
4. *Election* (1999) D & Co-Sc
5. *Meet the Parents* (2000) Un Sc
6. *Jurassic Park III* (2001) Co-Sc
7. *About Schmidt* (2002) D & Co-Sc
8. *The Assassination of Richard Nixon* (2004) Ex-P
9. *Sideways* (2004) D & Co-Sc
10. *Gray Matters* (2005) Ex-P
11. *Paris, je t'aime* (2006) Co-D
12. *I Now Pronounce You Chuck and Larry* (2007) Co-Sc

D.A. Pennebaker

D.A. Pennebaker fashioned his first film in 1953 with the short *Daybreak Express*, in which he married the sounds of Duke Ellington to footage taken from a moving subway car. He then made a number of short films before constructing his first feature length documentary, *Opening in Moscow* (1959). In 1959, Pennebaker joined a filmmaking collective known as Drew Associates who were dedicated to furthering the use of film in journalism. With fellow filmmakers Albert and David Maysles, Richard Leacock, and Robert Drew, Pennebaker helped to pioneer the revolutionary style of filmmaking known as *cinema verité*. (A 16mm synchronized camera invented by Pennebaker and Leacock would be one of the most important steps in defining this school of filmmaking.) Pennebaker then served as editor and sound recordist on *Primary* (1960), which focused on the Democratic Presidential Primary in Wisconsin. In 1963, Pennebaker co-directed *Crisis* (with Leacock and Drew), which documented the desegregation of the University of Alabama.

Pennebaker next turned his camera on pop icon Bob Dylan for his fly-on-the-wall account of the singer's tour of England, *Don't Look Back* (1967). The film, which did tremendous box-office business for a documentary, is often credited as being the first rock documentary. *San Francisco Examiner* critic Craig Marine says *Don't Look Back* is "easily one of the best documentaries on any subject ever made. It is also one of the most cinematically influential." Pennebaker then directed another groundbreaking music-oriented film, *Monterey Pop* (1968), which is credited as being the first concert film. That same year, Pennebaker joined forces with novelist-turned-director Norman Mailer for *Wild 90* (1968). (Pennebaker later served as cinematographer for two more Mailer-helmed fiascoes, *Beyond the Law*, 1968, and *Maidstone*, 1970.) Pennebaker then agreed to collaborate once again with Bob Dylan on the singer's own film, *Eat the Document* (1972). He served as an editor and cinematographer on the legendary project, which remains unreleased today. Next, Pennebaker shot and co-directed *One P.M.* (1972) with legendary French New Wave auteur Jean-Luc Godard.

Other Pennebaker-helmed projects include *John Lennon and the Plastic Ono Band: Live Peace in Toronto* (1969), *Company* (1970), *Ziggy Stardust and the Spiders from Mars* (1973), *The Energy War* (1977), *Town Bloody Hall* (1979), *Jimi Plays Monterey* (1986), and *101* (1989). In 1993, Pennebaker and his wife Chris Hegedus directed *The War Room*, which offered a behind-the-scenes look at Bill Clinton's Presidential campaign. This insightful documentary was critically lauded, and Pennebaker received his first Oscar nomination for his efforts. Pennebaker has since directed or co-directed a number of films, including *Searching for Jimi Hendrix* (1999), *Down from the Mountain* (2000), and *Moon Over Broadway* (1997), which the *New York Times* cited as the Best Documentary of the Year. Pennebaker also served as a producer and second unit director on the D.W. Griffith Award–winning film *Startup.com* (2001).

Favorite Films: The films of directors René Clair, Michael Powell, Robert Flaherty, Federico Fellini, Roberto Rossellini, Jean-Luc Godard.

ANDREW RAUSCH: *Tell me about your collaboration with Jean-Luc Godard, and how his film* One A.M. *ultimately became your film* One P.M.

D.A. PENNEBAKER: It started with my running into Godard at the Cinematheque in Paris, and we were talking about doing a project together. I suggested the idea that he go down and rig up a small village or town somewhere, and then we would appear without any idea of what he had in mind. The idea here was that things would happen, and the question was whether or not we could film this and capture the story in a film without knowing in advance what Godard had planned. It would be like a newsreel of a secret plan or something. [Laughs] And he thought that was interesting, but of course nobody wanted to put up any money for it, so it never got anywhere.

Then PBS decided they wanted to do something with Godard. We then came up with this idea of having Godard come and then two of us would work as his cameramen. How he would work wasn't really specified. It would be kind of loose and not really spelled out with any kind of script or anything. But he had a plan, and that was that we would shoot each scene

D.A. Pennebaker and rock legend Bo Diddley during filming of Pennebaker's *Sweet Toronto* (The Douglas Corporation, 1988).

with a four-hundred-foot roll complete; we would go right through the scene to the end on a single roll without stopping shooting. Then he would put all of these reels together, and that would be the film. At least that was the theory.

And then he got kind of sidetracked by *Wind from the East* [1970], and he either didn't have time or just lost interest in editing all of this material that we'd shot. So, I had a contract with PBS to deliver the film, so I had to finish it. So it started as *One A.M.*, which sort of loosely was *One American Movie*, and then it became *One P.M.* [Editor's note: *One Pennebaker Movie*.]

Your fellow cinema verité practitioners the Maysles brothers chose to have someone else edit their work so they could remain completely objective. You edit your own films. Isn't it a bit unrealistic and idealistic to believe that a film can ever be one-hundred-percent objective?

DAP: Well, I never really felt that was their true reasoning for not editing. [Laughs] Al doesn't edit because he simply refuses to edit. He can't do it. He's a cameraman, and an extremely good one. I've used him myself on several occasions, and I love him dearly. David did do some editing, but he worked with a number of people who came in and sort of took Al's work and made a film out of it. I think if fairly smart people who have some filmmaking talent perch on a film long enough, they'll finally figure out what it should be. As far as we're concerned — since there are so few of us — we're always trying to keep things really lean and not get into elaborations or expensive solutions. I think the people who shoot the film should edit it. They're the ones who at least know what they think happened, and that's probably as close as you're ever going to get to how the film should go. Whether in fact what they saw was not the big picture is really not that important. I don't think anybody ever really sees the big picture. I doubt that in our natural lives very many of the people responsible for what we do ever see more than a certain slant of any given thing. That's just the way things are. I think in the end the film should be what the filmmakers want it to be. And if they get something wrong, there are ways of checking it. We always screen it for the people we've filmed. I'm not talking about the things that embarrass them; they have to learn to live with that. And they do. They never change that. But if we have something happening at one time, and it really happened at another time, they can point it out and we'll correct it. We don't want to have something be wrong, even if we may think that it doesn't make a big difference in what the film's about. And most viewers will never know this. But since it is history, I feel a little like Herodotus; I want to know how many men there were in the Xerxes' armies!

In the end, I think it's a mistake to have someone else come in who didn't take part in the ongoing process of shooting the film and ask them to look at it and come up with an objective view.

You worked on a couple of films with Norman Mailer. What were those collaborations like?

DAP: They were interesting. Norman was a certain kind of person and a very good writer. He worked hard, you know? He was *not* a lazy writer. He could sit down and really push himself to write something. I thought at the time — and I thought this with Bob Dylan, as well — that if you could get him to sit down and do the work of making a film ... to sit down and edit it the way he might write a novel, that would be an interesting type of filmmaking. Well, I've now abandoned that course of thinking! [Laughs] It's too hard for them in the sense that they know they could — in that same span of time — turn out something worth $100,000. And the film — even if they do it really well — might not earn a cent. I think the economics of it makes them very unwilling to cast themselves into that role.

On the last film [*Maidstone*], Norman did finally spend a lot more time on it than he'd expected to. He did change what would have been a lot of easy decisions into a lot of hard ones. Unfortunately, I think it's going to take many years for people to kind of uncover the film. It's got some interesting things in it. It's fascinating because the leading actor, in a sense, tried to take the film hostage. And I know of only one Hollywood film where this happened — where the one person the film really couldn't be without said, "You're going to do it my way, or it's not going to get finished." And they had to kind of give way to it.

I understand that Mailer bit part of Rip Torn's ear off while filming that. What happened?
DAP: Rip was playing his own game there. Rip is a real soldier. He commits to the battle, he commits to the side, and nothing's going to sway him. *Maidstone* was about a film director who decides to run for President, and there's kind of a terrorist aspect throughout the film; there are a lot of people running around trying to kill him.

Norman announced that the film shoot was over. He had a big party out on Gardner's Island, and everybody came out to have a good time and get drunk. And Norman gave a speech thanking everyone for helping out, and informing them how smart a film it was going to be, and that it would really look wonderful. And while he was congratulating himself, Rip was wandering around. I didn't know what he was up to. He and a friend were carrying around a big hammer. I don't know why, but I had a camera and I had film in it. I really don't know why because I knew the film was over, and I was ready to go home. But I followed him around throughout much of the morning. And when Rip came upon Norman and his wife, he did this attack. As I said, the film was about someone trying to assassinate this man. Rip's reasoning was that it had to go beyond the reaches of just saying, "Okay, the film's all shot." It had to actually go as far as that attack. It was like a terrorist plan, really. Rip came up with a hammer, and he hadn't bothered to tell Norman what he was up to. He hadn't told me, either, so I'm still not sure how I knew to film this; it's always been a mystery to me. He hit him in the head with the hammer and they engaged in a struggle. Norman didn't know what the hell was going on. He thought Rip had lost his mind! [Laughs] His wife, Beverly, and his children were all screaming. And Norman bit his ear off. I was busy pulling focus there as if it were part of the film.

I guess I knew in some way subconsciously that this *was* part of the film. But there was no reason for me to think that. Norman didn't think that. Later, he was not even going to put it in the film. But, over time, he came to see that it was an absolutely crucial part of the film and that without it, the film was just pastiche and kind of a conceit on his part. In this case, what Rip did kind of took the film hostage. He had to do what he did, even though it wasn't part of any script or original concept of the film.

You frequently collaborate with your wife, Chris Hegedus. In any collaborative process, there are almost always a few disagreements. Do these collaborative squabbles ever carry over to your home life once the cameras are turned off?
DAP: When we work together on a film, we're partners. We're no longer man and wife. Maybe that's a fine distinction, but I know that as a husband I have certain responsibilities at home. When we're doing a film, the responsibilities are very particular and individual. You're working at a high creative speed. You're coming up with ideas, and they're getting rejected, and you know, it smarts a little. No one is eager to have their ideas turned down. On the other hand, you have to be open when someone else's ideas really seem to work. You have to form an attitude that this is an alliance, and that sometimes we're going to disagree and I'm really going to feel like crowning you, you know? [Laughs] But I also have to be open to whatever makes the film work better. In the end, the idea is king, and not any one person.

Denny Doherty of the Mamas and Papas performs in the concert film *Monterey Pop* (Leacock-Pennebaker, 1968).

Filmography for D.A. Pennebaker

1. *Daybreak Express* (1953) D & Cin
2. *Baby* (1954) D & Cin
3. *Brussels Loops* (1957) D & Cin
4. *Opening in Moscow* (1959) D & Cin
5. *Breaking It Up at the Museum* (1960) Co-D & Cin
6. *Yanki No!* (1960) Cin
7. *Primary* (1960) Ed & SED
8. *Mr. Pearson* (1962) Cin
9. *Crisis* (1963) Co-D
10. *Jingle Bells* (1964) Co-D & Cin
11. *Lambert, Hendricks & Co.* (1964) D & Cin
12. *You're Nobody Till Somebody Loves You* (1964) D & Cin
13. *Hier Strauss* (1965) D & Cin
14. *Don't Look Back* (1967) D, Sc, Cin, Ed
15. *Monterey Pop* (1968) D & Cin
16. *Beyond the Law* (1968) Cin
17. *Rainforest* (1968) Co-D & Cin
18. *Wild 90* (1968) Sc, A, Cin
19. *Keep on Rockin'* (1969) D, P, Cin
20. *Jerry Lee Lewis: The Story of Rock & Roll* (1969) D & Cin
21. *Alice Cooper* (1970) D & Cin
22. *Company* (1970) D & Cin
23. *Maidstone* (1970) Cin
24. *Eat the Document* (1972) Cin & Ed
25. *One P.M.* (1972) Co-D, Sc, P, Cin, Ed
26. *Ziggy Stardust and the Spiders from Mars* (1973) D & Cin
27. *The Energy War* (1977) Co-D & Cin
28. *Town Bloody Hall* (1979) Co-D, P, Cin
29. *Elliot Carter at Buffalo* (1980) Co-D & Cin
30. *DeLorean* (1981) Co-D & Cin
31. *Dance Black America* (1983) Co-D
32. *Rockaby* (1983) Co-D, Cin, Ed, SED
33. *Jimi Plays Monterey* (1986) Co-D, Cin, Ed
34. *Shake!: Otis at Monterey* (1987) Co-D & Cin
35. *Suzanne Vega* (1987) Co-D & Cin
36. *From Pole to Equator* (1987) Ed
37. *Sweet Toronto* (1988) D & Cin
38. *101* (1989) Co-D & Ed
39. *Jimi Hendrix* (1989) D & Cin
40. *Jerry Lee Lewis* (1990) Co-D & Cin
41. *Comin' Home* (1991) Co-D & Cin
42. *Little Richard* (1991) Co-D & Cin
43. *The Music Tells You* (1992) Co-D & Cin
44. *The War Room* (1993) Co-D, Cin, Ed
45. *Woodstock Diary* (1994) [TV] D & Cin
46. *Kleine Zeit* (1996) D & Cin
47. *Moon Over Broadway* (1997) Co-D, Cin, Ed
48. *Sessions at 54th* (1997) Cin
49. *Victoria Williams: Happy Come Home* (1997) Co-D & Cin
50. *Bessie* (1998) Co-D & Cin
51. *Depeche Mode: The Videos 86–98* [video: "Everything Counts"] (1998) D
52. *Searching for Jimi Hendrix* (1999) [TV] Co-D, Cin, Ed
53. *Down from the Mountain* (2000) Co-D, Cin, Ed
54. *Startup.com* (2001) P & SUD
55. *Only the Strong Survive* (2002) D, Cin, Ed
56. *The Best of Bowie* (2002) Co-D & Cin
57. *The Cutman* (2003) Ex-P
58. *Assume the Position with Mr. Wuhl* (2006) [TV] D
59. *Al Franken: God Spoke* (2006) Ex-P
60. *Addiction* (2007) Co-D

Michael Radford

Born in New Dehli, India, the son of a British officer and an Austrian mother, Michael Radford attended Worcester College, Oxford, where he studied to become an educator. After instructing for several years in Edinburgh, Radford applied to, and was accepted by, the National Film School. After graduating in 1974, Radford directed a number of documentaries, including *The Last Stronghold of the Pure Gospel* (1977) and *The Madonna and the Volcano* (1976), which took top honors at the 1976 Nyon Documentary Film Festival. In 1980, Radford crafted his first feature film, *The White Bird Passes*. However, it was his second feature, *Another Time, Another Place* (1983), which launched his career. The following year, Radford directed the critically-acclaimed adaptation of George Orwell's *1984* (1984). The film, which featured actors Richard Burton and John Hurt, won Radford the British Film Award for Best Director, as well as the prestigious Francois Truffaut Award. Although his next film, *White Mischief* (1987), was a commercial failure in its theatrical release, it has since gained cult status on video.

In 1994, Radford helmed *Il Postino*, the first Italian film ever made by an Englishman. The film became the highest grossing foreign language film in the history of cinema (although it has since been surpassed by *Life Is Beautiful*, 2000). The critically-acclaimed film received more than thirty-five international awards and was nominated for five Oscars, including Best Director and Best Screenplay nods for Radford. The filmmaker has since directed the romantic thriller *B. Monkey* (1998) and the groundbreaking improvisational film *Dancing at the Blue Iguana* (2000), starring Daryl Hannah, Jennifer Tilly, and Elias Koteas. Radford's most recent directorial outing was the impressive adaptation of William Shakespeare's *The Merchant of Venice* (2005), starring Al Pacino, Joseph Fiennes, and Jeremy Irons.

Favorite Films: *The Gospel According to St. Matthew* [1964], *Fat City* [1972], *Kagemusha* [1980], *Chinatown* [1974], *Shame* [1968], *The Double Life of Veronique* [1991], and *Contempt* [1963].

ANDREW RAUSCH: *You once observed, "The eyes are the most important thing in cinema." Could you elaborate on that?*

MICHAEL RADFORD: Well, Peter Brook says the theater is an exterior space where you can, in fact, create anything. An actor can walk into a black room and say, "Here is Russia...," and immediately you are in Russia. The cinema is more of a paradox because it is fundamentally an interior space. It's more about what is unsaid that determines things because it's such a concrete medium. I think if you look into an actor's eyes, the great ones are able to give you an interior life which needs no explanation. It's that interior life that informs the movie, and then the exterior of the movie becomes an expression, if you like, a metaphor for that interior life. That's why the eyes are the most important thing. In theater, the physical movements of the actor are important because everything must be absolutely rigid and precise. But it's the expression within the actor's eyes that determine the precision of a movie actor.

You've often stated that Another Time, Another Place *is your favorite of the films you've directed. What is it about that film which keeps it so close to your heart?*

MR: I guess it's because more people tell me they like it than any of the others! [Laughs] I guess I'm a whore for praise, just as most of us are.

But, being serious for a moment, I think there's a kind of purity in that film. I think I discovered what I was good at doing [with that movie], which is basically making a movie about small people with universal themes. And the movie moves like a chess game; it's like a series of very psychological moves, which lead to a very profound conclusion for a human being. And, I think, more than with any of the other films — maybe because it was my first film and I was struggling, throwing more of myself and my energy into that than I have ever thrown into a movie since — I felt I was able to make the world around the main character become an expression of their inner state. And that, to me, seems the most successful of my works at doing that.

You know, I'm always amazed that a small film that is essentially about agriculture has had such an effect on so many people — maybe not so much in the United States, but certainly in Europe.

You mentioned the purity you see within that film. It seems to me that most of your work has a lyricism, if you will, a certain purity. In a time in which so many filmmakers are corrupted by the process of filmmaking, how do you personally manage to maintain that vision?

MR: By turning down most of what is offered to me and by trying to keep myself as free as possible. Truthfully, it's difficult, and it's getting harder. In a sense, you have to be successful to continue. The success of *Il Postino* was a major advantage because it allowed people to see that, by doing what I did, I could make a film that could actually make money. But you can't always hit the nail right on the head with the general public. It's a bit hit-and-miss, and the determining factors are not always in your hands anyway. The latest film I made [*Dancing at the Blue Iguana*] will probably not be a success, but I am extremely proud of it in many ways.

I'd like to talk about Il Postino *for a moment. On that project, your leading man, Massimo Troisi, who was also your close friend, was dying. How difficult was it to balance the role of the filmmaker who must complete the film and that of the sorrowful friend?*

MR: It was almost unbearable because I know that at any moment I could have stopped the film, and I had to make that judgment at every single moment of the day — particularly as we got further along with the production and had more and more film in the can. Not only were the risks getting bigger, but every sacrifice would have been jettisoned had we stopped. I had to juggle that in my brain, and also I had to juggle the idea that we might be making this sacrifice for no reason at all, that the film might not only be a mediocre movie, but be a mediocre movie for the very reasons that we had in front of us — meaning that his being ill was not enabling us to work in a proper manner. I mean, I had him for an hour a day, and I had to shoot the film in an incredibly simplistic way. You'll notice that, in every scene, he walks in and sits down. He couldn't stand. He just didn't have the energy.

To see a friend suffering to that degree was unbearable. But somehow, because we both believed in the project so much, and we both knew that, for some reason, we had to finish this thing — and I don't know why we knew that, but we did — we kept on.

But, it was not good. It was not a pleasant experience.

On Dancing at the Blue Iguana, *you worked very extensively in character development. Could you tell me about that process?*

MR: Well, it's a process I had always wanted to try because I have always felt that making a film in the traditional manner — writing the script, then auditioning the actors — is a bit like playing a piece of composed music, recreating a symphony, if you will, whereas what we did is a bit like playing a jazz tune. Certain extraordinary things happen within the moment, and you'll never see it ever again.

We started with nothing. Again, it's like that statement by Peter Brook, which urges you to stare at the black hole and see what creative juices you have inside. We set out to answer a question, really, which was "How do we live the rest of our lives?" That's what we set out to try and answer.

The process was very simple, yet extremely complex. I first chose seven actors from an audition based on their capacities to do this sort of [improvisational] work. Not all actors are adaptive to it. And then we set to for eight months. The first month we just spent breaking down any kind of self-consciousness. Then we just began doing theater exercises and so forth, meanwhile developing characters. And then once the characters were really properly developed — each in their isolation — we started to draw the lines and connect the dots between them, trying to develop a series of stories which link those characters which have been created. That process took another four months or so.

A publicity photograph of director Michael Radford from the release of the acclaimed film *Il Postino* (*The Postman*) (Miramax Films, 1994).

If I may be critical of my own film, I think we hired too many actors to begin with, and thus didn't have enough time to fully develop all of the stories. I should have thrown out some of the actors, but I couldn't do that because I'd already had them with me for five or six months.

So I think there are people who look at this movie and accept it for what it is, taking on board the extreme reality of it and the profundity of the performances. Then there are other people who look at it and simply want more story. I guess it really depends on who you are as to whether you think the film is a masterpiece or a piece of rubbish, which I've seen both in critical reviews! [Laughs]

But the process was terrific for me and has changed my perceptions. Although I've always been very much sympathetic to actors, it has completely changed my vision of how one can direct in the cinema. It's also made me very aware that the more time you can give an actor, the more profound the performance you can get.

Being able to cast actors without having a preexisting screenplay and then creating characters around their improvisational creations must have been extremely liberating.

MR: It's extraordinarily liberating and psychically very good, for you become like a family. There are no holds barred and you're not afraid to fail. You're not afraid to indulge yourself and then pull yourself back in. There's an unparalleled atmosphere of extraordinary collaboration, and the cinema is an act of collaboration, so it felt quite wonderful. That atmosphere infected everyone who worked on the film, so when the crew came onboard, they, too, found themselves in a very special environment.

I'm going to be doing another such film in the near future, and I believe I learned a lot from the process that will allow for an even more extraordinary experience.

You once said, "A filmmaker should always remember that everything is a metaphor for something else." I find this statement fascinating. What did you mean by that?

MR: I think a filmmaker should not be careless because filmmaking is really about the exterior world which you create. I think the films that I like least are the ones in which the exterior world serves only as a backdrop for dialogue and action. It somehow reduces the film. Sure, you can tell a story that way. But where cinema starts to become magical—and become personal, I think—is when you're aware that the exterior world which you're filming, which has a concrete reality, is nevertheless informed by the inner world of the characters.

FILMOGRAPHY FOR MICHAEL RADFORD

1. *Fear* (1972) D & Sc
2. *Concerning the Surface* (1973) D & Sc
3. *Cold Night* (1974) D & Sc
4. *The Madonna and the Volcano* (1976) D
5. *The Last Stronghold of the Pure Gospel* (1977) D
6. *Three Men Up a Goat* (1979) D
7. *The White Bird Passes* (1980) D & Sc

Winston Smith (John Hurt) holds Julia (Suzanna Hamilton) in the "golden country" in the George Orwell adaptation *1984* (Atlantic Releasing Corporation, 1984).

8. *Van Morrison in Ireland* (1981) D
9. *La Belle Isobel* (1982) D
10. *The Making of The Pirates of Penanze* (1982) D
11. *Another Time, Another Place* (1983) D & Sc
12. *1984* (1984) D & Sc
13. *White Mischief* (1987) D & Co-Sc
14. *Homicide: Life on the Street* (1993) [episode: "Justice: Part 1"] D
15. *Il Postino* (1994) D & Co-Sc
16. *B. Monkey* (1998) D & Co-Sc
17. *Dancing at the Blue Iguana* (2000) D & Co-Sc
18. *Ten Minutes Older: The Cello* (2002) Co-D & Co-Sc
19. *The Merchant of Venice* (2005) D & Sc
20. *Flawless* (2007) D

Mark Romanek

After studying film at Chicago's progressive New Trier East public high school, and later as a Cinema Studies major at Ithaca College, Mark Romanek went to work as the second assistant director on Brian De Palma's underrated 1979 film *Home Movies*. While working on that project, Romanek met and became close friends with actor Keith Gordon, who also aspired to one day direct. This friendship would lead to their collaborating on the critically-acclaimed-but-largely-unseen film *Static* (1985). *Static*, the story of a television which allows communication with the dead, was co-written by Romanek and Gordon, starred Gordon in the lead, and served as Romanek's directorial debut. The film received a Grand Jury Prize nomination at the Sundance Film Festival.

Romanek then embarked upon a highly-successful career directing music videos for artists as diverse as Madonna, Nine Inch Nails, Fiona Apple, Beck, No Doubt, Macy Gray, David Bowie, and R.E.M. In 1996, Romanek won the Grammy for Best Music Video for Michael and Janet Jackson's "Scream." In 1997, the innovative director received the prestigious MTV Video Vanguard Award, honoring his career achievements as well as his advancement of the artform. Two years later, Tondo Books published a collection of images from his music videos entitled *Mark Romanek: Video Music Stills*.

Romanek co-wrote the Playboy Channel anthology film *Inside Out IV* (1992), on which he collaborated with several other noted music video helmers, including Nigel Dick and Antoine Fuqua. Romanek soon found himself being wooed by Hollywood, where he returned to direct his second film, *One Hour Photo* (2002), starring Robin Williams, Gary Cole, and Eriq La Salle. Critics praised Romanek for the picture's stylish look, and the film received a number of awards, including three major prizes at the Deauville Film Festival. Romanek then returned to crafting music videos, directing perhaps his finest video—for Johnny Cash's haunting "Hurt."

At the time of this writing Romanek was attached to direct several projects in various stages of production.

Favorite Films: *2001: A Space Odyssey* (1968), *The Conversation* (1974), *The Tenant* (1976), *Lenny* (1974), *The Godfather Part II* (1974), *Blade Runner* (1982), *McCabe & Mrs. Miller* (1971), *8 1/2* (1963), *Persona* (1966), *The Trial* (1963), *Citizen Kane* (1941), *Titicut Follies* (1967), and *The Killing of a Chinese Bookie* (1976).

Andrew Rausch: *Over the past few years your name has been attached to a number of films which stalled at some point. Could you tell me a little bit about these screenplays, your involvement with the projects, and about their premature demises?*

Mark Romanek: I adapted the script for *Arbus* from the Patricia Bosworth bio. Since the film takes place over several decades in New York City, it was prohibitively expensive to shoot

Emily Southwick (Jane Hoffman) and Ernie Blick (Keith Gordon) in a scene from Mark Romanek's 1986 film *Static* (NFI Productions, 1985).

correctly. Plus, the ideal and "bankable" actress for this role does not seem to exist. Since writing it, I've become unsure of the viability of the biopic concept. The only good ones I know are *Lenny*, *Raging Bull* (1980), *Andrei Rublyov* (1969), and *Citizen Kane*, which is semi-thinly veiled as fiction.

Urban Townies got fairly far along. It was a very original and stunningly well-written script by Jesse Wigutow exploring issues related to the creative process and suicide. However, once it became apparent that the producers had no intention of allowing the lead character to go through with the suicide (and, in fact, wanted to change it into a heartwarming "feel-good" film with the lead driving off into the sunset—literally), Brad and I said, "Go in good health," and moved on to other projects.

Paradise Falls was another tough and long education in the studio development system, which is a roll of the dice at best. An executive at Dreamworks had a script with a cool premise. I did months and months of research (both visual and literary) in an effort to help rework the film's plot. For example, I reread and took extensive notes on both the *Divine Comedy* and *Paradise Lost*. A writer not of my choosing was brought in to execute my ideas and, instead, chose to almost completely ignore them. Then, after eighteen months of work, the executive that initiated the project was fired, and the studio put the project into turnaround. A shame, that one. It could've been a mind-blower, but probably too expensive to do well.

Was there a singular moment in your life when you knew you wanted to be a filmmaker?

MR: I imagine that some guys my age saw the Beatles on Ed Sullivan and said to themselves, "I want to be in a rock band." When I was nine (and again later when I was thirteen)

I saw Kubrick's *2001: A Space Odyssey* and said to myself, "I want to be a film director." So Kubrick was, and continues to be, a massive inspiration for me. I admired the way the film was epic in scope, yet obscure and enigmatic in tone. I also admit to being intrigued by the myth surrounding the filmmaker.

Who else would you credit as being influences on your work?

MR: Well, Roman Polanski, Robert Altman, Federico Fellini, and Ingmar Bergman later became extremely important to me — although I've always had the most affinity for Kubrick's tone and style. I suppose what influenced me most was that each of these filmmakers had their own distinct *voice*; if you were to view a single shot from one of their films, you could instantly identify who had directed it. This is something I'm still in the earliest stages of trying to develop in my own work. I suppose the decade I spent making music videos was a sort of art school sketch pad — trying on different directors' styles to see what suited me as I started to develop my own series of themes, recurring motifs, and mannerisms.

It's interesting that you credit 2001 as being the film which made you want to become a filmmaker. In many ways, I think 2001 can be seen as a predecessor to the music video in that Kubrick was one of the first filmmakers to marry these beautiful musical arrangements to these breathtaking visuals.

MR: I suppose that's true. Kubrick's taste in music, and boldness in his use of music, was amazing — a huge influence. But that's just one of several ways the guy had balls the size of a small country. Kubrick was a cool New York Jewish hipster. He hung with Terry Southern and Peter Sellers, played drums, smoked weed, and married a moody bohemian ballerina in the fifties. Kubrick seemed a sort of cool Beat Generation nerd. When all is said and done, his films are just cool. He simply made the coolest films.

Was the transition from directing music videos to helming a major feature film a smooth one for you?

MR: It wasn't too bad. I felt ready to do it, and the logistical scale of the film was very manageable. The decade or so of music video-making gave me a certain confidence as far as the technical side of it went, which allowed me to concentrate on the actors' problems, and the nuances of the storytelling. I learned more during the editing of the film than during the shooting because that's where you find out what you did right, and — more often than not — what you didn't. Also, in the editing I learned a lot about film acting and what type of performance served the film overall, and what sort limited it.

The cliché of describing it as the difference between running a sprint and running a marathon is fairly apt.

How much different is it working with an accomplished actor like Robin Williams as opposed to a band or a musician?

MR: Well, it's a bit of apples and oranges. Many of the musicians I've worked with are, of course, as accomplished at their task as someone like Robin Williams is at his. The requirements of the formats [music video and feature film] are somewhat different, but the willingness to do the hard work, a general sense of full commitment, technique (with its requisite attention to detail), and tapping into and expressing genuine emotion are key. I try to glean from the artist — musician or actor — before we agree to work together, whether or not they possess any or all of these qualities. Some musicians aren't trained or experienced at being in front of a camera (their true gifts lie in the making of the music), and have to be reminded and/or quickly tutored on techniques, tricks, and shortcuts. Others, of course, are extremely gifted at expressing themselves in this way. I would say that a video can be more forgiving in this regard, in that a lot of film can be shot and the best little pieces (whether purposeful or accidental) can be assembled so that they spark off the music and each other and create the illusion of confidence and energy. Whereas, in a film, while one certainly does edit together an actor's best moment to create a performance, it's *far* harder to cobble something together. The actor really does need to deliver a committed performance. A certain amount can be faked. Editing can take a bad performance and make it seem passable, but the nuances of a great performance have to be there intact.

My experiences working with other big movie stars is limited, so I have nothing to compare to. But, I will say — and I hope this doesn't sound fawning — that Robin is possessed of all the above-mentioned talents in spades. He was happy to be the first to arrive and the last to leave whenever the job called for it. And with Robin you get the added bonus of laughing so hard between takes that you think you may pee your pants, which — on a tightly scheduled film — is a gigantic stress reliever.

One Hour Photo is quite different from most of the projects that Robin Williams is generally associated with. Was there any hesitation on Robin's part to do the film, or do you think these differences are what attracted him to the project?

MR: Funnily enough, we never really discussed this topic, and I would never want to put words in his mouth. I can only speculate that having done so many big-budget studio films, he may have felt that a smaller, independent project would be an invigorating change of pace. That said, if you look more closely at his dramatic work, his character in *One Hour*

Director Mark Romanek on the set of the Robin Williams–starrer ***One Hour Photo*** (Fox Searchlight Pictures, 2002).

Photo is not at all far afield from others he's connected with. He started his dramatic career with a stunningly dark PBS film based on Saul Bellows's *Seize the Day* [1986], which is an amazing film. He did a small, strange role in an adaptation of Joseph Conrad's *The Secret Agent* [1996]. His characters in *Awakenings* [1990] and *The Fisher King* [1991] have a good deal in common with Sy Parrish in *One Hour Photo*. Robin is attracted to isolated, lonely, outsiders roles, and he took to this one like a fish to water. And though the film is a bit creepy in places, it's not so nearly as dark as people imagine it might be. As for any hesitation, there seemed to be little. He read the script, watched my music video reel, asked to meet me for lunch. We did so, chatted for about forty-five minutes, and afterward he told his manager that he wanted to do the film. It was one of those weird, blessed, smooth developments.

FILMOGRAPHY FOR MARK ROMANEK

1. *Home Movies* (1979) Second AD
2. *Static* (1985) D & Co-Sc
3. *Inside Out IV* (1992) Co-Sc
4. *R.E.M. Parallel* (1995) [video: "Strange Currencies"] D
5. *Closure* (1997) [videos: "Closer" and "The Perfect Drug"] D
6. *Madonna: The Video Collection 93–99* (1999) [videos: "Rain" and "Bedtime Story"] D
7. *One Hour Photo* (2001) D & Sc
8. *The Best of Bowie* (2002) Co-D
9. *Weezer: Video Capture Device* [video: "El Scorcho"] (2004) D
10. *From Janet...: The Videos* [video: "Got 'Til It's Gone"] (2004) D
11. *Sonic Youth: Corporate Ghost* [video: "Little Troubled Girl"] (2004) D

David O. Russell

After crafting the offbeat indie films *Spanking the Monkey* (1994) and *Flirting with Disaster* (1996), screenwriter/director David O. Russell hit the big time with his first studio film, *Three Kings*, in 1999. The $50 million Warner Bros. film, a mixture of Robert Altman's *M*A*S*H* (1970) and *Kelly's Heroes* (1970), is truly one of the most independent-minded big-budget studio releases to date. Based loosely on screenwriter John Ridley's script *Spoils of War*, the film follows four American soldiers (played by George Clooney, director Spike Jonze, and rappers-turned-actors Ice Cube and Mark Wahlberg) searching war-torn Kuwait for gold bars owned by Saddam Hussein. The superb acting, sharp screenplay, and awe-inspiring camerawork of *Three Kings* brought Russell — a largely-unknown indie filmmaker — to the attention of critics and cineastes alike.

Shortly before our interview, Russell was given the opportunity to screen *Three Kings* in the White House for President Bill Clinton and a group of foreign diplomats. Humorously, Russell lied to an annoying *Newsweek* reporter, telling him that a real human body was used for a scene in which a bullet is shown tearing through a man's intestines. Unaware that he was being fed false information, the writer reported Russell's use of the corpse, creating a minor controversy. In 2000, *Three Kings* was named to *Cinescape*'s list of the top twenty-five actioners of all time.

After a five-year hiatus, Russell made a grand return in 2004 with not one but three projects. First, he served as executive producer on the Will Ferrell comedy *Anchorman* (2004). Then came his fourth and fifth directorial efforts, *I Heart Huckabees* and *Soldiers Pay* (both 2004). *Huckabees* was billed as an "existential comedy" and starred Dustin Hoffman, Lili Tomlin, Jude Law, and Naomi Watts. *Soldiers Pay* was a highly-controversial documentary about the Iraq war.

Favorite Films: *The 400 Blows* (1959), *The Celebration* (1998), and *The Graduate* (1967).

ANDREW RAUSCH: *A few months ago you had the opportunity to screen* Three Kings *in the White House for President Clinton. What was that experience like?*

DAVID O. RUSSELL: You know, the President actually went on Roger Ebert's show last month and said it was his favorite film of the year. I actually got to talk to him quite a bit. He loved the film and he talked about it. First of all, he said that it was not just an "entertaining film," but what he considered an important film because he thought Americans needed to know how the war really ended; they didn't really know that. He thought the film could be of use in educating the electorate in showing them what was involved in these interventions.

David O. Russell directing his second feature film, *Flirting with Disaster* (Miramax Films, 1996).

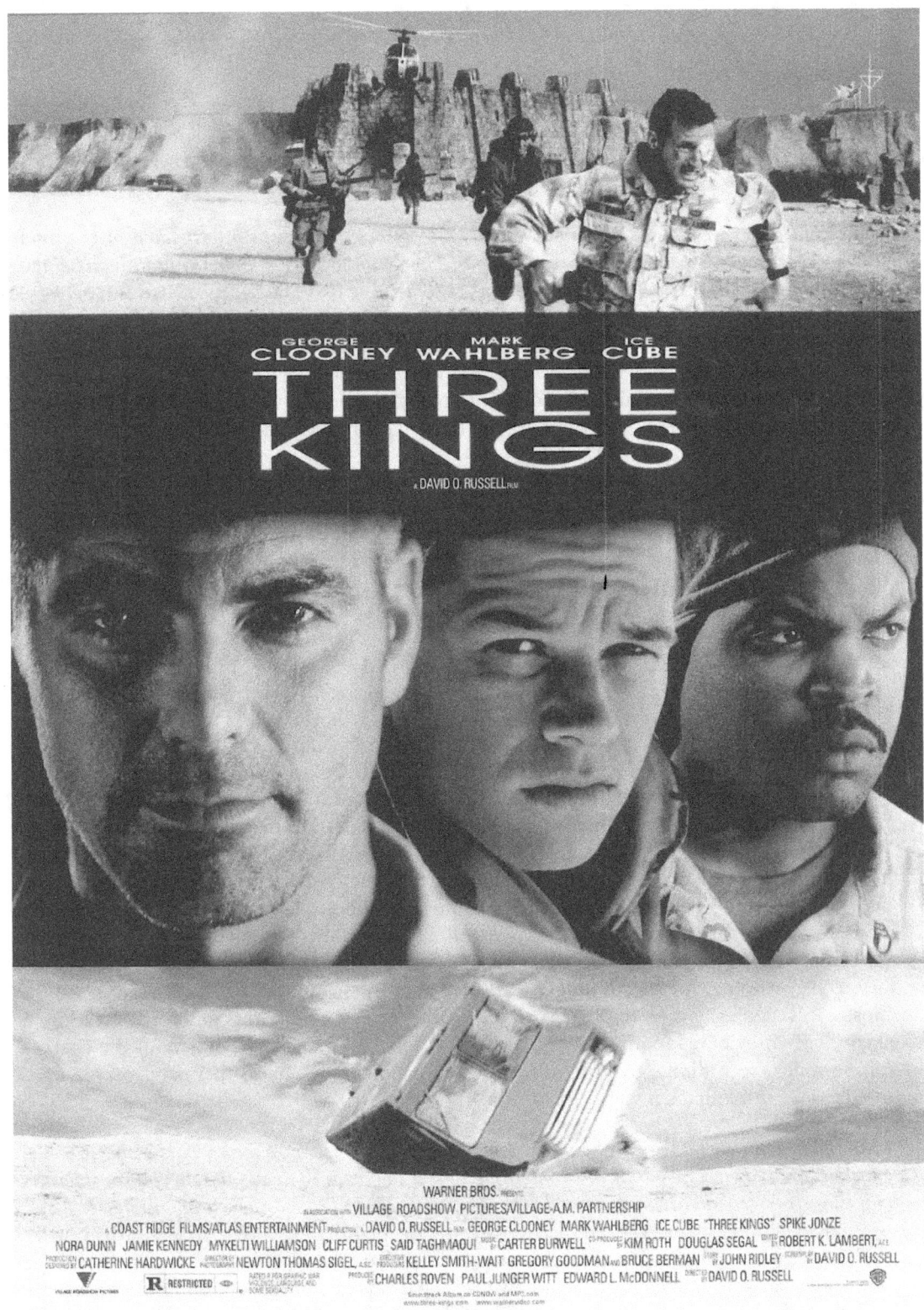

The poster for David O. Russell's *Three Kings*, starring George Clooney, Mark Wahlberg, and Ice Cube (Warner Bros. Pictures, 1999).

That must have been flattering.

DR: Oh, it was completely flattering. It was also a little odd because the movie is funny in ways that are uncomfortable, so people seemed careful about laughing at certain things in front of the President for fear that maybe they shouldn't. It was a very quiet screening, which was very deadly for me. [Laughs]

I particularly liked the scene in which Mark Wahlberg's character was interrogated by the Iraqi soldiers because, unlike most films, we're given the opportunity to see the enemy as human beings. These aren't the faceless dehumanized villains of something like The Sands of Iwo Jima *(1949); they're real people.*

DR: That was one of the ideas that motivated me. I felt that the war had been shown in a very superficial black-and-white fashion, and we never really saw the faces of the Iraqis who were being bombed and decimated. You know, many of them didn't like Saddam Hussein any more than we did. That was very much something which motivated me to do the film.

I understand you actually went out and interviewed some former Iraqi soldiers?

DR: Oh, yeah. We had *many* of them working on the film. A lot of the extras in the film are people who fought in the uprising against Saddam and escaped over the border, or people who were in Saddam's army and deserted. Some of them were captured and tortured.

Some of the camerawork in the film kind of reminded me of a young Sam Raimi. Were you a fan of his work at all?

DR: Well, I saw *Evil Dead* [1985]. What in particular? The swooping camera, right? To tell you the truth, I never really followed him very closely. I was probably more visually inspired by Oliver Stone or Mikhail Kalatozov.

Were you disappointed that Three Kings *didn't receive any Oscar nominations?*

DR: Well, yeah.... I have three thoughts on this. My first thought is that you can't really pay too much attention to that because it's really not a reason to make films. If that becomes your reason, it's definitely a bad sign. It leads to self–importance and a lot of other bad things. That's number one. Number two, this was a good year; there were a lot of good movies. Number three, I don't really think my movie is a natural for the Academy because I typically don't think they nominate movies as dark as *Three Kings* unless there's a virtuoso performance at the center of it — something that is all about one character. Maybe Hillary Swank [in *Boys Don't Cry*, 1999] or Robert De Niro in *Raging Bull* [1980] or Russell Crowe in *The Insider* [1999]. In those cases, it's really dark, but they can look at it and say, "Wow, this guy really acted up a storm!" My movie was too much of an ensemble for that. It really wasn't about the characters so much, so it didn't give the Academy that handle which helps them approach a dark movie. So, I think that's my analysis of it.

In the film, I think the violence is presented in a very responsible manner, as the effects of the gunshots are shown close-up. Is this something that is important to you, and do you consider the film industry's general attitude toward violence perhaps being reckless or irresponsible?

DR: Definitely. That was another motivator for making the movie for me. I had never really dealt with violence in a movie, and I decided that when I did, I wanted to resensitize it in some way — to make it alive in a new way. That was one of the key things that drew me to the material.

You once misled a journalist from Newsweek *by telling him that you used a real cadaver for those shots, which I think is kind of funny. Why did you tell him that?*

DR: He kind of pissed me off! He was asking me a bunch of kind of rude questions. In fact, he actually called me back after the interview to apologize. He was saying things like, "How do you think they're gonna market this movie? It just seems too hard to market." I was just, you know, shut up with those questions! The only reason I'm doing this interview is to help the movie, so if you like the movie, help me. Don't tell everybody, "Gee, how will they market this movie?" I was a little annoyed by that. I can't remember what else he asked, but then he asked me about the body, I just told him, "Yeah, those are real cadavers." [Laughs]

Then the Mortician's Association called us, all up in arms, saying that this was an unethical use of a corpse.

You're not going to lie to me are you? [Laughs]

DR: [Laughs] Probably not. You're not going to annoy me, are you?

I hope not. [Laughs] Well, I would have to agree with him in that I think Three Kings *is a really independent-minded film, which you don't expect to see coming from a studio. How did you manage to bypass studio interference and get what you wanted up on the screen?*

DR: The studio categorized me as a filmmaker, and they told me they've worked with other filmmakers in the past, like Oliver Stone or Martin Scorsese. Not that I'm comparing myself to those filmmakers, because I'm not, but the studio had worked with those directors

Dustin Hoffman and Lily Tomlin follow the clues in the existential comedy *I Heart Huckabees* (20th Century–Fox, 2004).

and they categorized me as being a filmmaker because I came out of the world of Miramax and Sundance. That was how they presented the proposition from the start. Secondly, they felt like they were protected by the action in the movie. I think they thought, well, if you want all of this childish weird shit, go ahead. Maybe we'll get him to change it later. They didn't really go after the politics or any of the provocative stuff. They understood this was not *The Green Mile* [1999] from the beginning. This was not a straight-ahead proposition. They pretty much accepted that, although they tried to get me to take out some of the stuff at the preview stage, but it all tested well — the internal organs and stuff like that, but since it tested well, they didn't have a leg to stand on.

What film for you best defines the word "cool" and why?

DR: I would say *Klute* (1971) defines the word cool for me. What makes it cool for me is that the character Jane Fonda plays is really sexy and yet really hard and very vulnerable. I also love that John Klute is played by Donald Sutherland, yet he ends up with this really cool, tough woman. He's a dweeb, but he's also really tough, smart, and soulful.

Filmography for David O. Russell

1. *Spanking the Monkey* (1994) D, Sc, Ex-P
2. *Flirting with Disaster* (1996) D & Sc
3. *Three Kings* (1999) D & Sc
4. *The Slaughter Rule* (2001) P
5. *Adaptation* (2002) A
6. *The Slaughter Rule* (2002) P
7. *Anchorman* (2004) Ex-P
8. *I Heart Huckabee's* (2004) D, Sc, P
9. *Soldiers Pay* (2004) D, Sc, P

John A. Russo

In 1968, long before the so-called "Independent Film Revolution," a group of unknown filmmakers from Pittsburgh set out to make a horror movie. Led by director George Romero and screenwriter John A. Russo, the team created a $114,000 masterpiece, *Night of the Living Dead*, about seven strangers who seek refuge from flesh-eating zombies. Despite its low budget, the black-and-white film was a huge success and has since continued to gain popularity, spawning countless imitations. Often touted as the most terrifying film ever made, the movie was listed by the National Film Registry as a classic in 1999. Respected film critic Leonard Maltin calls *Night of the Living Dead* the "touchstone modern horror film," warning, "Don't watch this alone!" The filmmakers then followed up their success with *There's Always Vanilla* (1972).

Russo then redirected his talents toward writing books, churning out a number of successful novels, including *Hell's Creation*, *Living Things*, *The Awakening*, *Blood Sisters*, and *Limb to Limb*. A number of Russo's novels have been adapted into films, such as *Return of the Living Dead* (1985), *Voodoo Dawn* (1990), and *The Majorettes* (1986), which Russo also produced and appears in. In addition, Russo is the author of *Making Movies: The Inside Guide to Independent Movie Production*, and has penned novelizations of *Night of the Living Dead* and Romero's *Day of the Dead* (1986). In 1990, special effects wizard Tom Savini helmed a remake of *Night of the Living Dead*, for which Russo served as co-writer and producer.

Not only a successful novelist and screenwriter, Russo is also an accomplished filmmaker in his own right. In 1981, Russo made his directorial debut with *Midnight*, which he adapted from his own novel of the same title. Russo later directed the sequel *Midnight 2: Sex, Death, and Videotape* (1993). That same year, Russo explored the theme of vampirism with *Heartstopper* (1993). After making two films in 1996, *Scream Queens* and *Santa Claws*, Russo appeared in Academy Award–winning director Peter Werner's Emmy-nominated mini-series, *House of Frankenstein 1997* (1997). Russo has also appeared as an actor in a number of other films, including *The Inheritor* (1990) and *I Married a Strange Person!* (1997).

In 1999, Russo committed what many aficionados saw as the Cardinal Sin when he co-directed *Night of the Living Dead: 30th Anniversary Edition*, for which he shot a number of new scenes in black-and-white and integrated them into the 1968 classic. For this new edition, Russo excised nearly fifteen minutes from the original film and added a new score. While some fans felt Russo's film was a great improvement over the original, others saw it as being the ultimate blasphemy.

Favorite Films: *Since You Went Away* (1944), *The Best Years of Our Lives* (1946), *Invasion of the Body Snatchers* (1956), *Forbidden Planet* (1956), and the films of John Ford.

ANDREW RAUSCH: *Where did the concept for* Night of the Living Dead *come from?*

JOHN RUSSO: Well, George and I were both working on different ideas when we weren't doing commercial film. He and I were usually the main ones working on this stuff. He and I were both single at that time, so we spent most of our free time at the studio. We were the ones who would sleep on the floor and work all night. Whenever we weren't doing commercials,

An advertisement for the John Russo–directed film *Midnight* (Independent International Pictures, 1982).

he'd go to one typewriter and I'd go to another one and we'd work on story ideas. We had already decided we were going to do some kind of film.

So, I had a couple of pages already done that opened in the cemetery that actually had kids in ghoul masks. Our first idea was that a saucer would land. It was kind of an early *E.T.* [1982], you know? The kids from outer space were gonna land and befriend these Earth kids, and they were gonna have a lot of powers that normal kids didn't have, running amok and causing havoc in the town. It was gonna be a sci-fi comedy, but we found out pretty quickly that we couldn't afford the special effects. Then George went away one weekend and wrote about half of a story, which opened in a cemetery. I had made the comment that cemeteries scare people and that would be a good way to open a film. I was working on another story about a kid who's running away from home. He's running through the woods and he steps through a pane of glass, like you use to grow hot-house tomatoes, only underneath is a rotting corpse. This was going to be about aliens who come to Earth in search of human flesh. George's story, which wasn't in screenplay form, got up to the point where it had the girl and it opened in the cemetery, and she was running from something and calling it a "thing." We all liked the story, but I said to George, "Who are they and what do they do?" He didn't know! [Laughs] So I said why not use my flesh-eating idea? It seems to me that they're people, so they must be dead people. Why not turn it around and make them flesh-eaters? He said that was good, so then we hashed that out. Then he said we couldn't show people coming up out of their graves, so I said, "Let's make them the recently dead. They're the only ones that can come back. That way we don't need all that special effects garbage." So, that's how it happened.

I took all the material and the ideas we had and wrote the script. By that time, I pretty much turned out to be the leader of the idea sessions. I don't know. It was like George was out of ideas or something, so people would get stumped and I'd say, "Well, here we've got Harry, and he's a coward. If something goes wrong during the escape attempt, he's not gonna stick. He's gonna try to save his own ass, so he'll probably board the damn door up when he wasn't supposed to." Things like that. So I took all these ideas and rewrote George's first ideas into screenplay form and then finished the second half of the screenplay.

Then George and I were at a friends' house, who was an investor, and George read the thing and said that something was bothering him. He didn't like it or something. Our friend read it and said, "There's nothing wrong with it. This is good." [Laughs] So George said, "I know what's bothering me. There needs to be another siege before the ghouls finally overtake the people in the house. There needs to be another minor attack." So we wrote that in, and that was it. We changed things as we went. We changed the ending a little bit. We wanted to put Judy Ridley in there because she was good-looking, and we thought the film needed some sex appeal because horror films had that at that time. It was originally written to be a guy. It was originally a cemetery caretaker who gets into the house, not the young couple. So we gave him a girlfriend and made him younger, just kind of writing her lines on the spur of the moment.

One of the things that I find appealing about Night of the Living Dead *is the combination of things you used to scare people. You had a touch of sci-fi, you had cannibalism, and the supernatural, all of which played upon people's natural fears of death.*

JR: I saw every film that came to town when I was a kid. We had three movie theaters in a small town. I saw all the horror films. You always hoped you'd see something good, and I never really did until *Invasion of the Body Snatchers*. We wanted to make something better than these things with the rubber monsters that Hollywood was cranking out at the time. The zombie movies were my least favorites because the zombies didn't do anything but walk around looking stiff and dead. Once in a while they'd throw someone against the wall. They weren't frightening like Frankenstein or Dracula or any of that stuff. For that matter, neither were mummies. They were about in the same category. They weren't very scary.

What we did that really turned the trick was making them flesh-eaters. Now zombies were really terrifying because they ate human flesh, and they could turn you into one. Everyone's afraid of death, but now you could have a sort of life in death that nobody wanted. [Laughs] I think another part of it was that using the recently dead tapped into those same feelings. You might bereave somebody who dies, but you don't really want to see them. You don't really want to touch them. People are afraid of corpses, and it played off of those fears. I think it's a mistake what's gone on since then, where zombies are green and decayed and horrendous-looking. I guess that has its place, but I think it was much more frightening using the minimal makeup that we did. I think it touched some deeper vibes in people.

Could you have ever imagined the film would become as big as it has over the years?

JR: Nobody could have imagined that because it's probably the only film there is that's been going on strong for thirty years. It's been in every format, and it's never been out of release. It's kind of a phenomenon in and of itself. If it would have had some kind of massive marketing campaign in the beginning, it probably would have been even bigger! I can't think of any other film that's had that run, not even any of the other famous horror films, like *Invasion of the Body Snatchers* or *Texas Chain Saw Massacre* [1974].

Barbra (Judith O'Dea), Ben (Duane Jones), and Tom (Keith Wayne) try to make some sense of things in the horror classic ***Night of the Living Dead***, written by John Russo (Continental Distributing Inc., 1968).

What is it about the horror genre that has drawn you back so many times as both a novelist and as a filmmaker?

JR: You can do good work in any genre. The thing about *Night of the Living Dead* is that the premise is outlandish, but we were true to the premise. The thing that makes it succeed is that once you've accepted the outlandish premise that the dead can rise and go after human flesh, we tried to make the people behave the way real people would behave in any kind of crisis. It's the same in *Stagecoach* [1939]; whenever you have a crisis, you have your cowards, you have your people with problems, and you have people who can be more brave than others. You have the whole gamut, so that's what we tried to do.

As far as horror, you can work with any aspect of the human condition. It's kind of fun to play with the horror genre, too. You just take the old myths and give them new twists and play with people's minds.

You recently directed Night of the Living Dead: 30th Anniversary Edition, *which integrated newly-filmed scenes into the thirty-year-old classic. What made you decide to do that?*

JR: I'm a trustee of the corporation that made the movie, so if there comes a chance to colorize it or to do anything.... I mean, I'm obligated to make as much money as I can for the shareholders. Beyond that, it was fun doing that. I wrote and directed the new scenes. Originally George was gonna direct it and we were gonna write it together, but he got involved with some other projects. When we got the money together and could finally do it, he was too busy.

But we had a great time doing it, and it looks absolutely terrific. It's really fun. This is no different from George Lucas going back and putting those scenes that he wanted to see in *Star Wars* [1977] back in there. It's really no different than a director's cut. What we tried to do were the things we had discussed thirty years ago but couldn't afford. One of the main things was that we desperately wanted an original score, and there was no way in hell we could afford that. We had to resort to library music, but now we've got a really good original score. We also wanted to explain why there were so many zombies surrounding this one little farmhouse out in the middle of nowhere. Where in the hell did they come from? We never explained that, but now we have. You see that they were the patrons and waitresses and so on that worked at a diner.

The other thing is, the reason we didn't have featured zombies—there should have been continuing zombie characters, and with the exception of Bill Heinzman and myself, there weren't—was because we could never count on the same person showing up for two days in a row to be an extra. I ended up being the zombie that got the tire in the head because I was there working on the crew. It was four o'clock in the morning and everybody else had gone home. I figured, well, I'll get into the goddamned make-up and still load magazines. Now we have featured zombie characters.

Everything integrates perfectly. Plus, we were able to fix a lot of things. The famous jump cut is gone now. Bill Heinzman came up with a way to edit that gets rid of that. There's been criticism from people on the internet who don't know anything about this. They *can't* know anything about it because they haven't seen it yet. But they're pissing and moaning that I should have my ass kicked and all that because we shortened the movie! Oh, my God! Well, if it was their movie and they had a chance to do this, they'd fall all over themselves to get to a camera. We judiciously shortened things, you know? If you just shave a few seconds off of the shots.... You don't even miss those few seconds, but it gives you time to add another key scene or character. This is just common practice. This is how you shave time off of anything. You don't even miss any of the stuff we took out. It's not like anything was devastated. It's all there, plus you get all this new stuff that's a lot of fun. It's entertaining as hell.

Do you think there are any subject matters that should be taboo for a filmmaker, or do you think the sky is the limit?

JR: No, I don't think anything should be taboo. It just depends on the handling of it. We need to learn about everything under the sun. It's just a question of taste, restraint, and manners.

Do you think there is a place for these films like Faces of Death *(1978)?*

JR: Oh, there's a place for it.... [Laughs] Right up the ass of the person who distributed it!

FILMOGRAPHY FOR JOHN A. RUSSO

1. *Night of the Living Dead* (1968) Sc & A
2. *There's Always Vanilla* (1972) P
3. *Midnight* (1981) D, Sc, S
4. *The Return of the Living Dead* (1985) S
5. *The Majorettes* (1986) Sc, S, P, A
6. *Drive in Madness!* (1987) A
7. *Night of the Living Dead* (1990) S & P
8. *Voodoo Dawn* (1990) Co-Sc & S
9. *The Inheritor* (1990) A
10. *Midnight 2* (1993) D & Sc
11. *Heartstopper* (1993) D & Sc
12. *Santa Claws* (1996) D, Sc, P, A
13. *Scream Queens* (1996) D & Sc
14. *I Married a Strange Person!* (1997) A
15. *House of Frankenstein 1997* (1997) [TV] A
16. *Night of the Living Dead: 30th Anniversary Edition* (1999) Co-D, Sc, Ed, A
17. *Children of the Living Dead* (2002) Ex-P
18. *Saloonatics* (2002) D, Sc, Ex-P

Tony Scott

In Peter Bogdanovich's seminal work *Who the Devil Made It*, the writer/director describes one filmmaker whose work was largely overlooked at the time it was produced because of its commercial success, saying the filmmaker's pictures "represent one of the most vivid, varied, yet consistent bodies of work in movies; ironically, too, perhaps the most typical American. Which maybe explains why his pictures don't date as so many do, even the best...." Of course, Bogdanovich was talking about the once-undervalued Howard Hawks, but he could have just as easily been describing helmer Tony Scott, whose work is generally completely disregarded by the critical intelligentsia because of its commercial appeal. Despite criticism that he has "sold out" to big-budget commercialism, Scott continues to walk the tightrope between artistic expression and commercial product with the greatest of ease.

Scott was a fine-art painter before coming to work for his brother Ridley's commercial production company in the early eighties. His feature debut was the 1983 vampire film *The Hunger*, which showcased the sleek stylishness his work would become known for in the years to come. A scan of Scott's credits conjures up some impressive films—his teamings with actor Tom Cruise on *Days of Thunder* (1990) and *Top Gun* (1986); his collaborations with screenwriter Quentin Tarantino on *True Romance* (1993) and *Crimson Tide* (1995); Robert De Niro as a starstruck stalker in *The Fan* (1996); Bruce Willis at his gritty best in *The Last Boy Scout* (1991); Denzel Washington's broken-down bodyguard avenging the abduction of Dakota Fanning in *Man on Fire* (2004). Most of Scott's films are testosterone-fueled thrill-rides brimming with bravura. The heated confrontations which typify so much of Scott's work are the stuff of cinematic legend: Kevin Costner versus Anthony Quinn in *Revenge* (1990); Denzel Washington squaring off against Gene Hackman in *Crimson Tide*; the witty Tarantino-scripted exchange between Dennis Hopper and Christopher Walken in *True Romance*, surely one of the past decade's most memorable cinematic moments.

Other directorial efforts on Scott's resume include *Beverly Hills Cop II* (1987), *Enemy of the State* (1998), *Spy Game* (2001), and *Domino* (2005). In addition to his work as a director, Scott works frequently as a producer. His production credits include *RKO 281* (1999), *Tristan & Isolde* (2006), and *The Assassination of Jesse James by the Coward Robert Ford* (2007).

At the time of this writing Scott was preparing to direct Denzel Washington and Val Kilmer in *Deja Vu* (2006).

Favorite Films: *Apocalypse Now* (1979) and his brother Ridley Scott's *Blade Runner* (1982). ("I know it sounds like nepotism, but I think it's a brilliant film.")

ANDREW RAUSCH: *What filmmakers have most influenced your work?*

TONY SCOTT: It was actually Roman Polanski that got me going into film—specifically his film *Knife in the Water* (1962). I was a painter in art school. My two gods were Hieronymus Bosch and Francis Bacon. Polanski embodied a lot of that darkness and strangeness inside his movies that I saw in those paintings.

To be honest, I'm a vampire. I steal things. We have a production company that shoots commercials and rock videos. I go in there and I watch my nephew. I watch people like David Fincher. It's really some of my contemporaries that I steal from and am inspired by. I've always got an eye on the youth and what they're doing, as well. I think *Enemy of the State*, just the way we handled and shot lots of the aerial stuff and the surveillance shots, was motivated by these younger guys who come from rock videos and commercials.

For television, we've got a series called *The Hunger*, which is an offshoot of the original movie. We did twenty-two episodes last year, and I did one of them. We did another twenty-two episodes this year, and I got David Bowie to be in mine, and to be the wrap-around host for all of them. In that, I'm trying to bridge that gap between MTV and half-hour dramas. I've been using all of these kids I vampire from to direct these episodes. The series is actually a lot weirder than the original movie. I think the original idea was actually a weak idea. It was sort of a "B" movie that got elevated to another level. It was arty, it was full of itself, it was indulgent. [Laughs] I got blacklisted after that. It took me four more years to get another movie.

What's David Bowie like to work with?
TS: He's brilliant. I haven't worked with him since the original, so it's been seventeen years. He's really become a different person now. He's got two lives now. His hobby and his

Tony Scott gives actor Tom Cruise direction on the set of the action film *Top Gun* (Paramount Pictures, 1986).

business right now is art. He buys paintings. He's also the editor for a big art magazine in Europe. He's very smart and very articulate. You know what I love about Bowie? He's a guy who's never content to just sit back and let it roll. He's always reaching and trying new stuff. Sometimes it misses and sometimes it hits, but he's never content to stop moving and stop thinking and stop trying to reinvent himself. That's why I'm a huge fan.

That must be refreshing after some of the big ego-inflated movie stars.
    TS: Yeah, it is. People start believing their own press and they stop reaching anymore. He never does. He's always reaching and struggling. That's why he's brilliant.

I think it's fair to say that a lot of your work is underrated. It seems whenever a film or a filmmaker reaches a certain level of success, it's kind of human nature to label them as being commercial and having no real value. It seems like that label has undeservedly been stuck on a lot of your films, regardless of the fact that there are some real gems there on your filmography. Does that ever bother you?
    TS: No, it never really bothered me. After *The Hunger* I got absolutely slammed. I was never even given credit for the fact that I could actually craft the movie. I understood the problems with the actual movie itself. When I went on to make *Top Gun*, I got equally as razzed! [Laughs] I got destroyed! Then it was an easy shot because there were few directors coming out of commercials and advertising and going into movies. There were very few American directors doing it. The press' first shot was, "It's a one-hundred-and-twenty-minute commercial. It's all style over content." *Top Gun* just got slammed! It got fucking destroyed! [Laughs] I think *Top Gun* was a good movie. It was a good, solid popcorn entertainment movie. It was fun. It was rock and roll.

Which of your films would you like to see get a second look?
    TS: *True Romance*. It didn't make a bean! I think maybe it was a turn-off because of the violence, although there are certainly enough other violent movies out there. I don't know. Maybe the audience didn't like the characters well enough to root for them.

It's an interesting film because there are no real clear-cut "good guys." Clarence and Alabama are definitely anti-heroes.
    TS: You know that was Quentin's first screenplay, and to be honest, I hold him responsible for the uniqueness of the characters in *Crimson Tide*. You know, he came in and did a rewrite. We all loved the story, but we weren't sure about the characters until Quentin came in and rewrote them completely.
    The best script I've ever had, which barely changed from the moment it hit my desk to the point the movie was finished, was *True Romance*. I'm not just saying that because it was Quentin, either. It was brilliant. The characters were so full and so well-drawn that it makes a director's life so much easier when you can go to the set and put your hand on your chest and say, "This fuckin' scene is brilliant. You guys are doing this scene and there's no variation here." And every actor just wanted to come to the set and do the words that were there on the page, you know? I can't remember one day where I struggled with an actor who wanted to change things. Everyday they came to work saying, "This is great!"

The scene between Christopher Walken and Dennis Hopper is easily one of the decade's most memorable. Did you know at the time how special that scene was?
    TS: I knew it was brilliant when I read it on the page. The first time I read it, I just died laughing. I read that in a little hotel in Italy at three a.m. while I was on the road shooting. I

said, "This scene is brilliant." It's kind of funny because, even though I wanted to make this movie great, it was actually one of the easiest two days' shooting of my career. The scene was so well-written, so well-crafted, and the actors were so good that I didn't have to move the camera because I had total confidence in them, just letting them run it. The camera was a "lock off" and I just let them do it, and I think it turned out great.

You had a remarkable cast. When you have Sam Jackson, Gary Oldman, Brad Pitt, and Val Kilmer playing bit parts, you know you've got an incredibly strong cast.

TS: When you have good material, every actor wants to do it. They all did it for scale. I let both Gary and Brad run with their characters. Gary said, "I've got a vision about who this guy is." He was just finishing a movie and there was this guy hanging around the set who was a Jamaican drug dealer who'd been living in New York for fifteen years. So he said, "This is the guy!" That was his idea. The same with Brad. He said, "This is one of my roommates!" [Laughs]

[Producer] Bill Unger told me that you sustained a prop gun injury while you were shooting True Romance. *What happened?*

TS: Chris Walken puts the gun to Dennis Hopper's forehead, or at least he was originally supposed to, just before he kills him. We were rehearsing it and when Chris went to pull the trigger, Dennis said, "Fuck that! I don't like this idea! This is scary shit! This is too close to home." [Laughs] I said, "Listen Dennis, I'll fucking do it!" I said I'd rehearse it and I'd do it. Well, the gun was one where it had a slide, and the slide came out about a quarter of an inch and it punctured a perfect hole in my forehead.

Mafia chieftain Vincenzo Coccotti (Christopher Walken) interrogates Clifford Worley (Dennis Hopper) in this memorable scene from *True Romance* (Morgan Creek Productions, 1993).

True Romance — both Quentin's script and the final film — seemed to have been very much influenced by Terrence Malick's Badlands *(1973).*

TS: *Badlands* is one of my favorite movies. I think *True Romance* was a tribute to *Badlands*, and I didn't try to disguise the fact. I loved the script for *True Romance*, and I loved *Badlands*, and I thought, "Here is a way to pay tribute." I've done that before in other films, such as *Enemy of the State*, which was a tribute to *The Conversation* (1974).

What's your take on Quentin Tarantino and Roger Avary's now infamous dissertation on the "homosexual subtext" of Top Gun?

TS: I pissed myself laughing! [Laughs] I thought it was brilliant. He called me up and said, "You ought to look at this before it comes out." I thought it was brilliant. I haven't spoken to Quentin in a while, but he's a brilliant writer and he's quite a visionary. Not in big ways, just in small ways. He just makes people live and breathe in a way that no one else has brought to the cinema in a long, long time.

I'm going to name some actors and actresses that you've worked with, and I'd like you to comment on each of them.

TS: All right.

Let's start with Anthony Quinn.

TS: Brilliant. He's still one of my lifelong friends.

Bruce Willis.

TS: I've only worked with Bruce on the one film. We were actually talking about doing something else, which is about a retired fighter pilot. That would have been with him and De Niro, but that seems to have disappeared at the moment.

I think you pulled one of his best performances out of him in The Last Boy Scout. *He looked so scuzzy in that role! I loved the whole scene with the dead squirrel!*

TS: He was great with the revision of that character. I've got to tell you, I wasn't sure at first. I thought it was too scuzzy, as you call it. But then, when we went to work, it turned out great.

Gary Oldman.

TS: That was a fun experience working with Gary. I love actors who have a vision about who the character is. When I first talked to him, he didn't know who the character was. Then he called me up one day and he said, "I know who this guy is! He's standing next to me!" [Laughs]

Robert De Niro.

TS: Robert De Niro is one of my gods in terms of the acting world. He is the strangest and the sweetest guy on two legs, and he is the most hard-working, well-prepared actor. He does huge amounts of preparation. You hear actors talking about doing prep for movies, but this guy is tireless in his pursuit of actually finding out who his character is. By the time he comes to the set, he's so well-prepped that he doesn't have to act. He just thinks it.

When we did *The Fan*, we shipped knife salesmen in from Dallas, New York, and San Francisco. We sat and talked about their wives, their kids, their favorite part of the house, and the clothes they wore. Anything and everything. That was the first time I'd experienced that level of preparation. I think that's why I was just so in awe. He's just so dedicated to the process because he loves movie-making. I'd love to do something else with him.

Gene Hackman.

TS: Gene's another actor I would put up there with Bob De Niro. Gene is someone else who does an enormous amount of preparation. I've done two movies with Gene now, and he's just so prepared. He does so much homework and has so much vision about who the character is. He's such a pro. He and De Niro are a real delight to work with.

But Gene's tough! [Laughs] I'm sure you can see it, but Gene's tough. He does not like indecision. He's very particular, but he's always right because he does so much homework and he knows exactly who his character is at any given point of the movie. And that's why I went back to him the second time. I love working with him.

Robert Duvall.

TS: I did one movie with Duvall, *Days of Thunder*, and I'd put him up there in the same category with Bob and Hackman. It's funny. The common denominator is that they all do a lot of homework, but they all do it in different ways. They all know exactly who they are when they come to the set, but Bob Duvall is a handful! [Laughs] He's tough.

Ellen Barkin.

TS: Ellen was great. She's a cactus, a real handful. She's a spitfire, but she's brilliant. I think she was great in *The Fan*. I've loved many of her movies.

You know what? It sounds like I'm saying all of these guys are great! I've only had one bad experience with an actor, so it's not a case of me being a smartass and saying I think I've chosen wisely and carefully. I've only had one bad experience in ten movies and I've always enjoyed their time, enjoyed their work, but I do a tremendous amount of homework before I cast someone in a movie. I always believe in casting into who somebody is in real life and

Lt. Commander Ron Hunter (Denzel Washington) and Capt. Frank Ramsey (Gene Hackman) square off in the Tony Scott thriller *Crimson Tide* (Hollywood Pictures Company/Buena Vista Productions, 1995).

not asking them to play act or to be somebody else. I mean, Gene Hackman was the commander of that boat in *Crimson Tide*. Denzel Washington was his right arm. I use these guys' inherent personalities and ask them to transport themselves into the military world.

Kevin Costner.

TS: *Revenge* was a brilliant experience for me, working with Kevin in Mexico. A tough environment. He's fun and he was a real supporter. What went wrong was in postproduction. I had a tough time with Ray Stark, but I thought Kevin was great in the movie. I've tried several times since to do projects with him, and I'm still looking.

Samuel L. Jackson.

TS: He's great. I feel like I'm sucking up by saying all these guys are great. But, you know, they are great. I've been very lucky. I've rarely had to compromise in ten movies who I wanted in my films. I can only say the guys are great. I fought for the people I wanted and I got them. It sounds like I'm sucking up, but I'm not. Sam Jackson is brilliant.

Critics might undervalue your work, but the great actors certainly don't. Thespians like De Niro and Anthony Quinn line up to work with you. How does that make you feel?

TS: Great! [Laughs] I started out my career where I was so pigeon-holed doing visual, mood-atmospheric pieces. Slowly the perception has changed. I think the turning point was *True Romance*. Even if people didn't like the movie, I think they saw that I knew how to work with actors; I knew how to get performances on the screen. My life started to change then. I think my biggest rush is watching great actors perform. And I'm always intimidated by them. I'm in awe of them. I always do my homework so I know exactly where I've got to be.

FILMOGRAPHY FOR TONY SCOTT

1. *Leaving Memory* (1969) D
2. *The Hitter* (1979) A
3. *The Hunger* (1983) D
4. *Top Gun* (1986) D
5. *Beverly Hills Cop II* (1987) D
6. *Revenge* (1990) D
7. *Days of Thunder* (1990) D
8. *The Last Boy Scout* (1991) D
9. *True Romance* (1993) D
10. *Cityscrapes: Los Angeles* (1994) A
11. *Crimson Tide* (1995) D
12. *The Fan* (1996) D
13. *Wild Bill: Hollywood Maverick* (1996) A
14. *The Hunger* (1997) D & Ex-P
15. *Clay Pigeons* (1998) Ex-P
16. *Enemy of the State* (1998) D
17. *RKO 281* (1999) [TV] P
18. *The Last Debate* (2000) Ex-P
19. *Where the Money Is* (2000) Ex-P
20. *Big Time* (2001) Ex-P
21. *Spy Game* (2001) D
22. *The Hire: Beat the Devil* (2002) D & Ex-P
23. *The Hire: Hostage* (2002) Ex-P
24. *The Hire: Ticker* (2002) Ex-P
25. *Six Bullets from Now* (2002) Ex-P
26. *Man on Fire* (2004) D & P
27. *Domino* (2005) D & P
28. *Tristan & Isolde* (2006) Ex-P
29. *The Assassination of Jesse James by the Coward Robert Ford* (2006) Ex-P
30. *Deja Vu* (2006) D & P

Alan Shapiro

Alan Shapiro directed his first amateur film at the age of twelve. While attending courses at New York University Film School, his first student film *Briefly ... Brian* (1978) garnered much praise, including winning Best Student Film at Cannes. Based on the promise he showed with that student film, Warner Bros. provided Shapiro with a scholarship and an apprenticeship under director Ken Russell on the set of *Altered States* (1980). In 1979, Shapiro directed the telefilm *Meeting Halfway*, featuring future filmmaker Keith Gordon.

Shapiro then had the (seemingly) good fortune of selling his original screenplay *Stonybrook* to Warner Bros., with himself attached as director. Then the unbelievable happened — Dustin Hoffman signed on to the project. This was, of course, every filmmaker's dream. However, the dream soon turned into a nightmare as Shapiro was asked to step down from the project, and a number of events (Hoffman's backing out being a major one) led to the project eventually being permanently shelved. When many other filmmakers would have given up, Shapiro climbed back on the proverbial horse and returned to work.

In 1984, Shapiro wrote and directed the Cable Ace Award–winning telefilm *Tiger Town* for Disney. He then served as producer on the time travel adventure *The Blue Yonder* (1985) before writing and directing another film for Disney. The heartfelt family film *The Christmas Star* (1986) told the story of an escaped convict (played by Edward Asner) who is befriended by neighborhood children who believe he's Santa Claus. Shapiro was then handpicked by acclaimed filmmaker Francis Ford Coppola to write and direct the two-hour pilot for his television series *The Outsiders*, which featured such up-and-coming actors as David Arquette, Michael Madsen, and Billy Bob Thornton.

In 1993, Shapiro officially arrived in Hollywood when he directed the hit thriller *The Crush*. The film, which marked the feature film debut of Shapiro's discovery, Alicia Silverstone, was nominated for three MTV Movie Awards. In 1996, Shapiro wrote and directed the big-budget film adaptation *Flipper*, starring Paul Hogan, Elijah Wood, and Isaac Hayes.

At the time of this writing Shapiro is in preproduction on a thriller entitled *The New Girl* (2006).

Favorite Films: *The Bicycle Thief* (1948), *City Lights* (1931), *The Wizard of Oz* (1939), *One Flew Over the Cuckoos Nest* (1975), and *The 400 Blows* (1959).

ANDREW RAUSCH: *Early in your career you sold a spec script,* Stonybrook, *to Warner Bros., with yourself attached to direct Dustin Hoffman in the film. You must have been extremely overjoyed at the time.*

ALAN SHAPIRO: Yes, I was. It was like the Hollywood stairway to heaven. Little did I realize that I had in fact stepped onto the "down" elevator which continued its descent to the sub-basement level, where I was rudely asked to leave.

You were removed from the project, which then suffered a number of setbacks and was ultimately shelved. How did this horrifying experience change your perceptions of the business?
AS: It was a marvelous education. It was a crash course — in slow motion — in Development Hell and a system where insecure movie stars and their minions can — and do — ruin everything.

When you discovered Alicia Silverstone for The Crush, *did you have any idea how big she would become?*
AS: I didn't know, of course, what the future would hold for Alicia (or anything, for that matter), but as I watched her on the set and in dailies I was increasingly astonished at both her talent and my good fortune in casting her out of oblivion. I believed when the world at large saw her performance they would be similarly impressed.

When The Crush *was aired on television, her character's name was changed from Darian to Adrian, which I found unusual. Why was that?*
AS: That was per Warner Bros., and done entirely outside of my involvement. I thought it was weird, too. Astute observation!

In his review of the film, Hal Hinson of The Washington Post *calls* The Crush *an "invitation to child abuse." Would you care to comment on that?*

Teen dream Adrienne Forrester (Alicia Silverstone) attempts to seduce older man Nick Eliot (Cary Elwes) in this memorable scene from *The Crush* **(Morgan Creek Productions, 1993).**

AS: [Laughs] That may be one of the kinder reviews. One labeled me a "leering pedophile." I was initially incredulous at the level of vitriol the movie incurred because it was always very tongue-in-cheek for me. Eventually I wore it as a badge of honor. To have successfully engendered so severe a response, I must have hit a few bullseyes.

Let's talk about Flipper. *There's an old filmmaking adage that says you never make a film on water, with kids, or with animals. On that film you worked with all three. I understand that was a pretty rough shoot?*

AS: The physical elements that were required on the production of *Flipper* contained every possible nightmare. I was a huge fan of Steven Spielberg and the making of *Jaws* [1975], the mythology of *Jaws*. So I knew all the great horror stories and I'd read every interview. I sort of called *Flipper* "*Jaws*-lite" because I started assembling the same team. First of all, I had Bill Butler as camera, and he shot *Jaws*. We were doing an animal water movie, in this case a yipping, happy animal. But it was the same elements—massive underwater shooting, on-the-water shooting, in-the-water shooting.... Then, lo and behold, my producer ends up being Sid Sheinberg, who was Spielberg's mentor.

Some of the anecdotes about making the movie are sort of very similar to things you heard about *Jaws*, which was all the nightmares, like shooting on water.... You set a shot and then all of a sudden it just drifts away! Then, it's an animal movie. And it's a *smart* animal. Smart animals, as opposed to a dumb animal, are much more difficult to work with because you ask them to do this one trick and then they get bored and don't want to do it anymore. They've done that and they're ready to move on. And as we know about film, it requires a lot of repetition. Go from A to B or whatever it is. So the dolphins were impossible, and this was a magnet for environmental political maniacs. And I happen to be a real animal person, but it's a lightning rod for that stuff. We were in the Bahamas for what turned out to be the worst hurricane of the century, so we were constantly getting killed by weather. It was one-hundred degrees with one-hundred-percent humidity *every* day. Since this was a totally exterior movie, we were outside from sun up to sun down. You had to wear space suits so you didn't get third-degree sunburn.

With kids involved you have very limited shooting times. You're in a third-world country. We were in the Bahamas, which was rugged in many respects. Just doing anything involved with water is really, really hard. Our schedule went from sixty days to eighty-something days. And everyday I thought I was going to be fired.

Luke Halpin, of the original television series Flipper, *appears in the film. How did that come about?*

AS: He was, like a lot of child actors, in a tragic downfall. He had some drug problems or whatever, and then he started working as a grip in the South Florida area. We were just talking in pre-production and somebody had mentioned that he was a grip. I said we should at least put him in the movie for sentimental reasons. He could probably use the work. He was thrilled. It was pretty emotional for him.

You also worked with Isaac Hayes on that film. What was he like to work with?

AS: Absolute sweetheart. One of my favorite moments—ever—was being on the set with Isaac and he was doing something I didn't like and I wanted him do it differently, so I asked him to do it differently. And he looked at me and he goes, "Hey, you da man." I thought, "Wow! Isaac Hayes is telling me that I'm the man. [Laughs] Okay. I could die today."

One of the criticisms of Flipper *was that it takes place in the Bahamas, yet there's only one central black character in the film.*

Fourteen-year-old Sandy Ricks (Elijah Wood) and his bohemian uncle, Porter (Paul Hogan), in Alan Shapiro's *Flipper* (Universal Pictures, 1996).

AS: Well, that's one more than any of the others were. It's funny. I mean, there were only so many central characters. There's the kid, the uncle, Paul Hogan, and then there's the love interest.... I mean, I felt pretty good about making him a black character. I didn't feel any pressure to, I just felt like I wanted to round it out a little. If it wasn't enough, I don't know.... There really weren't that many parts in that movie.

The one thing is that, when I took the job, this was a property. I didn't invent *Flipper*. There's only so much you can bring to it. I remember when I agreed to do it I said, "You know, the great thing about this is that it's *Flipper*, but the thing that sucks is also that it's *Flipper*." [Laughs] On the suck side, you know, what are you gonna do with *Flipper* that's gonna be really earth-shattering?

I mean, the one thing that I did do—and I couldn't believe I got it through—and had a blast writing it, was writing in this whole thing with the Hammerhead shark. This villain in the water for Flipper and this big fight that goes down and all this. Of course, the executives don't really know their heads from their butts, so they didn't really question it, and I just said, "Yeah, sure we can do that. Blah, blah, blah..." And then it comes to doing it and you're dealing with making that happen, which wasn't easy. We had to build this amazing animatronic shark and do digital stuff. So just as a filmmaker, it was kind of cool to get involved with all of that.

I've never been much of a Flipper *fan, but I thought the film was done quite well. It was one of the few adaptations of old television series that I've felt that way about. Most of them are very poor in both concept and execution.*

AS: For the record, I wasn't a *Flipper* fan either. I was doing another film at Universal, *Archie*, which was another rehash. I was doing something entirely different and they asked me if I would do *Flipper*. I resisted it and then sort of went into it. More and more it's getting hard to get a movie made, so if a big studio is saying, "Make this movie for us," you gotta do those things.

Like I said, there was a lot of cool stuff in it, just from a filmmaking view. I was very intrigued by doing *Jaws*-lite and living through some of the Spielberg mythology.

So anyway, that was sort of a long-winded way to say that it was never my life's dream to make *Flipper*! [Laughs]

Actually, there were some things I really liked about the movie. I don't dislike the film, it's just that it's —

AS: *Flipper*! [Laughs]

Right. It's just one of those things where you tend to have a predisposed idea about the film before you see it. If you don't like Flipper, *you're not going to be overly excited about seeing the film.*

AS: Oh, sure! And it's really easy to have an immediate defensive kind of cynicism about it like, "Oh, there's another stupid TV remake!" They're always doing these things. They make so much crap today. It's mostly crap. I call it "industrial waste." It's just feeding a big machine. There's so much greed. It's a really unfortunate time in the industry, I think. In my brief tenure in the business, which is twenty years, it has changed hugely.

What are some of the ways you've seen it change during that time?

AS: As the business has internationalized, more and more focus has gone on dumbing down the movies, if you will. They're much more interested in films that translate into multi-continents, like action, sex, big stars. So the films become dumber and dumber and more expensive. That is a function of the business internationalizing. It's much more domestic now. Think about the movies from my point of view that really inspired me and changed my life: *One Flew Over the Cuckoo's Nest* or *Midnight Cowboy* [1969] or *Summer of '42* [1971]. Those wouldn't be made today, and that's really sad.

FILMOGRAPHY FOR ALAN SHAPIRO

1. *Briefly...Brian* (1978) [TV] D
2. *Meeting Halfway* (1979) [TV] D
3. *Tiger Town* (1983) [TV] D & Sc
4. *The House on Sorority Row* (1983) CA
5. *The Blue Yonder* (1985) [TV] P
6. *The Christmas Star* (1986) [TV] D, Sc, P
7. *Crossing the Mob* (1988) [TV] Sc
8. *The Outsiders* (1990) D
9. *The Crush* (1993) D & Sc
10. *Flipper* (1996) D & Sc

Bryan Singer

New Jersey native Bryan Singer began making Super-8 films when he was thirteen. In the mid–1980s Singer attended USC film school, where he formed a filmmaking collective with composer/editor John Ottman and producer Kenneth Kokin. He then crafted a $16,000 short film entitled *Lion's Den* (1988), which starred Ethan Hawke. On the strength of this short, Singer received funding for his independent feature film debut, *Public Access* (1993). The film was met with critical acclaim and won both the Grand Jury Prize at Sundance and the Critics Award at the Deauville Film Festival. Although Singer found modest success with *Public Access*, nothing could prepare him for the reaction his second film would receive. With *The Usual Suspects* (1995) Singer not only avoided the "sophomore slump," but managed to create one of the decade's finest films. *The Usual Suspects* would ultimately win a slew of awards, including Oscars for screenwriter Christopher McQuarrie and leading man Kevin Spacey.

In 1998, Singer successfully salvaged the long-stalled Stephen King adaptation *Apt Pupil* (the film had been in the works, with various directors attached, for nearly fifteen years), which starred Brad Renfro and Academy Award–nominee Ian McKellen. Singer's study of evil failed to find an audience, however, and was met with less-than-glowing reviews. For his fourth film Singer brought another long-dormant project to life with *X-Men* (2000). "Once I start something, I always finish it," Singer says. "They had been trying to get *X-Men* made for thirty years, and they thought maybe if I got involved it might actually happen." Not only did Singer succeed in getting *X-Men* made, the film became one of the year's largest box office draws, raking in more than $100 million. (The film made $55 million in the opening weekend alone.) Singer then directed the film's sequel, *X2* (2002), which was another colossal hit. Singer then jumped ship from the *X-Men* franchise to go to work on the rival superhero film *Superman Returns* (2006).

"I love filmmaking, and I love the process," Singer explains. "And I would rather do nothing else. It's a privilege to be able to paint such big pictures, so to speak.... When a piece of acting jumps off the screen, or when an idea comes across and you see the finished set, or you see them cut together, and you say, 'Wow, that was just like I dreamed of. I'm so glad to be able to inspire that.' Because it really is a collaboration; it's hardly one person's picture. Most importantly, it'll be there forever. It'll be there long after I'm dead."

Favorite Films: *Lawrence of Arabia* (1962), *Close Encounters of the Third Kind* (1977), *The King of Comedy* (1983), *Pink Floyd's The Wall* (1982), *Friday* (1995), and *Willy Wonka and the Chocolate Factory* (1971).

ANDREW RAUSCH: *A lot of your work is very dark. I was wondering if you were a fan of film noir?*

BRYAN SINGER: I never grew up being a big fan of film noir, though I've gone back and been intrigued by films that have had anti-heroes and not-so-happy endings. If anything, I've merely been intrigued by them. Ultimately, film noir in a classic sense was never a genre that I followed, though.

Forgive me for making this observation, but you mentioned that two of your favorite films are Pink Floyd's The Wall *and* Friday. *Each of those films is, in its own way, notoriously linked to the drug culture. Do you smoke?*

BS: [Laughs] Not really, but I understand that world and I appreciate it. And characters that are high.... I mean, just showing people that are high or are smoking weed, like in *Dazed and Confused* [1993] or *Poltergeist* [1982], is one thing, but it takes a movie like *Friday* to truly capture the essence of that experience in that kind of detail. I admire that. If anyone can do that about any experience in a film, it's a good thing — you know, the way that Oliver Stone did with LSD in *The Doors* (1991).

The American Film Institute recently unveiled a list ranking the 100 greatest American films. What are your thoughts on such lists?

BS: At first you recoil at something like that because you look at your favorite movies that are not on that list. Then you look at some of your less favorite movies that somehow made it onto the list. But then, you stop and you say, "You know what? If this is gonna help

Bryan Singer on the set of his masterpiece, *The Usual Suspects* (Gramercy Pictures, 1995).

some kid out there get off their butt and rent *Citizen Kane* [1941], which is a fucking masterpiece, then it's worthwhile." I look at it like the Academy Awards; it's this pious kind of self-righteous view of what films are the "best," but then it also gets people to go and see films like *The Piano* [1993] and *Happiness* [1998] — things like that which they might not ordinarily see. Or even *The Usual Suspects* or *Gods and Monsters* [1998], for that matter. I think in that way, the Academy Awards, top-one-hundred lists, and critics in general serve a valuable function.

I was a little bit disappointed that The Usual Suspects *wasn't on the AFI's list.*

BS: Sure. I probably felt the same way, but then that's only in concept rather than practice. I look at *The Usual Suspects* differently than you might.

It's one of those unique stories where you take that very difficult challenge of making up a story with that *Rashomon* [1950] concept, and you actually pull it off. That's a very unique phenomenon that kind of all came together. I think *The Usual Suspects* is a very good film with a very great ending.

Your last two films, The Usual Suspects *and* Apt Pupil, *both had intense twist endings. Do those types of endings appeal to you as a viewer?*

BS: Absolutely. I think when you get into the predictable climax, I think the audience is ready to leave. I think it's a lot more fun to take the audience to a place where they really don't know what's going to happen; anything can still occur right up until the last frame. I think that's great. That's something I loved about *Raiders of the Lost Ark* [1981]. He saved the day, he got the Ark of the Covenant, and everything's put to bed. Then he asks, "Where's the Ark?" And they say, "We have top men working on it." He says, "What kind of men?" And they say, "*Top* men." Then you see the Ark being wheeled into this giant, cavernous space and you realize there's still another story there. I think that's always exciting. That's what I like about *The Usual Suspects* and *Apt Pupil*, for that matter — they're very unpredictable.

The Usual Suspects *is widely-regarded as one of the finest films of the past decade. Did you have any sense of just how special the film was when you were making it?*

BS: Not during the production, but during the test screenings, and as it was coming together, I saw the ending as being a very unique and special one. But one can never truly predict or interpret one's own work like that.

That final scene is definitely one of the most memorable in the history of cinema.

BS: I think it's a combination of the voices that are coming through, the story turn, and the music. I think those things really combine to create a nice effect.

When we hear Keyser Soze speak, we don't know that he's actually Verbal Kint. Pulling that off was ingenious. Were those lines actually spoken by Kevin Spacey?

BS: Yeah. Those were all Kevin.

I've been told that "Soze" is a Turkish word for "talk." Is that correct?

BS: It actually means "one who talks too much."

So this was intended as a clue that Verbal was Keyser Soze?

BS: Yeah. I don't know how many people figured it out, but the clue was there.

The order in which Kobayashi hands out the packages is the same order the characters in the film die. Was this scripted that way or was it something you came up with?

BS: No. I think I just stacked them that way on the day, but I can't remember whether that was intentional in relation to their deaths. I just remember that it made sense to me, but I don't remember if that aspect of it was intentional. I remember stacking them and saying, "This is the order they should be in," but I don't know why, though. Maybe. That's so weird that I can't remember....

Benicio del Toro's line, "He'll flip ya, flip ya for real," is a line from Straight, No Chaser *(1989). Whose idea was it to incorporate that line?*
BS: That was Benicio's. I didn't know that was from that other movie until just now, but I'll bet Benicio saw it.

I'm going to name some actors you've worked with, and I'd like to hear your thoughts on them.
BS: Okay.

Let's start with Ian McKellen.
BS: Ian's a great actor. He helps you forget everything that's remotely pretentious about being a movie actor and everything that's wonderful about being an actor. He truly loves the process. He loves acting.

I interviewed Ian a while ago when Apt Pupil *first came out. The thing that struck me as interesting is that he often plays these very powerful, sadistically evil characters to perfection, yet he's the nicest, most charming man you could ever hope to meet.*

Dean Keaton (Gabriel Byrne) and "Verbal" Kint (Kevin Spacey) take turns reading in a police line-up in *The Usual Suspects* (Gramercy Pictures, 1995).

BS: Yes. He's very sweet. You know, I just found out this past week that I'm going to be working with him again on *X-Men*. He's playing Magneto, the villain.

What are your thoughts on Kevin Spacey?

BS: He's a really terrific actor. A really serious actor who gives you his all. He's very, very intelligent. I think until *The Usual Suspects* he hadn't had a chance to break out. A lot of people still didn't know who he was, but I think he's always been a really tremendous actor, and I think he's always been recognized as such.

Gabriel Byrne.

BS: A very natural actor. He makes detail in his performances seem effortless. Very sympathetic and very handsome. In fact, more handsome with every passing year. He's also very underrated. Gabriel gave a performance in *The Usual Suspects* that is, especially in the light of Spacey's exposure, very worthy of recognition. In that movie, he did things that I didn't even see until I was editing, which were very subtle and very clever.

Kevin Pollak.

BS: A very talented actor. I just saw him again in *Casino* (1995), and it just reminded me how brilliant he is. He can be very dangerous sometimes for a comedian. You forget sometimes how tough he can be. That's why I was happy to cast him in that movie.

Brandon Routh, Kevin Spacey, and Bryan Singer discuss the scene they are about to shoot on the set of *Superman Returns* (Warner Bros. Pictures, 2006).

Brad Renfro.

BS: Brad is very smart and very natural. He's young and still getting his chops, but a very gifted and smart young actor. He thinks like a filmmaker. I think that's what he will be one day.

Apt Pupil *was one of the better Stephen King adaptations to date. Why do you think so many filmmakers have difficulty in successfully adapting his work?*

BS: They were just done by bad filmmakers or by filmmakers who were treating them like "B" genre pictures rather than serious movies.

What were some of the considerations that went into changing King's original ending?

BS: I found that to get to a place where Brad Renfro could be on a freeway overpass firing a rifle at cars, I thought you had to take the journey the book takes you on, which was multiple murder. They both become multiple serial killers. I felt that in book form, it was kind of fun. I thought it was a wild romp, but in a movie it would be a little exploitive, repetitive, and a bit corny. In dealing with the holocaust as an element in the story, it didn't feel right to go there. I felt it was much more chilling to show the beginning of that journey — the potential for Todd to become that type of creature, or even a different type of creature that's equally as dangerous. He was an upper middle class kid with good grades. He could even become President of the United States. No one knows what secrets he holds and just what he's capable of.

What do you see as being the single biggest problem with Hollywood?

BS: Writers' and actors' fees. Not that they don't deserve the money, mind you, because they do. They are the backbone of the movies, but the trouble is that their fees and their availability have become so strained that the days when you could develop a film with a writer until it was the best it could be, and the actors were available and under contract to be in that movie, are over. As a result, we force movies into production quickly. We hire writers to do brief polishes, and everybody's racing towards when Sharon and Tom will be available to do a movie. The writers are these high-paid guys who come in and do a quick polish for half-a-million dollars or more. But nobody puts the full developmental time into movies that they once did, and that's been the detriment of movies. That's what's wrong with Hollywood.

That sounds almost like a line from your film Public Access. *"That's what's wrong with Hollywood." [Laughs]*

BS: Yes, but it is absolutely what is wrong. I've watched it. If you look at the history of any shitty movie, you'll find out that it was stuff like that. Nobody stood there and just developed the damn thing until it was as great as it could be.

FILMOGRAPHY FOR BRYAN SINGER

1. *Lion's Den* (1993) D & Sc
2. *Public Access* (1993) D, Ex-P, Sc
3. *The Usual Suspects* (1995) D & P
4. *Cannes Man* (1996) A
5. *Apt Pupil* (1998) D & P
6. *Burn* (1998) Ex-P
7. *X-Men* (2000) D & Co-Sc
8. *X2* (2002) D, S, Ex-P, Un A
9. *Star Trek Nemesis* (2002) Un A
10. *House, M.D.* [episodes: various] (2004–2006) D & Ex-P
11. *Superman Returns* (2006) D & Ex-P

John Singleton

After winning three major awards while attending USC's Filmic Writing Program, screenwriter/director John Singleton secured a contract with Creative Artists Agency. Shortly thereafter, Columbia Pictures purchased his screenplay *Boyz n the Hood* (1991), with Singleton himself attached as director. With that film, which follows the lives of two friends growing up in war-torn South Central Los Angeles, Singleton established himself as a visionary filmmaker with a unique perspective. The project was well-received by critics, and earned Singleton Oscar nominations for Best Original Screenplay and Best Director. (Singleton was the first African-American filmmaker nominated for the Best Director statuette, as well as the youngest ever, at twenty-four.) For *Boyz*, Singleton also received Best New Filmmaker honors from both the MTV Movie Awards and the New York Film Critics Circle, as well as a Writers Guild nomination. The media quickly lumped Singleton together with other major African-American directors of the time — Spike Lee, Matty Rich, and Robert Townsend — dubbing them the "Black Pack." (The filmmaking careers of Singleton and Lee have since outlived those of Rich and Townsend.)

As Hollywood has churned out a slew of unimaginative *Boyz n the Hood* rip-offs over the past decade, Singleton himself has moved on; he has since directed seven very distinctive films: *Poetic Justice* (1993), *Higher Learning* (1995), *Rosewood* (1997), *Shaft* (2000), *Baby Boy* (2001), *2 Fast 2 Furious* (2003), and *Four Brothers* (2005). The filmmaker, who credits influences as diverse as Akira Kurosawa and Marvin Gaye, has also appeared in a number of film and music video cameos; directed the $2 million video for Michael Jackson's "Remember the Time," starring Eddie Murphy; created his own video game; and co-written a book. In addition, Singleton has directed a number of high-profile television commercials and has produced a number of films, including *Woo* (1998), *Hustle & Flow* (2005), and *Black Snake Moan* (2006).

At the time of this writing Singleton was working on a number of projects, including a film about Marvel superhero Luke Cage and an adaptation of Tom Clancy's novel *Without Remorse*.

Favorite Films: *Shaft* (1971), *Raiders of the Lost Ark* (1981), *E.T. the Extra-Terrestrial* (1982), *The Seven Samurai* (1954), *Jaws* (1975), *The Empire Strikes Back* (1981), *Raging Bull* (1980), *Do the Right Thing* (1989), *Halloween* (1978), and *Cinema Paradiso* (1988).

MICHAEL DEQUINA: *Judging from your favorite films, I'm guessing you're a big Steven Spielberg fan?*

JOHN SINGLETON: Did I mention *Jaws*? I can't emphasize that enough. That, and *Raiders of the Lost Ark*.

Let me tell you a story I haven't told anyone. I don't care if you print it or not. I haven't even told Spielberg this, but I'm going to tell him one day. I saw *Raiders of the Lost Ark* at the Chinese Theater when I was thirteen years old. I'm watching it, and I had to go to the bathroom. But I didn't want to leave, you know what I mean? So I took this cup — this lemonade cup — and I pissed in the cup. But when I reached down to piss in the cup, it was the first time I noticed I had pubic hair. While I was watching *Raiders of the Lost Ark* I realized I had my first pubic hair! [Laughs] I became a man watching *Raiders of the Lost Ark*!

Did you do any writing or directing prior to film school?

JS: I didn't do a lot of writing, but I made films. I basically read up on what filmmakers did when they were young, and then I did everything that they did. I'd read that Steven Spielberg had made eight Super-8 movies when he was in junior high school and high school, so that's what I did — I made Super-8 movies. I got the equipment from the junior college; I started taking junior college classes while I was in high school in cinematography just so I could get the equipment, and I started shooting little films. By the time I was in the twelfth grade I'd made four or five films.

My teacher had graduated from USC Film School. I had visited USC Film School when I was in the eleventh grade, and after reading a book about George Lucas I said, "That's it. I've got to go to USC." I then started hanging around the USC campus. I had to get into USC, and there was nothing that could stop me — except for my grades; I had a B average. But what pushed me over the top was that I had personalized my application; I had ingratiated myself to the staff of the school. They didn't have anybody there that looked like me, and they had very few people who had a real passion.

Everybody at that time wanted to be George Lucas or Steven Spielberg; when you're young and you're going to school and just finding yourself, you barely get the time to know who you are. I had a good sense of who I was, and that was even more solidified when, just a few weeks before attending film school, I met Spike Lee. I saw *She's Gotta Have It* [1986], and I met Spike outside the theater. He took the time to talk to me, and I said, "I'm starting film school in about a week. Just watch." [Laughs] Cocky, you know? In the writing classes they always said "write what you know." I was like, "What do I know?" I'd already written about my family and how fractured it was, and I thought I should write about my friends and growing up in my neighborhood. I had written a proposal when I was in high school to get into USC about the three films I was going to make. One of those was about three friends growing up in South Central Los Angeles, and the different paths they take. And that idea from high school turned out to be *Boyz n the Hood*. I had keyed into the things that were specific about the area where I was from, and just ran with it as my entry into the business. It helped that I was influenced by hip-hop culture and, at that time, very few people film-wise had any type of hip-hop attitude or element to their work. There was a whole other massive pop-culture movement happening out there that had not been reflected in film. So one of the things I did in my pitch to Columbia, which is how I got the $6 million steward, is I said, "This movie is like *Easy Rider* [1969]! It hasn't been made yet. Everybody out there is waiting for this movie, but you guys have never made a movie like this. I'm going to make it!" I learned early on that if you talk big and you can back it up, you can be successful in any business.

You became the youngest filmmaker in history to receive an Oscar nomination for Best Director. What was it like to suddenly hear people mentioning you in the same breath with Orson Welles?

JS: Knowing film history, I was like, "No, I'm not going to crash and burn and be ostracized in the end the way he was. I'm going to do what I have to do to make movies, and make *good* movies."

John Singleton on the set of his first film, *Boyz n the Hood* (Columbia Pictures, 1991).

Did you start getting a lot of offers after the success of Boyz n the Hood?

JS: Not really. They didn't know what to do with me. There was a whole thing at the time where everyone was saying, "Let's find the next John Singleton." That could have been a young black kid, a young white kid.... Just a young talented filmmaker who would make a movie for nothing and make a shitload of money. Since that time they've attempted to do it with different people. They build them up to tear them down. They're always looking for the next wunderkind, whether it's Quentin Tarantino or Spike Jonez.... a visionary. They build you up and then say, "Well, he really wasn't shit." [Laughs] And you can't get mired into that shit. You just have to do what you've gotta do, and continue on.

You mentioned that Boyz n the Hood *came from your own childhood. Where did* Poetic Justice *come from?*

JS: It just came from my imagination. It's funny. I have issues with that film, but then at the same time, in retrospect it was great because, even at twenty four years old, I didn't make too bad a film. I could have done something ten times more violent. I mean, *Boyz n the Hood* wasn't violent, but I could have done an action movie. Instead I chose to make something more introspective. It wasn't a perfect film, but it was thoughtful in a sense, but it was still street. I think it shows my maturity as a filmmaker.

My only problem with the film is that I wrote it so quickly. If I had focused more and taken more time with the script, it would have been ten times better. It was a journey. Any filmmaker who takes some kind of journey in terms of their career ends up making a road movie or something where there's some sort of travel. That's what I was doing with *Poetic Justice*.

When I came back to *Higher Learning*, this was after the riots and everything, and my attitude was like, "You know what? Fuck everybody! I'm going to make something that makes

Justice (Janet Jackson) and Lucky (Tupac Shakur) in a scene from John Singleton's street romance *Poetic Justice* (Columbia Pictures, 1993).

a statement, but at the same time fucks with everybody's heads." It wasn't going to be an all-black cast. I wanted to make it very multi-ethnic and deal with different characters and their issues of race and sexuality ... loneliness, as well as the desire to belong. I dealt with all of those things through the characters in that film. That's why — after six years— that movie still holds up to anything that's out now! You see that kid Remy and you're like, "Damn! That's exactly like what's happening at all of these schools with the shootings and everything." Thank God I made it before Columbine! I would never have been able to release that film after that.

Then with *Rosewood*, I was on my way to making a different movie. Rosewood came about because Jon Peters called me — and nobody really ever calls me to do a film — and he said, "I've got this article I'd like you to read and turn into a movie." I read the article about Rosewood in *Esquire* and I went to visit the survivors, who were now in their eighties and nineties. I had my heart set on making this other film, but I had never met anybody who had gone through what those people had. And being a city kid, I had issues with the South. I was like, "Fuck the South. I'm not going down South." And this old black woman told me, "Either you're going to make this movie, or Steven Spielberg's going to make this movie. We want you to make this movie." So I did it. *Rosewood* was good, and it marked another maturity for me as a filmmaker, although it was a low point for me financially in regards to the box office. It wasn't really a film that was accepted in its theatrical release — by anybody. The subject matter was just too disconcerting. But on video and DVD the movie has had a life of its own. That and *Boyz n the Hood* are the two movies that people most often come up to me and talk about; especially the older people come up to me and say, "*Rosewood* was a really good film, and you really did a good job making that movie."

How did Shaft *come about?*

JS: *Shaft* had been in the works around the time I made *Higher Learning*. I had wanted to do it since *Boyz n the Hood*; I was like, "We should do another *Shaft* movie." MGM purchased the rights for me to direct and produce from Turner, who controlled the rights to MGM properties from way back. Once they bought the rights from Turner, they found that this could be a lucrative film property. Ted Turner then put out a mandate saying they would not sell the rights to any more films to anyone. So it started at MGM as a $25 million movie. It was going to be Richard Roundtree as the original Shaft, a new guy as the son of Shaft, and Lauryn Hill as the daughter. With Richard Roundtree's character I was planning to basically make "Shaft Meets the Dark Knight Returns"; basically, he's dying, and he's going on this last adventure. I was set on Richard Roundtree still kicking ass. But MGM didn't believe in the project, so they gave it back to me in turnaround to set it up somewhere else.

Then I got a call from Scott Rudin who says, "Hey, I dig this. We should do this together." We partnered up on this movie. We ended up being like oil and water, but we still made a great film. It was hell to get it done, but at the same time I look at it as my only pure Hollywood movie. It was my baby that ended up becoming just a big Hollywood blockbuster. I can't say it was hard to make the movie, because I had more resources than I'd ever had before. That was good, but it was also bad because I saw how the so-called "other half" lives and I had less respect for it. How can you have passion when it's almost like a cushy job? You get paid all this money and you have all the fucking time in the world to shoot a page and a half! "I was like, I have to go back to shooting three pages a day!"

You tend to use a lot of performers who are non-actors; people like Ice Cube, Janet Jackson, Tyrese, Gordon Parks.... What do they bring to these projects?

JS: They bring flaws that breathe. There's a possibility of being too perfect. But people who don't act bring flaws that actually breathe and bring those characters to life. That's what I love.

Filmography for John Singleton

1. *Boyz n the Hood* (1991) D, Sc, Un A
2. *Poetic Justice* (1993) D, Sc, P
3. *Beverly Hills Cop III* (1994) A
4. *Higher Learning* (1995) D, Sc, P
5. *Your Studio and You* (1995) A
6. *Michael Jackson: Video Greatest Hits — HIStory* (1995)
7. *Rosewood* (1997) D & Sc
8. *Woo* (1998) Ex-P
9. *Shaft* (2000) D, Sc, P, Un A
10. *Baby Boy* (2001) D, Sc, P
11. *2 Fast 2 Furious* (2003) D, Sc, P
12. *Baadasssss!* (2003) A
13. *Time Out* (2004) Ex-P
14. *Hustle & Flow* (2005) P
15. *Four Brothers* (2005) D, P
16. *Black Snake Moan* (2006) P
17. *Illegal Tender* (2007) P

Kevin Smith

Kevin Smith's 1994 debut film *Clerks* was a festival favorite, receiving praise and awards at both Cannes and Sundance, and quickly established the young New Jersey filmmaker as a major force in the independent film world. Smith then fell victim to the "sophomore slump" with his follow-up film, *Mallrats* (1995), which was panned across the board. Smith soon returned to form, however, with his third feature, *Chasing Amy* (1997). With this Ben Affleck–starrer, which is arguably one of the finest films of the nineties, Smith displayed a newfound maturity while still delivering the laughs he's become known for. Smith and his cast received critical praise for their work on the film and were recognized from a variety of awards groups, including the Independent Spirit Awards, the British Independent Film Awards, and the MTV Movie Awards. That same year Smith made headlines when he was enlisted by Warner Bros. to pen a script for a new Superman movie which would be directed by Tim Burton. Burton would ultimately reject Smith's script, leading to a longstanding feud in the press between the two filmmakers.

Not content to rest on his laurels, Smith tackled theology in his ambitious fourth outing, *Dogma* (1999). The controversial religious farce, which starred Affleck, Matt Damon, Chris Rock, and George Carlin, was perceived as being blasphemous by many. The film then caught the attention of the Catholic League, who called for a boycott. Smith's next movie, *Jay & Silent Bob Strike Back* (2001), was arguably his lightest. With this film, which Smith initially saw as being the last entry in his "Jersey Cycle," he revisited many of the characters from his four previous pictures.

Smith then wrote and directed the light comedy *Jersey Girl* (2004). With this film about the relationship between a single father and his young daughter, Smith wanted to make a slightly more serious movie than those he had made previously. Sadly, the film soon became caught up in a media backlash against its lovebird stars Ben Affleck and Jennifer Lopez. After Affleck and Lopez's previous pairing (*Gigli*, 2003) bombed, Miramax held *Jersey Girl* back nearly a year and then recut it significantly to reduce Lopez's screen time. These cuts did little to lure audiences to see the movie, and, as a result, damaged the film itself.

As a filmmaker, Smith is a quadruple threat: he writes, directs, acts, and produces. Aside from his own pictures, Smith has done some script doctoring, and also wrote an as-of-yet-unproduced script based on *The Six-Million Dollar Man*. Smith executive produced 1997's *Good Will Hunting*, which went on to make over $100 million for Miramax. In addition, he has also written storylines for a number of comic books, including *Jay and Silent Bob*, *Daredevil*, and *Clerks*.

At the time of this writing, Smith was in postproduction on his sixth film, *Clerks 2* (2006).

Favorite Films: *Jaws* (1975), *JFK* (1991), *A Man for All Seasons* (1966), *The Last Temptation of Christ* (1988), and *Do the Right Thing* (1989).

ANDREW RAUSCH: *Here's a question you've probably never been asked in an interview before.... I know that you're a big Run-DMC fan. I was wondering which of their films you enjoyed the most:* Krush Groove *(1985) or* Tougher Than Leather *(1988)?*

KEVIN SMITH: [Laughs] Hands down, *Krush Groove*! Come on, man. It's like the secret origin of Run-DMC and the Fat Boys.

A lot of your work feels very personal. You've said that Clerks *was, in some ways, very autobiographical for you. I remember reading in the* Playboy *interview that some of* Chasing Amy *was autobiographical in terms of the emotions Holden is feeling. Is there ever a sense of self-consciousness or embarrassment after baring your soul in a film?*

KS: Not really. The films are, more or less, therapeutic for me in as much as I get to work through the immature idiosyncrasies that hold most guys back from becoming men. That's what the films are generally about to me — the struggle with maturity, and the effort to leave youth behind.

What was the first film that really had an impact on you?

KS: I would have to say that *Jaws* was the first film that really had an impact on me, as I was five and would be forever after that afraid of sitting on a toilet, let alone going in the ocean. There's water in the toilet, sharks swim in water. I rest my case. I have a pool now, and I don't go in it as much as I'd like to because I'm sometimes still seized by the irrational notion that a shark could show up at any moment.

Aside from the paranoia the flick instilled, I remember, even at five, digging on the craft (that camera half in, half out of the water), the performances (Robert Shaw will forever remain

Kevin Smith as actor, alongside Jason Mewes, in his 1999 comedy *Dogma* (Lions Gate Films, 1999).

one of my favorite actors), and the dialogue. Guys sitting around shooting the shit — as Brody, Quint, and Hooper do during their night onboard the Orca — would later become a mainstay of the kind of static, conversational filmmaking that I do.

Years later, Richard Linklater's *Slacker* [1991] would have almost as great an impact. It served as an example of a flick that I could make myself — regional, talky, and not very visually complicated.

Your love of Jaws *is certainly evident in the number of homages you've incorporated into your work. Several of the characters in your films are named after characters in* Jaws.

KS: Yeah, *Jaws* is just one of those flicks I can pay neverending homage to. It's practically a flawless film.

Star Wars *(1977) is another film that often rears its head in your work, from the "Death Star Theory" of* Clerks *to a character making reference to "the Holy Trilogy" in* Chasing Amy. *What is it about the* Star Wars *films that appeal to you?*

KS: I was a hardcore *Star Wars* geek when I was a kid — had all the figures, joined all the fan clubs, played Star Wars incessantly — but grew out of it when I hit my teens. *The Empire Strikes Back* [1980] still held a place in my heart, though, as it's the best of the three, and almost a perfect film.

In the late eighties and early nineties, nobody was talking about *Star Wars* anymore. It was pretty much regarded as merely a sweet trio of sci-fi flicks, revolutionary and profitable, that had waned in popularity over the years. It didn't seem to have the fanatical fanbase that *Star Trek* had, so there weren't really any "Warsies" to speak of, keeping the flame burning, and most had given up hope of ever seeing the oft-spoke-about remaining six flicks. When I was writing *Clerks*, I remembered all the movie-dissecting discussions I'd ever had with my friends, particularly about *Star Wars*. Even though a long-diminished passion of mine, it still wound up as the focus of the occasional film gab session. It seemed natural to include a version of these ruminations on the trilogy, as Dante was more or less my stand-in, and the film is kind of autobiographical, at least in setting and character. Hence, the "Death Star Contractors" scene was written.

It's probably the biggest misconception about me in regards to the flicks I've done — that I'm a massive *Star Wars* fan. I'm not, really, although, as mentioned, I do love *Empire*. It was just a cultural holdover/touchstone from my youth that was a funny basis for a discussion the characters could have while trying to kill the time in the convenience store.

What filmmakers do you credit as being your biggest influences?

KS: I'd have to say that Jim Jarmusch and Hal Hartley had the biggest influence on what I do. *Stranger Than Paradise* (1984) was a film that I watched over and over again and thought, "Man, the camera hardly moves." That was very liberating for a guy who has zero visual flair or talent to see. And the way Hartley's characters spoke — as if on stage most times — made me feel okay with putting huge, unrealistic speeches in my characters' mouths. Richard Linklater may have been the director whose work kicked me in the ass enough to start thinking about being a filmmaker, but Jarmusch and Hartley made filmmaking seem more accessible to a neophyte filmster from New Jersey.

Let's talk about your involvement with Good Will Hunting *for a moment. Matt Damon and Ben Affleck had shopped the script around Hollywood for a number of years before you came onboard and finally helped them get the film made. I think the film is brilliant. What did you see in the screenplay that no one else had seen?*

KS: Actually, Castle Rock first saw something in it. The boys took their script out on the spec market and sold it rather quickly for a boatload of money to Castle Rock. However, once there, it sat. And sat. And sat. Castle Rock over-developed it, bringing in people like Rob Reiner and William Goldman to offer the boys suggestions in plotting a flick that didn't really need a plot. Then came the capper: Andy Scheinman, one of the partners in Castle Rock, wanted to direct it himself. Ben and Matt didn't want this, as Scheinman was chiefly an executive, and his only directing credit was *Little Big League* [1994].

Ben and Matt strongly objected to Scheinman directing, and took the stand that they wouldn't make the flick if he was involved. This made it difficult for Castle Rock because part of the boys' deal was that they were attached as stars, pay or play.

In their frustration, they told Ben and Matt that they could take the script out for two weeks and shop it around again. If they sold it, great. If not, it would be directed by Scheinman and they'd be out on their asses, thus losing their chance to even be in the flick, let alone the stars.

That's where Scott Mosier and I came in. Ben asked us to give it a read and see if we could bring the script to Miramax. We read it and fell in love with it immediately. However, getting it into Miramax was going to be iffy. Number one, the price tag was about a million bucks. Castle Rock had bought it for eight hundred thousand, and there were about two hundred thousand in turnaround costs—a price Miramax had never paid for any script. And number two, Miramax had already passed on the project, by way of Cary Woods, the producer of *Scream* [1996] and *Beautiful Girls* [1996], who'd been set up at Miramax back then.

Long story short, Scott and I got it to Harvey Weinstein, told him to read it immediately, and begged him to consider buying it regardless of the cost. He read it over a weekend and wrote the check on Monday. We were named executive producers. The end.

Let's talk about Dogma, *which is causing quite a furor right now. How did a nice Catholic boy like yourself end up making a film like* Dogma? *[Laughs]*

KS: I made *Dogma* because I am a nice Catholic boy. But more importantly, because I'm a nice Christian boy, too. The movie is a celebration of my faith and spirituality, with some dick and fart jokes thrown in for good measure. If you're going to preach for two hours, you'd better entertain in the process.

At the time of this interview Dogma *has not yet been released. There has already been quite a bit of controversy concerning the project. What are your thoughts on this?*

KS: As far as the controversy goes, I've learned to dismiss it. It all comes from one guy who isn't keen on how I choose to celebrate my faith in God and Christ, who—I might add—is condemning a movie he hasn't even seen. If you look at it from the perspective that he's just a guy who's not a fan, it's easier to deal with. There are plenty of people out there who aren't fans of the other flicks I've done, either. The only thing that makes Bill Donohue [the head of the Catholic League] any different is that he's using his distaste for the flick as a platform to raise money for his organization.

What type of advice would you give to aspiring filmmakers?

KS: The advice I always give to anybody who wants to be in film is chiefly this: script, script, script. Were it not for the script for *Clerks*, my film career would have stalled quite quickly. The fact of the matter was, we had a film with shoddy, wooden acting; flat, ugly visuals; and obvious amateurity. But critics and audiences forgave the shortcomings because they enjoyed the script. Everything else can sag a little, if the script is interesting enough.

But more than that, I'd say it takes a certain degree of reasonable unreasonability to be

Oscar winners Matt Damon and Ben Affleck as fallen angels Loki and Bartleby in Kevin Smith's *Dogma* (Lions Gate Films, 1999).

a filmmaker. People will tell you that it isn't reasonable to think you can make a movie if you've never done it before. They'll tell you it's not reasonable to think little ol' you can access one of the toughest careers to break into, one in which the odds of failure are far higher than the odds of success. They'll insist it's not reasonable to want to be a filmmaker because that only happens to other people. And it's at the moment that you have to prove them right. It is unreasonable — all of it! But that's okay, because you've got your reasonable unreasonability firmly grounded. You're daring to accomplish the near-impossible, and you can't attempt it without being aware of how not reasonable you're being. Reasonable people don't risk tens of thousands of dollars on a dream. Reasonable people don't hurl themselves into a technology they know very little about, outside of theory and book reading. Reasonable people aren't so arrogant as to assume that anyone wants to hear whatever story it is they might have to tell. And that's why not everyone is a filmmaker.

FILMOGRAPHY FOR KEVIN SMITH

1. *Mae Day: The Crumbling of a Documentary* (1992) D, Sc, P, A
2. *Clerks* (1994) D, Sc, Ed, P, A
3. *Mallrats* (1995) D, Sc, A
4. *Drawing Flies* (1996) P & A
5. *Chasing Amy* (1997) D, Sc, Ed, A
6. *A Better Place* (1997) P
7. *Good Will Hunting* (1997) Ex-P
8. *Overnight Delivery* (1998) Un Sc
9. *Space Ghost Coast to Coast* (1998) A
10. *Independent's Day* (1998) [TV] A
11. *Dogma* (1999) D, Sc, Co-Ed, A
12. *Scream 3* (2000) A
13. *Coyote Ugly* (2000) Un Co-Sc

14. *Law and Order* (2000) A
15. *Clerks: The Animated Series* (2000) A
16. *Chasing Kevin* (2000) A
17. *Vulgar* (2000) Ex-P & A
18. *Jay and Silent Bob Strike Back* (2001) D, Sc, A, Ed
19. *Starwoids* (2001) A
20. *Now You Know* (2001) A
21. *The Concert for New York City* (2001) [TV] Co-D
22. *Clerks: Sell Out* (2002) Sc & A
23. *The Flying Car* (2002) [TV] D
24. *Daredevil* (2003) A
25. *Jersey Girl* (2004) D, Sc, Ex-P, Ed
26. *Clerks: The Lost Scene* (2004) D & Sc
27. *Clerks 2* (2006) D, Sc, P
28. *Southland Tales* (2006) A
29. *Catch and Release* (2006) A
30. *Zack and Miri Make a Porno* (2008) D, Sc, P

Betty Thomas

Nicknamed "the Midnight Queen" because of her penchant for late-night shoots, Betty Thomas is one in only a handful of female A-list directors working in the film industry today. Thomas' career began as an actress appearing in such nondescript "B" movies as *Chesty Anderson, USN* and *Jackson County Jail* (both 1976). After a brief appearance in the Robert Zemeckis comedy *Used Cars* (1980), she was cast in the role she is most generally associated with — Sgt. Lucy Bates on *Hill Street Blues*. For her work on the popular Steven Bochco–produced television series, Thomas received an impressive seven Emmy nominations, winning one. She was also awarded the prestigious Q Award by the Viewers for Quality Television.

Shortly after the cancellation of *Hill Street Blues*, Thomas redirected her energies, focusing on a second career as a filmmaker. Her first two stints behind the camera were for the television series *Midnight Caller* and *Mancuso, FBI*. Thomas then made her feature directorial debut with *Only You* (1992), starring Andrew McCarthy and Helen Hunt. For her work on the HBO series *Dream On*, Thomas was nominated for yet another Emmy in 1993 — this time as a director. The following year, Thomas adapted Joyce Wadler's *My Breast* (1994), for which she received her ninth Emmy nomination.

After her successes on the small screen, Thomas was promoted to the big leagues, helming *The Brady Bunch Movie* (1995). This would be the first in an impressive string of hit films for Thomas. She then made a brief return to cable television, where she directed *The Late Shift* (1996) for HBO. This successful telefilm garnered Thomas a tenth Emmy nomination, as well as a Directors Guild Award. She then teamed up with irreverent shock jock Howard Stern for the biopic *Private Parts* (1997). The following year, Thomas directed Eddie Murphy in the hit family film *Doctor Dolittle* (1998). She then continued her winning ways with the Sandra Bullock vehicle *28 Days* (2000). She has since directed the comedies *I-Spy* (2002) and *John Tucker Must Die* (2006).

Not one to rest on her laurels, the award-winning actress and filmmaker has also found success as a producer. In 1998, Thomas produced the Deborah Kaplan/Harry Elfont co-directed teen comedy *Can't Hardly Wait*, which became a moderate hit, raking in just over $25 million theatrically. Her second production venture was the record-breaking actioner *Charlie's Angels* (2000), which she executive produced. Thomas' most recent production efforts have been the Ben Affleck–starrer *Surviving Christmas* (2004) and *Guess Who?* (2005).

Favorite Films: *Ishtar* (1987), *Showgirls* (1995), *Troll 2* (1990), *Mannequin 2: On the Move* (1991), *Bride of Chucky* (1998), *Joe Versus the Volcano* (1990), and *Jaws 3-D* (1983).

ANDREW RAUSCH: *As an A-list director working in a male-dominated industry, do you ever feel that you're treated differently because you're a woman?*

BETTY THOMAS: No, I don't feel like it. I could be wrong. The only thing I can think of is that jobs directing big action films don't generally go to women. I guess that's okay, since those aren't usually the ones I'm interested in.

If one didn't know, they'd never guess that Dream On *or* Private Parts *were directed by a woman, as they're both very much male oriented, maybe even sexist to a degree.*

BT: That is interesting. I think the people who hired me for those jobs were very smart people; smart men, if you will. [Laughs] Ivan Reitman hired me for *Private Parts* for a number of reasons. I guess one of them was probably that I had just made *Late Shift* with him, and he loved *The Brady Bunch*. Ivan also knew that Howard [Stern] responded much better to women than he does to men. I wasn't really a Howard Stern fan before that movie.... I think what you want to do is to not have a fan of someone direct a movie about that. But then, I guess that can work backwards if you were to have someone who knew nothing about baseball direct a movie about baseball. I guess the idea is that you're better off not being the sexist guy if you're going to direct a sexist piece. I think women have a great insight into that.

That was Howard Stern's first job as an actor. What was working with him like?

BT: He was good because he just kept saying, "What do you want? What should I do? How do I do this? What do you mean 'find the moments that reveal me'?" It was a great experience because Howard was completely open, and he totally understood that he didn't really know what he was doing here. He was very much open to learning. He was one of those really smart people who just say, "Show me how to do this. I'll figure it out." And it turned it out that he was pretty much right.

Why do you think The Brady Bunch *succeeded where a lot of other television adaptations have not?*

BT: Well, I'm not sure that's true. Right now *Charlie's Angels*, which I produced, is making a lot of money. Several of them have worked. If they didn't work, they wouldn't make them. They make money. This is what these companies are about—this is a moneymaking business. That's why they make them over and over again.

But the reason I thought *The Brady Bunch* was different was because there was an actual idea behind it. This was a movie made for a reason, with an idea behind, which was about something. So, that was different. It wasn't my idea. This was an idea which had emerged before I came to the film, but this was what made you look at the movie. This was a satirical film, and I loved the idea of making it.

Betty Thomas as actress in the 1988 comedy *Troop Beverly Hills* (Weintraub Entertainment/Columbia Pictures, 1988).

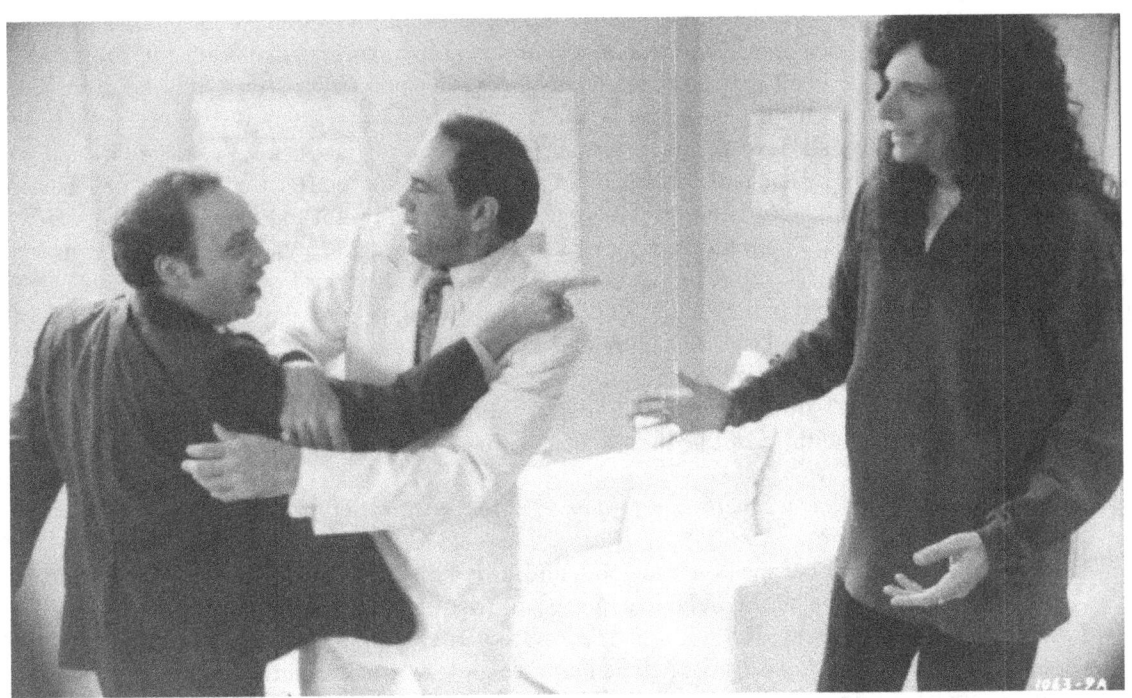

WNBC exec Vin Vallesecca (Reni Santoni) holds back an angry Kenny "Pig Vomit" Rushton (Paul Giamatti) from attacking shock jock Howard Stern (himself) in this scene from *Private Parts* (Rysher Entertainment/Paramount Pictures, 1997).

What made you pass on directing the sequel?

BT: I don't do sequels. But that's not just a blanket statement. I think the reason most directors make that statement is because you've already done your hit on that idea. Is there another? I don't have another take on it. That was it. You saw it. I shot my wad. How can you think the same thing twice? I just feel that you shouldn't make a film if you're not making it for a reason.

Do you feel that you have to have a specific reason for directing every project you take on?

BT: Oh, yeah. I think you have to have a reason for every movie you do—some reason that will let you spend a year of your life on that film. It can be a practical reason, or it could be something deep. Whatever it is, you've got to have a reason. That way, no matter what happens with the movie, you can always look back and remember why you chose to do that particular project.

These days a lot of talented directors who can't act to save their lives choose to appear in their own films. You, on the other hand, are a very accomplished actress, yet you don't appear in your films. Why is that?

BT: You might get some disagreement on the "talented directors who can't act to save their lives" part! [Laughs]

Well, I'm not talking about guys like Woody Allen. There are a few directors out there who shall remain nameless who have no business acting.

BT: I just have no interest in it. I think it's stupid. I've already had that dream, and I've already fulfilled that dream. I don't have to fulfill it in my own movies. [Laughs] These other people, I guess, weren't so lucky. Maybe that's why they're doing it.

When you were making The Late Shift, *what was it like directing a movie about people who were still very much alive, and have you run into any of the central characters since the film's release?*

BT: Yeah, it's all been very positive. That was a very positively received film, despite the fact that it showed a very negative aspect to one of the main characters. I've talked to Warren [Littlefield]; I've talked to Dave [Letterman]; I've talked to [Jay] Leno; I've talked to stepdaughters of people.... [Laughs] In fact, I had to work with Dave after that on *Private Parts*. In the beginning, I talked to Leno on the phone, and he didn't want to look at the movie. He said he wouldn't see it. Then, recently, while I was on the set of *28 Days*, he called me. At first I thought it was a joke; I thought someone was pretending to be Jay, but it wasn't. It was Jay. It turns out that he liked it very much, and he thought the guy who played him did a terrific job. I think everyone did. Dave has never said that to me, and he will never say that, but he did make a lot of fun of the movie, and he did give it a lot of attention. And, I guess, he did work with me. I don't think it's his style to reveal too much about himself. I doubt that he was terribly pleased with it, but he didn't cut me out of his life, either.

Kathy Bates turned in a wonderful performance in that picture. From a director's standpoint, what was she like to work with?

BT: Kind of scary because she's so good, and such a big deal. You know, you think you're going to treat everyone the same, but you are still sort of starstruck. That was something I had to get over. I thought, "How can I direct Kathy Bates?" That seems stupid. But, as you know, I did direct her, and I think I helped her to become even more outrageous in the beginning. [Laughs] I think she may have been holding back a little until she realized that I didn't want her to. As soon as I spoke to her without being afraid, there was no stopping her. She is tremendously wonderful. She's very intuitive. She just gets it, you know? She completely becomes the person she's playing.

I found the casting of impersonator Rich Little for Johnny Carson very interesting. He is at once the absolutely perfect logical selection and also a seemingly odd choice since he's not that well known for his acting.

BT: Well, he's the closest thing you can get to actually using Johnny Carson. It wasn't really about acting so much as it was feeling like Johnny was in the room in some way. It was a tough call, but there wasn't anyone else we could think of who could give you the feeling of Johnny actually being in that room. And I actually thought his acting was pretty darned good.

Considering the family-oriented subject matter of Doctor Dolittle, *I was wondering how much concern there was on your part that the scandal involving Eddie Murphy might affect its reception?*

BT: Listen to this: what scandal?

Kathy Bates portrays Jay Leno's manager Helen Kushnick in Betty Thomas' ***The Late Shift*** (Home Box Office, 1996).

The Eddie Murphy/prostitute scandal.

BT: What scandal? [Laughs]

[Laughs] Oh, I understand now. What was directing Eddie like?

BT: He's fun. He's quiet and he's very shy. The cool thing about Eddie is that he's incredibly intuitive. You really begin to trust his sense of comedy, and even his sense of reality and acting. I found myself trusting him completely. After awhile he would say, "I'm acting with a tennis ball on a stick. There's nothing here, and I'm starting to feel like a fool." I knew as soon as he said those things that I had to address that because there was something really wrong. When he said that, I had to step back and ask myself what I could do to help him to feel more involved with a character that's not there. I really grew to trust him in every way, even in those moments when you go, "Oh, come on, Eddie, just do it." I'm not saying that didn't cross my mind, but on the other hand I got to where I could work with him in figuring out what was wrong. I guess people expect Eddie to be improvising all the time, and he does improvise a lot, but he doesn't do it all the time. He actually just picks spots for it, and you have to tell the cameraman not to stop filming no matter what happens. [Laughs] A lot of that stuff is gold.

I'd like to switch gears here for a moment and talk about 28 Days. *I found the soap opera sequences to be quite humorous, and I would imagine that shooting those and parodying that medium was a lot of fun.*

BT: That was great fun. *Days of Our Lives* let us borrow their sets. We used real soap opera wardrobes, and we also used actors who were used to doing soap operas. They improvised quite a bit. I would suggest a situation to them, and they would make something out of nothing. I just gave them a room, a wardrobe, and a vague situation, and they would just go! It was really a lot of fun. I had no idea how much fun that was going to be. We tried not to make fun of soap operas, but still have fun with that whole genre. It was great, great fun. I think even the crew had a good time working on that stuff.

FILMOGRAPHY FOR BETTY THOMAS

1. *Tunnel Vision* (1976) A
2. *The Last Affair* (1976) A
3. *Jackson County Jail* (1976) A
4. *Chesty Anderson, USN* (1976) A
5. *The Fun Factory* (1976) A
6. *Dog and Cat* (1977) [TV] A
7. *Outside Chance* (1978) [TV] A
8. *Loose Shoes* (1980) A
9. *Used Cars* (1980) A
10. *Hill Street Blues* (1981–1987) A
11. *Nashville Grab* (1981) [TV] A
12. *Homework* (1982) A
13. *When Your Lover Leaves* (1983) [TV] A
14. *Prison for Children* (1987) [TV] A
15. *Midnight Caller* (1988) D
16. *Mancuso, FBI* (1989) D
17. *Troop Beverly Hills* (1989) A
18. *Dream On* (1990–1993) D
19. *Only You* (1992) D
20. *On the Air* (1992) D
21. *My Breast* (1994) [TV] D
22. *The Brady Bunch Movie* (1995) D
23. *The Late Shift* (1996) [TV] D
24. *Howard Stern's Private Parts* (1997) D
25. *Doctor Dolittle* (1998) D
26. *Can't Hardly Wait* (1998) Ex-P
27. *28 Days* (2000) D
28. *Charlie's Angels* (2000) Ex-P
29. *I-Spy* (2002) D
30. *Surviving Christmas* (2004) P
31. *Guess Who?* (2005) Ex-P
32. *The Loop* (2006) D
33. *That Guy* (2006) D
34. *John Tucker Must Die* (2006) D

Robert Towne

There is a strong case to be made that Robert Towne is the most gifted scribe ever to write for film. There can be little doubt that he is one of the finest ever. While many extremely gifted wordsmiths have crafted one or two excellent screenplays in their lives—an extraordinary feat in itself—the prolific Towne has written or co-written many standout screenplays in his storied career. The legendary screenwriter has received four Best Screenplay nominations: *The Last Detail* (1973), *Shampoo* (1975), *Greystoke: The Legend of Tarzan, Lord of the Apes* (1984), and the brilliant *Chinatown* (1974), winning for the latter. Making this accomplishment even more impressive are the three screenplays which Towne has contributed to without receiving credit that were also nominated by the Academy for Best Screenplay: *Bonnie and Clyde* (1967), *The Godfather* (1972), and *Reds* (1981). In addition, *Chinatown*, *Bonnie and Clyde*, and *The Godfather* all appear on the American Film Institute's list of the one hundred greatest films in the history of American cinema. Other films Towne has penned or added his midas touch to include *Marathon Man* (1976), *Dick Tracy* (1990), *Days of Thunder* (1990), *The Firm* (1993), *Mission: Impossible* (1996), *Armageddon* (1998), and *Mission: Impossible II* (2000).

About his work, Towne is humble. "One could fairly describe screenwriting as a frivolous pastime in the scheme of things in the world," Towne has said. "I'm not inventing a vaccine to save humanity, or a bomb to destroy it. I'm just telling a bunch of little stories."

Trading his job behind a desk for one behind the camera, Towne made his directorial debut in 1982 with *Personal Best*, the odd story of lesbian Olympic track stars. His second directorial effort was the popular Mel Gibson starrer *Tequila Sunrise* (1988). In 1998, Towne's third film, the masterful Steve Prefontaine biopic *Without Limits*, was released to critical acclaim. Although the film was not a box office success—due in part to a rival Prefontaine picture released the year before—Towne's film was highly entertaining and well crafted. Despite the tremendous success Towne has enjoyed as a screenwriter, his path as a helmer has not been quite so smooth; the screenwriter was to have directed his scripts for *Greystoke* and *The Two Jakes* (1990), but was ultimately removed from both projects. (Both of which, it should be noted, became abysmal failures after his departure.)

Still considered Hollywood's premiere scribe, Towne continues to write and perform script polishes, commanding a hefty fee for his work. Towne's most recent directorial effort was *Ask the Dust* (2006), which was produced by Tom Cruise and stars Colin Farrell, Salma Hayek, and Donald Sutherland.

Favorite Films: *Grand Illusion* (1938), *Winter Light* (1963), *The Four Feathers* (1939), and *Rules of the Game* (1939).

Actor Billy Crudup and director Robert Towne discuss a scene on the set of the Steve Prefontaine biopic *Without Limits* (Warner Bros. Pictures, 1998).

ANDREW RAUSCH: *You have said of directing that once you step onto the set, "you realize what a joke total control is, and what it really means." What did you mean by that?*

ROBERT TOWNE: Well, what I mean is that so much of the time, motion pictures are done with so many variables: weather, locations, which are subject to change; your actors can surprise you because you almost never have rehearsal time like you would with a play. When you're shooting a film, what you actually walk away with is some kind of combination of rehearsal and performance, which is why the number of takes. It's not quite performance level. It's kind of a twilight zone. You don't really know what you're going to get; you're going to be surprised. Sometimes these surprises are good, and sometimes they're not so good. The point is that everything can change, and I think you have to be ready to change with it. A movie is always slightly out-of-control for this reason. So you have to be prepared to opportunely exploit these things which are out of your control, and somehow make them work for you.

It may be an actor doing something you don't expect them to do—project something you don't expect. Even as you're doing it, you try to figure out how that can work for the movie.

Budd Boetticher, who is one of my favorite filmmakers of all time, makes a cameo in Tequila Sunrise. *How did that come about?*

RT: We had become friendly, and I wanted him to be in it. I'm an admirer of his, too.

After you parted ways with both Greystoke *and* The Two Jakes, *the films kind of fell apart. Although it may not be politically correct to say so, I would think the normal human reaction to their failures would be one of satisfaction. Was this the case for you?*

RT: I can honestly tell you that I've never really watched either film, and I don't feel anything one way or the other about it. Particularly in the case of *Greystoke*, I just feel like it was a tremendous lost opportunity, so I don't get any satisfaction from that at all.

Despite your not seeing the films, you probably have some idea of how the producers decided to approach them. How might you have approached them differently?

RT: I really don't know much about their decisions. The only thing I know about *Greystoke* is that most of my original script dealt with a child being raised by apes. I understand in the finished film, that's about five minutes of the movie, so there was a little shift of emphasis.

Considering some of the things that went down with The Two Jakes, *do you think actors are sometimes given too much power over a film?* [Editor's note: Towne was reportedly fired from the project at the request of his long-time friend and collaborator Jack Nicholson.]

RT: I don't know. You know, I would have to say that largely depends on the actor, and that time in the actor's life. I mean, can you say that Mel Gibson had too much power over *Braveheart* [1995]? Sometimes that's true, and sometimes it isn't. I think the balance of power.... There was a time — before I was in film — when the producers had all the power, the [Daryl] Zanucks and the [David O.] Selznicks, and people like that. Directors had dramatically less power. I still think that, all in all, directors have more power than anyone else associated with the film, although obviously there are examples where actors have more power than the directors.

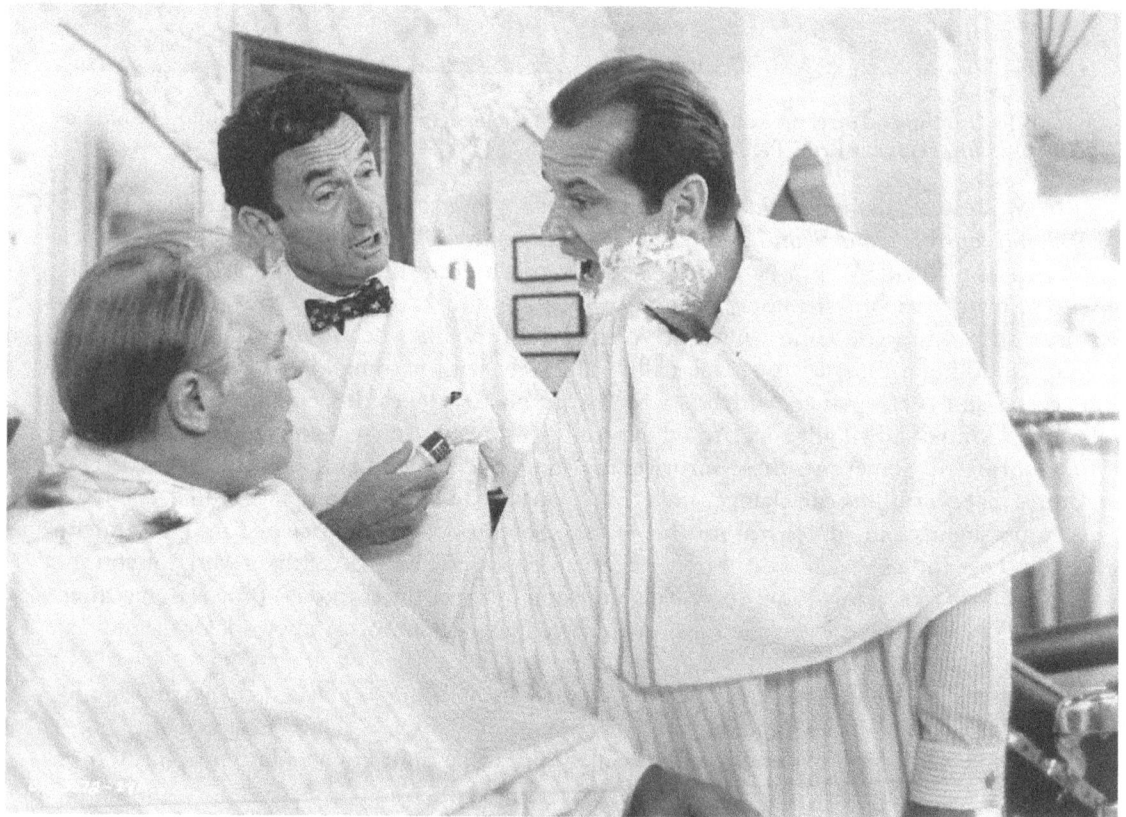

A banker getting a haircut (Doc Erickson) and Barney the barber (George Justin) incur Jake Gittes' (Jack Nicholson) wrath in this scene from *Chinatown*, written by Robert Towne (Paramount Pictures, 1974).

I think one of the advantages of the past—where the producers had the most power—was that there was generally more concern about the screenplay. Since the predominant power shifted to the directors, there has been less attention paid to the writing.

You've now worked within the film industry for more than three decades, and written or co-written some of the most significant films ever made. How would you assess the current state of the film industry?

RT: It's hard to say, because it's constantly changing. I think it's harder than ever to get movies made, unless they're kind of big "tent pole" movies. I think, generally speaking, mainstream movies are not as good as they've been in the past. Independent movies, while they can be quite good, are often highly self-indulgent. So, when there's too great a split from the so-called commercial movies and the so-called artistic movies, you get this; movies are either shamelessly pandering or agonizingly self-indulgent. I think, while there are dramatic exceptions, you're seeing that to a greater degree now than you have in the past.

In what is primarily considered a young man's game, where veteran filmmakers and screenwriters are often discarded like yesterday's trash in exchange for the wunderkind of the week, how do you explain the tremendous long-term success that you've found—and continue to find—in the film industry?

RT: Desperation? Necessity? I don't know. There are surely other older people working in the field who are as successful as me.

Well, you know, I'm speaking in terms of tradition. If you go back throughout the history of cinema, you find many fine filmmakers who were pretty much shut out of the industry after a certain age: Orson Welles, D.W. Griffith, King Vidor, John Ford....

RT: Ford was working well into his sixties, wasn't he? I don't know. Christ, Andrew. I've worked very hard for a long time. Who and what am I to answer that question? You could probably answer that question better than I could. I don't know.

I think that one part of my longevity—quite seriously—is necessity and desperation. Owing to personal need, I had to work, quite frankly, for financial reasons. That led me to things I had never planned to do, never thought I would do, or never thought I *could* do—*Mission Impossible*, *Days of Thunder*, and even *The Firm*. What happens in that situation is that you learn that you can, and you're constantly learning new things. I guess that forces you to stay flexible, doesn't it?

John Milius once told me that no matter how different a writer's works may seem on the surface, that he constantly finds himself unconsciously revisiting certain themes. Do you see any such recurring themes in your own works?

RT: Well, I can give you one, and it's a very general kind of thing. I think if you look at it, you'll see that there's a level of consistency. I have rarely, if ever, written anything where a man or woman's profession was not central to the story. It was a private detective in *Chinatown*, a hairdresser in *Shampoo*, life in the military in *The Last Detail*, a lawyer in *The Firm*, an expert secret agent in the *Mission Impossible* movies, a race car driver, men and women who are track stars. All of them were defined by their profession and had to somehow work or deal with their profession in the fabric of their life, or their life within the fabric of their profession—that conflict between a man's life and his work.

As different as these things may seem, I think you'll find that to be a common denominator. I think that's the most obvious one I could point out, without sounding either stupid or self congratulatory. [Laughs]

Dale "Mac" McKussic and Nick Frescia (Kurt Russell) are old friends who wind up on opposite sides of the law in Robert Towne's action thriller *Tequila Sunrise* (Warner Bros. Pictures, 1988).

As a viewer, do you have any guilty pleasures?

RT: I'll tell you a film that is really not very good that has stupidly memorable moments in it, and that's *The Bodyguard* (1992), with Kevin Costner and Whitney Houston. I mean, I don't know how good a movie you can call *Ghost* (1990), but it's certainly memorable. I think the guilty pleasure movies usually have some stunning presence or performance or some sort of chemistry that, in spite of the ragged filmmaking in certain areas or maybe a story that doesn't quite hold together, has such a level of credibility or passion that you just can't help but be drawn into it. That's what "B" movies in the forties used to have that made them so much fun. Some of them are very good, very efficient.

FILMOGRAPHY FOR ROBERT TOWNE

1. *Last Woman on Earth* (1960) Sc & A
2. *Creature from the Haunted Sea* (1961) A
3. *My Daddy Can Lick Your Daddy* (1962) Sc
4. *The Young Racers* (1963) 2AD
5. *The Tomb of Ligeia* (1965) Sc
6. *Bonnie and Clyde* (1967) Un Sc
7. *Villa Rides* (1968) Sc
8. *Drive, He Said* (1971) Un Sc & A
9. *The Zodiac Killer* (1971) A
10. *The New Centurions* (1972) Un Sc
11. *The Godfather* (1972) Un Sc
12. *Cisco Pike* (1972) Un Sc
13. *The Last Detail* (1973) Sc
14. *The Parallax View* (1974) Un Sc
15. *Chinatown* (1974) Sc
16. *Shampoo* (1975) Sc & Un A
17. *The Yakuza* (1975) Sc
18. *The Missouri Breaks* (1976) Un Sc
19. *Marathon Man* (1976) Un Sc

20. *Orca: The Killer Whale* (1977) Un Sc
21. *Reds* (1981) Un Sc
22. *Personal Best* (1982) D, Sc, P
23. *Swing Shift* (1984) Un Sc
24. *Greystoke: The Legend of Tarzan, Lord of the Apes* (1984) Un D & Sc
25. *8 Million Ways to Die* (1986) Un Sc
26. *Tough Guys Don't Dance* (1987) Un Sc
27. *The Pick-Up Artist* (1987) A
28. *The Bedroom Window* (1987) P
29. *Tequila Sunrise* (1988) D & Sc
30. *Frantic* (1988) Un Sc
31. *Dick Tracy* (1990) Un Sc
32. *The Two Jakes* (1990) Un D & Sc
33. *Days of Thunder* (1990) Sc & S
34. *The Firm* (1993) Sc
35. *Love Affair* (1994) Sc
36. *Crimson Tide* (1995) Un Sc
37. *Mission: Impossible* (1996) Sc
38. *Armageddon* (1998) Un Sc
39. *Without Limits* (1998) D & Sc
40. *In the Company of Spies* (1999) Ex-P
41. *Mission: Impossible II* (2000) Sc
42. *A Decade Under the Influence* (2003) A
43. *Ask the Dust* (2006) D & Sc

Robert Weide

According to Robert Weide, he knew he was destined to become a filmmaker when he was rejected from USC's film school for the third time. A huge Marx Brothers fan, Weide produced the documentary *The Marx Brothers in a Nutshell* in 1982. After that, he produced and/or directed a number of successful documentaries and comedy specials, including *W.C. Fields Straight Up* (1988) and *The Lost Minutes of Billy Crystal* (1987), which starred Rob Reiner and Billy Crystal. In 1992, Weide co-executive produced Larry Gelbart's *Mastergate* for Showtime, which starred James Coburn, Bruno Kirby, and Burgess Meredith.

After becoming close friends with novelist Kurt Vonnegut, Weide wrote and produced his first feature film, *Mother Night* (1996), which he adapted from Vonnegut's novel. The film was directed by Keith Gordon and starred Nick Nolte, John Goodman, and Alan Arkin.

In 1999, Weide was nominated for a Best Feature Documentary Oscar for his tour-de-force, *Lenny Bruce: Swear to Tell the Truth*. The Robert De Niro–narrated documentary was also nominated for two Emmys, winning one in the category of Editing. (The other category the film was nominated in was Outstanding Non-Fiction Special.) His mockumentary *Larry David: Curb Your Enthusiasm* (1999) has since spawned the award-winning HBO television series *Curb Your Enthusiasm*, which Weide produces and directs.

At the time of this writing, Weide was working on a documentary about the life and works of Kurt Vonnegut.

Favorite Films: *Duck Soup* (1927), *Annie Hall* (1977), *Bound for Glory* (1976), and *Scenes from a Marriage* (1973).

ANDREW RAUSCH: *I think your passion for the Marx Brothers is evident through the name of your production company— Whyaduck Productions.*

ROBERT WEIDE: Well, yeah, that's where the name comes from. My joke about that name when people ask, I tell them that Whyaduck was actually my family name before it got changed to Weide at Ellis Island. And a lot of people say, "Really?" [Laughs] I say, "No, not really." A lot of people think it's from the duck on *You Bet Your Life*, but it's not. It's actually from their first movie *Cocoanuts* (1929) in a scene where Groucho is explaining to Chico how to find his way to an auction. He says, "You'll see a river, you'll cross a bridge, and you'll come to a viaduct...." And Chico's saying, "Whyaduck? Why-a-no-chicken?"

So the Marx Brothers film was my first movie back in 1981. I incorporated then and used this name Whyaduck, thinking that would be my company for the Marx Brothers film and then I would dissolve it afterwards. But I found that people remembered that. Even if they forgot my name, they remembered Whyaduck.

What are some of your favorite Marx Brothers films?

RW: It's hard to analyze this stuff too much. It all comes down to a visceral reaction. All of their early films are wonderful—*Animal Crackers* [1930], *Horsefeathers* [1928], *Duck Soup*, which is sort of the classic. It sounds like I'm name dropping, but last year Kurt Vonnegut invited me out to his country house, and we were just hanging out like a couple of college roommates. One night he said to me, "What would you consider the ultimate Marx Brothers film?" I said, "I guess it would be *Duck Soup*." So we got into his car, went to a video store, and brought back *Duck Soup*. I think he had seen it once when it was released in the thirties—he would have been a kid then—but we just watched it and laughed like a couple of idiots.

You recently worked with Robert De Niro on the Lenny Bruce documentary. What was De Niro like to work with?

RW: He was terrific. He's not a guy who invites you in on a personal level. There's not a lot of backslapping and kidding around. He basically shows up and does his work.

A publicity still from Robert Weide's faux documentary *Larry David: Curb Your Enthusiasm*, which later spawned the hit series *Curb Your Enthusiasm* (Home Box Office, 1999).

Strictly business.

RW: Yeah, he's strictly business. I'm certain among his close friends and the people within his circle; he's a very personable guy. It's not that he was unfriendly either. He was perfectly friendly.

When he arrived, I asked him, "Do you want to spend any time beforehand going over some of this or even talking about Lenny?" He said, "No, let's go to work," and that was it. He went into the booth and put on the headphones. It was interesting. My wife has an acting background, and she kind of pinned this. She said that an actor who works as internally as De Niro really needs a character to sink his teeth into. If you just give him copy for narration and it's just Bob De Niro reading copy off a page, it maybe isn't so interesting. What's funny is—and I think I can tell this story because it has a happy ending—when he first came into the room and started to read the copy, it was very flat and very monotone. Frankly, I was worried. I thought, Oh, geez. I went for the name. He doesn't really do anything like this. Reading copy is an entirely different art than finding a character and acting.

To his credit, if I asked him to do the same line ten times, he gladly did it. I even offered him line-readings, which he gladly accepted. I thought, "Oh, my God! I'm giving line-readings to Robert De Niro! How did that happen?" It was pretty overwhelming. Now here's what happened that was interesting—about halfway through the film, the narration starts to take on this sort of Martin Scorsese-ish element when we get to the point where Lenny's busted for the drugs in Philadelphia on a trumped-up charge, and an attorney approaches him and says that for $10,000 he can pay off the judge and the attorney and all of this. Well, the narration started to sound like something out of *Casino* [1995] or *Goodfellas* [1990]. It was like, [narrating like De Niro] "When an attorney made a bribe offer to Lenny, Lenny refused and went to the press...." It started to sound like a Scorsese film, and De Niro really got into it. It was really good. And from that point on, he just sailed through the narration beautifully. I think he found the character of the narrator, so to speak.

So what happened was, he got to the end and I said, "Bob, now that we're really in the swing of this, do you wanna go back and do those first few pages over again?" He said yes, and he nailed every one. So, ultimately, I was extremely happy with the narration, and I think he did a great job. But there was that first ten minutes when I was in a bit of a panic attack.

Was De Niro familiar with Lenny Bruce at all?

RW: I asked him about that. I said, "Were you a big Lenny Bruce fan? Did you know a lot about him?" He said, "No. Probably about as much as the next guy." So what happened was, I sent him a copy of the film. I think it had my voice on it as a scratch narration track. I think he just responded to the story and the material. God knows he did it for not a lot of money. I think he just liked the project and felt good about being attached to it. So I was thrilled and honored.

Robert Weide's documentary *Lenny Bruce: Swear to Tell the Truth* received an Academy Award nomination for Best Documentary (Home Box Office, 1998).

Were you a fan of De Niro's work prior to the documentary?

RW: Oh, yeah! Who's not? I think he's one of the best guys out there. There was a lot of time spent trying to figure out who would be the best narrator for this film. I did not want to go for an obvious choice. HBO and I were going back and forth. They were suggesting comedians they thought were cut from Lenny's cloth. I said, "If I go with a comedian, I would rather have it be somebody who has nothing in common with Lenny." Someone like Steve Martin, or I even thought about John Cleese for a while. But I said ideally I wanted to go for someone who was not even a comedian and maybe shared some sort of spiritual connection with Lenny by being somewhat of a rebel or something. But we were watching a film one day—me and a couple of people from HBO—and an HBO exec named Anthony Radswell, who, unfortunately, passed away himself this past year, suggested De Niro as narrator. We were watching the film and there was a picture of Lenny in the film where he actually looked like a young De Niro. And somebody said, "Look, Lenny looks like De Niro in that photo." And Anthony said, "Hey, what about De Niro?" My jaw just dropped and I said, "Oh, my God! That's *exactly* the right choice. I don't even know why, but that's exactly right!"

As an expert on the subject, what are your thoughts on the Fosse biopic Lenny *(1974)?*

RW: I quite like it. I was a teenager when Lenny died, so I certainly knew nothing about his life or his career during his lifetime. I do remember seeing that film with my mother because it was rated-R and I was fourteen. That was kind of odd, seeing it with my mother. Especially during the lesbian sequence! [Laughs] That film really got me interested in Lenny. I maybe knew a little bit about him before that, but I saw the film and thought, "Wow! What an interesting story!" Then, of course, I wanted to go out and buy all of the Lenny Bruce records and read everything I could. There were certain obsessions in high school, and they remain my obsessions today. Fortunately I've been able to make a living off of them. The big four were the Marx Brothers, Kurt Vonnegut, Lenny Bruce, and Woody Allen. There were more after that, but those were the big four during my real formative years. Those were all characters who later played a role in my making a living.

But yes, *Lenny* just struck a chord with me. Again, it's like those Marx Brothers films— I can't tell you why they appealed to me other than that they just go right to the marrow of me in the same way that hearing a single note of Billie Holliday's voice does. Hearing Ella Fitzgerald or Sarah Vaughn — I appreciate them and I like them and have a lot of their CDs and I listen to them a lot, but Billie Holliday just goes right to my gut. The Marx Brothers go right to my gut. Lenny Bruce goes right to my gut. Kurt Vonnegut goes right to my gut.

FILMOGRAPHY FOR ROBERT WEIDE

1. *The Marx Brothers in a Nutshell* (1982) P
2. *The Great Standups* (1984) [TV] D
3. *The Lost Minutes of Billy Crystal* (1987) [TV] D
4. *W.C. Fields Straight Up* (1988) P
5. *Mort Sahl: The Loyal Opposition* (1989) D
6. *Mastergate* (1992) [TV] Ex-P
7. *Mother Night* (1996) Sc & P
8. *Lenny Bruce: Swear to Tell the Truth* (1998) [TV] D
9. *Larry David: Curb Your Enthusiasm* (1999) [TV] D & P
10. *Curb Your Enthusiasm* (2000–) D, Ex-P, A

Wim Wenders

Before discovering the craft of filmmaking, German director Wim Wenders studied medicine, philosophy, and painting, and also earned a living as an engraver. Wenders' career in the film industry began in 1967 with his brief employment at the Dusseldorf office of United Artists. The aspiring filmmaker then enrolled in the newly-founded Graduate School of Film and Television, located in Munich. Having already made several short films, Wenders completed his first feature film, *Summer in the City*, in 1970. The following year he made his big-league debut with his adaptation of Peter Handke's novel *The Goalkeeper's Fear of the Penalty Kick* (1971). That same year, Wenders joined forces with a dozen other German filmmakers to establish the production and distribution company Filmverlag der Autoren. The following year, the artist established his own Wim Wenders Produktion. In 1976, Wenders established Road Movies Filmproduktion, which he operates with producer Chris Sieverrich.

Wenders' 1977 film *The American Friend* garnered accolades and brought him to the attention of Francis Ford Coppola, who later served as executive producer on Wenders' *Hammett* (1982). During that long and troubled production, Wenders also crafted *Lightning Over Water* (1980), which he co-directed with Nicholas Ray, and *The State of Things* (1982), for which he received critical praise and a handful of international awards (including the Golden Lion at the Venice Film Festival). In 1984, Wenders' film *Paris, Texas* was awarded the prestigious Golden Palm Award at the Cannes Film Festival. For his work on the film, Wenders received the award for Best Direction at the British Academy of Film and Television Awards.

In 1987, Wenders enjoyed a banner year, receiving Best Director honors at the Cannes Film Festival for his film *Der Himmel uber Berlin*, and also publishing his first book, *Written in the West*. In 1991, Wenders took a stab at science fiction, helming the William Hurt–starrer *Until the End of the World*. In 1997, the prolific auteur directed the acclaimed film *The End of Violence*, which garnered Wenders his seventh Golden Palm nomination. For his breakthrough documentary *The Buena Vista Social Club* (1998), Wenders was showered with praise and received his first Oscar nomination. Wenders then directed a star-studded ensemble, which included Mel Gibson, Jeremy Davies, Mila Jovovich, Jimmy Smits, Peter Stormare, and Amanda Plummer, in the ambitious fable *The Million Dollar Hotel* (2000).

In addition to his work as a filmmaker, Wenders has served as both chairman and president of the European Film Academy, and teaches film at the Academy of Film and Television.

Favorite Films: *Breathless* (1960), *The Rules of the Game* (1939), *The Wild Child* (1969), *Down by Law* (1986), *The Lusty Men* (1952), *The Woman in the Window* (1944), *The Lovers of Pont Neuf* (1991), *Blade Runner* (1982), *Only Angels Have Wings* (1939), *The Man Who Shot Liberty Valance* (1962), and the entire catalogues of Anthony Mann and Yasujiro Ozu.

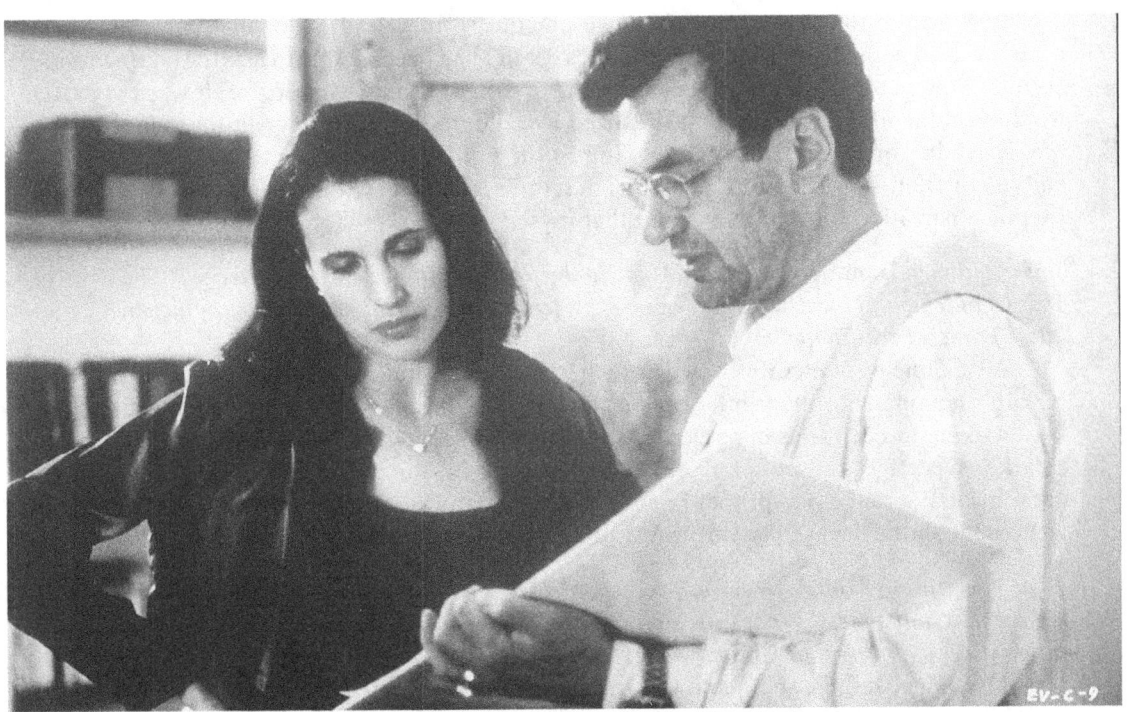

Actress Andie MacDowell and director Wim Wenders on the set of the film *The End of Violence* (Metro-Goldwyn-Mayer Inc., 1997).

ANDREW RAUSCH: *You have a well-documented fascination with the American West. Have you ever considered directing a western film?*

WIM WENDERS: I look at *Kings of the Road* [1976] and *Paris, Texas* as my westerns. I'm not interested in directing period films anymore, so a straight western would be out of the question.

You once said, "Originality now is rare in the cinema, and it isn't worth striving for because most work that does this is egocentric and pretentious." I find that statement fascinating, and I wondered if you might elaborate on that for me?

WW: Did I say that? I no longer remember the context. I find that a pretty pretentious remark, to tell you the truth.

Was it at all intimidating directing accomplished filmmakers Samuel Fuller or Nicholas Ray, and did you approach them any differently than you would any other actor?

WW: There was nothing intimidating about it, on the contrary. Otherwise I wouldn't have made four films with Sam Fuller as an actor. It was a sheer privilege. And a pure pleasure, especially listening to all of Sam's stories for hours and hours after every day of shooting. Sam was a relentless storyteller and an amazingly disciplined actor. With Nicholas Ray, that was a slightly different story, insofar as I had witnessed Nick teach acting classes. I was very much in awe of Nick's highly subtle and emotional work with actors. I did learn a lot from Nick, especially when he directed me in *Lightning Over Water*, where we would take turns being each other's director.

After Lightning Over Water *debuted at Cannes, you re-edited the film considerably, excising nearly thirty minutes from the movie. What factors led to your decision to recut the film?*

WW: My editor, Peter Przygodda, had practically finished the film all on his own. I had been involved with *Hammett*, and after Nick's death I had been unable to face the editing room. So the film was told in the third person, so to speak, by a neutral observer. It was only after we showed the film at Cannes that I realized I would never forgive myself, for the rest of my life, if I didn't bring myself to tell the film in the first person; and that I owed that to Nick and to our friendship. So I re-edited it from scratch, all alone, without even an assistant. And I wrote a narration for it and recorded that myself, too.

You mentioned Hammett, *which leads me to my next question. To what degree was* The State of Things *autobiographical regarding your experiences on* Hammett *and your conflicts with producer Francis Ford Coppola?*

WW: *State of Things* was based on experience, sure, but not so much on *Hammett*, and certainly not on my conflict with Coppola. It was rather about two different worlds of filmmaking, working in Europe as opposed to working in Hollywood. It was a bleak film, made from a dark perspective, and out of a hole that I felt I was in. But still, I didn't fill it with autobiographical material. (Except that Friedrich Munroe was driving my own car, an Oldsmobile Delta 88 with the license plate of "SAM SP8." That was the most personal touch.)

After The Million Dollar Hotel *was released, Mel Gibson made some disparaging remarks regarding the film in the press. What was Gibson like to work with on the film, and was there any indication during filming that Gibson was unhappy?*

WW: Mel liked the shoot and was impressed by how fast we proceeded. I had two weeks with him, and he didn't work for a single day longer. He didn't really believe we could do it. He was great to work with — very precise, very relaxed, no problem whatsoever — and I still think that Skinner is one of his best performances.

I would agree.

WW: I'm proud of it, that's for sure. And I know *Million Dollar Hotel* is amongst my best work. The rest doesn't matter much anymore. Mel regretted to have said in public what he should have kept for himself. But he sure likes and dislikes movies for other reasons than me....

Of what accomplishment in your career are you the most proud?

WW: With the exception of *Hammett*, I controlled all my films and produced or co-produced them all. So I can only blame myself for all mistakes, be proud of some of my flops and suspicious of some of my successes.

What is the one question you've never been asked in an interview, but have always wanted to answer?

WW: The one question that nobody ever asks is "Have you ever felt you were repeating yourself?"

Do you?

WW: When I was working on *Hammett*, I got very involved in Dashiell Hammett's life. At some point, really at the height of his success, he mysteriously stopped writing and never published anything again for a long, long time. I finally found an explanation in an interview of his in which he said that the very moment he realized he had begun to copy himself and to only repeat what he knew he could do best, he just *had* to stop working. I was very impressed with the rigidity of his approach, and the honesty involved. I've been very much aware of that problem in my own creative output, and have tried to avoid the trap of producing what everyone was expecting from me. After *Paris, Texas* I felt that pressure very acutely. So I decided to shoot a film that would be the total opposite — no straight narrative, no story, really, a film made without a script, more like you would produce a poem, feeding mostly on the unconscious and on gut feelings. After *Wings of Desire* I made a science fiction film, *Until the End of the World*. I shot a number of documentaries, or journal-like films, in order to work very differently.

You get used to a certain power in fiction films: fifty people standing behind you, trucks around the block, you call the shots, and your vision overrides everything. Standing on the street alone, or maybe with just a crew of two or three around you, with no other guideline than reality itself, that seemed like a great cure to me — a counter-balance to the addictive fiction-driven world of movies. So while I was working very consciously against repeating myself, I didn't notice that I was doing just that, nevertheless. And working for a whole year on the digitalization of my entire catalogue, which exposed me at length to all my old films again, I couldn't help accepting that I had been telling the same stories over and over again, in whatever disguise they were trying to hide. I was a bit stupefied at first, I must say, about the tricks my subconscious played

Mel Gibson as Detective Skinner in Wim Wenders' romantic whodunit *Million Dollar Hotel* (Lions Gate Films, 2000).

on me. But I slowly learned to live with it, so to speak, and to forgive myself, realizing I was in good company, after all. All my favorite directors, in the past and in the present, had but a couple of stories they were varying all the time. No way to deny that. Some even had just one story, like my cherished Yasujiro Ozu. There was nothing wrong with that. The only condition was not to rely on "style" or "method" as your source of inspiration, but to keep digging in the well that had provided your very first efforts. I guess that was something Hammett had found impossible to do. The well had run dry.

Filmography for Wim Wenders

1. *Schauplatze* (1967) D, Sc, P
2. *Same Player Shoots Again* (1967) D, Sc, P
3. *Silver City* (1968) D, Sc, P
4. *Polizefilm* (1968) D, Sc, P
5. *Alabama: 2000 Light Years from Home* (1969) D, Sc, P
6. *Three American LPs* (1969) D, Sc, P
7. *Summer in the City* (1970) D, Sc, P, A
8. *The Goalkeeper's Fear of the Penalty Kick* (1971) D, Co-Sc, P
9. *The Scarlet Letter* (1972) D, Co-Sc, P
10. *Alice in the Cities* (1973) D, Co-Sc, P
11. *The Island* (1974) D, Sc, P
12. *Wrong Move* (1975) D & P
13. *Kings of the Road* (1976) D, Sc, P
14. *The American Friend* (1977) D, Sc, P
15. *Lightning Over Water* (1980) Co-D, Sc, P, A
16. *Reverse Angle* (1982) D, Sc, P
17. *Chambre 666* (1982) D, Sc, P
18. *The State of Things* (1982) D, Co-Sc, P
19. *Hammett* (1982) D
20. *Paris, Texas* (1984) D & P
21. *Tokyo-Ga* (1985) D, Sc, P
22. *Wings of Desire* (1987) D, Co-Sc, P

23. *Notebook on Cities and Clothes* (1989) D, Sc, P
24. *Until the End of the World* (1991) D, Co-Sc, P
25. *Arisha, the Bear and the Stone Ring* (1992) D, Sc, P
26. *Faraway, So Close!* (1993) D, Co-Sc, P
27. *Lisbon Story* (1994) D, Sc, P
28. *Beyond the Clouds* (1995) Co-D & Co-Sc
29. *A Trick of the Light* (1996) Co-D, Co-Sc, P
30. *The End of Violence* (1997) D, Co-Sc, P
31. *Go for Gold!* (1997) P
32. *Buena Vista Social Club* (1998) D, Sc, P
33. *Willie Nelson at the Teatro* (1998) D & P
34. *The Million Dollar Hotel* (2000) D, Co-Sc, P, Un A
35. *Half the Rent* (2002) P
36. *Junimond* (2002) P
37. *Ode to Cologne: A Rock 'n' Roll Film* (2002) D & Sc
38. *Ten Minutes Older: The Trumpet* (2002) Co-D, Co-Sc, A
39. *U-2: The Best of 1990–2000* (2002) [video: "Stay"] D
40. *The Soul of a Man* (2003) D & Sc
41. *Narren* (2003) P
42. *Land of Plenty* (2004) D, Sc, S
43. *La Torcedura* (2004) Ex-P
44. *Don't Come Knockin'* (2004) D & Sc
45. *The Palermo Shooting* (2008) D, Sc, P

Kevin Williamson

Kevin Williamson's story is the stuff of legend. In a few short years, Williamson went from being an in-debt waiter and struggling actor to one of the hottest screenwriters in Hollywood. In the late eighties, Williamson took a screenwriting course at UCLA extension. Shortly thereafter, he wrote and sold his first script, *Killing Mrs. Tingle*.

Williamson's next script was *Scary Movie*, which he later retitled *Scream* (1996). Despite *Scream*'s basic by-the-numbers structure (the textbook three-act structure), Williamson managed to transcend the horror genre with one of the freshest entries in recent memory. By exposing the basic formulas and clichés of the classic horror film, he knowingly revitalized the time-worn strategies. The film, directed by Wes Craven, went on to earn more than $100 million—the most ever for a horror film—and single-handedly breathed new life into the dying horror genre. However, Williamson is a reluctant savior. "I don't think I saved it," Williamson has said. "I think it just sort of came back for a few days. And it will be gone again, you know? Everything's a cycle. If I didn't do it, someone else was going to."

Williamson has been busy ever since, penning *I Know What You Did Last Summer* (1997), *The Faculty* (1998), *Scream 2* (1997), and the treatment upon which *Halloween: H20* (1998) was based. In addition, Williamson is also the creator and producer of two network television series, *Dawson's Creek* and the short-lived *WasteLAnd*. Williamson was originally slated to helm *The Faculty*, which Robert Rodriguez went on to direct.

In 1998, Williamson was named at number thirty-one on *Entertainment Weekly*'s "The Power List," comprised of the one hundred people who "wield the most power in the entertainment world." In 1999, Williamson made his directorial debut with his first screenplay, *Killing Mrs. Tingle*, retitled *Teaching Mrs. Tingle*.

Williamson then took a five year hiatus from the film industry before reteaming with *Scream* director Wes Craven for the film *Cursed* (2005).

Favorite Films: *Halloween* (1978), *Jaws* (1975), *Terms of Endearment* (1983), *All About Eve* (1950), and *The Sound of Music* (1965).

Andrew Rausch: *In* Scream, *the killer says something rather interesting. He says, "Movies don't create psychos. Movies make psychos more creative." In light of the Columbine shooting and the now-annual finger-pointing at movies like Oliver Stone's* Natural Born Killers *(1994), I think this statement is as poignant as ever. The media constantly tries to blame cinema for this type of behavior. What are your personal thoughts on this subject?*

Kevin Williamson: That's interesting that you pointed out that one line because I don't think enough people have pointed it out. Because that was the whole theme of the movie. The entire movie was based around that line. That was my statement. *Scream* was my way of saying you can't blame the movies. *Scream 2* actually places blame, putting it upon the parents.

I recently saw you on Politically Incorrect, *and the age-old question of whether or not movies imitate life or vice-versa was discussed. There was a woman on there that you argued with a little bit on that subject.*

KW: Oh, that dumb idiot from Orange County? [Laughs] Sorry. I fought with her all the way out to the parking lot. She actually thinks that kids will watch *Dawson's Creek* and *want* to be gay. She really, really believed that.

That's ridiculous.

KW: I know! Afterwards, I went up to her and I said, "Tell me that you were just saying that to push buttons. Tell me you were just saying that to cause a stir on *Politically Incorrect* and that you truly don't believe that." And she did. She really believed that. I said, "M'am, with all due respect, I don't even know how to respond to you because that's such a ludicrous—" Oh, my God. I said, "Do you really believe that little kids everywhere are looking at what happened to Mathew Shepherd and saying, 'Oh, that's cool?'" Like they're saying, "That's really cool. I can't wait to be Mathew Shepherd." I just said, "M'am, you're crazy."

We've all heard stories about people, such as James Whale, who were forced out of Hollywood because of their homosexuality. Would you say that things are getting better for gay people working in the film industry?

Casey Becker (Drew Barrymore) receives a terrifying call in the horror classic ***Scream***, written by Kevin Williamson (Dimension Films, 1996).

KW: Yeah, I think so. I think everything is a step forward, even if it may seem like a step backward at the moment. I think it's still a step forward because it's causing some kind of resistance, which creates a better movement later. It's sort of a checks-and-balances situation. I really do think things are always moving forward. Even right now I think they're moving forward. I have never — as a gay man working Hollywood — had any problem because of my being gay. I mean, there has been just a *little* bit.... I've noticed that I've encountered, just this year, a little bit of network brass that seem a bit homophobic, but never to any detriment. It's just guys being guys. I just sort of laugh at them and keep on going, and we seem to have a good repore, but honestly, I have never experienced any sort of mistreatment due to my sexuality.

With Scream, *you kind of rejuvenated the horror genre. Since then, there have been a number of rip-offs. What are your thoughts on those?*
KW: There was a lot about *Urban Legend* [1998] that I actually liked. Because that's the closest thing — to me — to being a *Scream* rip-off. If you read the script, you'll see that they really took the formula. The writer did a very clever thing. He told a fresh enough story with the urban legend, and he basically used the formula I used. That's why I think that was the most by-the-book rip-off there's been. I thought a lot of it was successful, although I've always thought the ending was a big problem. I think they should have taken a lot more care with the third act. But the first two acts, at least in the script, read really well. I only watched part of the movie, though; I never watched the whole thing.

After Scream *came out, horror was fresh again for about a minute. Then came a slew of rip-offs repeating the same things over and over again, and the genre has almost put itself back into a coma.*
KW: Isn't that the way it always works? Anytime you have a hit, there are ten more movies just like it. Then it's fizzled out again. It's because they make them so fast. I thought *I Know What You Did Last Summer* was made too quickly. I thought that script needed a rewrite.

Because of scheduling conflicts, you weren't able to work on the upcoming Scream 3 *(2000), although it is based on your original treatment—*
KW: Not really. It's not anymore. It was going to be, but they rewrote it so much that nothing I wrote exists any longer.

Are you happy with the film?
KW: I haven't seen it yet, but they sent me one of the early drafts. When I got to page thirty I stopped reading it. I haven't seen the movie yet, so I don't know where to begin. However, I do know that they wrote another six drafts after the one I read. So, what I understand from [producer] Kathy Conrad, it has improved a great deal.

Does it make you at all sad not being able to personally oversee the last part of your trilogy?
KW: Yes. If I still think about it, I'll cry.

I really like the idea of a movie-within-a-movie, with the fictitious Stab 3 *being shown in* Scream 3. *I thought that was rather ingenious. That was your idea, wasn't it?*
KW: Yeah, that was all mine. I think they decided to keep that. They're still making *Scream 3*, so who knows? There was this wonderful moment I had in the treatment where Sidney is confronted with all the sets of *Stab 3*, which are basically the sets of [the first] *Scream*. So, you sort of relive all that. In my original treatment's ending of the movie, which I don't think they filmed, Courtney Cox was now a screenwriter/producer of *Stab 3*. And she's given up a career in journalism for this career in Hollywood, which is very unfulfilling. She got really

successful. So, in a weird way, Courtney Cox sort of became Kevin Williamson, and the director of the movie sort of became Wes Craven. Courtney and this director were major characters in my treatment. I think what happened at the end of the movie, after all the mayhem happens, a reporter comes on, and this all takes place on the set of Julie's house. And the end was, again, Julie takes the microphone away from the reporter and hands it to Courtney Cox and she starts giving the live report. The third movie would have ended the way the first one ended.

I'm sure you won't be involved, but do you see them trying to milk any more sequels out of the Scream *franchise?*
    KW: I don't know. I guess it'll depend on the success of *Scream 3*. I know that Wes is not interested. I know that I'm not interested. None of the actors are interested. So I have a feeling if they do make a *Scream 4*, it'll be some new series. They'll just use the title.

You've described Scream *as being an homage to* Halloween. *As a fan of the series, what was it like working on* Halloween: H20?
    KW: It was a blast! I got to work with Jamie Lee Curtis! I'm madly in love with her.... [Laughs] And she knows it! And she just manipulates me like crazy. She can just walk into a room and kiss me, and then I'll just have to sit there for two days and just be stunned.

I'd read that at one point they considered an alternate ending for Halloween: H20?
    KW: There was a big argument concerning [executive producer] Moustapha Akkad. He owns the character Michael Myers, and that's his life's blood. That's the only way he really makes money, so he would not let us kill Michael Myers. Jamie Lee Curtis said, "I'm not gonna do this if I don't get to kill him. There's no reason for me to come back if I don't get to kill him." So we had a big fight on our hands. We were like, "We've got to kill him. We've got to satisfy the audience." They go, "Well, kill him. Stab him. Let him lie there dead." Because he wanted to bring him back for another movie. Jamie Lee Curtis said she wouldn't do the film unless she got to cut his head off. She said, "I've got to chop his head off."
    So me and Jamie went to Moustapha and pitched to him how we wanted to kill Michael. Then we also pitched to him how they could resurrect him and bring him back in *Halloween 8*. I came up with a way he could survive. I pitched that to him, he liked it, and they actually filmed it for the opening of part 8. And Jamie Lee Curtis agreed to let herself be filmed and appear in the first minute of *Halloween 8*.

The Faculty *seemed very much influenced by* Invasion of the Body Snatchers *(1956). Were you a big fan of that film?*
    KW: Very much so. In fact, it's one of the only science fiction movies I ever got into. I'm not a big science fiction freak.

How much did that script change after you came in and began working on it?
    KW: The funny thing is, the original script that I was given, everything was changed. And then, from my original draft, I wrote twenty-two drafts of that movie. Then two other writers came on after me and wrote several more. Then Robert went through them himself and took a scene from each of my drafts, mixed with scenes from their drafts, and he put it all together.

What was Robert Rodriguez like to work with?
    KW: A dream. I loved him. Once again, a classic case of Kevin falling in love with a director and he can do no wrong. That man was so brilliant to me, you have no idea. He was the nicest guy. So respectful. We had the best time, and now we're really good friends.

Screenwriter-director Kevin Williamson on the set of *Teaching Mrs. Tingle* (Dimension Films, 1998).

You recently directed your first movie, Teaching Mrs. Tingle, *which I liked quite a bit. What was that experience like?*

KW: It was one of those things where I thought, "You know, I may never get another chance to direct, so I'd better have fun and make the most of it." And I really did. I can honestly say that I showed up to the set everyday just bouncing off the walls because I was just so thrilled to be directing a movie. I just tried to put everything I knew into it — all my love, all my passion. I tried to make sure everyone had a good time, and I think we accomplished it. You can ask Katie [Holmes]. We had the best time of our lives making that movie.

FILMOGRAPHY FOR KEVIN WILLIAMSON

1. *Another World* (1990) A
2. *Dirty Money* (1994) A
3. *Hot Ticket* (1996) A
4. *Scream* (1996) Sc
5. *I Know What You Did Last Summer* (1997) Sc
6. *Scream 2* (1997) Sc, Ex-P, A
7. *Dawson's Creek* (1998) Sc, S, Ex-P
8. *Halloween: H20* (1998) Un Sc & Ex-P
9. *The Faculty* (1998) Co-Sc
10. *WasteLAnd* (1999) Sc, S, Ex-P
11. *Teaching Mrs. Tingle* (1999) D & Sc
12. *Scream 3* (2000) CC
13. *Glory Days* (2002) Sc & Ex-P
14. *Cursed* (2005) Sc & P
15. *Backwater* (2005) Sc & P
16. *Venom* (2005) P

Robert Wise

Few artists in the history of the medium have mastered their craft so well as filmmaker Robert Wise did. The four-time Oscar winner (well, five actually, if you count the Irving G. Thalberg Memorial Award he received in 1967) was responsible for many of the finest films ever captured on celluloid. Before stepping into the role of director, Wise served as editor on such landmark films as *The Hunchback of Notre Dame* (1939), *Citizen Kane* (1941), and *The Magnificent Ambersons* (1942), on which he also worked as uncredited co-director. While most filmmakers have one specific strength, the versatile Wise moved from genre to genre with ease. In a career spanning an unbelievable eight decades, nearly everything Wise touched turned to gold. He fashioned classic films in nearly every genre (and in some cases the definitive example of that field): horror (*The Haunting*, 1963), science fiction (*The Day the Earth Stood Still*, 1951), drama (*Somebody Up There Likes Me*, 1956), spectacle (*Helen of Troy*, 1956), musical (*West Side Story*, 1961, and *The Sound of Music*, 1965), action (*Run Silent, Run Deep*, 1958), western (*Blood on the Moon*, 1948), and the list goes on. When the American Film Institute composed their list of the one hundred greatest films in the history of American cinema in 1998 ("100 Years, 100 Films"), both *West Side Story* and *The Sound of Music* made the cut, with *Citizen Kane* occupying the top spot.

While the likes of D. W. Griffith, King Vidor, John Ford, and Wise's mentor Orson Welles suffered from age discrimination and eventually found themselves unable to work, the remarkable Wise directed his fortieth film, *A Storm in Summer* (2000), at the age of eighty-five. Making this feat even more impressive, the film, which Wise made for Showtime, was nominated for three Emmys. In addition, the screenplay, penned by the late Rod Serling, received a Writers Guild Award.

Sadly, Robert Wise passed away on September 14, 2005. But he left behind an amazing body of work. This brilliant filmmaker is gone, but his legacy lives on.

Favorite Films: *Apocalypse Now* (1979), *The Godfather* (1972), and *All About Eve* (1950).

ANDREW RAUSCH: *Budd Boetticher once suggested to me that Orson Welles might possibly be the most overrated filmmaker in history. Having worked with Welles, what are your thoughts on this observation?*

ROBERT WISE: I don't think that's so. I worked with the man. I edited his first two films, *Citizen Kane* and *The Magnificent Ambersons*, and I think he was absolutely brilliant. For me, the fact that he was only twenty-five years old when he made *Citizen Kane*, which has been called the greatest film ever made — to me, that justifies his praise and testifies to his talent.

Yeoman First Class Mueller (Jack Warden) comes to the aid of the injured Commander "Rich" Richardson (Clark Gable) in Robert Wise's *Run Silent Run Deep* (United Artists Corporation, 1958).

Welles left for Rio before post-production was completed on The Magnificent Ambersons. *The members of the Mercury Theatre group and yourself were left to complete the film. Tell me a little bit about that.*

RW: He had to go to Rio, and we were left to finish editing the film. You see, with *Citizen Kane* we hadn't screened it for a test audience. But the studio decided they wanted to have a test screening for *The Magnificent Ambersons*, and it was a disaster. The audience didn't like it at all, and they laughed at a lot of it at inappropriate times. A lot of the audience walked out. It was just terrible. And this was a very long film, so we decided to take it back and do some editing and try to cut out some of the places where the laughs were bad. We did that, and then we took it out again for another screening. This time things were a little better, but there were still some bad laughs, so we had to cut it again. We cut it three times.

Finally, we had cut so much that there was a continuity problem, so we had to add a scene with Georgie and his mother. Since Orson wasn't around, I was asked to direct that scene. I did, and we added that to the film. When we screened it the fourth time, there were no walk-outs and no bad laughs. Everything seemed to play all right, so that's the way the picture went out.

Welles had a well-documented resentment toward the film because of the alterations the studio ordered. Did Welles ever direct any of that resentment toward you?

RW: I don't think so. I think he understood that I was the editor and I was working under the studio's direction. I was working with Jack Moss, who was Orson's man on the picture. So I don't think Orson had any resentment toward us. I think he understood that we were just doing what we had to do.

In his essay "The Day the Earth Stood Still: Dramatizing a Political Tract," film analyst James Shaw asserts that producer Julian Blaustein, screenwriter Edmund North, and yourself, all of whom he calls New Deal Democrats, "sought to impart a rational response to the McCarthy era following World War II," thus making what he felt was a political statement. Do you agree with this, or is this a case of overanalysis?

RW: I think overanalysis. [Laughs] I don't think there's anything to that.

Does it ever amuse you when scholars search for subtext that perhaps doesn't exist?

RW: Oh, sure. [Laughs]

You know, the interesting thing about The Day the Earth Stood Still was the casting. Originally, Julian Blaustein, Eddie North, and I had envisioned Claude Rains for the lead role in *The Day the Earth Stood Still*. Fortunately for us, as it turned out, he was unavailable; he was performing in a play in New York.

I got a call from Daryl Zanuck, who was running the studio, and he said, "I just signed a talented young actor that I'd like you to consider for the lead role in your picture." So I met Michael Rennie, I liked him, and I cast him. That turned out to be a big break for us. Instead of having an actor who had done other films and who people had seen before, we had a brand new fresh-faced actor to do the film. I actually think the film had much more credibility with Michael than it might have had with Claude Rains.

I recall reading that you had problems with the War Department regarding the film's theme of peace. Is that correct?

RW: Yeah. For some reason or another, we needed some tanks for the film. When we sent the script over to the War Department, they didn't like it! [Laughs] They didn't like the peace message in it, and they refused to let us use the tanks.

Luckily, someone suggested that we request the tanks from the National Guard in Virginia. We went over and spoke with them about it, and they had no problems with it. So all the tanks which appear in the picture were from the National Guard in Virginia.

In 1956, you directed the Rocky Graziano biopic Somebody Up There Likes Me. *Was it a daunting task to make a film about the life of someone who was still very much alive?*

RW: Well, it was all right. Paul Newman and I spent time with him in New York. We studied him: the way he spoke, the way he walked.... We met some of his friends and spoke with them. We got to know him pretty well. Then we were able to get ahold of an interview with Rocky that was on tape so Paul could listen to it and study the way Rocky spoke.

Before his untimely death, actor James Dean was slated to play Graziano in that picture. How do you think the film might have been different with Dean in the leading role?

RW: Oh, I have no idea. I really can't say, but I think Paul Newman did an excellent job. He's really quite good in that picture.

You co-directed West Side Story *with Jerome Robbins. Since you had already directed twenty-seven films prior to that, and Robbins had already worked extensively in theater, were there any disagreements regarding a difference in vision?*

RW: Actually, it was a pretty smooth collaboration. Jerry decided that unless he could do more than simply repeat his work as choreographer from the stage play, then he'd rather not work on the film. I was a producer, as well as the director, and I decided the best thing for the film would be to have Jerry onboard as a co-director. I thought, he could do the musical and dance parts of the film, and I could do the book part. That worked quite well for about sixty percent of the shooting.

Then we began running behind schedule, and the studio decided to take Robbins off the film. Fortunately for me, he had rehearsed all the remaining dance numbers, and all of his staff stayed on to assist me, and I was able to continue and finish the show.

What are your thoughts on Jan De Bont's remake of your film, The Haunting?

RW: I didn't see it, but I hear it was terrible. I've had many people tell me over the years, "Mr. Wise, you made the scariest film I've ever seen, and you don't show anything. How did you do it?" It's all by suggestion; where, in the remake I've been told that everything is shown. I cannot imagine how this could be as effective.

You once called The Sand Pebbles *the most difficult film you ever made. What were some of the challenges you faced working on that film?*

RW: The big obstacle was working on a boat, and filming on water. I'd never done that before. That was something I found quite difficult.

Also, we had problems with showing the Yangtze River because we weren't allowed into China at that time. We were forced to shoot outside Hong Kong, which has no river. But there were places where they had little juts of land and islands, and I was able to place my camera in such a way that it looked like the Yangtze River.

What was Steve McQueen like to work with?

RW: Steve was fine. A great guy. No problem at all. He did a great job in the film, and received his only Academy Award nomination. He didn't win, but he was nominated.

Let's talk about another musical you directed, The Sound of Music. *At one time that film was the biggest money-maker of all time. Does the continued success of that film ever amaze you?*

RW: We took the film out for a couple of advance screenings in the Midwest. We took it to Chicago one night, and to Minneapolis the next. Once we got the audience reaction and saw the preview cards, which were sensational, we were sure we were going to have a very successful picture, but we had no idea it was gonna go through the roof like it did.

Three years after The Sound of Music, *you collaborated with Julie Andrews for another musical,* Star! *(1968). Although* Star! *received seven Oscar nominations, it didn't receive the accolades* The Sound of Music *had, nor was it a box-office success. What was your reaction to that?*

RW: Well, it was very disappointing. I think *Star!* is an awfully good picture, but for some reason it just didn't catch on. It was a biographical film about Gertrude Lawrence. I think it's a damned good picture, but it just didn't seem to work for the audiences ... or the critics, I'm afraid.

That film was later re-released in a substantially shorter version titled Those Were the Happy Times. *What was your involvement with this second version?*

RW: I had no involvement at all. The studio said they wanted to try to do something with it, so I turned it over and let them make the changes. I took my name off of it. They cut it with my film editor, but again, I had no involvement. I didn't like the version they made, either.

In 1996, you made your debut as an actor in John Landis' aptly titled film The Stupids. *How on earth did you become involved with this project?*

RW: John called me and said he was filming up in Canada and had a part with one or two lines in it for me. I was intrigued by this, so I said, "Sure. I'll do it." They flew my wife and I up to Canada, and I shot my scene in two days. Mainly, the thought of going to Canada appealed to me.

At first, I was a little nervous about being in front of the camera instead of behind it. But I think I did all right. I don't think I caused John too many headaches! [Laughs]

The film industry is a place where age discrimination is practiced routinely, yet you directed your fortieth film, A Storm in Summer, *at the age of eighty-five. What's your secret?*

RW: Well, I don't know if there's any secret, but I was thrilled by the offer to make this film. I love directing films. It's been my whole life, so when they came to me with the script and told me that Peter Falk was attached, I liked the idea and I said, "Sure, I'd like very much to make this film."

The film turned out quite good, I thought, and was nominated for three Emmys. I was quite pleased with *A Storm in Summer*. It was my fortieth film, and it will be my last.

FILMOGRAPHY FOR ROBERT WISE

1. *Of Human Bondage* (1934) Un SE Ed
2. *The Gay Divorcee* (1934) Un SE Ed
3. *The Informer* (1935) Un SE Ed
4. *Top Hat* (1935) Un SE Ed
5. *The Story of Vernon and Irene Castle* (1939) Un Co-Ed
6. *Bachelor Mother* (1939) Ed
7. *5th Ave Girl* (1939) Ed

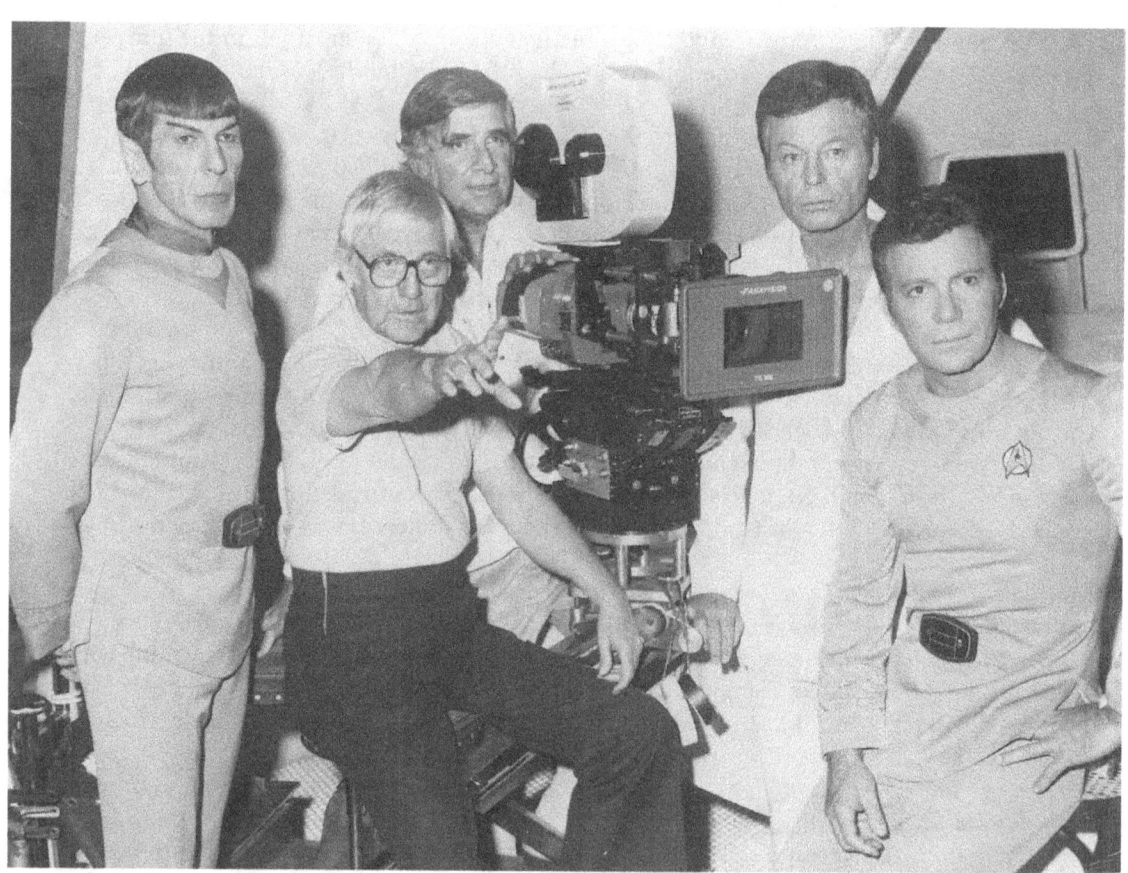

Leonard Nimoy, Robert Wise, Gene Roddenberry, Deforest Kelly, and William Shatner in a publicity photograph for the release of *Star Trek: The Motion Picture* (Paramount Pictures, 1979).

8. *The Hunchback of Notre Dame* (1939) Ed
9. *My Favorite Wife* (1940) Ed
10. *Dance, Girl, Dance* (1940) Ed
11. *Citizen Kane* (1941) Ed
12. *The Devil and Daniel Webster* (1941) Ed
13. *The Magnificent Ambersons* (1942) Un Co-D & Ed
14. *Seven Days' Leave* (1942) Ed
15. *Bombardier* (1943) Ed
16. *The Fallen Sparrow* (1943) Ed
17. *The Iron Major* (1943) Ed
18. *The Curse of the Cat People* (1944) D
19. *Mademoiselle Fifi* (1944) D
20. *The Body Snatcher* (1945) D
21. *A Game of Death* (1945) D
22. *Criminal Court* (1946) D
23. *Born to Kill* (1947) D
24. *Mystery in Mexico* (1948) D
25. *Blood on the Moon* (1948) D
26. *The Set-Up* (1949) D
27. *Two Flags West* (1950) D
28. *Three Secrets* (1950) D
29. *The House on Telegraph Hill* (1951) D
30. *The Day the Earth Stood Still* (1951) D
31. *The Captive City* (1952) D
32. *Something for the Birds* (1952) D
33. *The Desert Rats* (1953) D
34. *Destination Gobi* (1953) D
35. *Return to Paradise* (1953) P
36. *So Big* (1953) D
37. *Executive Suite* (1954) D
38. *Helen of Troy* (1956) D
39. *Tribute to a Bad Man* (1956) D
40. *Somebody Up There Likes Me* (1956) D
41. *Until They Sail* (1957) D
42. *This Could Be the Night* (1957) D
43. *Run Silent, Run Deep* (1958) D
44. *I Want to Live!* (1958) D
45. *Odds Against Tomorrow* (1959) D & P
46. *West Side Story* (1961) Co-D & P
47. *Two for the Seesaw* (1962) D
48. *The Haunting* (1963) D & P
49. *The Sound of Music* (1965) D
50. *The Sand Pebbles* (1966) D & P
51. *Star!* (1968) D
52. *The Baby Maker* (1970) Ex-P
53. *The Andromeda Strain* (1971) D & P
54. *Two People* (1973) D & P
55. *The Hindenburg* (1975) D & P
56. *Audrey Rose* (1977) D
57. *Star Trek: The Motion Picture* (1979) D
58. *Wisdom* (1986) Ex-P
59. *Rooftops* (1989) D
60. *All Night the Sun Shines* (1992) P
61. *The Stupids* (1996) A
62. *A Storm in Summer* (2000) [TV] D

Steven Zaillian

Steven Zaillian began his career in the film industry working as an editor, cutting films like *Breaker! Breaker!* (1977) and *Kingdom of the Spiders* (1977). He received his first break as a screenwriter with *The Falcon and the Snowman* (1984), which was directed by John Schlesinger. His second produced screenplay, *Awakenings* (1990), was directed by Penny Marshall and garnered Zaillian his first Best Screenplay nomination. Zaillian then used his newfound screenwriting success to position himself as a filmmaker. Zaillian made his directorial debut with *Searching for Bobby Fischer* (1993), which he also wrote. The film, starring Ben Kingsley, Joe Mantegna, and first-time child actor Max Pomeranc, was met with critical acclaim but failed to find an audience. That same year, Zaillian received his second Best Screenplay nomination for Steven Spielberg's *Schindler's List* (1993), this time winning the Oscar.

Zaillian's status as both a screenwriter and a director has continued to grow. Besides penning screenplays like *Jack the Bear* (1993), *Clear and Present Danger* (1994), and *Mission: Impossible* (1996), Zaillian also works as a hired gun, performing uncredited rewrites for such noted films as *Crimson Tide* (1995) and *Black Hawk Down* (2002), as well as two more Spielberg collaborations—*Amistad* (1997) and *Saving Private Ryan* (1998). Although often credited with rewriting the lackluster *Twister* (1996), Zaillian is quick to point out that this was not the case. "For three weeks I wrote scenes and faxed them to Oklahoma, where the film was being shot," Zaillian explains. "Unbeknownst to me until much later, every page I sent was completely ignored because the director was perfectly happy with the script he already had. The production company was not. Anyway, the point is, there isn't a word I wrote for *Twister* that actually made it into the film."

In 1998, Zaillian once again found himself in the director's chair, helming the John Travolta/Robert Duvall–starrer *A Civil Action*, which he also wrote and executive produced. After David Mamet's initial draft was discarded, Zaillian was hired by producers to adapt the screenplay for the long-awaited *Silence of the Lambs* (1991) sequel, *Hannibal* (2001). In 2003, Zaillian received an impressive third Oscar nomination for *Gangs of New York* (2002), which he co-wrote with Jay Cocks.

Zaillian has since co-written the Sydney Pollack–helmed thriller *The Interpreter* (2005), and returned to directing with *All the King's Men* (2006), which stars Sean Penn, Jude Law, and Kate Winslet.

Favorite Films: *The Bicycle Thief* (1948), *The 400 Blows* (1959), *In Cold Blood* (1967), *To Kill a Mockingbird* (1962), *McCabe & Mrs. Miller* (1971), *The French Connection* (1971), and *Salesman* (1969).

Director Steven Zaillian and child actor Max Pomeranc on the set of *Searching for Bobby Fischer* (Paramount Pictures, 1993).

ANDREW RAUSCH: *You've collaborated with Steven Spielberg a few times now. What is he like to work with?*

STEVEN ZAILLIAN: Writers don't threaten the good directors. They aren't afraid to rely on them. And they get the best work out of them.

Spielberg and I had a very satisfying collaboration. We respected each other. And we both, I think, realized early on that if we could be honest with each other and ourselves and stay vigilant, we could play on each other's strengths and check our weaknesses.

The two films you've directed at this point in your career have been screenplays that you've written. Do you see yourself ever directing another writer's work?

SZ: I can't write any scene without picturing it. I see the room, the characters in it, what they're wearing, what's in their hands, where they move, how they sound, et cetera, over and over as I write it. I can't put it on paper otherwise. Then, when the time comes to actually direct it, I have some confidence, having written (and seen and experienced) it, that I can answer just about any question that comes up. Since directing requires one to answer literally hundreds of questions each day, this helps a great deal.

So, no, I've never seriously considered directing someone else's script because, without having "seen it" as it was written, I'd have a much more difficult time convincing myself that I was any kind of expert on the subject.

As a writer, you've worked with a number of talented filmmakers, such as Penny Marshall, Philip Noyce, Martin Scorsese, John Schlesinger, and, of course, Steven Spielberg. How much have you learned as a director from having worked with them?

SZ: I was very lucky that my first experience collaborating with a director was John Schlesinger on *The Falcon and the Snowman*. He actually *likes* writers. Of course, that shouldn't be a remarkable statement, but, sadly, it is. He said to me once that his favorite part of making films was the time spent discussing the story with the writer in the months prior to shooting. It was a rude awakening then, some years later, when I learned this wasn't always—or even usually—the case. The irony is that it took a writer/director to teach me this lesson.

I consciously made some decisions after that: whenever possible, if it's something I really care about, make sure I have the option to direct it; if it's something I care about that already has a director involved, make sure it's one I admire. If it isn't either one of those things, then don't get involved, or at least not emotionally. Just do the work, do it well, but don't fall in love with it.

You learn a lot without realizing it when you stay with a film through its production. The one big thing I know I've learned from the good directors I've worked with is this: they share an ability to approach a scene confidently and to commit to a strong visual idea, rather than just covering everything. It takes guts, skill, and intuition to do this. You're saying, "You down there, take away the net!" But when you're wrong, you're dead; you've got nothing to fall back on. But more often you're right because you've thought about it, or you've trusted your instincts and your instincts aren't bad, and it becomes what's memorable about the style of the film.

You've performed uncredited rewrites for a number of films. Is this something you enjoy?

SZ: There are two very different kinds of projects for me. Three, actually. Those I write and direct, which take about three years. Those I write for others to direct, which take several months to a year. And rewrites, often uncredited, which are done very quickly—a few weeks to a couple of months—which I do sometimes as a favor and sometimes for money, which helps when I disappear back into one of those three-year projects.

I know that I'm very lucky to be able to do this, to go back and forth among these different kinds of writing. Frankly, after writing and directing a film, the last thing I feel like doing immediately is writing and directing another. It just takes too much out of you—too much consideration day in and day out, too much thinking about the same things over and over. A short-term rewrite, at that moment, sounds very good. Of course, after a rewrite or two, the more personal long-term projects start looking good again. Going back and forth between them is really ideal, and I'm grateful I'm able to do that.

The actual work, of course, it quite different, too—the nature of it. My projects are all-encompassing, in terms of the writing and emotional investment. Rewrites, on the other hand, usually have a much smaller target; there's something specific someone wants me to address—a certain aspect of the story, for instance, or the main character or the third act....

A lot of times today producers will line up three or four talented screenwriters to come in one after another to take a pass at a script. Again, Crimson Tide *is a good example of this, where Michael Schiffer, Tarantino, Shane Black, Robert Towne, and yourself all contributed. Sometimes this works well, as it did on that project, and sometimes it doesn't. Many purists believe that a singular vision is always best and that bringing in more writers often blurs the focus of the work. What do you think? Do too many cooks spoil the broth, or does this genuinely better the material?*

SZ: I think it's rare that a script is greatly improved by a long succession of writers. Can it be marginally improved? Yes. Can it be ruined? Yes. What it cannot be, I don't think, is made into something it isn't intrinsically, no matter how many writers are brought in. There's something fundamentally wrong, I think, with this theory that you can bring in one "kind" of writer for this, and another "kind" for that, and on and on, as if the script were some kind of building renovation and we were various tradesmen with overlapping skills. It almost never works. You end up with the Winchester Mystery House.

Having said that, it did work once in something I was involved with: *Clear and Present Danger*. John Milius, Donald Stewart, and myself, all working independently, contributed individual strengths to that film. We all, I think, recognized this, and we felt a kind of joint pride of ownership.

You began working in the film industry as an editor. What, if anything, did you learn from editing that eventually lent itself to writing and directing?

SZ: I think writing's a lot like editing, certainly in terms of the shaping of stories. One thing I learned in the editing room is that less is usually more. The right image or look can replace a page of dialogue. Another thing I found is that you can often throw away the first reel of badly-written films and no one will notice. This is because they spent ten minutes setting up the story before actually beginning to tell it. Just put up reel two.

When I'm writing, I consciously try to begin as late in the story as possible and end it as soon as possible. I try to determine what the story is really about and try to find the characters in the middle of it. In the case of *Schindler's List*, for instance, there's a great deal of information known about Schindler, and described in the book, before he arrived in Krakow. His childhood, his hometown, his marriage, his failed businesses, etc. It was tempting, and seemed necessary at first, to show at least some of this. Of course, it wasn't. It was much better to find him already involved in the main action, knowing nothing about him, and then gradually, through the story, come to understand him. So that's how I started it.

Liam Neeson portrays businessman-turned-humanitarian Oskar Schindler in *Schindler's List*, written by Steven Zaillian (Universal Pictures, 1993).

People have accused me of constructing screenplays out of too many short scenes rather than fewer long ones. I certainly don't do this to drive up the cost of shooting, which it does; I do it because it's how I think and see things—and maybe because of things I've learned in editing rooms.

On Searching for Bobby Fischer, *you worked with Max Pomeranc, who did a wonderful job. What are some of the challenges to directing a young child with little or no acting experience?*

SZ: Max's greatest strength as an actor was that he wasn't an actor. I went to great — sometimes ludicrous — lengths to keep it that way as long as possible, to preserve that innocence, that un-studiedness. I didn't want him to memorize his lines — which was all right to him because it would have seemed like homework — so that he could "discover" what he was going to say as each day's scenes unfolded. This, of course, was more time-consuming and required more film, but worked very well. Conrad Hall, the cinematographer on the film, was fond of saying Max was the best method actor he'd seen in years. "He's like Brando!" By doing this, things happened — moments, gestures, little truths — that could never have been planned. It felt true because it was true.

All the kids in *Bobby Fischer* were acting for the first time. They were figuring it out as we went along. It requires patience, creating situations that feel real for them, reminding them they can refer to things in their own lives for inspiration, respect and love, and lots of film.

Filmography for Steven Zaillian

1. *Breaker! Breaker!* (1977) Ed
2. *Kingdom of the Spiders* (1977) Ed
3. *Starhops* (1978) Ed
4. *The Falcon and the Snowman* (1984) Sc

Chess genius Josh Waitzkin (Max Pomeranc) waits for his opponent to make his move in this scene from *Searching for Bobby Fischer* (Paramount Pictures, 1993).

5. *Awakenings* (1990) Sc
6. *Schindler's List* (1993) Sc
7. *Searching for Bobby Fischer* (1993) D & Sc
8. *Jack the Bear* (1993) Sc
9. *Clear and Present Danger* (1994) Co-Sc
10. *Crimson Tide* (1995) Un Sc
11. *Primal Fear* (1996) Un Sc
12. *Mission: Impossible* (1996) S
13. *Amistad* (1997) Un Sc
14. *Saving Private Ryan* (1998) Un Sc
15. *A Civil Action* (1998) D, Sc, Ex-P
16. *Hannibal* (2001) Sc
17. *Black Hawk Down* (2002) Un Sc
18. *Gangs of New York* (2002) Co-Sc
19. *The Interpreter* (2005) Co-Sc
20. *All the King's Men* (2006) D, Sc, P
21. *American Gangster* (2007) Sc & Ex-P

Index

About Schmidt 176
Abraham, F. Murray 74–75
Ace Ventura: Pet Detective 112
Ackroyd, Dan 102
Adjani, Isabelle 45
The Adventures of Robin Hood 50
Affleck, Ben 233, 235, 237, 239
The African Queen 53
Agutter, Jenny 96
Aiello, Danny 73
Airheads 112
Akkad, Moustapha 262
Aldrich, Robert 1
Alfred Hitchcock Presents 102
Ali, Muhammad 105, 151
Alien 144
Alien Apocalypse 29
Alive 92
All About Eve 259, 264
All That Jazz 87
All the King's Men 270
Allen, Woody 125, 126–128, 241, 253
Aloha, Bobby and Rose 161
Altered States 216
Altman, Robert 26, 102, 105, 194, 197
Amadeus 95
Amarcord 56
Amazing Stories 82
American Beauty 171
American Cinema 1
American Cinematheque 96
American Dream 125
The American Friend 107, 254
American Gothic 171
American Hot Wax 161, 163, 164
American Me 161
American Movie 126
American Pie 179
American Pop 12, 14
Amistad 66, 270
The Amityville Horror 167
Anchorman 197
Anderson, Wes 6
Andrei Rublyov 193
Andrews, Julie 267
Anger, Kenneth 161
Anglade, John-Hugues 10–11
Animal Crackers 251
The Animation Show 112
Aniston, Jennifer 112

Annie Hall 96, 126, 250
Another Time, Another Place 187, 188
Antonioni, Michelangelo 24, 177
Any Given Sunday 79
Apocalypse Now 7, 12, 14, 107–108, 155, 156, 158, 171, 209, 264
Apollo 13 56
Apple, Fiona 192
Apt Pupil 221, 223, 226
Arbus 192
Arbus, Diane 14
Archie 220
Arkin, Alan 250
Arkoff, Samuel Z. 56
Armageddon 244
Armed and Dangerous 129, 131
Arquette, David 216
Arruza 34, 36
Arruza, Carlos 34, 36
Art, Acting, and the Suicide Chair 107
Ash Wednesday 92
Ask the Dust 244
Asner, Edward 216
The Asphalt Jungle 12, 18, 19
The Assassination of Jesse James by the Coward Robert Ford 209
The Assassination of Richard Nixon 176
Assault on Precinct 13 40, 42
Astin, Sean 110
The Austin Chronicle 116
Avalos, Stefon 169
Avary, Roger 7–11, 171, 175, 213
The Avenger 18, 21, 23
The Avengers 45, 48
Avildsen, John G. 118
L'Avventura 24, 150, 178
The Awakening 203
Awakenings 196, 270
Azoff, Irving 164

B. Monkey 187
Baby Boy 227
Back Door to Hell 96, 99
Back to School 88
The Bad News Bears 139
Bad Timing 141
Badlands 112, 161, 213
Bahr, Fax 107
Bakshi, Ralph 12–17, 113

Baldwin, Alec 24, 26, 114
Ball, Lucille 52
Bancroft, Anne 104
Band, Albert 6, 18–23
Band, Charles 18
Barbeau, Adrienne 40
Barkin, Ellen 24, 214
Barry Lyndon 7
Barrymore, Drew 129, 260
Bartel, Paul 102
Bartock, Dennis 96
The Base 129, 131
Basinger, Kim 50
Bassett, Angela 61
Bates, Kathy 45, 48, 242
*batteries not included 82
Battle Beyond the Stars 59
Battle of Algiers 126, 129
Battleship Potemkin 56
Beach Boys 96
The Beast 7
Beast from Haunted Cave 96, 97
Beatles 152, 193
Beatty, Warren 102, 105, 161
Beautiful Girls 236
Beaver and Buttface 116
Beavis and Butthead Do America 112, 113, 114
Beck 192
Becker, Harold 24–28
Becker, Josh 6, 29–33
Beebe, Dick 144, 146
Before Sunrise 92, 93, 139, 141
Before Sunset 139
Bellows, Saul 196
Bender, Lawrence 10, 100
Bennett, Michael 88
Benny & Joon 45, 46, 47
Benton, Robert 102, 105
Berg, Peter 76
Bergman, Ingmar 24, 89, 155, 194
Best Seller 50
The Best Years of Our Lives 29, 107, 203
Bester, Alfred 43
Beverly Hills Cop II 209
Beyond JFK: The Question of Conspiracy 125
Beyond the Law 181
The Bicycle Thief 96, 150, 178, 216, 270
Biel, Jessica 7, 9

The Big Brass Ring 107, 108–110
The Big Country 29
The Big Sleep 56
Big Trouble in Little China 40, 41
Big Wednesday 155, 158
Bigelow, Kathryn 87
Bill, Tony 103
Bird, Laurie 96
Black, Shane 272
Black Caesar 50
The Black Cat 144
Black Hawk Down 270
Black Love 134
The Black Marble 24
Black Pack 227
Black Snake Moan 227
Blade Runner 48, 71, 192, 209, 254
The Blair Witch Project 64, 166, 167–169
Blast Off Girls 137
Blaustein, Julian 266
The Blob 66
Blood and Sand 34, 37
Blood Feast 134, 135, 136
Blood Feast 2: All You Can Eat 134
Blood on the Moon 264
Blood Sisters 203
Bloody Mama 56
The Blue Yonder 216
Bochco, Steven 239
Body Bags 40
Body Snatchers 50
The Bodyguard 248
Boetticher, Budd 3, 6, 34–39, 245, 264
Bogart, Humphrey 53
Bogdanovich, Peter 3, 56, 58, 102, 105, 106, 209
Bogosian, Eric 139
Boileau, Pierre 45
Bones 71
Bonnie and Clyde 244
Boone, Richard 18
The Boost 24
Bosworth, Patricia 192
Bound for Glory 250
Bowie, David 192, 210–211
Boxcar Bertha 58, 59
Boylan, Grace Duffie 171
Boys Don't Cry 200
Boyz n the Hood 227, 228, 229, 231
The Brady Bunch Movie 239, 240
Branagh, Kenneth 127
Branded 50
Brando, Marlon 149, 155, 157, 158–159, 178, 274
Braveheart 246
Brazil 71
Breaker! Breaker! 270
Breathless 161, 162, 254
Breiman, Valerie 76
Brennan, Paul 150
Bride of Chucky 239
The Bridge on the River Kwai 29, 134
Briefly...Brian 216
Briggs, Joe Bob 134
Bringing Up Baby 102, 105

Broderick, James 125
Broken Blossoms 96
Bronson, Charles 58
Brook, Peter 187, 189
Brooks, Albert 102
Brooks, Mel 102
The Brother from Another Planet 71, 72
Brown, Mary Kay 113
Bruce, Lenny 251, 252–253
A Bucket of Blood 56
The Buena Vista Social Club 254
Bulletproof 71
Bullfighter and the Lady 34, 35
Bunuel, Luis 177, 180
Buried Alive 66
Burroughs, William 167
Burton, Tim 112, 233
Bus 174, 150
Byrne, Gabriel 42, 224, 225

Cabaret 7
Cabot, Susan 58
Caged Heat 57
Cagney, James 74
Calley, John 163
The Cameraman 76
Cameron, James 56, 59
Campbell, Bruce 29, 32
Candy, John 131
Cannibal Holocaust 169
Cannibal! The Musical 118
Can't Hardly Wait 239
Cape Fear 16
Capote, Truman 149
Capra, Frank 66, 82
Captain America 12
Captain Nice 102
Carlin, George 233
Carmen Jones 139
Carney, Art 129
Carnival of Souls 61, 63
Carpenter, John 40–44, 87, 88–89
Carrey, Jim 66
Carrie 179
Carson, Johnny 67, 242
Carter, Chris 50
Casablanca 35, 50, 61, 96, 129
Cash, Johnny 192
Cash, Rosalind 125
Casino 252
Cassavetes, John 102
Castle, William 144, 145
Catch-22 102
Cazale, John 11
The Celebration 197
Celebrity 127
The Cell 79
Cellular 50
A Century of Women 125
Chan Is Missing 139
Chaplin, Charles 118, 121, 178
Charlie's Angels 239, 240
Chase, Chevy 47, 102
Chasing Amy 233, 234
Chechnik, Jeremiah 45–49
Chelsea Walls 92, 94–95
Chesty Anderson, USN 239
China 9, Liberty 37 96, 99

Chinatown 144, 162, 187, 244, 246, 247
The Chocolate War 87, 90
The Christian Licorice Store 161, 163
Christine 40, 43, 97, 88
The Christmas Star 216
Christo in Paris 150
Christo's Valley Curtain 149
Church, Thomas Haden 179
The Cimarron Kid 38
Cinderella 18
Cinefantastique 129
Cinema Paradiso 227
Cinescape 18, 197
Citizen Kane 6, 19, 26, 61, 109, 139, 192, 193, 223, 264
Citizen Ruth 176
Citizen Toxie: The Toxic Avenger Part IV 118, 121
City Hall 24
City of Lights 176, 216
A Civil Action 270
Clair, René 182
Clancy, Tom 227
Clash by Night 178
Class of Nuke'Em High 118
Clayton, Jack 177
Clear and Present Danger 155, 157, 270, 273
Cleese, John 252
Clerks 233, 234, 235, 236
Clerks 2 233
Clinton, Bill 123, 155, 181, 197–200
A Clockwork Orange 7, 112
Clooney, George 197
Close Encounters of the Third Kind 66, 221
Clouzot, Henri-Georges 45
Cobura, James 107, 250
Cockfighter 96, 97
Cocks, Jay 270
Cocoanuts 250
Cohen, Etan 112
Cohen, Larry 3, 50–55
Cole, Gary 192
Collateral 66
Color Me Blood Red 134
Coltraine, John 14
Columbine 231
Columbo 50, 54
The Comancheros 35
Combs, Sean 79
Coming Soon 82
Commando 129, 131–133
Company 181
Conan the Barbarian 155–156
El Condor 50, 53
The Conformist 129
Connery, Sean 45, 48
Conrad, Joseph 108, 155, 156, 196
Conrad, Kathy 261
Contempt 187
The Conversation 192
A Conversation with Gregory Peck 125–126
Conversations with Moviemakers of Hollywood's Golden Age at the American Film Institute 3

Cook, Elisha, Jr. 148
Cool and the Crazy 12
Cool World 12, 15
Coonskin 12, 13, 15
Coppola, Francis Ford 14, 56, 57–58, 107, 108, 155, 158, 216, 254, 256
Corbucci, Sergio 18, 20
Corman, Roger 3, 56–60, 97, 99
Costner, Kevin 209, 215, 248
Cotton, Joseph 19
Cox, Courtney 261
Crane, Joseph 19
Craven, Wes 61–65, 259, 262
Crawford, Travis 149
Creature 144
Creature from the Black Lagoon 144
Crimes of Passion 66
Crimson Tide 209, 211, 215, 270, 272
Crisis 181
Critters 2 82
Crowe, Russell 200
Crudup, Billy 245
Cruise, Tom 24, 25, 66, 209, 210, 244
Crumb, Robert 12, 113
The Crush 216, 217–218
Crying Freeman 7
Crystal, Billy 250
Cube, Ice 116, 197, 231
Curb Your Enthusiasm 250
Curse of the Blair Witch 166
Cursed 61, 259
Curtain, Jane 102
Curtis, Jamie Lee 262

Dacascos, Mark 131
Dad 92
Damon, Matt 233, 235, 237
Dancing at the Blue Iguana 187, 188–189
Dangerfield, Rodney 88
Dante, Joe 56, 57, 59
Darabont, Frank 66–70, 82
Dark Star 40
Dassin, Jules 24
David, Larry 251
Davies, Jeremy 254
Davis, Bette 50–53
Davis, Miles 14
Davis, Stan 32
Dawn of the Dead 7
Dawson's Creek 259, 260
Day of the Dead 203
Day of the Dolphin 102
The Day the Earth Stood Still 146, 264, 266
Daybreak Express 181
Days of Our Lives 243
Days of Thunder 209, 214, 244, 247
Dazed and Confused 93, 139, 141, 142, 222
Dead Poets Society 92
Dead Silence 171
Dean, James 266
Death in Venice 150
Death Race 2000 56

De Bont, Jan 267
Deep Impact 76
Déjà Vu 209
Delpy, Julie 93, 141
Dementia 13 56, 57
DeMille, Cecil B. 136
Demme, Jonathan 56, 57, 58, 96
Demon Knight 71
De Niro, Robert 56, 80, 209, 213, 214, 215, 250, 251–253
De Palma, Brian 87, 88, 161
Depp, Johnny 45, 46
Desperation 82
De Toth, Andre 53
Devil in the Flesh 150
Diabolique 49
Les Diaboliques 45, 49
Dial M for Murder 7
Diaz, Cameron 76
Dick, Nigel 192
Dick Tracy 161, 244
Dickerson, Ernest 71–75
Diddley, Bo 182
Dillinger 155, 159
Dingeldein, Phil 1–2
Dinner for Five 76
Direct Mail Copy That Sells! 134
Dirty Harry 155
The Divine Comedy 193
Django 20
Do the Right Thing 71, 73, 227, 233
Doctor Dolittle 239, 242
Dr. Mordrid 18
Dr. Strangelove 108
Doctor Zhivago 129, 162
Dodsworth 96
Dog Day Afternoon 11
Dogma 233, 234, 236, 237
Dogtown 107
Doherty, Denny 185
Domino 209
Donahue, Bill 236
Donahue, Heather 167
D'Onofrio, Vincent 92
Don't Look Back 181
Don't Look Down 61
The Doors 222
Dorff, Stephen 144
Double Indemnity 26
The Double Life of Veronique 187
Down by Law 254
Down from the Mountain 181
Downey, Robert, Jr. 87
Dracula 2000 61
Dream On 144, 239, 240
The Dreamlife of Angels 92
Dressed to Kill 87
Drew, Robert 149, 181
Drew Associates 181
Duck Soup 250, 251
Dunaway, Faye 7, 40
Dusty and Sweets McGee 161, 163
Duvall, Robert 76, 89, 214, 270
Dylan, Bob 14, 181

E.T. 205, 227
Eastwood, Clint 34, 38, 142, 157
Easy Rider 56, 96, 228
Eat the Document 181

Eating Raoul 102
Ebert, Roger 120
Ed McBain's 87th Precinct 50
Eddie Murphy Raw 71
8½ 192
Eisenstein, Sergei 5
Eisner, Michael 163
Elf 76, 80
Election 176, 177, 178–180
Elfont, Harry 239
Elizabeth 146
Ellington, Duke 181
Elliot, T.S. 156
Ellis, Bret Easton 7, 9
Elvis 40
Elwes, Cary 217
Ely, Ron 38
The Empire Strikes Back 227
The End of Violence 254, 255
Enemy of the State 209
The Energy War 181
Entertainment Weekly 259
Epitaph 99
Epps, Omar 71, 72
E.R. 86
Eraserhead 139
Erickson, Doc 246
Erin Brokovich 178
The Erotic Witch Project 168
Escape from L.A. 40
Escape from New York 40
Esquire 106, 164
Evans, Robert 165
Evel Kneivel 157
The Evil Dead 29, 200
Excalibur 7
The Exorcist 167
Explorers 92
The Eyes of Laura Mars 40

Face of Fire 18
Faces of Death 208
The Faculty 259, 262
The Falcon and the Snowman 270
Falk, Peter 54, 268
Fall of the House of Usher 56
Fallen Champ: The Untold Story of Mike Tyson 125
The Fan 209, 213
Fangoria 82
Fantasy Film Festival 82
Farewell to the King 155
Farrell, Colin 244
Farrell, Sharon 52
Fast Food Nation 139
Fat Boys 234
Fat City 187
Faulkner, William 158
Favreau, Jon 76–81, 107
Fazio, Ron 122
FeardotCom 144, 145
Feeney, F.X. 107, 109
Fellini, Federico 14, 24, 56, 155, 182, 194
Fender, Freddy 18
Ferrell, Will 76, 80, 197
Fiennes, Joseph 187
Fiennes, Ralph 45, 48
Fighting Mad 96

Fire and Ice 12
Firestarter 129–130
The Firm 244, 247
First Family 102, 103, 105
Fishburne, Laurence 42
The Fisher King 196
A Fistful of Dollars 20, 96
Fitzgerald, Ella 253
Five Easy Pieces 12
Five Guns West 56
Flaherty, Robert 182
Fletcher, Louise 129
Flight to Fury 96, 99
Flipper 216, 218–220
Flirting with Disaster 197, 198
The Fly II 66, 82
The Fog 40
Fonda, Jane 202
Fonda, Peter 56
Foote, Horton 125
Forbidden Planet 40, 144, 203
Ford, John 1, 24, 34, 118, 155, 171, 172, 247, 264
Ford Fairlane 164
Foreman, George 151
Forman, Milos 102
Fosse, Bob 87, 253
Foster, Jodie 87
The Fountain Society 61
Four Brothers 227
The Four Feathers 244
The 400 Blows 19, 45, 61, 197, 216, 270
Foxx, Jamie 66, 79
Fraker, William 163
Franklin, Carl 59
Freddy's Nightmares 82, 144
Freebie and the Bean 161
Freed, Alan 164
Freeman, Alfonso 69
Freeman, Morgan 66, 68, 76
The French Connection 270
Friday 221, 222
Friday the 13th 41
Friends 76
Fritz the Cat 12
Frog Baseball 112
From Here to Eternity 162
Fuller, Samuel 255
Fuqua, Antoine 192
Futuresport 71
Fuzzbucket 82

Gable, Clark 265
Gaghan, Stephen 126
Galecki, Johnny 45, 174
Gallagher, Peter 144, 146
Gangs of New York 270
Garcia, Andy 107
Garciadiego, Paz Alicia 48
Garfinkle, Louis 18
Garris, Mick 82–86
The Garry Moore Show 102
Gast, Leon 150, 151
Gattaca 92
Gaye, Marvin 227
Gelbart, Larry 250
The General 66
Geronimo 155

Get Smart 102
Geto Boys 116
Ghost 248
Ghosts of Mars 40
Ghoulies 2 18
Giamatti, Paul 179, 241
Giant 162
Gibson, Mel 87, 120, 244, 248, 254, 256, 257
Gigli 233
Gimme Shelter 149, 153
The Girl, the Body, and the Pill 136
The Girl Who Returned 118
Glen or Glenda 107
Glenn, Scott 18
Glover, Danny 125
Glover, John 90
Goalkeeper's Fear of the Penalty Kick 254
God Told Me To 50
Godard, Jean-Luc 149, 152–153, 161, 181, 182–183
The Godfather 12, 71, 76, 102, 171, 244, 264
The Godfather Part II 56, 71, 176, 192
Gods and Monsters 223
Goldman, William 235
Gone with the Wind 120
The Good, the Bad, and the Ugly 176
Good Will Hunting 233, 235–236
Goodfellas 162, 252
Goodman, John 250
Gordon, Keith 87–91, 192, 193, 216
The Gore Gore Girls 134
The Gospel According to St. Matthew 187
The Graduate 6, 102, 103, 104, 197
Gramm, Phil 129, 130–131
Grand Illusion 56, 244
Grant, Cary 105
Graver, Gary 110
Gray, Macy 192
Gray Matters 176
Graziano, Rocky 266
Great Expectations 92
Green, Hilton 83
The Green Mile 66, 68, 202
Gregory's Girl 7
Grey Gardens 149
Greystoke 244, 245–246
Il Grido 178
Griffith, Bill 113
Griffith, D.W. 5, 247, 264
Grimaldi, Alberto 53
Grodin, Charles 103, 105
Grumpy Old Men 102
Guess Who? 239
Guillermon, John 53
Guilty as Sin 50

Hackman, Gene 161, 209, 214, 215
Hale, Gregg 166
Hall, Conrad 274
The Hall of Mirrors 139
Halloween 40, 41–42, 134, 144, 227, 259, 262
Halloween: H20 259, 262

Hallowell, Geri 9
Halpin, Luke 218
Hamilton, Suzanna 190
Hamlet 92
Hammett 254, 256
The Hamptons 126
Handke, Peter 254
Hanks, Tom 66, 69
Hannah, Daryl 187
Hannibal 270
Happiness 223
Happy Together 45
A Hard Day's Night 9
Hardcore 155
Harlan County, U.S.A. 125
Harlin, Renny 169
Harold and Maude 45
Harris, Souter 24
Harry Potter 135
Hartley, Hal 235
The Haunted Palace 56, 57
The Haunting 264, 267
Hawke, Ethan 42, 92–95, 139, 141, 221
Hawks, Howard 1, 40, 102, 129, 209
Haxan 167
Hayek, Salma 244
Hayes, Isaac 216, 218
Heart of Darkness 108, 155, 156
Hearts of Darkness: A Filmmaker's Apocalypse 107–108
Heartstopper 203
Heaven Can Wait 102, 105
Heavy Traffic 12, 13, 15
Hegedus, Chris 181, 184
Heinzman, Bill 207
Helen of Troy 264
Hell Night 66
Hell Up in Harlem 50
The Hellbenders 18, 20
Hellman, Monte 56, 96–101
Hell's Creation 203
Hendrix, Jimi 149
Henry, Buck 3, 6, 102–106
Henry: Portrait of a Serial Killer 167
Hercules and the Amazon Women 29
Hercules and the Maze of the Minotaur 29, 30
Hercules and the Princess of Troy 18
Herz, Michael 118, 121
Herzfeldt, Don 112
Hewitt, Peter 87
Hey Good Lookin' 12
Hickenlooper, George 96, 107–111
Higher Learning 227, 229
Hill, Debra 40
Hill, Walter 144
Hill Street Blues 239
The Hills Have Eyes 61
Hinson, Hal 217
His Girl Friday 40, 45
Hitchcock, Alfred 1, 7, 29, 31, 45, 49, 82, 83, 173
Hocus Pocus 82
Hoffman, Dustin 103, 104, 201, 216–217

Index

Hoffman, Jane 193
Hogan, Paul 216, 219
Holden, William 137
Holiday, Billie 253
Hollywood Boulevard 57
The Hollywood Knights 161, 162
Holmes, Katie 87, 263
Home Movies 87, 192
Homicide 86, 125, 126
Honey, I Blew Up the Kid 18
Hooper, Tobe 40
Hopkins, Anthony 89
Hopper, Dennis 56, 209, 211, 212
Horowitz Plays Mozart 150
Horsefeathers 251
The Hottest State 92
House of Frankenstein, 1997 203
House on Haunted Hill 144, 145–148
Houston, Whitney 248
Howard, Ron 56
Hughes, John 46
Humanoids from the Deep 56
Humphrey, Hubert 149
The Hunchback of Notre Dame 264
The Hunger 209, 210, 211
Hunt, Helen 239
Hurd, Gale Ann 59
Hurt, John 190
Hurt, William 254
Hussein, Saddam 200
Hussey, Olivia 83
Hustle & Flow 227
The Hustler 25, 130
Huston, John 18, 19, 157
Huston, Walter 178
Hutton, Timothy 24

I Am a Fugitive from a Chain Gang 178
I Bury the Living 18
I Heart Huckabees 197
I Know What You Did Last Summer 259, 261
I Love Trouble 89
I Married a Strange Person! 203
I Miss Sonia Henie 102
I-Spy 239
Idiocracy 112
The Idiot 177
If I Had a Hammer 29
In Cold Blood 270
In the Mouth of Madness 40
The Incredible Hulk 12
The Inheritor 203
Inside Out IV 192
Inside the Actors Studio 31
The Insider 200
The Interpreter 270
The Invaders 50, 51
Invasion of the Body Snatchers 203, 205, 262
The Iron Giant 178
Iron Man 12
Irons, Jeremy 187
Ishtar 135, 239
Islands 150
It's a Wonderful Life 66, 96
It's Alive! 50, 167

It's All True 26
Ivanhoe Donaldson 24

Jack of All Trades 29
Jack the Bear 270
Jackson, Janet 192, 230, 231
Jackson, Michael 192, 227
Jackson, Peter 16, 118
Jackson, Samuel L. 212, 215
Jackson County Jail 239
Jagger, Mick 107
Janssen, Famke 144
Jarmusch, Jim 235
Jaws 155, 175, 218, 220, 227, 233, 234–235, 259
Jaws 2 87
Jay & Silent Bob Strike Back 233
Jennings, Peter 154
Jennison, Gordon 32
Jeremiah Johnson 155, 157, 158, 171
Jersey Girl 233
JFK 233
Jimi Plays Monterey 181
Jimmy the Boy Wonder 134
Joanov, Phil 87
Joe Versus the Volcano 239
Joe's Bed-Stuy Barbershop 71
John Lennon and the Plastic Ono Band: Live Peace in Toronto 181
John Tucker Must Die 239
Johnson, Ben 159
Jones, Duane 206
Jones, Spike 197, 229
Jones, Tommy Lee 40
Jovovich, Mila 254
The Judge 82
Judge, Mike 112–117, 118
Juice 71, 72
Jules et Jim 162
Juliet of the Spirits 61, 129
Jungle Fever 71, 73
Jurassic Park 134
Jurassic Park III 176
Justin, George 246

Kael, Pauline 109, 149, 155
Kagemusha 187
Kain, Khalil 72
Kalatozov, Mikhail 200
Kaplan, Deborah 239
Kattan, Chris 148
Kaufman, Andy 50
Kaufman, Lloyd 3, 118–123
Keaton, Buster 118
Keeping On 125
Keitel, Harven 12, 100
Keith, David 129
Kelly, Deforest 268
Kelly, Sarah 139
Kelly's Heroes 197
Kennedy, John F. 125, 149
Kershner, Irvin 40
Key Largo 96
The Killing 19
The Killing Box 107
The Killing of a Chinese Bookie 192
Killing Zoe 7, 10–11
Kilmer, Val 209, 212
King, Stephen 61, 63, 66, 67, 68,

69, 70, 82, 84, 86, 129, 130, 221, 226
The King of Comedy 221
King of the Hill 112, 115
King Solomon's Mines 134
Kingdom of the Spiders 270
Kings of the Road 255
Kingsley, Ben 270
Kinski, Klaus 144–145
Kirby, Bruno 250
Kiss Me Deadly 71
Klute 202
Knife in the Water 209
Kodar, Oja 107, 110
Kokin, Kenneth 221
Koppel, Ted 123
Kopple, Barbara 125–128
Korin, Judy 125
Koteas, Elias 187
Krause, Brian 85
Kristofferson, Kris 92
Krush Groove 71, 234
Kubrick, Stanley 19, 82–83, 87, 130, 172, 177
Kurosawa, Akira 6, 155, 177, 227
Kushnick, Helen 242

LA Weekly 161
Lalee's Kin 150
Lancaster, Burt 31
Landis, John 82, 267
Larry David: Curb Your Enthusiasm 250
La Salle, Eriq 192
The Last Boy Scout 209, 213
The Last Broadcast 169
The Last Detail 244, 247
Last House on the Left 61, 62
Last Night at the Alamo 139
The Last Stronghold of the Pure Gospel 187
Last Tango in Paris 178
The Last Temptation of Christ 233
The Late Shift 239, 240, 242
Law, Jude 270
Law and Order 144
Lawrence of Arabia 12, 29, 129, 221
Leacock, Richard 149, 181
Lean, David 24, 155
Learned, Michael 108
Leary, Denis 174
Lee, Spike 71, 72–73, 227
Lee, Stan 121
The Legend of Boggy Creek 169
Legere, Phoebe 122
Leigh, Jennifer Jason 66
Lemieux, Rachel 2
Lenny 192, 193, 253
Lenny Bruce: Swear to Tell the Truth 250, 251–253
Leno, Jay 242
Leonard, Robert Sean 92
Leone, Sergio 20, 34, 37–38, 96
Lester, Mark L. 129–133
Leto, Jared 12
Letterman, David 242
Lettich, Sheldon 29
Levinson, Barry 54
Levy, Eugene 131

Lewis, Herschell Gordon 3, 134–138
Lewis, Joseph H. 1
Lewis, Juliette 45, 48
Life and Times of Judge Roy Bean 155, 157
Life Is Beautiful 187
Life with Father 102
Lightning Over the Water 254, 255–256
Liman, Doug 76, 79
Limb to Limb 203
Lincoln, Abraham 117
Link, William 54
Linklater, Richard 3, 93, 139–143, 235
Lion's Den 221
Liotta, Ray 171
Little, Rich 67, 242
Little Big League 235
Little Big Man 171
Little Cigars 21, 22
Littlefield, Darren 242
Living Things 203
Livingston, Ron 112, 171
Loeb, Lisa 92
Loggia, Robert 131
Lopez, Jennifer 79, 233
Lord of the Rings 12, 14, 15–16
The Lost Minutes of Billy Crystal 250
Louis-Dreyfuss, Julia 45
Lovecraft, H.P. 56
The Lovers of Pont Neuf 254
The Low Life 107, 108, 110
Lucas, George 82, 153, 155, 161, 162, 207, 228
Lunatics: A Love Story 29
The Lusty Men 254
Lynch, David 112

M 7
MacDowell, Andie 255
Machine Gun Kelly 56, 58
MacPherson, Don 48
Macy, William H. 48, 50
Mad 69
Made 76, 77, 79
Madonna 24, 33, 192
The Madonna and the Volcano 187
Madsen, Michael 216
Magnani, Anna 178
The Magnificent Ambersons 26, 107, 264, 265
Magnum Force 155
Maidstone 181, 183–184
Mailer, Norman 149, 181, 183–184
The Majestic 66, 69, 70
The Majorettes 203
Making Movies: The Inside Guide to Independent Movie Production 203
Malcolm X 73
Malcolm X 71, 72, 73
Malice 24, 25, 26
Malick, Terrence 161, 162, 213
Malkovich, John 156
Malle, Louis 118
Mallrats 233

Malone, William 144–148
The Maltese Falcon 19
Maltin, Leonard 1, 155, 203
Mamas and Papas 185
Mamet, David 270
Mamoulian, Rouben 34, 37
A Man for All Seasons 233
The Man from Elysian Fields 107
The Man from Laramie 177
Man on Fire 209
The Man Who Shot Liberty Valance 254
Mancuso, FBI 239
Mann, Anthony 177, 254
Mannequin 2 239
Mansion of the Doomed 18
Manson, Charles 29
Mantegna, Joe 270
Marathon Man 244
Marcello, I'm So Bored 155
Marciano, Rocky 76
Marine, Craig 181
Mark Romanek: Video Music Stills 192
Marshall, Penny 270, 271
Martin, Steve 252
Martini, Steve 82
Marty 29
Marvin, Lee 159
Marx, Chico 250
Marx, Groucho 250
Marx Brothers 250
The Marx Brothers in a Nutshell 250
Maryjane 161
*M*A*S*H* 197
Mason, Connie 135
Mason, James 105
Massacre at the Grand Canyon 18
Mastergate 250
Masterson, Mary Stuart 45
Matheson, Tim 66
Maverick 34
Maximum Overdrive 130
Mayor of Sunset Strip 107
Maysles, Albert 3, 125, 149–154, 181, 183
Maysles, David 125, 149, 181, 183
MC Hammer 116
McAdams, Rachel 64
McBride, Joseph 108–110
McCabe & Mrs. Miller 26, 176, 192, 270
McCarthy, Andrew 239
McCarthy, Eugene 105
McConaughey, Matthew 139
McCormack, Patty 2
McElhone, Natascha 144, 145
McKellen, Ian 224
McLean, Barbara 34
McQuarrie, Christopher 221
McQueen, Steve 267
Mean Streets 12, 14, 59, 76, 161
Meet Marlon Brando 149
Meet the Parents 176
Meeting Halfway 216
Meltdown 45
The Merchant of Venice 187
Mercury Rising 24

Meredith, Burgess 250
Metalstorm: The Destruction of Jared-Syn 18
Mewes, Jason 234
Michaels, Lorne 112
Midnight 203, 204
Midnight 2 203
Midnight Caller 239
A Midnight Clear 87, 92
Midnight Cowboy 220
Milius, John 108, 155–160, 247, 273
Miller, Arthur 149
Miller's Crossing 76
The Million Dollar Hotel 254, 256, 257
A Minute to Pray, a Second to Die 18
Mission: Impossible 244, 247, 270
Mission: Impossible II 244
The Mist 67
Mr. Stitch 7
Mitchell, Elvis 120
Mitchell-Smith, Ilan 90
Miyazaki, Hayao 118, 120
Mo Better Blues 71, 72
Mobsters 143
Mommy 1–2
Monday Night Mayhem 71
Monte Hellman: American Auteur 96
Monte Walsh 163
Monterey Pop 181, 185
Moon, Wally 99
Moon Over Broadway 181
Moore, Julianne 48
Morales, Sylvia 125
Moreau, Jeanne 178
Morgan, Trevor 172
Morrissey, Paul 102
Mosier, Scott 236
Moss, Jack 265
Mother Night 87, 89–90, 250
Movie Maker 149
Muhammad and Larry 150
Murphy, Audie 18, 19, 34, 38
Murphy, Cillian 64
Murphy, Eddie 61, 227, 239, 242–243
The Music Lovers 134
Music of the Heart 61
Mutrux, Floyd 161–165
My Breast 239
My Darling Clementine 56
My Dinner with Andre 118
My Generation 126
My Neighbor Totoro 118, 120
My Son Liveth 171
Myrick, Daniel 166–170
Mysterious Ways 171

Napoleon 45
National Lampoon's Christmas Vacation 45, 46–47
National Lampoon's European Vacation 46
Natural Born Killers 7, 259
Neeson, Liam 273
Never Die Alone 71

Index

The New Adventures of Mighty Mouse 12
The New York Times 120, 149, 154
New York Undercover 144
Newman, David 102, 105
Newman, Lorraine 164
Newman, Paul 266
Newsweek 197
The Newton Boys 92, 139, 141–143
Nichols, Mike 102, 103, 104, 105, 178
Nicholson, Jack 56, 96, 98, 99, 246
Nicholson, James H. 56
Nickerson, Jimmy 80
Night of the Living Dead 203, 204–207
A Nightmare on Elm Street 41, 61, 63
Nightmare on Elm Street 3: Dream Warriors 63, 66
Nights of Cabiria 12
Nimoy, Leonard 268
Nine Inch Nails 192
1984 187, 190
1941 155
Nixon, Richard 129, 131
No Doubt 192
Nolte, Nick 89–90, 250
North, Eddie 266
Northern Exposure 171
La Notte 176
Noyce, Phillip 271
NWA 116
NYPD Blue 86

Oates, Warren 96, 97, 98
O'Bannon, Dan 40
Odd Jobs 171
O'Dea, Judith 206
Of Mice and Men 34
O'Fallon, Peter 171–175
Office Space 112, 113, 116
Oldman, Gary 212, 213
The Omen 167
On the Waterfront 107
One Flew Over the Cuckoo's Nest 92, 162, 216, 220
One Hour Photo 192, 194–196
101 181
One P.M. 181
The Onion Field 24
Only Angels Have Wings 40, 254
Only You 239
Opening in Moscow 181
Ophuls, Max 19
Orgazmo 118
Orson Welles — Spain 149, 152
Orwell, George 187
The Other Side of the Wind 108
The Others 82, 84, 144
Ottman, John 221
Outcast of the Islands 96
The Outpost 61
The Outsiders 216
Owens, Jesse 37
The Owl and the Pussycat 102
Oz 125, 126
Ozawa 150
Ozu, Yasujiro 254, 257

Pacino, Al 7, 10–11, 24, 26, 27, 161, 187
Pakula, Alan 178
Paradise Falls 193
Paradise Lost 193
Paris, je t'aime 176
Paris, Texas 92, 254, 255
Parker, Trey 118, 120
Parks, Gordon 231
Party of Five 171
The Passion of Martin 176
Patton 130
Payne, Alexander 3, 176–180
Peckinpah, Sam 18, 20, 34, 37, 96, 99–100, 137, 142
Penn, Sean 24, 270
Pennebaker, D.A. 3, 181–186
People 176
The People Under the Stairs 63
People's Tribunal 125
A Perfect Murder 7
Perkins, Anthony 83, 84
Perrotta, Tom 176
Persona 192
Personal Best 244
Persons Unknown 107
Peters, Jon 7, 23
Phantasm 7
Philadelphia 56
Phone Booth 50
The Piano 223
Picture This 107
Pierson, John 166
Pink Floyd's The Wall 221, 222
Pirahna 56, 57
The Pit and the Pendulum 18
Pitt, Brad 15, 212
The Player 105
Plummer, Amanda 254
Poe, Edgar Allan 56, 117
Poetic Justice 227, 229, 230
Poitier, Sidney 37
Polanski, Roman 194, 209–210
Politically Incorrect 260
Pollack, Sydney 157, 270
Pollak, Kevin 225
Pollock, Jackson 14
Poltergeist 222
Pomeranc, Max 270, 271, 274
Post, Don 144
Il Postino 187, 188, 189
Powell, Michael 182
Powers, Tyrone 37
Prefontaine, Steve 244, 245
Prehysteria! 18
Presley, Elvis 40
Previn, Soon-Yi 125
Price, Vincent 146
Primary 181
Princess Yang Kwei-fei 118
Private Parts 239, 240, 241
Profiler 171
Protocol 102
Przygodda, Peter 256
Psychiatry in Russia 149
Psycho 83
Psycho III 84
Psycho IV: The Beginning 82, 84
Pterodactyl 129

Public Access 221, 226
Pulp Fiction 7, 8, 71, 112, 162, 171, 174, 175

Quarks 102
The Quatermass Experiment 40
The Queen of the Night 45, 48
Quicksilver Highway 82
Quinn, Aidan 46, 61
Quinn, Anthony 29–30, 209, 213, 215

Radford, Michael 187–191
Radner, Gilda 102
Radswell, Anthony 252
Raging Bull 71, 79, 80, 139, 193, 200, 227
The Ragman's Daughter 24
Raiders of the Lost Ark 223, 227–228
Raimi, Sam 29, 200
Rains, Claude 266
Rambone 117
Rappaccini 118
Rashomon 107, 223
Rausch, Andrew J. 35, 119
Ray, Nicholas 254, 255–256
Rea, Stephen 144
Reality Bites 92
The Red Badge of Courage 18, 19
Red Ball Express 37
The Red Baron 56
Red Dawn 155, 156
Red Eye 64
Red River 61
Redford, Robert 103
Redgrave, Vanessa 76, 171, 172
Reds 92, 244
Reel Conversations 107
Reeves, Steve 18, 21, 23
Regarding Heiny 116
Regarding Henry 116
Reiner, Rob 235, 250
R.E.M. 192
Renfro, Brad 226
Rennie, Michael 266
Renoir, Jean 19
The Replacements 76, 79
Reservoir Dogs 79, 96, 100
The Resurrection of Broncho Billy 40
Return of the Living Dead 203
The Return of the Magnificent Seven 50
Return of the Seacaucus 7 139
A Return to Salem's Lot 50
Revenge 209
Reyes, Lucha 48
Rich, Matty 227
Ride in the Whirlwind 96, 98
Riding the Bullet 82
Ridley, John 197
The Rifleman 34
The Right Stuff 92
Ringu 144
Rio Bravo 40
Ripstein, Arturo 45
The Rise and Fall of Legs Diamond 34

Ritt, Martin 178
RKO 281 209
Roach, Hal, Jr. 34
Robbins, Jerome 266–267
Robbins, Tim 66, 68
Roberts, Jeremy 32
Roberts, Julia 105
The Robot Wars 21
Rock, Chris 233
Rocky 118
Rocky Marciano 76, 79–80
Rocky V 118
Rodat, Robert 45
Roddenberry, Gene 268
Rodriguez, Robert 67, 112, 262
Roeg, Nicholas 102, 156
Rolling Stone 120
Rolling Stones 12, 149, 153
Romancing the Bone 117
Romanek, Mark 192–196
Romeo & Juliet 123
Romero, George 7, 203, 204, 205, 207
Room at the Top 177
Roos, Don 45, 49
Rope 29, 31
Rosemary's Baby 161, 163
Rosewood 227, 231
Rossellini, Roberto 182
Roundtree, Richard 231
Routh, Brandon 225
Rudin, Scott 231
Rudy 76
The Rules of Attraction 7, 9
Rules of the Game 107, 244, 254
A Rumor of Angels 171, 172
Run-DMC 234
Run Silent, Run Deep 264, 265
Running Fence 149
Running Time 29, 31–33
Rush, Geoffrey 144, 146, 147
Russell, David O. 197–202
Russell, Ken 216
Russell, Kurt 40, 248
Russo, John A. 203–208
Ryan, Meg 131
Ryan, Robert 178

Saint Jack 56
The St. Valentine's Day Massacre 56
Salesman 149, 270
San Francisco Examiner 181
Sanchez, Eduardo 166
The Sand Pebbles 267
The Sands of Iwo Jima 200
San Giacomo, Laura 175
Santa Claws 203
Santoni, Reni 241
Sarris, Andrew xiii, 1–3
Saturday Night Fever 118
Saturday Night Live 102, 112
Saving Private Ryan 45, 66, 155, 270
Saving Ryan's Privates 117
Savini, Tom 7, 8, 203
Sayles, John 56, 71, 72
A Scanner Darkly 139
Scared to Death 144

Scarface 10–11, 74, 116
Scenes from a Marriage 250
Schaefer, Christen Harty 125
Schecter, Danny 125
Scheider, Roy 87
Scheinman, Andy 235
Schiffer, Michael 272
Schindler's List 31, 270, 273
Schlesinger, John 270, 271–272
School Daze 71
School of Rock 139
Schrader, Paul 155
Schumacher, Joel 50
Schwarzenegger, Arnold 131, 132
Scofield, Paul 31
The Scooby Doo Project 168
Scorpio Rising 161
Scorsese, Martin 14, 16, 56, 58, 59, 79, 161, 162, 201, 271
Scott, George C. 24, 25, 76, 129, 130
Scott, Randolph 34
Scott, Tony 3, 172, 209–215
Scream 61, 147, 236, 259, 260, 261
Scream 2 63, 259, 260
Scream 3 63, 261
Scream Queens 203
Sea of Love 24, 27
The Searchers 71
Searching for Bobby Fischer 270, 271, 274
Searching for Jimi Hendrix 181
Seconds 176
The Secret Agent 196
The Seduction 66
Seinfeld 174
Seize the Day 196
Sellers, Peter 194
The Sentinel 96
Serendipity 102
Sgt. Kabukiman NYPD 118
Serial Mom 134
Serling, Rod 264
The Serpent and the Rainbow 62
Seven Men from Now 34, 35
The Seven Samurai 71, 176, 227
The Seventh Seal 56
Shaft 227
Shakespeare, William 109, 122–123, 187
Shakur, Tupac 71, 73–74, 230
Shalit, Gene 120
Shame 187
Shampoo 244, 247
Shapiro, Alan 216–220
The Shark Tank Redemption 68–69
Shatner, William 268
Shaw, James 266
Shaw, Robert 234
The Shawshank Redemption 66, 67–68
She Came to the Valley 18
She-Wolf of London 82
Sheen, Martin 108, 129
Shepherd, Mathew 260
She's Gotta Have It 71, 72, 228
Shine 146
The Shining 84, 86, 130, 167
Shoot the Piano Player 61, 96, 162

The Shooting 96, 98, 99
Short Circuit 134
Showdown 18
Showdown in Little China 129
Showgirls 239
Shrek 135
Sideways 176, 179
Siegel, Don 1, 34, 38–39
Siegel, Joel 120
Sieverrich, Chris 254
Silence of the Lambs 56, 270
Silver, Joel 144, 146, 148
Silverstone, Alicia 12, 216, 217
Since You Went Away 203
Singer, Bryan 221–226
The Singing Detective 87
Singleton, John 6, 227–232
Six in Paris 149, 152–153
The Six-Million Dollar Man 233
Slacker 93, 139, 235
Slater, Christian 76
Sleepwalkers 82, 84, 85
Sling Blade 107, 110–111
Sloane, Michael 70
Smith, Chris 126
Smith, Kevin 118, 139, 233–238
Snow Falling on Cedars 92
Soldiers of Music 150
Soldiers Pay 197
Some Came Running 139
Some Folks Call It a Sling Blade 107, 110–111
Somebody Up There Likes Me 264, 266
The Sopranos 76
Sorbo, Kevin 30
Sorcerer 7
Sorkin, Aaron 26
The Sound of Music 259, 264, 267
South Park: Bigger, Longer, and Uncut 112
Southern, Terry 197
Spacey, Kevin 221, 223, 224, 225
Spanking the Monkey 197
Spartacus 29
Spencer, Scott 87
Spice Girls 8–9
Spice World 8
Spider-Man 12
Spiegel, Scott 67
Spielberg, Steven 30–31, 66, 82, 84, 155, 161, 162, 169, 172, 218, 220, 227–228, 270, 271
Spy Game 209
Stack, Robert 114
Stagecoach 207
The Stand 82, 84, 86, 166
Stanton, Harry Dean 96, 97, 98
Star! 267
The Star Is My Destination 43
Star Trek 235
Star Trek: The Motion Picture 268
Star Wars 175, 207, 235
Starlog 82
Starman 40, 43
Starr, Ringo 152
Startup.com 181
The State of Things 254, 256
Static 192, 193

Index

Stealing Candy 129
Stefano, Joseph 83
Steinbeck, John 158
Stephen King's The Shining 82, 83–84
Stern, Howard 239, 240, 241
The Steve Allen Show 102
Stevens, George 34
Stevens, George, Jr. 3
Stewart, Donald 273
Stockwell, Dean 18
Stoltz, Eric 7, 10
Stone, Oliver 87, 155, 200, 259
Stone, Sharon 45
Stonybrook 216–217
A Storm in Summer 264, 268
Stormare, Peter 254
La Strada 12, 150
Straight, No Chaser 224
Straight to One 92
Stranger Than Paradise 235
Strasberg, Lee 10
Streep, Meryl 61
Strode, Woody 37
The Stupids 267
Sturges, Preston 121
Suburban Roulette 134, 136
SubUrbia 139, 140
Suicide Kings 171, 173–175
Sullivan, Ed 193
Summer in the City 254
Summer of '42 220
Sunset Boulevard 107
Superman III 116
Superman Returns 221, 225
Supernova 144
Surviving Christmas 239
Surviving the Game 71, 74
Sutherland, Donald 202
Swank, Hillary 200
The Sweet and Lowdown 126
Sweet Toronto 182
Swingers 76–77, 78, 79
Syngenor 144

Tales from the Crypt 66, 82, 144, 146
Tall Tale 45
Tanen, Ned 165
Tape 92, 93, 139
Taps 24, 25
Tarantino, Quentin 7, 8, 33, 56, 67, 79, 96, 100, 118, 134, 174–175, 209, 211–213, 229, 272
Targets 58
A Taste of Blood 134, 136
Taxi Driver 14
Taylor, James 96, 98
Taylor, Jim 176
Teaching Mrs. Tingle 259, 263
The Tenant 192
Tequila Sunrise 244, 245
Terms of Endearment 259
Terror Firmer 118
Testi, Fabio 96
The Texas Chainsaw Massacre 40, 134, 206
That Was the Week That Was 102
There Goes My Baby 162

There's Always Vanilla 203
There's Something About Mary 121
They Live 40
The Thing 40
Thinnes, Roy 51
The Third Man 61, 66, 107
Thirtysomething 171, 172
This Ain't Bebop 112
Thomas, Betty 239–243
Thomas, Henry 83
Thornton, Billy Bob 110–111, 216
Thou Shalt Not Kill...Except 29
Three Kings 197–202
Thurman, Uma 45, 92
Tiger Town 216
Tilly, Jennifer 187
A Time for Dying 34
Titicut Follies 192
To Die For 102
To Kill a Mockingbird 125, 270
Tolkien, J.R.R. 12, 15
Tomlin, Lily 201
Top Gun 209, 210, 211
Torn, Rip 184
Toro, Benecio del 224
Touch of Evil 40, 107
Tougher Than Leather 234
Town and Country 102, 135
Town Bloody Hall 181
Towne, Robert 3, 56, 244–249, 272
Townsend, Robert 227
The Toxic Avenger 118
Toxic Avenger: The Novel 118
The Toxic Avenger: Part II 118
The Toxic Avenger III: The Last Temptation of Toxie 118, 122
The Train 31
Training Day 92
Trancers 66
Travers, Peter 120
Travolta, John 8, 24, 270
The Treasure of the Sierra Madre 35, 61, 176
The Trial 192
Tricia's Wedding 129
The Trip 56
Tristan & Isolde 209
Troisi, Massimo 188
Troll 18
Troll 2 239
Troma's War 118
Tromeo & Juliet 118, 121–123
Troop Beverly Hills 240
The Troublemaker 106
Truck Stop Women 129, 130–131
True Romance 7, 100, 209, 211–213, 215
Truffaut, François 155
Turner, Ted 231
28 Days 239, 242
Twilight of the Mayas 129
Twister 270
2 Fast 2 Furious 227
The Two Jakes 244, 245–246
Two-Lane Blacktop 96, 161
Two Mules for Sister Sara 34, 38–39
2001: A Space Odyssey 66, 71, 139, 192, 194

Two Thousand Maniacs 134, 136
Tyrese 231

Ulrich, Skeet 139
Unforgiven 29
Unger, Bill 212
Universal Soldier: The Return 144
Unsolved Mysteries 114
Until the End of the World 257
The Untouchables 161, 164
Up in Smoke 161, 164, 165
Urban Cowboy 164–165
Urban Legend 261
Urban Townies 193
Used Cars 155, 239
The Usual Suspects 221, 222, 223–224

Vampire in Brooklyn 61
Vampires 40
Van Cleef, Lee 53
Van Der Beek, James 7, 9
Van Doren, Natalie 68
Van Horn, Patrick 78
Van Sant, Gus 102
Variety 161, 162
Vaughn, Sarah 253
Vaughn, Vince 24, 76, 77, 78, 79
Very Bad Things 76
Vidor, King 34, 247, 264
Village Voice 161
Vincent, Jan-Michael 158
Viridiana 176
Vision Quest 24
Vogue 45
Vonnegut, Kurt 87, 89, 250, 251
Voodoo Dawn 203

W.C. Fields Straight Up 250
Wadler, Joyce 239
Wahlberg, Mark 197, 200
Waiting for Godot 96, 97
Waking Life 92, 93, 139
Waking the Dead 87
Walkabout 107
Walken, Christopher 92, 171, 175, 209, 211–212
Wallach, Eli 178
Wambaugh, Joseph 24
The War Room 181
Warden, Jack 265
Washington, Denzel 209, 215
The Washington Post 110, 217
WasteLAnd 259
Waterland 92
Waters, John 134, 146
The Way We Were 35
Wayne, John 29, 34, 35, 37
Wayne, Keith 206
Webb, Charles 104
Weide, Robert 87, 90, 250–253
Weiler, Lance 169
Weinstein, Harvey 236
Weir, Peter 171
Weld, Tuesday 92
Welles, Orson 5, 26, 107, 108–110, 149, 152, 153, 156, 172, 173, 228, 247, 264–265
Wenders, Wim 254–258

Werner, Peter 203
Wes Craven's New Nightmare 61, 63
West Side Story 264, 266–267
The West Wing 26
Whale, James 260
Wharton, William 87
What's Happening! The Beatles in the USA 149
What's Up, Doc? 102, 105–106
When We Were Kings 150, 151
The White Bird Passes 187
White Heat 74
White House Madness 129
White Mischief 187
White Rush 129
Whitmore, James 18
Who the Devil Made It 3, 209
Wicked Stepmother 50–53
The Wicker Man 134
Wigutow, Jesse 193
Wild 90 181
The Wild Bunch 18, 20, 96, 176
The Wild Child 254
Wild Man Blues 125, 126–128
Wild Palms 87
Wild Strawberries 107
Wilder, Billy 24, 82, 177
Willeford, Charles 96, 97

Williams, Robin 92, 192, 194–195
Williams, Tennessee 109
Williamson, Kevin 61, 63, 259–263
Willis, Bruce 24, 209, 213
Willy Wonka and the Chocolate Factory 221
Wilson, Dennis 96
The Wind and the Lion 155
Wings of Desire 257
Winkler, Charles 80
Winkler, Irwin 80
Winslet, Kate 270
Winter Light 244
Winters, Shelly 56
Wise, Robert 3, 6, 26, 264–269
Wishmaster 61, 63
With Love from Truman 149
Witherspoon, Reese 177, 180
Without Limits 244, 245
Without Remorse 227
The Wizard of Oz 216
Wizards 12, 13, 113
The Woman in the Room 66–67
The Woman in the Window 254
Woo 227
Wood, Ed 6
Wood, Elijah 216, 219
Woods, Cary 236

Woods, James 24
Woodstock '94 125
Written in the West 254

X, Malcolm 73
The X-Files 50
X-Men 221, 225
X2 221
Xena: Warrior Princess 29

Yankee Doodle Dandy 50
Young, Sean 24
Young Guns 143
The Young Guns 18
The Young Indiana Jones Chronicles 66
Youth in Poland 149

Zaillian, Steven 270–275
Zane Grey Theater 34
Zathura 76
Zemeckis, Robert 144, 155, 239
Ziggy Stardust and the Spiders from Mars 181
Zimmerman, Bonnie 89
Zinnemann, Fred 163
Zoltan, Hound of Dracula 18, 20
Zombiegeddon 118, 119
Zwerin, Charlotte 149

www.ingramcontent.com/pod-product-compliance
Lightning Source LLC
Chambersburg PA
CBHW080935020526
44116CB00034B/2718